ELITES IN SOUTH ASIA

ELITES
IN SOUTH ASIA

EDITED BY
EDMUND LEACH
AND
S. N. MUKHERJEE

CAMBRIDGE
AT THE UNIVERSITY PRESS
1970

Published by the Syndics of the Cambridge University Press
Bentley House, 200 Euston Road, London N.W.1
American Branch: 32 East 57th Street, New York, N.Y.10022

© Cambridge University Press 1970

Library of Congress Catalogue Card Number: 78-101446

Standard Book Number: 521 07710 9

Printed in Great Britain
at the University Printing House, Cambridge
(Brooke Crutchley, University Printer)

CONTENTS

MAPS

PREFACE

The Editors wish to express their thanks to the Master and Fellows of St John's College, Cambridge, for the facilities which they provided in April 1968 and which made it possible to hold the Seminar of which this book is the final outcome. They also wish to thank all those connected with the Cambridge Centre of South Asian Studies who helped in the organization of this enterprise, but in particular they wish to record their thanks to Mr B. H. Farmer, the Director of the Centre, and to Mrs C. Brown, the Director's Secretary. Further, they wish to record their thanks to all those who participated in the Seminar itself, not only those who contributed papers but those who offered comments in the open discussions. Many of the contributions from this last category of collaborator were extremely valuable, and some have been incorporated, unacknowledged, in the text of the revised papers which we now submit for our readers' approval. Finally, the Editors, in their personal capacities, would like to record their thanks to the various members of the staff of the Cambridge University Press who have helped to guide the project from typescript to printed page.

E. R. L.
S. N. M.

EDITORS' INTRODUCTION

All the papers in this collection were originally prepared for a two day seminar held at St John's College, Cambridge, in April 1968 under the auspices of the University Centre of South Asian Studies. The seminar carried the general title 'Elites in South Asia', but the contributors were allowed to decide for themselves just what they should mean by the term 'elite', and they have taken full advantage of this latitude. Some of our authors have used the term in Pareto's sense to mean those who exercise influence within any specialized sector of society: in this sense there may be elites among artists or schoolmasters or trade union officials quite regardless of their social class origins or their political status; others concern themselves exclusively with a political elite considered as a decision-making segment of an economically powerful ruling class; others again have had in mind Mosca's model of an open ruling class—the Power Elite of C. Wright Mills—which recruits its members from many different sectional elites within the total society on a more or less transient basis.

In the history of sociological thought the concept of 'elites' has been closely bound up with the theory of the 'circulation of elites' which derives from Mosca and Pareto and which, in its historical origins, stands in polar opposition to the Marxist theory of permanent struggle between fixed classes of owners and producers. In practice, the two types of theory are not necessarily mutually incompatible. Elitist analysis is concerned with how individuals are recruited into positions of personal influence as part of a political process. In Marxist analysis, on the other hand, the emphasis is on the nature of political domination and its ultimate dependence on the control of strategic institutions within the economic infra-structure of society. An integration of the two lines of approach is perfectly feasible, but nothing of this sort has been attempted in this book. The various elites which are described are simply samples drawn from different Indian localities at different historical periods. Collectively they demonstrate that political influence may derive from many different sources—from scholarship or mercantile skill as well as caste status or property in land—but they do not add up to an integrated whole. Our authors have not described, or attempted to describe, the Power Elite of contemporary India.

Even so, the papers do share one important common parameter; all are concerned with Indian elites in the context of British influence and its aftermath, and in this particular the problems which they delineate are by no means peculiar to the Indian subcontinent. Nearly all the 'developing countries' of contemporary Asia, Africa and Latin America are entangled with their post-colonial heritage even though in the Latin American case the colonialist phase itself is now receding into the background. The history of political elitism in all these countries has been similar. In the immediate post-colonial period power first came into the hands of men who had been educated according to the cultural and political conventions of the oppressors whom they had helped to overthrow. Their political respectability depended on a double criterion; they needed to have demonstrated their hostility to the colonial power, yet they also had to exhibit professional competence of a kind which the colonial authorities would themselves recognize. Nehru, the jailbird, terrorist, agitator, who overnight became an honoured international statesman, Prime Minister of India, admired as a Harrovian and graduate of Trinity College, Cambridge, is but one example among many. An Oxbridge, L.S.E. or Sandhurst background, plus a pre-Independence sentence of imprisonment, has been almost a prerequisite for post-Independence leadership in any British ex-colonial territory, and very similar principles apply to the former colonial territories of France and Holland. This phase is transient and is itself a developing process. In India, as early as the second decade of this century, influence began to shift away from anglophile, ultra-Anglicized servants of the Raj into the hands of nationalist leaders of 'non-co-operation' and 'civil disobedience'. Both groups were members of the same social class with much the same kind of background education, but the nationalists constituted among themselves an elite of a new kind, and it was to members of this latter group that the British finally handed over the reins of political authority. Since Independence this devolution has proceeded further. Ultimate power still rests with a limited elite who are members of a quite narrowly defined social class, but the principles of recruitment to this elite tend to change. Close familiarity with the values of English upper middle class culture becomes less and less relevant.

   In the light of the importance of elites in the contemporary political situation, it was appropriate that the seminar should examine other Indian contexts in which membership of an elite has depended on social background rather than economic circumstance, and several of the papers in this collection in fact have this orientation. But, in practice, for most of our authors, theory has been of minor relevance; the word 'elite' then implies no more than 'the men at the top', whatever the particular context of discussion happens to be.

   Spear starts the ball rolling with a step back into pre-British India. His *mansabdars* were the 'feudal barons' of the Mughal Emperors; they were an elite in that they were 'a selected cross-section of the landed aristocrats of India'. Spear both compares and contrasts the role of this elite in Mughal India with the part played by the Civil Service both in modern Britain and in British India. His argument implies that, at least in embryo, the *mansabdari* came close to being a bureaucracy in the Weberian sense, a view which surely stretches this ideal type concept some way beyond its normal limits? However, Spear's most significant point is the emphasis which he places on the interdependence of *mansabdar* authority and Mughal authority. Because of this relationship they could not survive the establishment of British rule. In sharp contrast, more orthodox, formally bureaucratic, civil service elites have often shown themselves remarkably resilient in the face of drastic changes of regime.

Stokes's paper is a re-analysis of a paradox of the Indian Mutiny period, the circumstance that it appeared to the British officials of the time that: 'the agricultural labouring class—the class who above all others have derived the most benefit from our rule were the most hostile to its continuance. Whilst the large proprietors who have suffered under our rule almost to a man stood with us.'

Stokes examines the background to this proposition as revealed by the history of land and taxation policy in the region between Delhi and Agra during the period 1840–57. He shows on the one hand that, owing to misunderstanding of the social facts, the policy of the British officials often had precisely the opposite consequences to what was intended, but he also shows that land law innovations did not, as is commonly supposed, simply impoverish the 'traditional elite' of rural landlords in favour of the urban trading and money-lending classes. It tended rather to induce a circulation of property rights among different sectors of the traditional elite so that advantage and disadvantage were roughly balanced. Consequently, in the crisis situation of 1857, the 'local magnate class' did not act as a unity: 'the breakdown of British authority so far from throwing the elite wholly on the side of rebellion split it raggedly down the middle, so that even within the same district magnate and peasant proprietors of the same caste could react in quite opposite directions'.

With Mukherjee, Dobbin and Johnson we move to problems of elitism in the nineteenth-century cities of Calcutta, Bombay and Poona. Here the distinction between ruling class and political elite becomes more meaningful. Mukherjee tries to relate the politics of Calcutta to the class system and caste structure of the city at that period. Dobbin describes the situation in Bombay where elite groups of varied origin were competing against each other to achieve political domination. Although she closes her study at 1883, her conclusions seem highly topical. She observes that even a century ago the men who achieved political eminence on the all-India stage, and even internationally, often failed to maintain control of the local politics in their home city. This can still happen, but the significance of such inconsistency may be very different in the context of an independent India from what it was under the aegis of the British Raj. Johnson's paper comes to grips directly with the key issue: 'The first Indian nationalists came from small well-defined social groups occupying privileged positions within their own provinces. Although differing from each other in many ways these provincial elites were drawn into continental politics by shared interest in British rule.'

The problem to be solved is: what gave one such potential power group the necessary advantage over its rivals? Johnson takes the Chitpavan Brahmins of Maharashtra as a case in point. He examines the 'distinctive contribution Chitpavan Brahmins made to Indian political life', but he also examines the sources of their short-lived success. His conclusion is that the significant factor was not caste as such, but the development within certain sections of this caste of an English-educated elite. Education gave these people the political know-how to operate effectively with British-derived institutions. Admittedly, their high caste status gave them an initial advantage in gaining access to a British-style education, but they then used their educational advantages to try to maintain Brahmin domination, an objective in which they were ultimately unsuccessful.

Gray's paper is a contemporary study designed to show what has happened to the traditional feudal aristocracy in Andhra Pradesh in the circumstances of post-Independence India. The conclusion seems to be that the old guard squirearchy have shown themselves very resourceful in adapting themselves to the new political institutions, or perhaps to adapting the new institutions to themselves. A large part of Gray's paper is taken up with a case study of a single village, and one cannot help wondering how far the author is justified in using this example as a basis for his wider generalizations.

Bernstorff's contribution is likewise strictly contemporary. She makes a detailed study of the thirty-four candidates who stood for the seven constituencies in the Old Town of Hyderabad during the general election of 1967. Her conclusion is that the candidates 'represent a new elite which is not linked to the established elites. However, they belong to a small stratum in Indian society, the educated middle class.' 'Educated' in this context means, of course, 'educated into a partly Anglicized culture'. This is an important finding, though not unexpected, but one could have wished that our author had developed her conclusions rather further. 'By education and occupation none of [the candidates] can be considered as belonging to the lower classes...

No candidate is from a scheduled caste, but a few belong to lower Shudra castes. Politics provide a channel for social mobility, but the climb is slow...'

Dalton is concerned with the intellectual development of M. N. Roy from an early nationalist phase, through his career as a Marxist, when he was quite explicitly alienated from the Indian nationalist tradition, to the final phase when he renounced Communism and identified himself as a 'radical humanist'. Dalton's thesis is that in the amalgam of Indian and European ideas which contributed to Roy's thought it was the elements derived from Gandhi and traditional Hindu mysticism which ultimately became dominant. Roy, argues Dalton, is not to be regarded as a solitary eccentric; the evolution of his thinking is matched elsewhere: 'Radical humanism, which is synonymous with the mature political and social thought of M. N. Roy, will be considered here as the ideology of an intellectual elite'.

A sentence on the first page of Shils' paper sets its theme: 'in the land of the *guru* the profession which has taken over his obligations is held in low esteem by those who practise it and by others'. In India, as elsewhere, the academics form an important elite; yet, compared with their Euro-American counterparts, they seem to carry little influence and receive extremely meagre material rewards. Shils maps out the anatomy and depressing implications of this situation, which, for a country struggling to achieve economic modernity, may be extremely serious. But he does not despair. Despite the shortcomings of the academics 'something does get done, and India, as we know it, would not exist without them'.

The two final papers, those of Das Gupta and Bagchi, are both concerned with economic elites and are nicely contrasted. Das Gupta's piece relates to a period before the establishment of British political authority but is concerned with Indian entrepreneurs who made their fortunes by engaging in trade with Europeans. Bagchi, on the other hand, focuses attention on the period 1900–30 when the British political power was fully dominant. He re-examines the conventional proposition that the economic stagnation of India under the British is properly attributed to such factors as caste restrictions and other-worldly value systems. The evidence, he suggests, points to quite other conclusions. He shows how the British used their political influence to help British companies maintain a stranglehold on the Indian economy; and it was the inefficiency of British-controlled enterprise rather than the lack of initiative on the part of Indian industrialists which was ultimately responsible for the persistence of economic backwardness in India right through the first half of the twentieth century. In this paper, as in others, we meet with the phenomenon that, under colonial conditions, an elite group which partly adopts the value system of the alien rulers stands to gain very markedly in the process. In the case of British India, one outstanding example of this process was the industrial success of the Parsis. Bagchi has looked at the relevant historical evidence through the eyes of an economist, and more sociologically minded readers may find his analysis only partly convincing. Even so he clearly establishes his case that the conventional explanations which attribute to the Parsis a special capability for business efficiency cannot be sustained.

And that may be the right point at which to stop. The merit of the seminar to which these papers were originally contributed was that it was inter-disciplinary. Historians, sociologists and economists with a common territorial interest met to discuss a common theme. As was to be expected the level of communication was not always very high. The sociologists thought that the historians and the economists were simple-minded, the historians thought the sociologists were ignorant, but all the participants, as well as the readers of this book, were faced with kinds of evidence which was unfamiliar and were compelled to recognize that the facts of Indian social history fit very badly with the conventional cliches of Indian social historians. The sundry authors have not shown that anything is generally true about the elites of South Asia; they have, however, demonstrated that quite a number of things are not true, and that wholly negative conclusions may in the end be very worth while.

E. R. LEACH

S. N. MUKHERJEE

THE MUGHAL 'MANSABDARI' SYSTEM

PERCIVAL SPEAR

In this paper it is proposed to consider the *mansabdari* system as a pattern of a Mughal elite. But before doing this it would seem right to define more closely the sense in which the word 'elite', now almost as diverse in meaning as such words as 'democracy' or 'freedom', is understood.

If we take the word to mean a directing group or class, it has then to be decided in what field this group is to operate. There are elites in different departments of life and at different levels of life. There are general local elites like the country gentry of Victorian and Hanoverian England. But they were not the only elites, for there were religious, professional and mercantile bodies as well. There cannot always be said to be only one elite in each sphere of life. In the religious field, for example, in nineteenth-century Britain there was an Anglican and Scottish Presbyterian elite, with Free Church and Roman Catholic bodies as well. In the world of learning there was the elite of Oxbridge, which overlapped into the worlds of the Church and education. There was also a scientific body overlapping to some extent with Oxbridge, but also independently growing in London and elsewhere. The fact of overlapping does much to confuse the issue. A striking example of this is the near monopoly of the I.C.S. by Oxbridge graduates as the result of the introduction of the examination system and the manœuvres of Benjamin Jowett and Sir Charles Trevelyan. Did Oxbridge then rule India or was it an influence *on*, rather than an actual regulator of, the Indian government?

It would seem that a line should be drawn between influence and control. An elite is a body which controls a particular sphere of life, though it may be influenced by other elites at other levels or in different departments of life. If this be taken as a working definition, and the question of interlocking elites, such as Oxbridge in relation to the government, the Church or India in Victorian England, is ignored, we can proceed to frame questions about the chosen elite itself. We shall first want to know something of its composition, how it was arranged and what work it performed. How was this elite recruited? which raises the question whether it was an elite within an elite, an expression of something more fundamental than itself. From this point its method of self-management and retention of power can be considered and finally the reasons for its collapse.

The *mansabdars* were the governing class of the Mughal Empire. They illustrate the fact that the Mughal Empire was not what used to be called an Asiatic despotism, or, in other words, an irresponsible and all-powerful autocracy. Not many oriental monarchies have been wholly irresponsible and few have been all-powerful. The distinction between Asiatic and other despotisms should in fact be relegated to the limbo of historical jargon. Despotisms are despotisms without geographical labels and they, like other political forms, are subject to classification and analysis. An absolute despotism, where the despot can really do what he likes, is in fact a very rare thing. All despots are to a greater or lesser degree the prisoners of the elites which create and sustain them. The Ching emperors of China were dependent on the mandarinate and the mental prisoners of Confucian and Chinese traditions. The apparently irresistible Sultans of Turkey had sharp checks in the Janissaries, the resources of provincial governors and the mental authority of Islamic law. So it was with the Mughal empire. The Emperor Babur, though a descendant of Taimur, had something of a feudal relationship with his Turkish *begs*. His most difficult tasks in India were to persuade his followers to face the hot weather in India after the overthrow of Sultan Ibrahim of Delhi in 1526, and the next year to face the Rajput host of Rana Sangha of Mewar. His son Homayun was virtually the head of a confederation of jealous aristocrats, Turkish, Afghan and local. With the help of some he conquered Gujarat and Bengal; by the action of others he lost the whole empire and fled to political asylum in Persia. His return in 1555 was a modest affair, helped by a temporary political vacuum in north India, and there was nothing in his position, his powers or his personality to suggest that he would long retain his restored position.

It was his son Akbar who really made the empire. He did this not merely by military prowess, although he was a magnetic leader and skilful general. He turned the Mughal government from a foreign imposition by rulers with an alien culture into an Indian regime by means of a political deal with the Rajputs and a new approach to Hindus in general. He converted the old type of empire with its loosely knit feudatories dominated by a powerful personality at the centre into a bureaucracy working to rule and by decree, and operated by a salaried and graded officer corps.[1] A later example of the confederal type of feudal despotism can be seen in the eighteenth-century Afghan Empire of Ahmad Shah Abdali. By military prowess and skill in managing discordant tribes he blew up in a few years an empire

---

[1] See V. Smith, *Akbar the Great Mogol*, 2nd ed., Oxford, 1902, pp. 354–67.

which included, besides Afghanistan proper, Baluchistan, Sind, the Punjab, Kashmir and Badakshan. His successors lacked Ahmad Shah's talents and within thirty years this empire had shrunk again to the confines of Afghanistan and Badakshan, with the single addition of Peshawar.[1] It was this bureaucracy (which was organized on the *mansabdari* system) which distinguishes the Mughal Empire from all Indian regimes after the Gupta Empire in the fourth and fifth centuries A.D.

We are fortunate in having a first description of the system by Abu'l Fazl, secretary and confidant[2] of Akbar, who himself had probably much to do with its development, in his political and administrative encyclopedia, *The Ain-i Akbari*. Much more information was given by later writers of the Mughal period which has provided modern scholars with materials both for reconstruction and for argument. The forms of the system with its titles indeed persisted in Hyderabad, Deccan, until the absorption of that state by India in 1948. But this was only an administrative fossil. The content and significance of the system had long disappeared. Thus it has been left to twentieth-century scholars to reconstruct its mechanism and operations.

Certain germs of the system, which provided characteristic features later, are to be found in Turkish central Asian practice. A decimal system was used to classify their horsemen; thus a *khan* commanded 10,000, a *malik* 1,000, and an *amir* 100. Here is to be found both the decimal notation and the idea of numbers determining rank.[3] In the spacious time of Taimur nominal and actual numbers coincided. A *khan* actually did command a sizeable army. But with the break-up of the Empire after Taimur's death in 1404 these numbers could no longer be maintained. Poverty prevented maintenance of the full quota, but pride forbade a reduction in title. So we find officers with high titles commanding small forces. Thus, in the time of Sultan Balban, the *malik* Baq Baq, governor of Budaon (an important position) had the formal command of 10,000, but actually only 4,000 troopers. And these, according to the historian Barani, formed an unusually large contingent.[4] The Delhi Sultanate was relatively powerful until 1398, but thereafter the gap between the title of command and the number commanded became so wide that there was no real relation between the two. This persisted until Babur's day.

It was Akbar who used these materials as the basis for his graded bureaucratic system. From them he took the idea of rank indicated by

[1] See P. Sykes, *History of Afghanistan*, 2 vols, London, 1940, II, 351–91.
[2] V. Smith, *Akbar the Great Mogol*, p. 380.
[3] M. Athar Ali, *The Mughal Nobility under Aurangzeb* [Ali, *Aurangzeb*], London, New York, 1966, p. 38.
[4] *Ibid.* pp. 39–40.

numbers, and of numbers indicating the command of troops. To this
he added a graded system of distinction between rank and obligation to
produce troops, and a complete dependence of the *mansabdars* on the
government for their maintenance. In the former rather haphazard
arrangement a *khan* who commanded a *tomam* or army of 10,000 troopers
composed his forces with the followers of ten *maliks* with a thousand men
each. Under Akbar's system the commander of 5,000 (*panch hazari*) or
any other number was entirely responsible for the number of troops
which the figure represented. The contingent was inspected, the horses
were branded with the government mark, and he was penalized if he
failed to maintain the right number of men or horses or to keep those
he had up to standard. A further vital feature of Akbar's system was the
financial dependence of the *mansabdars* on the government. For some
years Akbar paid all these officers in cash, collecting the land revenue
directly through his own officers or *karoris*. His successors found this
impracticable in their conditions and substituted for it the system of
land assignments.[1] While the government remained vigorous this proved
as effective a means of control as that of cash payment. A *mansabdar's*
salary was determined by a calculation taking into account both rank
and military obligation. Once determined, the officer was given an
assignment on the land revenue of a given area. It was not, in fact as
well as in theory, a landed estate or a permanent property, but merely
a lien on the revenue of that area in lieu of a cash salary. It was, again
in fact as well as in theory, resumed at death or dismissal, and a strict
account made of the officer's assets against his probable loans from the
treasury. In a country where most money was raised from the land in
periodic payments, loans for immediate expenses were an integral part
of the whole economic structure. The needs of the *mansabdar's* family
after his demise were often met by a revenue-free grant of a small
parcel of land, perhaps a single village, known as *altamgha*. Nor did the
mansabdar, once more in fact as well as in theory, retain the same land
assignment throughout his tenure of office. They were frequently
changed, so that he had no opportunity to develop personal contacts in
one area before his assignment was moved somewhere else. He might
send his own agents to the new area, but often used men on the spot
who knew the local conditions. In either case his relationship to the
land was that of cash–nexus, not of landlord–tenant. His relationship
to the government was that of a salaried officer subject to orders, and
financially tethered to the treasury, which calculated the revenue
value of lands against his paper salary, and the chancery which issued
the necessary grants.

[1] The use of this term, with the special meaning attached to it, we owe to W. E. Moreland,
India at the death of Akbar, London, 1920, e.g. pp. 67, 72, 80, 84.

The *mansabdar* was thus quite definitely an imperial official, subject to orders, and controlled from the centre by very effective financial sanctions. We may now note how the service was organized. According to Abu'l Fazl, His Majesty (Akbar) by divine inspiration chose the numbdr 66 for the number of grades from the Commander of Ten (*Dahbashi*) to the Commander of Ten Thousand (*Dah Hazari*).[1] Only the royal sons, however, held commands of over Five Thousand, so that this figure and rank (*Panch Hazari*) was in fact the highest rank for a subject. The inspiration of the number 66 lay in the fact that under the Arabic system of *abjad* or numerical notation, 66 represents the numerical value of the word Allah. In practice, there were thirty-three grades within the same numerical limits. It has already been noticed that the figure attached to the *mansab* did not mean that that number of troops were required of the officer or that he would be paid for their upkeep. It was, in fact, a definition of rank and status like the words colonel and lieutenant-general in the army, or captain and admiral in the navy. Within the system there were such refinements and gradations, related to what may be called the pay and allowances field, as made the whole system very complicated. There was a wide field, in fact, for 'adjustments' and 'fiddling'. Besides the personal rank of the *mansabdar* called *zat*, there was also a second figure called *sawar*, or horseman. This was never more than the *zat* rank and usually less.[2] Only rarely did it not exist at all. The *sawar* rank related to the number of horsemen the officer must provide, but it was not the exact number. Though related to the actual number required it could also vary, so that this figure not only indicated a service obligation, but a rank within the particular *mansab* itself. It was a rank within a rank. The usual proportion of horsemen required to the number of the *sawar* rank was one-fifth, until the time of Shah Jahan who upgraded it.[3] Thus a man with a *sawar* rank of 3,000 would be required to produce 600 horsemen. You could be, for example, a *mansabdar* with a *zat* rank of 4,000, a *sawar* rank (within the *mansab* rank) of 3,000, actually maintaining 600 horsemen. But the refinements are not yet complete, for how many horses should a trooper provide? There were three grades in this requirement, of one, two, or three horses (*yak, du, sih aspah*). There was a standard proportion in this regard, the 1,000 horsemen required of a particular *mansabdar*, for instance, being divided in 300 with three horses each, 600 with two horses each and 100 with one horse each, making 2,200 horses in all.[4] But these numbers could be varied and

[1] *Ain-i Akbari*, Book II, Ain 3, tr. H. Blochmann, 2nd ed., Calcutta, 1927, I, 247–59 [*Ain*].
[2] I. H. Qureshi, *Administration of the Mughal Empire*, Karachi, 1966, pp. 92–3.
[3] *Ibid.* pp. 96–7.
[4] *Ibid.* p. 98.

even doubled,with corresponding variation of salary, so here again was wide scope for adjustments of claims, for promotions and demotions. An example of the working of the system is given by Dr Qureshi in the following terms.[1] A *mansabdar* with a *zat* rank for his *mansab* of 5,000 was called a *Panch Hazari*. Supposing that his *sawar* rank was also 5,000 (common but not invariable), he would, under the system outlined above, have to maintain 1,000 troopers (one fifth of his *sawar* rank). These troopers would have between them 2,200 horses, in the proportions mentioned above, and the *mansabdar* would be paid for their maintenance. The horses were regarded as government property; they were branded with the government mark, and were inspected from time to time.

There was one more complication. The above description assumed that the *mansabdar* in question is paid for twelve months in the year. But this was by no means always the case. Payments could vary from twelve months to as little as five. When a salary was thus reduced, the obligations of the *sawar* rank were correspondingly less. Thus, if the holder of a *sawar* rank which required the maintenance of 1,000 troopers (as above) was paid for only nine months in the year instead of twelve, the troopers' requirement would sink to 750, and the normal horse requirement to 1,650. Thus obligations could be varied within a *sawar* rank itself by the manipulation of pay as well as horse maintenance, just as obligations within the *zat* rank could be varied by manipulations of the *sawar* rank. All these variations of obligations also affected rank and status. When these refinements are realized, it can be seen how complicated the system in fact was, and what a field it contained for claim and counter-claim, for plot and counter-plot. Indeed, had not most of the *mansabdars* been absent from the court on civil or military employments, it is difficult to see how the system could have survived in the welter of claims and resentments which would have accumulated at the centre. As it was, these distinctions served as so many cords of varying strength to bind the serving *mansabdar* to the system by hopes of advancement and fears of ceremonial setbacks. The whole system was ingeniously devised to cloak differences of obligation and the realities of service beneath dignified titles. It was a way of reconciling family and tribal aristocratic pride with the discipline of a bureaucratic system. There is perhaps some analogy with the proliferation of titles in Europe as a cover for the loss by the nobles of hereditary office and power.

These were the devices by which the Empire sought to harness into its service a restless territorial aristocracy diverse in race, creed, community and culture. And what were the motives which induced these

[1] *Ibid.* pp. 98–9.

men to submit to these controls, appearing at the imperial court with bowed heads and a humility which they would scorn as craven weakness in their own country?[1] One such motive, and I think a major one, was ambition. The imperial service offered a career open to talent, with no officer barred up to provincial governorships and the chief ministries. To remain outside the system meant relegation to one's estates, nothing more than a local celebrity, and no chance of independence through rebellion because of the strength of the system which was being boycotted. While some families, like that of Asaf Khan, the brother-in-law of Jahangir, seemed to have something of a lien on high office, it remained true until the end that immigrant adventurers and local men without influence could and did rise to high office. Appointments never became the monopoly of a group of families as in Venice, and the hereditary element, though present, was not as great as might have been expected. It may also be noted, in reverse, as it were, that, as prospects waned and inducements grew less with the growth of financial stringency in the later Empire from about 1690 onwards, so positive loyalty declined also. A second motive was that of class or clan solidarity. A quite small group such as the Sayyids of Barha, famous for their bravery, but not previously conspicuous in public affairs, found that the imperial service extended and magnified their influence. Other groups of existing standing or reputation, like the Rajput chiefs, found it more satisfying to be ornaments and props of an all-India empire than the rulers of usually distracted courts in distant and barren Rajasthan. Raja Man Singh was a confidant of Akbar as Raja Jai Singh was of Shah Jahan. A tribal group like the Afghan Rohillas of Rohilkund thought the same. Without the empire they were little more than successful marauders, looked upon with suspicion and hostility by the people of their own chosen area of settlement. Within its service they had status, prestige and the possibility of unlimited influence.

A further motive, and a strong one, was that of personal loyalty to the emperor. This arose partly from their personalities, which were remarkable from the coming of Babur in 1526 to the death of Bahadur Shah I in 1712. Such characters provided a powerful catalyst for the Indian desire and capacity for personal devotion. It was fostered by Akbar's skill in throwing a mystique of divinity around the emperor's person and office in line with Persian precedent. The idea also accorded with the general respect for authority in the subcontinent and the acceptance, emotional as well as intellectual, of the belief that a hierarchical society should have a reverential head. Finally perhaps

[1] See Bernier, *Travels in the Mogol Empire*, 2nd ed., revised, London 1934, pp. 260–70, for a description of court etiquette.

may be mentioned the Persian culture which the *mansabdars* shared, overlaying the various local cultures of the communities from which they had sprung. For Persian in the Mughal period was not only a linguistic and administrative convenience—Persian revenue terms and the use of Persian as a diplomatic language found their way into the Hindu far-south—but a cultural magnet as well. It exercised that fascination which one civilization sometimes exercises over another, leading to admiration, imitation, emulation and a desire to achieve the sense of 'belonging'. And this it did in spite of the handicap of being a language imported by foreign conquerors professing a foreign and unloved creed. Persian values in literature, art, administration, manners and deportment were generally accepted by the upper classes as conferring a title to gentility and good taste, a sense of being 'with it'. To use a homely comparison it presented the sort of fascination for backwoods nobles and chiefs that Beau Nash's school for manners at eighteenth-century Bath did for the bucolic and crude gentry of the shires. Granted this fascination for things and ideas Persian, it is to be noted that the Persian ethos was redolent with the idea of authority, of semi-divine monarchy (going back to the pre-Muslim kings and heroes like Chosroes and Rustum), of rank and order, of bureaucracy and imperialism.

The numbers of the *mansabdars* varied less than one might expect. The *Ain* at the end of Akbar's reign listed 1,800 *mansabdars*, of whom 133 held *mansabs* from 1,000 to 5,000. This was the class denominated *amir* or noble, hence the anglicism of 'omrah' for a Mughal noble from the Arabic plural of *amir*. By Shah Jahan's time there was a jump to 437 in this group. Thereafter the increase was slow, reaching 486 by 1678 and 575 by 1707.[1] Considering that during Aurangzeb's reign the empire absorbed two large Muslim kingdoms in the Deccan, parts of Maharashtra and the Carnatic coastal strip, this was a very moderate increase indeed. It suggests that there was a corps of about 500 high officers, comparable to the higher ranks of the British I.C.S., which really ran the Empire. If we recollect that the I.C.S. (or its earlier equivalents) numbered in all ranks from 800 to 1,200 and then subtract the junior members, we get a total for the British-Indian elite not unlike that for the Mughal.

The composition of the *mansabdar* order was as varied as its ranks and gradations. There was first a division between foreign and home-born officers. W. E. Moreland calculated that 70 per cent of Akbar's *mansabdars* were either foreign-born or the sons of foreigners. The remaining 30 per cent were, in the higher ranks, about equally divided between Hindus and Muslims.[2] This foreign element continued

---

[1] Ali, *Aurangzeb*, p. 9.   [2] W. E. Moreland, *India at the death of Akbar*, pp. 69–70.

to the end, the last effective minister of Shah Alam in the 1770s being a Persian immigrant, Mirza Najaf Khan. But their share of appointments tended to decline in favour of men of foreign origin settled for one or two generations. This process was helped by the Empire's expansion in the Deccan which brought in both Deccani Muslims and Marathas. The men of lineage, with their pride of race and clan, tended to keep themselves separate from the country-born, known as *sheikhzadas*. The broad conclusion is that the administration in its higher reaches was in foreign or semi-foreign hands. In the lower ranks, outside the *mansabdari* system, Hindus, as always, predominated. In this respect the British did not replace an indigenous administration by a foreign one, but replaced one foreign regime by another. The trouble, from the Indian point of view, was that it was more foreign and more strict.

But distinctions amongst the *mansabdar* order did not stop there. Among the foreign officers the most prominent were Iranis and Turanis, Persians and Turks. India had long been regarded, since the days of the Sultanate, as a happy hunting ground for enterprising adventurers and emigres. Muslim minority regimes were always on the look-out for promising recruits, uncommitted to any cause and uninvolved in local politics. Babur's Turkish antecedents gave the Turanis a flying start, so to speak, and the unsettled state of Central Asia as well as the openings in India encouraged a steady stream of immigrants. Persia was under the strong Safavi dynasty, but there were still dissidents or aspirants who thought they could better themselves in India. The Turanis had consanguinity and vigour in their favour, the Iranis cultural prestige and intelligence, while both had the advantage, from the government's point of view, of detachment from local issues and interests. Then there were the Afghans, both from their homeland and those already settled in India. But they were not favoured by the emperors, both because it was an Afghan regime which the Mughals had ousted from India after a thirty-year struggle, and because they were considered turbulent and unreliable. Thus the leading factions of the late empire were the Turanis and Iranis, the Afghans only becoming prominent in imperial politics when they emerged as allies of the Afghan invader Ahmad Shah Abdali in the 1750s. In the last years of effective empire it was a Persian, not an Afghan, who directed the state. It was an Afghan who blinded Shah Alam.[1]

Within India itself the Indian Muslims were known as *sheikhzadas*, of whom a half to a quarter claimed the more prestigious name of *Khanzadas* or sons of former *mansabdars*. This Indian Muslim element numbered,

[1] Ghulam Qadir, grandson of the Afghan chief Najib-ad-daulah, who was at one time a supporter of the Afghan invader Ahmad Shah and later chief Mughal minister for nine years.

according to the *Ain*, about 15 per cent of the whole number of higher officers. If we reckon the descendants of foreign officers as country-born, the proportion by 1700 had perhaps doubled, the balance being made up of Hindus and the really foreign.[1] At first drawn mainly from Turkish families in northern India, they were reinforced in Aurang-zeb's time by officers of the Deccan kingdoms who were bribed to change sides by the offer of a *mansab* or who were taken into service after the extinction of the kingdoms. This process was facilitated by the Indian tradition that it was honourable to serve a *de facto* ruler and therefore no dishonour to serve the conqueror of your previous master. Thus Mughal rulers often took the supporters of a rival into service immediately after a decisive battle and it was common for such an event to lead to an avalanche of changed allegiances.[2] It was the *khidmat* or service, which was honourable, rather than allegiance *à outrance* to a particular person. This tradition of Indian public life may perhaps help to explain the epidemic of changing sides which has recently occurred in some Indian legislatures. It was no disgrace to join the winning side provided it really won.

The last constituent of the service was the Hindu element. In Akbar's time they, like the *sheikhzadas*, numbered about 15 per cent of the whole service in its higher ranks.[3] Then they represented Akbar's political deal with the Rajput chiefs and mostly belonged to those clans. There were a few others like the Khattri Raja Todar Mal, the revenue minister, and the Brahmin wit, Raja Birbal. In the seventeenth century the Rajput connection continued, even throughout Aurangzeb's reign. But towards the end their numbers were augmented by the same Aurangzeb who attracted chiefs from the allegedly implacable Mara-thas with offers of *mansabs*. They came in sufficient numbers to form a distinct element in the whole corps. Unfortunately for Aurangzeb this policy did not pay off as Akbar's similar policy had done with the Rajputs; the Marathas had a different social organisation so that a chief could not necessarily carry his followers, who in the Rajput case were related clansmen, with him.[4] In the reign of Shah Jahan there were only thirteen Maratha *mansabs* of a thousand or more *zat* or 2·9 per cent of the total. In the years 1679 to 1707 there were ninety-six, or 16·7 per cent of the total.

Recruitment to the order was nominally in the hands of the emperor. On occasion a young man from abroad would present himself at the imperial durbar and catch the emperor's eye. He would be enrolled in

[1] Ali, *Aurangzeb*, pp. 16–18.
[2] E.g. after Aurangzeb's defeat of his brother at the battle of Samugarh in 1658.
[3] W. E. Moreland, *India at the death of Akbar*.
[4] Ali, *Aurangzeb*, p. 29.

the *ahadis*,[1] or personal troops, a kind of gentlemen's cadet corps, and from there, if first impressions were confirmed, be given a *mansab*. Or he might be given the command of ten straight away. No doubt on occasion the emperor would confer *mansabs* on men of whom reports of good service had come in, or who had caught his eye on campaign or in battle. There were also 'diplomatic' appointments, appointments with political overtones, like those of Rajput chiefs, Maratha Sirdars and Deccani Muslims. But many, and probably most in the lower ranks, must have been the result of the 'interest' of some group or individual who had the ear of the emperor. Existing *mansabdars* must certainly have interested themselves in their relations' prospects, and high officers must have been anxious to increase their influence by securing the appointment of connexions and dependents. In the circumstances it is surprising that the *khanzada* body was not larger than it was. Their failure to form a close oligarchy of the 'ins' suggests the keenness of competition for entry and imperial or ministerial sagacity in keeping the appointment options open.

The functions of the *mansabdars* covered the whole range of government except the judicial, which was reserved to the Muslim officers, the *maulvis* and the *qazis*. But as the law officers were interpreting a static system rather than enacting change through legal means, there was little occasion for a clash. Their work was declaration rather than legislation. The executive was largely independent of the judiciary, for the law officers had no collective organisation and could only record individual *fatwas* or opinions. Public opinion as to Islamic propriety was, apart from the imperial authority, the only real check on their actions. Then there were the confidential advisers or privy councillors of the emperor (the *lal purdahris*);[2] they held the high offices of state, such as that of *wazir* and the various *bakshis*; they were governors of provinces (*subadars*) and districts (*faujdars*); they commanded armies and forts. In the ranks below a thousand *zat* the positions they held were naturally subordinate, but like young I.C.S. officers they were on their way up. Officers such as *dewans* and lesser military commanders who must have mixed with them in the course of duty may be compared to the uncovenanted services of British India in relation to the I.C.S. There were, indeed, no hard and fast rules barring particular cadres from specified offices or posts, but it is clear that there was little hope of a high appointment for anyone who had not first acquired a *mansab*.

The *mansabdari* system disappeared with the Mughal Empire itelf.

---

[1] See *Ain* Book II, Ain 4, tr. H. Blochmann, 2nd ed., Calcutta, I, 259.
[2] Literally, those who had the privilege of passing through the red curtained doorway which led from the Hall of Public Audience to that of Private Audience.

Its hierarchy of ranks and the system of title-giving continued in Hyderabad state, whose head himself held the hereditary Mughal title of *Nizam-ul-mulk* or Regulator of the Kingdom, but it was a titular extension only, with none of the essence of assignment salaries, obligatory maintenance of contingents and executive duties. It was merely the framework of a post-Mughal Hyderabad peerage. It cannot be said that its collapse was a cause of the imperial fall; rather it was coterminous with it. Both dissolved together under the impact of forces which undermined them both. In the first place the system depended upon a tight control from above, by the emperor and his ministers. This control began to weaken in the later years of Aurangzeb, towards the end of the seventeenth century. The evidence for this is strong, including the complaints of the emperor himself. Indeed Aurangzeb himself can, in the second half of his reign from 1681 to 1707, which he spent in the Deccan, be described as the first of the later Mughals. Disregard or evasion of orders increased. In the emperor's absence, local crises like the rising of the Jats, the Mewatis and the Sikhs had to be settled on the spot. Apart from the declining authority of an ageing emperor there was a crisis in assignments. The demands of Deccan, politics required the creation of many more *mansabdars* both Muslim, Deccani and Maratha. But the disturbed state of the Deccan as a consequence of the destruction of the Muslim kingdoms of Golkonda and Bijapur and the Maratha kingdom of Sivaji seriously reduced the revenue available for the necessary assignments. So *mansabdars* increasingly received assignments whose revenue was insufficient to meet their *sawar* obligations. There arose a queue of *mansabdars* awaiting the award of any assignments.[1] As the economic crisis deepened *mansabdars* whose assignments were changed in the normal working of the system, became more and more reluctant to give them up. As the central government declined in authority it became more and more difficult for the government officers to enforce transfers. Indeed, since they themselves were often suffering from the same economic stringency and the same political uncertainties, they became less and less anxious to do so. Aurangzeb's prolonged residence in the Deccan and advancing age was the first cause of this decline, but its progress was accelerated by the wars of succession of 1707, 1712, 1713 and 1720–1 which first substituted puppets for rulers on the throne and then a clearer balance of rival factions without the strength to restore discipline.[2] Thus from about 1690 onwards to 1750 the *mansabdari* service was being transformed

---

[1] Ali, *Aurangzeb*, pp. 92–4. Aurangzeb thus expressed the shortage, 'There is only one pomegranate to serve a hundred sick men'.

[2] See W. Irvine, *The Later Mughals, 1707–1739*, 2 vols., Calcutta and London, especially Chapters IV, V, VI, VII and X.

from an official cadre to a title-holding group without power or inner cohesion. Former assignments increasingly became *jagirs* whose holders used their revenue to raise private armies for personal ventures. In Bengal the *zamindari* system developed out of the ruins of assignments. Bureaucracy dissolved into a disorderly system of personal fief holders with shifting loyalties and vaulting personal ambitions. The dissolution was completed by the destruction of the central authority at the hands of rival factions and the successive establishment of independent states in different parts of the empire.[1] These developments, however, were only the last nails in the coffin of the system. It had already been struck down by the enfeeblement of the necessary imperial regulator, which deprived it of the life-blood of discipline and authority, and by a creeping economic palsy which paralysed its executive limbs.

Looking now at the *mansabdari* system as an elite it seems clear that it can only be so described in a rather special sense. First comes the question of relationships. Can it be called an elite in itself or was it itself the product of an elite? Was it, in fact, the hen or the egg? On the one hand there is no doubt that the *mansabdars* governed the empire; they were both the sword and the pen of the emperor. The government could not have been stable without them. It would have become as in the days of Babur and Homayun, a dictatorship depending on the vagrant loyalties of numerous chiefs of diverse origins. Had some military genius revived the empire in the mid-eighteenth century it would have been an unstable regime of this sort unless he revived a disciplined bureaucracy as well. On the other hand it is to be noted that the *mansabdars* possessed no principle of unity amongst themselves, no cohesive spirit which could on occasion produce united action and impose itself on the emperor himself. Impositions occurred but they were by individual ministers using their backing as chiefs, such as the two Sayyids of Barha. Each had a second loyalty to race or clan (Turk, Rajput, Afghans etc.), to whose factions they adhered when factions arose. In this respect they had not got as far as the barons of King John or Henry III. To take an Indian parallel, one may note the slaves of the early Turkish sultanate. Though their origin was predatory and their status servile, their abilities won them high office, and they had enough corporate consciousness to intervene on occasion as a body in state affairs. The Janissaries of Turkey were a comparable and longer lived body. In British India, members of the Civil Service, though kept in strict subordination, developed a *persona* of their own because of their virtual irreplaceability. Service opinion was a factor to be reckoned with, and if their power of positive independent action was not great

---

[1] For these factions see Satish Chandra: *Parties and Politics at the Mughal Court (1707–1740)*, Aligarh, 1959.

their ability to obstruct and delay was considerable. Amongst the
Sikhs the army was an elite with its own *persona*; after Ranjit Singh's
death it made and unmade governments in rapid succession. In the
contemporary world there are many military elites which possess this
function of initiation and policy-making.

The fact must be faced that the *mansabdars* did not possess this power.
They had, so far as I can see, no *persona* of their own. They were the end
product of the straining of the real political elite through the sieves of
selection, discipline and honour. Their source was the whole body of
aristocratic chiefs in the country of all persuasions. The emperor, as it
were, took a portion of the pack and used it to control the remainder.
Their link was with him, and not, as in the later Civil Service, partly
at least with each other. That was why the system collapsed as soon as
the emperor's authority declined. In this respect they can perhaps be
compared to the British Civil Service in relation to the middle class.
The Service grew up as a specialist selection from the middle class,
which was the ruling group of the country. In one sense the Service was
an undoubted elite but in another it was only a reflection of or pro-
jection upon public affairs of the dominant middle class. This analogy
must not be pushed too far however, for there were also important
differences between *mansabdars* and Whitehall officials. One is that the
Civil Service has certainly some *persona* of its own, though it is also
subordinate to another body. Another is that while the Civil Service
'regulator' was the middle class from which it came, the *mansabdari*
'regulator' was the emperor to whom they looked. If the British middle
class declined, the character of the Civil Service would change; in the
other case it was when the emperor's authority declined that the
mansabdari system collapsed.

My conclusion is that the *mansabdars* constituted a genuine elite but
one which was of a secondary type. They never developed a personality
of their own and owed their effectiveness to the control of the emperor.
They derived from a larger class from which they were selected. They
were, in fact, a selected cross-section of the landed aristocrats of India.
They neither created the empire in the beginning, nor prevented its
fall at the end. Their origin was derivative and their role secondary.
With these qualifications they were a real force, forming a bureaucracy
which held India together more effectively than any previous regime
since the Gupta dynasty of the fourth and fifth centuries A.D. If assignments had not been substituted for cash payments at the end of Akbar's
reign, the *mansabdars* might have developed an *esprit de corps* reminiscent
of that of the Indian Civil Service of the nineteenth century; as it was
they remained dependent on the emperor. They carried the name and
authority of the emperor to places which had never known them before.

They did not create regimes or direct policy; what they did was to buttress efficiently the regime by regulating affairs, so making effective its authority and implementing its policy. There could have been no Mughal Empire without the *mansabdars*, but there could have been no *mansabdars* without the Mughal emperors.

SOURCES

The principal authorities for this chapter are:

The Ain-i Akbari of Abu'l Fazl, vol. I, trans. by H. Blochmann, 2nd ed., Calcutta, 1927.

The Ma'asir u'l Umara of Shah Nawaz Khan, trans. H. Beveridge, Bibliotheca Indica, Asiatic Soc. of Bengal (New Series), 1911–14.

W. Irvine, *The Army of the Indian Mughals*, London, 1903.

W. E. Moreland, *India at the death of Akbar*, London, 1920.

W. E. Moreland, *From Akbar to Aurangzeb*, London, 1923.

Abdul Aziz, *The Mansabdari System and the Mughal Army*, Lahore, 1945.

Satish Chandra, *Parties and Politics at the Mughal Court (1707–40)*, Aligarh, 1959.

Sir J. Sarkar, *Mughal Administration*, Calcutta, 1920.

Sir J. Sarkar, *History of Aurangzeb*, 5 vols., Calcutta, 1912–30.

I. H. Qureshi, *The Administration of the Mughal Empire*, Karachi, 1966.

M. Athar Ali, *The Mughal Nobility under Aurangzeb*, New York, 1966.

TRADITIONAL ELITES IN THE GREAT REBELLION OF 1857: SOME ASPECTS OF RURAL REVOLT IN THE UPPER AND CENTRAL DOAB

ERIC STOKES

Rural revolt in 1857 was essentially elitist in character. Things may have been otherwise in the cities and towns, where as at Aligarh (Koil) 'the low Muhammedan rabble' could become a potent revolutionary force. But in the countryside the mass of the population appears to have played little part in the fighting or at most tamely followed the behests of its caste superiors. The dominant castes and communities that took the lead in rebellion were a minority of the population, and, of these, the owners of land were a still smaller group. Figures for the classification and enumeration of population have to be treated with reserve, but it is interesting to note, for example, that in Aligarh district in 1872 landowners numbered some 26,551 or 2½ per cent of the total population.[1] In Mathura district where cultivating proprietary brotherhoods of Jats were thick on the ground the proportion was higher, some 6½ per cent. Roughly 47,000 owners (including non-agriculturalists) controlled an adult male agricultural population of 129,000 cultivators; in other words one in three male agriculturalists owned land.[2] It was one in six in the Ganges Canal Tract of the Muzaffarnagar district where the landowning castes—Tagas, Jats, Rajputs, Sayyids, Sheikhs, Gujars, Borahs, Marhals and Mahajans—comprised one third of the population.[3] In Mainpuri district the Rajputs formed just over 8 per cent of the population and held about one half of the land.[4] Even, therefore, where 'village republics' owned the land, as in the Jat *bhaiachara* settlements in northern Mathura or in the western portions of Meerut and Muzaffarnagar districts, the proprietary body

---

[1] *Statistical, Descriptive and Historical Account of the N.W. Provinces...*, ed. E. T. Atkinson (hereafter referred as *Gazetteer N.W.P.*), Vol. II, pt. 1, p. 390.
[2] *Report on the Settlement of the Muttra District N.W.P.* by R. S. Whiteway, Allahabad, 1879 (hereafter cited as *Muttra S.R.*), p. 25.
[3] *Settlement Report of the Ganges Canal Tract of the Muzaffarnagar District* (Allahabad, 1878), by A. Cadell, p. 10 ff.
[4] *Gazetteer N.W.P.* IV, 386 ff.

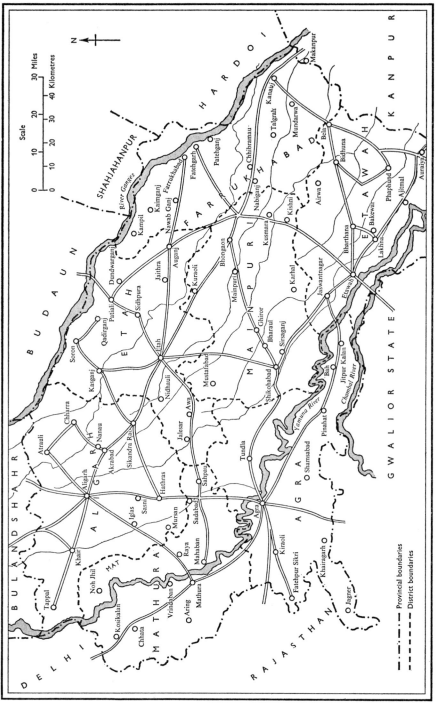

Map I. The Agra region.

was very much a rural elite. This fact deserves emphasis since it is all too easy to view the peasantry as a rural proletariat.

Most accounts trace the rural rebellion to the revolutionary effects upon the traditional landholding classes of British legal and institutional innovations. The rendering of the *malguzari* right (the right to engage for the government revenue) freely alienable and saleable is held to have resulted in a vast transfer of land rights and the displacement of much of the traditional elite—whether magnate or village *zamindars*—by the urban trading and money lending classes and by office-holders drawn from the literate castes.[1] Unquestionably there was a high rate of transfer of proprietary title (though not, of course, of actual cultivating possession), not only in the early fumbling period of British rule but in the later pre-Rebellion decades when the administrative machine was functioning more regularly. In some districts the rate ran as high as 2 per cent per annum, so that, as in Aligarh district, title to more than 50 per cent of the land could change hands in the two decades after 1838.[2] But although the non-agricultural classes made extensive acquisitions, increasing their hold up to as much as 18 per cent of the total cultivation (as in Saharanpur district by 1868), their gains were nothing like proportionate to the transfer rate. As Cohn has found in the Varanasi (Benares) region a large portion of the transfers represented a circulation of property within the traditional elite. The breakdown of British authority so far from throwing this elite wholly on to the side of rebellion split it raggedly down the middle, with the result that, even within the same district, magnate or peasant proprietors of the same caste could react in quite opposite directions. In Meerut district the Jats of Hapur *pargana* fought stoutly on the British side; to the west on the other side of the Hindan river in Baraut and Barnawa *parganas* they rose in their thousands, driving off the British columns sent from Meerut and pouring supplies into rebel-held Delhi. In the Muzaffarnagar district the Sayyid communities in the eastern *parganas* stayed quiet, while on the other side the Muslim gentry rose to support the Thana Bhawan rising of September 1857 when the green flag of Islam was raised and a *jihad* proclaimed against the white infidel. These are complexities that confute the generalized simplest accounts but they are still susceptible of historical explanation.

Strong armed clan communities such as the Jat clan settlements in western Meerut and Muzaffarnagar or those of the Gujars in western Saharanpur or the Pandir Rajputs of southern Saharanpur flared readily into rebellion, probably out of resentment at the heavy dif-

---

[1] S. B. Chaudhuri, *Civil Rebellion in the Indian Mutinies*, Calcutta, 1957, p. 21. S. N. Sen, *Eighteen Fifty Seven*, Calcutta, 1957, pp. 32–5.
[2] *Aligarh Settlement Report*, Allahabad, 1882, para. 182, p. 65.

ferential revenue assessment laid upon them.[1] But the critical factor in rural reactions was the presence or absence of a thriving magnate element heavily committed by interest to British rule. Nowhere were objective conditions more ripe for revolt than among the Sayyids of the Ganges Canal Tract of eastern Muzaffarnagar. Their losses of land to the urban moneylender had been on a spectacular scale, rising in some *parganas* such as Khatauli to as much as 56 per cent between 1840 and 1860. But the danger of revolt was stayed by the leadership of a few thriving Sayyid families who, aided by office-holding under the British, had built up considerable estates. The same phenomenon of magnate leadership is observable in south-eastern Meerut and in the Buland-shahr district. Here the Jats unlike their kinsmen near the Yamuna (Jumna) followed the lead of the Jat raja of Kuchesar, Gulab Singh, who held a vast estate of more than 270 villages.[2]

What were the conditions that permitted the emergence of a pros-pering, collaborating magnate class? A simple answer would be that where *zamindari* (roughly undivided freehold) tenures were numerous, a market in land titles was more readily created and supplied the conditions of mobility in which a new, active landlord class could emerge. Eastern Muzaffarnagar mirrored such conditions. In contrast, where cultivating proprietary brotherhoods (*bhaiachara*) held the land, they were not readily ousted by outsiders; mobility of titles was con-sequently much lower, as the lighter transfer rate in the Jat areas indicate. More important than the tenurial structure of the individual village was perhaps the supra-village organization of the clan area (*khap* or *ilaqua*), which M. C. Pradhan has shown has persisted ten-aciously to the present.[3] Not only did this help to keep outside encroach-ment at bay, but supplied a powerful political weapon for joint action among village communities. Nevertheless the difficulty which Jats or Gujars faced in revolt was the generalization of resistance to embrace other clans and groups. In the absence of individual leadership capable of welding, say, a whole district together, the rebellion of peasant communities would remain isolated and confined to their particular localities.

The critical factor remained, therefore, whether for the promotion or suppression of revolt, the action of magnate elements. Impoverished gentry could sometimes fill the gap in leadership, like Khairati Khan of Parasauli in Muzaffarnagar, an old Pindari who apparently placed

[1] I have treated these questions in greater detail in 'Rural Revolt in the Great Rebellion of 1857 in India: A Study of the Saharanpur and Muzaffarnagar Districts', *Historical Journal*, Vol. XII (1969), no. 4.

[2] See E. Stokes, 'Nawab Walidad Khan and the 1857 Struggle in the Bulandshahr District', *Bengal Past and Present*, Diamond Jubilee Number, 1967.

[3] M. C. Pradhan, *The Political System of the Jats of Northern India*, Bombay, 1966.

himself at the head of the Jat rising in late August 1857, but generally such men proved too lacking in scale and resources and themselves looked to magnate leaders. Thus in Bulandshahr district disaffected Muslim gentry like the Sayyids of Shikarpur rallied to the standard of Nawab Walidad Khan of Malagarh, a fallen nobleman who was related by marriage to the Delhi dynasty and well versed in public affairs. For a time Walidad rendered himself formidable, and the British were fortunate that there were few of his calibre in the Central and Upper Doab. But in this region most of the magnate class in fact stayed quiet or actively assisted the British. The notion that the traditional elite was driven *en bloc* into rebellion needs, therefore, critical re-examination.

Aligarh district makes an interesting study in this respect. 50 per cent of the land changed hands between 1839 and 1858, spurred by a heavy average revenue demand of Rs. 2-3-1 to the cultivated acre. The moneylending and trading classes registered considerable gains, strengthening their grip from 3·4 per cent of the district in 1839 to 12·3 per cent in 1868. Yet their overall gain of 9 per cent looks modest when viewed against total transfers which evidently in the main took the form of a circulation of proprietary rights within the traditional landholding castes. Circulation took place in two ways: first in the passage of land from village proprietors to magnates, and secondly, among village proprietors themselves.

Now it may seen odd to speak of the gains of the magnate class in a district where British administrative action in the pre-Mutiny decades would appear to have been so sharply directed against them. Thornton's settlement of 1839 was notorious for its deliberate attempt to curb the Jat chieftains of Hathras and Mursan by instituting a sub-settlement, wherever possible, with the village communities. The British themselves were agreeably surprised that the magnates should stick by them in the crisis of 1857 in view of the severe mauling the magnates had supposedly received at their hands.

W. H. Smith commented in his settlement report on Aligarh in 1874:

Scarcely one member of any of the old and powerful families of the district joined in the disturbances: on the contrary, some of these gave what assistance they could with undoubted readiness: some, like Thakur Gobind Singh, nobly exposed their lives in our cause, while others afforded aid only perhaps because they doubted the policy of refusing. Strangely enough...those of the greater families who had lost most by our rule, turned out our firmest friends in the time of trouble and need. Thakur Gobind Singh, the son of the very man whose fort we had taken and whose power we had crushed (in 1817)...was eminently loyal. He never hesitated from the first, but aided us with his followers, fought in our battles, and kept order on our behalf. Raja Tikam Singh, the son of Bhagwant Singh, whose independence we had forcibly destroyed, assisted us throughout to the utmost of his ability, though his own power had been largely reduced by the policy pursued at the last settlement by Mr Thornton. Without the aid of these two men Hathras would have been plundered, and our footing in the district for the time at least have been lost...[1]

The damage that Thornton's anti-*talukdar* settlement inflicted on the magnate interest in Aligarh was in fact, however, superficial. With the Mursan raja, Tikam Singh, the settlement was a generous one. Not only was he compensated with a fixed allowance or *malikana*—usually $22\frac{1}{2}$ per cent—of the revenue demand paid by the village proprietors (*biswadars*), but he was allowed to continue the work of collection himself, the villagers paying *malikana* directly to him. The financial arrangement worked to his advantage, as Thornton acknowledged:

instead of a vague title, and an income insufficient for his expenses, especially as it was never fully collected, the former [*viz.* the Raja] has now been recorded as zamindar of more than one-third of the pargana, and as hereditary talukdar with defined rights in the remainder; his income has been considerably increased, and there is every ground for hope that he will fully realise it.[2]

Given the circumstances that the Raja had pitched up the demand to such a height before Thornton's revision that the villages were falling heavily into arrears, there was much to be said from his viewpoint for an arrangement which guaranteed the coercive force of the courts for the collection of his fixed percentage of a punitively heavy demand.[3]

In contrast, so far from stabilizing and securing the village communities, Thornton's settlement completely defeated his intentions. Its close definition of landed rights seems to have been the signal for a revolution in proprietary titles, which according to Smith acquired for the first time a saleable value. In this revolution it was the magnate class as well as the moneylending and trading classes that forged ahead.[4] In the Hathras *tahsil*, where 'a vast revolution of property' took place, the Jats as a caste held their own without loss over the thirty years 1839–68, despite the fact that the transfers in the period amounted to some 66 per cent of the land:

Thirty-four per cent only of the land is now in the hands of those who occupied it at last settlement, and the majority of this belongs to Raja Tikam Singh, who has alone remained unaffected by the prevailing changes ...In fact, the old village occupants, the preservation of whom was Mr

[1] W. H. Smith in *Aligarh Settlement Report*, para. 55, p. 19.
[2] Cited Smith, para. 335, p. 118.
[3] For Mursan settlement, see Thornton's report in *Allygurh Statistics* by J. Hutchinson, Rurkee, 1854.   [4] Smith, paras. 186–7, pp. 67–8.

Thornton's chief care and thought, have been almost crushed out of the subdivision, and new men, to a large extent Bohras and Banias, have taken their place.

Not all the *talukdars*, however, were as fortunate as the Mursan raja. Many of the smaller *talukdars* like Thakur Jiwa Ram of Mendhu and Raja Narain Singh of Husain foundered while Tikam Singh was extending his estates, buying in the *biswadars* of four villages and so converting his hold to full ownership (*zamindari*).

The village bodies suffered fearfully. The *talukdari* settlement, with its additional increment of *malikana*, laid on them burdens too grievous to be borne. An assessment that was avowedly based on extracting 80 per cent of the rental assets left them a helpless prey of the Hathras banias and the village *saukars*. More than a third of the *talukdari* villages were sold up entirely, and a further third lost more than a half of their land.[1] But the alienation statement for 1838–68 shows the main sufferers to have been the Rajput brotherhoods, who over the period lost 51 per cent of their land, their losses (of 35,284 acres) balancing almost exactly the bania gains.

Other parts of the district illustrate the same transfer of rights out of the hands of the village proprietors. In Sikandra Rao Rajput transfers were again enormous, amounting to some 41 per cent in *pargana* Akerabad and 57 per cent in *pargana* Aligarh. But the take-over of the Husain taluk by the moneylending Rajput Jadon family of Mathura (under Raja Pirthi Singh of Awa) from the Porach Rajput family, and other internal caste transfers of this kind, disguise the extent to which property changed hands. In the upshot the Thakur (Rajput) loss appears as no more than 13·4 per cent.

Unfortunately the statistics do not allow us to distinguish with any great clarity the twin processes of circulation within castes which it has been suggested occurred, first the transfer of land from village communities to magnates, and secondly the movement of land within village communities themselves. Where the first process predominated, it seems more than likely that the magnates remained pro-British and were able to smother rebellion. The *talukdari parganas*, Hathras, Koil, Sikandra Rao, and Atrauli were of this kind. Disturbances, of course, did break out. Mangal Singh and Mahtab Singh, Rajput *zamindars* of Akrabad (*tahsil* Silkandra Rao) 'after the plunder of Akrabad *Tehseel* Treasury by sepoys, permitted the destruction of the records by their own people, refused all aid to the *Tehseeldar*, and generally lived a life of open rebellion'.[2] Yet they were countered by 'the most influen-

---

[1] Smith, para. 340, p. 119.
[2] W. J. Bramley, Mag. Aligarh to A. Cocks, Sp. Commr., 17 Nov. 1858; cited S. A. A. Rizvi, (ed.), *Freedom Struggle in Uttar Pradesh*, Lucknow, 1957–61, V, 868.

tial of Pundir Thakurs of Sikandra Rao, Jawahir Singh of Akerabad and Kundan Singh of Nai', who 'behaved remarkably well and afforded continuous and valuable aid'. The Kundan Singh at the end of August 1857 was made *nazim* of the *pargana*, and with a body of 1,500 of his own followers reinstated the *tahsildar* and maintained him in that position until authority was thoroughly re-established. When he died two years afterwards 'his sons and nephews were left among the most prosperous zamindars in the tahsil'.[1]

On the western side of the district in the thickly settled Jat *parganas* abutting Mathura district, the two processes were still more confused since the *talukdari* areas ran cheek by jowl with the Jat clan *khaps*. While Gobind Singh was raising the Jat Horse for service on the British side, Mohammad Ghaus Khan, who had taken over the leadership of the Muslim revolt in Koil city (Aligarh), was appealing to the Jat peasantry for supplies and promising that the district of Koil would be theirs.[2] Proprietary brotherhoods notoriously stood up better to a heavy revenue demand than single *zamindari* estates, but, assuming they had also withstood other forms of landlord encroachment by raja or bania, their resentment usually took the form of direct rebellion. This happened at Iglas and Khair. At Iglas the Jat communities 'under the guidance of one Amani Jat, ex-pattidar of Gahon...who had then come to the surface and dubbed himself Raja had the audacity to attack the trained troops of the Gwalior Contingent'. The same body of Jats from the Lageswan region in *pargana* Hasangarh joined in the attack on the government offices in Khair. Here on 20 May Rao Bhopal Singh, head of the Chauhan Rajputs of the *pargana*, had deposed the *tahsildar*, only to be surprised, caught and hanged by Watson, the Magistrate, and his European volunteers on 1 June. The sequence was that 'before the middle of the month the Chohans of the pergunnah, intent on revenge, called in the Jats to their help, attacked Khyr, plundered and destroyed nearly all the Government buildings, as well as the houses of the Bunyahs and Mahajuns'.[3] What bound together Jat and Rajput—hereditary enemies—in fitful alliance?

In *tahsil* Iglas small *taluks* were intermingled with village estates held by Jat proprietary brotherhoods working one of the finest tracts in the district. These *taluks*, such as Biswan, Kanka, Kajraut, and Gorae, each of a dozen villages or so, had stood up better here than elsewhere, but were probably too small to smother the rebellion of village communities. The severity and, above all, the unequal incidence of the

[1] Smith, para. 55, p. 19; para. 72, pp. 24–5. *Gazetteer N.W.P.* ed. E. A. Atkinson, II i, Allahabad, 1875, 509.
[2] S. A. A. Rizvi (ed.), *Freedom Struggle in Uttar Pradesh*, V, 668, 686.
[3] Bramley to Cocks, 17 Nov. 1858, *op. cit.* para. 10, cited *Freedom Struggle in Uttar Pradesh*, V, 658–9.

revenue demand placed the village communities under cruel pressure. Where additionally a heavy *malikana* was exacted by the *talukdar* the *biswadars* or sub-proprietors laboured under what was later acknowledged to be 'an almost unendurable burden'.[1] Land rights changed hands freely, as much as 52 per cent of the *tahsil* being subject to transfer between 1838 and 1868. The industrious Thakurel branch (*got*) of Jats which held the *chauwan gaon* or fifty-four villages of Lagaswan had undoubtedly suffered inroads from the moneylender. But total Jat losses in the *tahsil* do not appear to have been heavy over the thirty years of the settlement; apparently they parted with some 9,500 acres of their 110,000 acres, 3,500 being confiscated for rebellion in 1857.

W. H. Smith acknowledged that the Jats had put up a 'tough resistance' to the encroachment of the moneylending Brahmin and bania, and in 1868 they still held three-quarters of the land in the *tahsil*. Their most burning grievance was evidently the inequity of the revenue assessment.

That the Jats of Lagaswan should have sunk their traditional feud and leagued with the Chauhan Rajputs of Khair under Rao Bhopal Singh is testimony to their hatred of British rule. The Chauhan Rajputs had still stronger cause for rebellion. In *tahsil* Khair as a whole the Rajputs labouring under a revenue rate of Rs. 2-1-3 on the cultivation had lost almost 30 per cent of their land, while the Jats, whose holdings had equalled theirs, lost a mere 5 per cent. In Khair *pargana* itself the Chauhan Rajputs had in distant times held the whole area together with the neighbouring *parganas* of Chandaus and Murthal. By 1857 the head of this branch, Bhopal Singh, was reduced to a single village, and, 'urged by the vain hope of recovering the former influence of the tribe', led the attack on the Khair *tahsil* offices.[2]

All these are instances where land transfers, induced for the most part by a heavy revenue demand, failed to throw up a rising landlord element from among the traditional landholding castes. The fact that the banias made significant gains, largely at the expense of the unthrifty Rajput communities, sharpened no doubt the bitterness of loss, and made them a target for vengeance. But of themselves they hardly supply the main explanation of the pattern of rebellion. The really violent and persistent disturbances came from the *bhaiachara* Jat communities of the western *parganas* which continued into the Mathura district up to the Yamuna (Jumna) river and among whom bania gains were lowest.

The hard core of Jat settlement lay in *pargana* Noh Jhil in the Mathura district among the Nohwar and Narwar *gots*. Here the clan community

---

[1] *Aligarh S.R.* p. 85, para. 250.   [2] Smith, *Aligarh S. R.* para. 88, p. 31.

was to be found in its full perfection,[1] and the strength of its organization enabled it to withstand a stiff rate of revenue assessment and keep out the moneylender. In the early years of British rule (1809) it was remarked 'there is not a mahajan in the pargana, and the zamindars are so notoriously refractory that no man of property will become security for them'.[2] Immediately after the rebellion J. R. Best, the Officiating Collector, noted that where the *bhaiachara* system prevailed it was almost impossible for capital to force its way. Even well after 1857 when confiscations and commercial conditions had promoted land owning by the trading classes, Whiteway, the Settlement Officer, could still report in the early 70s that 'mahajans and bankers...have much less influence here than in most other parts of India'.[3]

Mark Thornhill, who had charge of the district at the outbreak of disturbances, considered Noh Jhil 'perhaps the worst Pergunnah of Muttra. It was the first that went into rebellion and the last to submit.' From this and other examples of peasant rebellion he determined on drastic measures:

However paradoxical it may appear it is a matter of fact that the agricultural laboring class—the class who above all others have derived the most benefit from our rule—were the most hostile to its continuance, whilst the large proprietors who have suffered under our rule almost to a man stood by us. As soon as I had realised this fact I brought it strongly to the late Mr Colvin's notice and urged that the Government must reverse its policy and throw itself on the large proprietors and repress the peasantry.[4]

In Noh Jhil he ordered the confiscation of twenty-two villages and proposed to confer them on the Mathura banking family of the Seths in reward. He carried out similar extensive confiscations elsewhere, but even in the pro-magnate atmosphere of the aftermath of revolt such sweeping proposals produced a reaction. Vansittart, the Special Commissioner, mounted a crusade to reverse the anti-peasant policy not only in Mathura but also in Agra and Etawah districts, resting himself on Burke's argument that he knew not how to draw up an indictment against a whole people. His thesis was simple: 'The main cause of rural rebellion was not the hatred of our rule but a summary adjustment by the sword of those feuds which had arisen out of the action of our Civil and Revenue laws on proprietary rights in land.'[5] Yet

[1] Cf. B. H. Baden-Powell, *The Indian Village Community*, 1896, p. 281ff.

[2] *Muttra S. R.* by R. S. Whiteway, p. 251.

[3] *Ibid.* p. 249. For Best's comments, J. R. Best to G. F. Harvey, 8 Dec. 1858; Post-Mutiny Records, Com. (Agra) Revenue 1859, bundle 2 (ii), File no. 35. U.P. State Archives, Allahabad.

[4] Mark Thornhill to W. Muir, Secy. to Govt., 15 Nov. 1858; Post-Mutiny Records, Com. (Agra) Judicial I (iii), File 49 (File 126/I 1857).

[5] Henry Vansittart to Muir, 28 Aug. 1858; *ibid.* Com. (Agra) Revenue 1859, bundle 2 (ii), File no. 35.

British rule could not be so readily exculpated, for 'the money-lenders and the mortgagers or purchasers of land' whom he saw as the enemy were scarcely in evidence in Noh Jhil or other strongly held *bhaiachara* clan areas. Alienation of land to outsiders was too slight to justify the sack of the Noh Jhil *tahsil* offices on 4 June by a crowd said to number 20,000 men,[1] which proceeded to destroy the records. One cannot but feel that the swingeing revenue assessment was the root of the matter.

This was to be seen in the *parganas* to the south of Noh Jhil. In 1881 Robertson, the Secretary to Government, reflecting on the settlement of 1839–69, wondered how the north eastern *parganas* of Mathura had stood a revenue rate (Rs. 2-8-3) even higher than that of Aligarh after revision (Rs. 2-6-3). But the rate rose progressively southwards, falling at Rs. 2-3-2 in Mat-Noh Jhil, Rs. 2-8-2 in Mahaban, Rs. 2-13-0 in Sadabad, and Rs. 3-1-8 in Sahpau.[2] Few communities could stand this degree of imposition, especially when they had not the tight clan organization of the Noh Jhil Jats or their standards of high farming. In Sahpau the village communities crumbled. The alienation statements shows 'the frightful extent to which the hereditary zamindars have been supplanted',[3] the majority of the alienations occurring in the twenty-five years between 1833 and the Mutiny. The result was 'the replacement of the hereditary yeomen...by a body of grasping traders and speculators who are not connected with the soil by ancient traditions, and who look upon the land merely as good investment for their capital'. But it is clear from the population figures that Jats were not strongly settled here (they were but 11 per cent of the population in 1872 as against some 53 per cent in Noh Jhil). The major losses during the 1833 settlement were borne by the Rajput communities, much as in *parganas* Hathras and Khair, to the advantage principally of non-resident Brahmin classes. In *pargana* Sadabad the position was different. Here the Jats formed the largest caste (some 28 per cent) and still were the most considerable landowners in 1873 (when they held 36 per cent), but the fact that they retained 73 per cent of the total *sir* or demesne lands, as against Brahmins 12 per cent and Thakurs 11 per cent, suggests their losses at some stage had been heavy. McConaghey, the settlement officer in 1873, inferred that the damage had largely been done during the first few years of British rule when Raja Bhagwant Singh of Mursan had been set aside and the revenue engagements taken with the village communities, who then proved unequal to the task of management. By 1873 just under half the land was in the possession of

[1] *Freedom Struggle in U.P.*, V, 686, 691. Also Vansittart to Muir, 2 Oct. 1858, Com. (Agra) Judicial I, File no. 2/1857.
[2] *Gazetteer N.W.P.* ed. Atkinson, VIII, Allahabad, 1884, 127.
[3] M. A. McConaghey in *Muttra S. R.* p. 129.

non-resident owners, half again of which can be identified as belonging to non-agricultural classes, Brahmins, Banias and Dhusars.[1]

Sahpau and Sadabad *parganas* were disturbed in May 1857 during that spontaneous, universal upsurge of anarchy that so flabbergasted Mark Thornhill, the magistrate. In late June he was able to take punitive measures in the Sadabad area, but on his enforced withdrawal shortly afterwards 'all the country round Sadabad rose, headed by one Deokaran, and plundered the *tahsil* and police station'. This was a Jat rising, but its details are obscure.[2] Better known are the peasant rebellions in the Mahaban *pargana*, which Thornhill's description has made celebrated.[3] Between 1838 and 1857 some 32 per cent of the land in *pargana* Mahaban was subject to transfer, the greater part going to strangers rather than other sharers. McConaghey estimated that in 1808 the Jats held at least three-fourths of the *pargana*; by 1874 their possessions had been reduced to one-third, that is, a loss of a half. The chief gainers were Brahmins, who extended their possessions from roughly 16 per cent in 1808 to some 32 per cent by 1874, and also banias who acquired some 15 per cent. It is not possible to date these gains, and, since a further 25 per cent of the *pargana* was alienated between 1858 and 1874, the extent of Jat losses needs to be kept in proportion. Now it is true that many of the Brahmin acquisitions as in Sahpau went to the non-agricultural class in Mathura and other towns, but in Mahaban it would appear that the principal beneficiary was the Brahmin Pachauri family of Mahaban itself 'whose importance dates from the time of Puran Chand, whose son Mukand Singh and grandson Ballab Singh were tahsildars in this district'.[4] Ballab Singh was recorded as a loyalist in 1857 who 'accepted the tahsildarship of P[h] Muhobun and with the aid of sowars he was authorized to raise managed to restore order in the P[h] in his own estates'.[5] The Jats traditionally made provision for their Brahmin priests by the grant of land, and the Pachauri family had claims to gentility, unlike that of Jagdispur (*pargana* Mahaban) or Salahpur Chandwara (*pargana* Sadabad) or Chhahari (*pargana* Mat), who advanced through moneylending.

After a punitive expedition to depose the celebrated Devi Singh of Tappa Raya who had set himself up as raja and sacked the *tahsil* offices, it was possible to restore and maintain order in this and neighbouring *parganas* through the use of collaborating agents. Thornhill

[1] *Muttra S. R.* p. 138.   [1] *Gazetteer N.W.P.* VIII, 227.
[2] Mark Thornhill, *Personal Adventures and Experiences...during...the Indian Mutiny*, 1884, pp. 102 ff.
[3] *Muttra S. R.* p. 155.
[4] Statement of persons who have rendered valuable services to Govt...dtd. 19 May 1858, sgd. J. R. Best; Com. (Agra) Judicial I 1857, File no. 1.
[5] *Muttra S. R.* p. 31.

appointed Raja Pirthi Singh of the Jadon family of Awa, to the office of *nazim* of Sadabad,[1] while Raja Tikam Singh of Mursan was given charge of *pargana* Mahaban where he still retained rights as *talukdar* in the small *taluks* of Ar, Sonkh, and Madim. According to Thornhill the recipe of governing through the great landholders worked the charm: 'the position from perfect anarchy was brought to perfect order and the entire revenue collected' even in the absence of British authority, except from *parganas* Noh Jhil, Kosi and part of Sahar.[2]

Here again then, in *parganas* Mahaban and perhaps Sadabad, the Jat colonies were too interspersed with magnate elements prepared to rally to the British to sustain a protracted resistance.

It should not be supposed, of course, that the traditional magnate class always rallied to the British. Where it did so, as in the person of the Mursan raja or the Lalkhani Bargujar house of Chhatari whose possessions spilled over from Bulandshahr into Aligarh district,[3] one may reasonably assume that it had successfully adjusted itself to the novel conditions of landholding introduced by British rule. Such adjustment was far from automatic. It is a remarkable feature of the Central Doab that, while on the Yamuna side the magnates largely sided with the British, on the Ganges side they went over to the rebels. In some measure they were undoubtedly influenced by their proximity to the stronghold of rebellion across the Ganges in Rohilkhand and Oudh, with bridge-heads across the river at Farrukhabad and Kanpur; but this supplies no sufficient explanation of why the rajas of Etah and Mainpuri threw in their lot with the cause of revolt. A detailed examination would be out of place here, but a brief examination of Mainpuri district and a quick glance at Etah may offer some pointers.

Between 1840 and 1857 some 32 per cent of the cultivated areas of Mainpuri district changed hands, although the proportion lost by the original owners was probably nearer 25 per cent. The transfers effected, however, a much smaller displacement of caste. Rajputs, easily the largest landholders, held 48 per cent of the villages in 1840 and still retained 44 per cent in 1870; while Brahmins rose from 14 to 18 per cent, and banias from $1\frac{1}{2}$ to $3\frac{1}{2}$ per cent. The value of land remained low and the settlement officers concluded that it was only after 1858 that

[1] Prithi Singh is a representative figure of a new entrepreneurial magnate class emerging from the ranks of the traditional elite. By the 1880s the raja of Awa's estates were 'reputed to be among the wealthiest in Upper India', paying some Rs. 3,75,000 in revenue; *Gazetteer N.W.P.* VIII, 72, and *Aligarh S. R.* 1882, para. 73, p. 25. For services in Rebellion, G. Couper to Offg. Commr. Agra, 2 Mar. 1859; Com. (Agra) Revenue Dept. 1860, bundle 3 (ii), File no. 40.

[2] M. Thornhill to W. Muir, Secy. to Govt. 15 Nov. 1858, *Gazetteer N.W.P.* VIII, 170.

[3] For the Chhatari family, see Stokes, 'Nawab Walidad Khan and the 1857 Struggle in Bulandshahr District', *Bengal Past and Present*, Diamond Jubilee Number, 1967, pp. 44 ff.

'capitalists' entered the land market. Assuming that Brahmin and other gains could be accounted gains of the trading classes, during the whole term of settlement between 1840 and 1870 the latter rose no more than 10 per cent.[1] There would therefore seem to be little that was typical of the classical revolutionary situation in Mainpuri. Yet Tej Singh, the raja, declared against the British and actively participated in military operations against them.

It is usual to suppose that, as one of the most sorely stricken victims of the anti-magnate policy of the Thomasonian era of the 1840s, Tej Singh had every justification.[2] But, as we have seen in Aligarh, this policy by no means spelled disaster to the magnate class. There high cultivation and a high revenue demand had generated a quasi-commercial market in land titles, while at the same time part of the traditional elite had transformed itself into a successful magnate element and more than kept its footing alongside the trading classes.

Conditions were clearly different in Mainpuri district. Tej Singh did not hold sway over densely settled cultivating brotherhoods, as may be seen from the very low numbers of *bhaiachara* estates. The Rajputs while holding a half of the district as late as the 1870s formed but 8 per cent of the population, and constituted more of a gentry or 'sturdy yeoman' class. Absentee ownership was high, characterizing three-fourths of the villages, and cultivating proprietors worked only 14 per cent of the total cultivated area as *sir* or home farm, Rajputs holding some 7 per cent. Apart from the Raja of Mainpuri and the Raja of Eka (heading the Pratabner branch), the Chauhan Rajputs, who played the critical role in the 1857 rising, were most strongly entrenched in small estates in the fertile central tracts of the district. The question before 1857 was whether they could hold their traditionally dominant position against other Rajput clans as well as other castes. The evidence suggests that they were forced to give ground on the western side of the district while maintaining their hold elsewhere. In what became Mainpuri *pargana* in the central region, for instance, the Chauhan proprietors (outside the twenty-three villages owned by large landholders) jostled for room. Property was extensively subdivided owing to the number of shareholders who traditionally took to military service to supplement their income. But no more than some 8 per cent of the cultivated area was subject to transfer, and the Rajputs still held 61 per cent (Chauhans 55 per cent) in 1870 as against 62 per cent in 1840. In Bhongaon *pargana*, further east, the transfer rate was higher, with about a quarter of the cultivation changing hands between 1840 and the rebellion, but the Rajput holdings remained steady from

[1] *Mainpuri Settlement Report*, Allahabad, 1875, pp. 17, 51–2.
[2] Cf. J. W. Kaye, *History of the Sepoy War*, II, 1864, 161 ff.

1840 to 1870 at 39 per cent. The Brahmins increased their hold from 17 to 25 per cent but mainly at the expense of the Kayaths and Lodhas. In Kishni *pargana*, bordering on Farrukhabad, the Chauhans in fact managed to increase their hold from 44 to 50 per cent over the settlement period.

On the western side of the district the story was different. The Mustafabad *pargana* marched with Agra and Mathura districts. Over the settlement period Rajputs dropped from 53 to 48 per cent, but Chauhan losses were more severe, their holdings falling from 46 to 36 per cent. Even Brahmin holdings dropped slightly from 9 to 8 per cent. The principal gainers were of the Marwari caste, a sure sign of intrusive commercial forces whose activity was so much more marked on the Yamuna side of the Doab. Transfers in this rich *pargana* ran extremely high, as much as 40 per cent of the land changing hands in a single decade between 1840 and 1850, while the revenue demand fell sharply on the cultivation at Rs. 2-3-2.

In Ghiror *pargana*, which stood between Mustafabad and Mainpuri, the Chauhans had again suffered, losing land to the moneylending Rajput Jadon family of Awa and to Brahmins from Kanauj, mainly it seems before 1857.

The Chauhan Thakurs still form the largest body of proprietors although their possessions have been sadly curtailed since the commencement of our rule. The members of the Partabner branch have suffered most severely, and the splendid estates of Usnida, Pachawar, Karaoli, Harhai, half Himmatpur, and Nahal Katengra with its six subordinate villages have passed away from them for ever for a mere song, before they were thoroughly acquainted with the rigid working of our system. It is distressing to see such men reduced to the position of cultivators when they might have been saved by more careful and lenient treatment. The Jadon Kunwars of Awa and Chaudhri Jai Chand of Binsiya now own their ancestral properties and are their masters.[1]

British officials later took the view that there was no mass rising of the agricultural community in Mainpuri as in Mathura district, but rather a struggle for the mastery between two landholding castes, the Chauhans and the Ahirs.

In this District there seems to have been no such thing as a national attempt at the subversion of the Government authority. No sooner did the mutiny commence, the Ahir tribe resumed their predatory habits and were followed by the Chowhan Rajpoots...All restraints were cast off and every malcontent found an opportunity for avenging old wrongs or recovering former possessions. Then followed the struggle for the mastery between the two tribes, and ended in the subversion of the Ahirs by the Chowhans. It was

[1] *Mainpuri Settlement Report*, p. 145.

owing in great measure to these incessant commotions that so many estates were ruined, and the prevalence of anarchy and suspension of authority were prolonged for so long a period.[1]

On this western side of the district, opposing the British presence at Agra, rebellion presented a ragged front. There was no clean division among the major caste groups; instead they fractured internally into collaborating and hostile elements. The Ahirs of Bharaul in Shikohabad *pargana* successfully repulsed Tej Singh, the Mainpuri raja, while their caste brethren, Ram Ratan and Bhagwan Singh of Rampur village, 'kept the whole pergunnah [of Mustafabad] in a state of rebellion and fought against British rule'.[2] Similarly, on Tej Singh's behalf 'the famous Ristee Ram of Khyrnuggur...with Soonder Singh, his uncle, headed several marauding expeditions into Furozabad and Moostufabad which contributed in no small degree to the anarchy and disorder which prevailed in these Perghunnahs'. Yet other Chauhans of Mustafabad *pargana* remained faithful to the politics of collaboration. It is noticeable that those like the Uresar family under Kunwar Gajadhar who 'did good services during the mutiny' were also those who had been 'more provident' than their Chauhan caste brethren and 'succeeded in retaining their ancestral land intact'. Bijai Singh, head of the Milauli family, was a similar 'shrewd and intelligent native gentleman, who, while most of his fellow caste-men were squandering away their hereditary lands, has succeeded in amassing considerable wealth and in acquiring fresh property'.[3]

It is against this background of Chauhan fearfulness for their traditional dominance, that Tej Singh's defection from the steadfast fealty of his ancient house to the British Raj must be judged. Apparently nature and circumstance had not lent him the capacity of adjustment that magnates nearer the Yamuna (Jumna) displayed. Edmonstone's picture of the Mainpuri house in 1840 as sunk in illiteracy, incompetence and corruption was a loaded one, but even a more favourable view would hardly suggest the dynasty had bred up a race of improving landlords. The *talukdari* sub-settlement struck an irretrievable blow. Although framed on terms similar to those of the Mursan raja in Aligarh, it had far less favourable results. It appears to have left the raja heavily dependent on his *talukdari* income rather than that derived from the small number of his estates recognized in full *zamindari*. Devoid of commercial aptitude or opportunity his position necessarily

[1] E. J. Boldero, Collr. to W. H. Lowe, Secy. Sudder Board of Rev., 17 Dec. 1858; Com. (Agra) Revenue 1859, bundle 2 (ii), File no. 35.
[2] Report by H. Chase, Joint Mag. 27 May 1859; Com. (Agra) Rev. Dept. 67/I of 1859, bundle 2 (iii), File no. 44.
[3] *Mainpuri Settlement Report*, p. 61. Also G. E. Lance, Offg. Collr. to G. F. Harvey, Commr. Agra, 1 Feb. 1859; N.W.P. Political Progs. 19 Mar. 1859, no. 147.

rested on his powers of lordship, of which he was deliberately stripped. The Mursan raja had been allowed to continue the direct collection of his dues from his taluk, but in Mainpuri the raja was purposely set aside. He was left to draw his *malikana* from the district treasury and at a blow lost all power to intervene in 133 out of his 184 villages. Given the fact that his estates were situated in the portion of the district least given to cash-crop farming, with lower transfer and lower revenue rates, there was little prospect of his riding the blow.[1]

The Etah raja, Dambar Singh, was similarly placed. He was left with but nineteen of his 147 estates in *zamindari* possession, and from the rest was given what appeared to be a generous *malikana* of 29 per cent. Yet by 1852–3 he was being compelled to mortgage ninety-seven villages, so serious was his financial disarray.[2] When the British were evicted from the district in June 1857 he faltered into rebellion. Etah was again a comparatively backward region with a relatively low standard of agriculture. It too presented no favourable milieu for the emergence of an enterprising magnate element able to adapt successfully in face of the institutional pressures being exerted against the old forms of lordship. As we have seen elsewhere, it was the presence or absence of such an element that appears to have been critical in determining political allegiance in 1857. In large areas of Mathura and Aligarh districts it was able not merely to hold down tumultuous peasant revolt but to forward valuable sums in land revenue to the beleaguered British authorities in Agra. Where it had failed to emerge and a declining, aggrieved aristocracy held sway, districts smarting much less severely from the economic and social dislocation of British rule could be carried into rebellion.

[1] Tej Singh's defection was also prompted by personal factors. The young raja had been installed in 1851, but his right to succeed was disputed by his uncle, Bhawani Singh, whose appeal was pending before the Privy Council at the outbreak of revolt. Tej Singh was reputed weak and dissolute, and had been placed under check by A. H. Cocks, the district officer. Bhawani Singh was thought to have been loyal, but informed official opinion in the district later came to the conclusion that he had persuaded Tej Singh to revolt and then played a clever double game. See on the question *District Gazetteer of United Provinces, Vol. X. Mainpuri*, ed. E. R. Neave, Allahabad, 1910, pp. 174–5. Also N.W. Provinces Political Proceedings, 13 May 1859, no. 116, 11 Aug. 1859, nos. 68, 69, 24 Sept. 1859, nos. 199, 218. For the financial position of the Mainpuri raja compared with the Mursan raja, see N.W.P. Pol. Progs. 13 May 1859, nos. 116, 119, 1 Sept. 1859, nos. 12, 13, 8 June 1861, no. 29. Also N.W.P. Revenue Proceedings, 18 July 1842, no. 3, cited *Parliamentary Papers*, 1857–8, XLII, 297 ff.

[2] Com. (Agra) Judicial I (ii) 1857, File no. 13. Statement of Debts filed on Estates of Raja Dambar Singh.

CLASS, CASTE AND POLITICS
IN CALCUTTA, 1815–38

S. N. MUKHERJEE

I

Some years ago Professor Morris-Jones suggested that contemporary Indian politics should be looked upon as a tale of three political idioms, 'modern', 'traditional' and 'saintly'.[1] In this paper I shall attempt to show that, in Calcutta in the 1820s and 1830s, the politics of the Bengali elites of the *bhadralok* class, was conducted in two idioms, which I shall also call 'modern' and 'traditional'. The term politics is used here to mean collective human action performed with a power perspective. In politics men aim at gaining authority and influence over certain areas of human activity. This concept of politics does not preclude the role of ideas; many men were inspired, stirred into action by some great ideas, but they all aimed at gaining power, if only to implement their ideas. In the nineteenth century the political destiny of Bengal was controlled by the British, and no section of the population (with the exception of a small segment of the Bengali Muslim peasantry led by the revivalist *Faraidis*)[2] was willing or able to challenge the British authority, least of all the Calcutta elite. There were, however, many less important areas of power which were controlled by the Indians and the elite groups competed to gain this control.

By the 'modern' idiom of politics I mean agitation through the press, public meetings, and petitions to settle public issues. The public issues that were important to the Indians were concerned with English education, *sati*, the right of the Indians to sit as jurors, the defence of private property, and the demand for a better position for Indians in the British India administration. The two main groups involved in agitation on such public issues were described as 'liberals' and 'tories' in a contemporary magazine.[3] Although this view has been accepted by some modern historians[4] I shall endeavour to show that such

[1] W. H. Morris-Jones, 'India's political idioms', in C. H. Philips (ed.), *Politics and Society in India*, London, 1963, p. 135.
[2] Ziya-Ul-Hasan Faruqi, *The Deobond School and the demand for Pakistan*, Bombay, 1963, pp. 17–18.
[3] *Alexander's East India Magazine and Colonial and Commercial Journal*, London, Vol. 1, Dec. 1830 to June 1831, p. 48.
[4] A. F. S. Ahmed, *Social ideas and social change in Bengal 1818–1835*, Leiden, 1965, pp. 27–31.

political labels had only a limited application in the 1820s and 1830s of the last century in Calcutta.

There was another area of collective activity, almost hidden, in which the Calcutta elite were engaged. This activity was beyond the control and knowledge of the British administrators. In this area caste rules were important, particularly those rules concerning marriage, pollution and inheritance. It seems that in the eighteenth century all matters related to caste were settled through 'caste cutcherries',[1] and leading men in Calcutta like Madan Datta and Nubkissen competed with each other to gain control of such 'cutcherries'.[2] In the nineteenth century the 'cutcherries' were replaced by *dals* (*de facto* social factions). The *dalapatis* (leading members of the *dals*) tried to control men by using the instruments of social sanction of excommunication, through the *dals*. I shall call such activities politics conducted through a traditional idiom, since they involved competition among elite groups in order to gain control over men and matters. This fits Morris-Jones's definition of the 'traditional' language of politics, it is the language 'of a particular kind of highly developed status society' and it is acted upon more than it is spoken about.[3]

During the first three decades of the nineteenth century no other Indian elite group was so active in public affairs and in such numbers as the elites of the *bhadralok* class in Calcutta; even Bombay was a decade or two behind Calcutta in this respect. In 1815 Rammohun Roy established his *Atmiya Sabha*, the first organization of its kind, which deliberately set out to reform Hindu religion and society; the members discussed both the nature of God and his various attributes and debated on social problems concerning caste, pollution and *sati*. In 1817 many well-to-do Bengalis, some of whom were very orthodox, joined with some non-official Europeans to establish the Hindu college, which had a far-reaching effect on the social history of Calcutta and Bengal. This was to be followed by the foundation of the School Book Society and the School Society which played a prominent part in improving primary education in Calcutta if not in Bengal. They printed new text-books, opened new types of schools which held annual examinations, laying the foundations for a new educational system. The emphasis was on English, mathematics, geography, natural sciences and English history, at both the primary and the higher level. Many schools and higher educational seminaries, like the Bishops' College, Rammohun's Anglo-Hindu School, the Oriental Seminary, the Sanskrit College and, most important, the

---

[1] H. Verelst, *View of the Rise, progress and present state of the government in Bengal, including a reply to the misrepresentation of Mr Bolts and other writers*, London, 1772, pp. 27–8.

[2] For the rivalry between the two families, see N. N. Ghosh, *Memoirs of Maharaja Nubkissen Bahadur*, Calcutta, 1901, pp. 141–9.

[3] Morris Jones, 'India's political idioms', p. 138.

Calcutta Medical College, were established during this period. An Indian press both in English and in vernacular languages was established in 1818; by the end of a decade it had refined itself into an effective political weapon, maintaining a small but steady circulation and providing a livelihood for a fairly large number of journalists and printers. Pamphlet wars were waged between rival groups, agitating for and against the abolition of *sati* or debating on the Bengali's right to alienate property without the family consent. Calcutta Town Hall witnessed many spectacular public meetings, often attended by up to 1,000 men, where European free traders joined with the Indians to protest against such issues as the restrictions on a free press, and administrative reforms.

Rammohun's *Atmiya Sabha* was to be used as a model by his supporters and his opponents. Many *sabhas* and *samitis* (societies) were formed during this period to further the cause of social and religious reform, for literary discussions and above all for political agitation. Although a large number of such societies were founded by the young students of the Hindu College, more serious ones were organized by their elders. One such organization was the *Dharma Sabha*, which was formed in 1830 in the wake of great agitation against the abolition of *sati*. Lord Bentinck inadvertently gave the Bengalis a chance to learn the techniques of agitation which were to be used later for more worthy causes. Finally, in 1838 the European free traders, Indian *zamindars*, Hindus and Muslims, conservatives and reformers united to defend the landed property in Bengal. The orthodox members now had the opportunity to put their experience in the *Dharma Sabha* to better use. This interest in public affairs, unusual by Indian standards in the early nineteenth century, sprang from a social transformation brought about by a number of factors, chiefly the economic changes in the eighteenth century. The society was being transformed from a status and relatively closed society where social and political relationships were determined by caste and customs, to a relatively open and competitive society where social relationships were largely shaped by class. However, caste remained important—social prestige was still attached to it and inheritance laws were determined by caste. Indian politics in Calcutta during this period, 1815–38, were shaped by both class and caste, and, since rural Bengal left its mark on Calcutta despite rapid urbanization, the 'traditional' language of politics was as important as the 'modern' language of politics.

II

In the late-eighteenth and the early-nineteenth centuries Calcutta, like Forster's Chandrapore, was divided into two worlds, southern or European and northern or native. The vast differences between the European town and the 'black town', as the Indian quarter was called, struck many European observers.[1] The European town was, as Sir William Jones said, 'large, airy and commodious', the houses were 'in general well built and some of them equal to palaces'.[2] The 'black town' in contrast was overcrowded with men living in badly built, unimpressive houses; with few exceptions even the houses of the opulent Indians were not built to please the eye.[3]

At the apex of the social and political pyramid were the Europeans of the southern part of the city. Although the two worlds were not yet as segregated as they were in Forster's Chandrapore, European contact with the Indians was more official and less social. The aloofness of the Europeans was scoffed at in the eighteenth century by the famous Indo-Muslim historian, Ghulam Hussein,[4] and Rammohun Roy,[5] the social reformer, was aware of it. However, the Europeans were not a homogeneous body; many non-official free traders, journalists, business-men, and missionaries, men like David Hare, James Silk Buckingham and William Adam, had a greater contact with upper classes of Indian society. Indians on their part were eager to establish such contacts and many ventures in education, journalism, religious reform and business, were jointly started by the Indians and the non-official Europeans.

The vital statistics of Calcutta have never been very reliable. Even the census of 1872 could not be accepted as accurate.[6] Thus it is not possible to make a satisfactory numerical study of the process of urban-ization. We have no reliable set of figures from which we could measure the rate of population growth of Calcutta, the rate of literacy, the changes in age groups, occupational patterns, sex ratio, and the reli-gious composition of the population. But, ever since 1752 when Holwell first put out his figures, many attempts had been made to enumerate and classify the population of Calcutta. Earlier estimates gave very

---

[1] C. Finch, 'Vital statistics of Calcutta', *Journal of the Statistical Society of London* (*J.S.S.L.*) Vol. 13, 1850, p. 168.

[2] S. N. Mukherjee, *Sir William Jones: a study in eighteenth-century British attitudes to India*, Cambridge, 1968, p. 77.

[3] C. Finch, 'Vital statistics of Calcutta', pp. 168–9.

[4] Ghulam Hussain, *Sair Mutaqharin* (Eng. trans.), Calcutta, 1789, Vol. 2, pp. 587–91.

[5] S. N. Mukherjee, 'The social implications of the political thought of Raja Rammohun Roy' in R. S. Sharma (ed.), *Kosambi Memorial volume*, Patna, in the press.

[6] W. H. Hunter, *A statistical account of Bengal*, Vol. 1, *Districts of 24 Parganas and Sundarbans*, London, 1875, p. 17.

high figures for the Indian population of Calcutta.[1] However, we have more reliable statistics for Calcutta from about 1821. It was then reported that there were 179,917 people living in Calcutta, of whom 118,203 were Hindus, 48,162 Muslims, 13,138 Christians and 414 Chinese.[2] This figure was much lower than the one given by Dwarkanath Tagore to R. Montgomery Martin and the figure supplied by the magistrates.[3] But, when we compare these figures with the estimates made in 1837 by W. Birch, the Superintendent of Police in Calcutta, on the basis of the reports made by the assessors of the house tax, it seems that the assessors in 1821 were not very far out.

Table 1[4]

English	3,138	Western Hindus	17,333
Euro-Asians	4,746	Bengali Hindus	120,318
Portuguese	3,181	Moguls	527
French	160	Parsees	40
Chinamen	362	Arabs	351
Armenians	636	Mugs	683
Jews	307	Madrasees	55
Western Muslims	13,677	Native Christians	49
Bengali Muslims	45,067	Low Castes	19,054
		Total	229,714

Two interesting facts emerge from these figures. Between 1821 and 1837, the population of the city of Calcutta grew very rapidly, by nearly 50,000. Although the rate of population growth was marginal by twentieth-century standards, the figures do indicate that Calcutta was a growing and thriving city, where many men came looking for jobs.

[1] The following estimates were made by various people in the nineteenth century. 1801: 1,625,000; 1802: 600,000; 1810: 10,000,000; 1819: 750,000. See William Adam, *Reports on the state of education in Bengal* (1835 and 1838) (ed. A. N. Basu), Calcutta, 1941, p. 5.

[2] *Census of India 1961: Report of the population estimates of India (1820–1830)* (ed. D. Bhattacharya and B. B. Bhattacharya), New Delhi, 1963, pp. 234–5. It was estimated that another 100,000 entered Calcutta daily, excluding the handful who travelled to and from the city by carriages and horses. The number was reached by the estimate of the houses in Calcutta and checking the people at each important entrance to the City. As far as we know these figures have never been cross-checked with the consumption of salt and other methods used by James Prinsep in Benaras.

[3] Tagore's informers suggested that there were 53,005 houses, in which some 300,000 people lived. See R. Montgomery Martin, *Statistics of the Colonies of the British Empire in the West Indies, South America, North America, Asia, Australasia, Africa and Europe. From the official records of the Colonial Office*, London, 1839, p. 209. For the figures for the years 1822 and 1828 see *Census of India, 1961*, pp. 234–5, *P.P.H.C.* 1831, V. 320A, Appendix no. 42,762; and A. F. S. Ahmed, *Social ideas and social changes in Bengal 1818–1835*, p. 11.

[4] C. Finch, 'Vital statistics of Calcutta', p. 172. Please note that the total number given here excluded the people who entered the city daily and also those who lived in the suburbs of Calcutta.

This fact is partially confirmed by the imperfect set of figures that we now have on sex ratios and age groups. As far as can be ascertained, the majority of people in Calcutta were male and adult. According to one estimate there were 61·6 Hindu women to 100 Hindu men and a corresponding figure for Muslim women was 50·8. Calcutta also had fewer children than an average European city.[1] The process continued in the latter part of the nineteenth century.[2] If increasing male immigration is a sign of urbanization then the process started very early in Calcutta.[3]

Another interesting fact emerges from these figures. Although Calcutta always had a heterogeneous population consisting of many communities from the very beginning, the bulk of the population were Bengali Hindus. Bengali Muslims formed the second largest community in Calcutta. According to figures given for 1798, the Muslim population in Calcutta increased at a faster rate than the Hindu population between 1798 and 1837.[4] This is confirmed by the fact that owing to lack of protein in the diet and ritual bathing in the Ganges the mortality rate was higher among Hindus than among Muslims.[5] But this slightly higher rate of increase among Muslims did not change the social structure of Calcutta. The 'black town' remained predominantly a Bengali Hindu city. The total Bengali Muslim population was still less than half the total Bengali Hindu population.

What is more significant, however, is the fact that the upper and middle part of the social and economic pyramid of Indian society in Calcutta was dominated by Hindus. Only a small number of Muslims took an interest in public affairs and had some weight in society, either because they were rich merchants and landowners, or because they were *vakils* in the Sadr Dewani Adalat or teachers at the Calcutta Madrasa or Fort William College. Some of these men, like Maulavi Karim Hussain, played an active and useful role in the committees of the Calcutta School Book Society and Calcutta School Society. But the majority of leading Muslims were non-Bengalis. It is interesting to note that some of the Muslim members of the School Book Society were eager to promote the interest of 'Hindostani' in both Persian and

[1] C. Finch, *loc. cit.* p. 173.
[2] It was estimated in 1866 that the majority of the population belonged to the age group of 16–40. In 1872 Hunter suggested that 67 per cent of the population were male adults. *Report on the Census of Calcutta 1866*, Calcutta, 1866, pp. 15–16. Cf. W. W. Hunter, *A statistical account of Bengal*, Vol. 1, pp. 38–44.
[3] Kingsley Davis, *The population of India and Pakistan*, Princeton, N.Y. 1951, pp. 139–41.
[4] Abstracting from Police magistrate's reports, Hamilton suggested that there were, in Calcutta, in 1798, some 14,700 Muslims and some 56,460 Hindus. W. Hamilton, *The East India Gazetteer*, London, 1815, p. 137.
[5] C. Finch, 'Vital statistics of Calcutta', pp. 174–5. Cf. W. H. Sykes, 'On the population and mortality of Calcutta', *J.S.S.L.*, Vol. 8, 1845, p. 51.

Nagari scripts and of a school situated in an area dominated by the non-Bengali Muslim community.[1] This fact needs some explanation. Ever since 1870 when W. W. Hunter published his famous work on *The Indian Musalmans*,[2] there had been a widely accepted thesis about the so-called 'Muslim backwardness' in Bengal and in India. It is generally thought that the Muslims were dispossessed when the British took over the administration of the province. The successive administrative reforms took away the remaining privileges held by the Muslims, consequently the community remained hostile towards British rule, and their rather conservative religion strengthened their dislike of western rule, western education and western culture. So, we are told, the Muslim response being totally negative, they failed to produce a leadership willing to inaugurate English education and social reform among the Muslims. Some scholars have even cited the Muslim peasant revolts as examples of this kind of Muslim response.[3]

The administrative reforms started by Warren Hastings and consolidated by Cornwallis dispossessed many powerful men in Bengal. But under the Mughal rule, in the *suba* of Bengal, Muslims never had a monopoly in all branches of administration. Undoubtedly, they held the highest executive positions in government and controlled the army and the administration of criminal justice (*nizamet*). But the Hindus were not a deprived class. They monopolized the administration of the revenue (*dewani*). A reading of *Sair Mutaqharin* shows that a considerable number were employed as *foujdars* and as generals in the army. Some of the most reliable men in the Nawab's army were Hindus.[4] In 1844, when the Bengali *bhadralok* were pleading earnestly for a better share in the administration of British India, through their Bengal British India society, they drew up an impressive list of Hindus employed in high positions during Mughal rule.[5]

The administrative reforms, which culminated in the Cornwallis system, swept away established native agencies such as *ameens*, *quanungoes*, *roy royans*, etc. Undoubtedly, in some branches of administration the Muslims were more adversely affected than the Hindus. Thus the establishment of the Company's army, with Hindu *sepoys*, meant unemployment among the Muslim soldiers.[6] The reforms introduced by

---

[1] W. Adam, *Reports on the state of education in Bengal*, pp. 12–13.

[2] W. W. Hunter, *The Indian Musalmans*, London, 1870.

[3] A. F. S. Ahmed, *Social ideas and social change in Bengal*, pp. 18–19. Cf. A. R. Mallik, *British Policy and the Muslims in Bengal 1757–1858*, Dacca, 1961, pp. 166–93.

[4] Ghulam Hussain, *Sair Mutaqharin*, Vol. 2, pp. 187–91.

[5] The Bengal British India Society, *Evidences relative to the efficiency of native agency in the administration of the affairs of this country*, Calcutta, 1844, p. ix. Robert Orme wrote that Aly Verdy Khan 'preferred the service of gentoos in every office and dignity of the state excepting in the ranks of the army'. R. Orme, Vol. 11, p. 53.

[6] Ghulam Hussain, *Sair Mutaqharin*.

Cornwallis in the administration of justice reduced the number of Muslim *vakils* (agents or law officers). In the eighteenth century the majority of the *vakils* were Muslims, but after the introduction of the Cornwallis system only 25 per cent were Muslims.[1] Muslim 'nobility', associated with the Court, lost all power and prestige when Murshidabad was reduced to a district headquarters. Their rather emotional letters, which have survived in the records, pleaded with sucessive governor generals for small monthly pensions, often as little as Rs. 40, to maintain their large families and servants who stayed behind even after their fall from power.[2]

The Hindus were also adversely affected by the administrative reforms, the great *roy royans, naib dewans, foujdars*; men like Alumchand, Manickchand and Mohanlal, who managed the affairs of the state under the patronage of the Nawabs, vanished from the scene. Rammohun Roy describes this loss of political consequence[3] for the Hindus under the British rule.

Table 2[4]

Year	Europeans	Natives	Total
1800	7,719	49,322	57,041
1810	10,715	77,125	87,840
1820	11,676	121,238	132,914
1830	15,701	96,897	112,598
1840	16,303	102,055	118,358
1850	26,803	126,910	153,713
1851	27,159	138,142	165,301

The administrative reforms and the economic changes brought about by new land laws and trade opened up opportunities for men who came from a stratum of traditional society which consisted largely of Hindus. The available statistics show that a large number of Indians were employed by the East India Company's government, the majority in the Revenue and Judicial Departments. Table 2 gives the figures for Indians and Europeans employed in Bengal in the civil administration from 1800 to 1851. It is important to remember that the Indo-Britons (Anglo-Indians) are not classified separately from the Europeans.

Although the number of Indians employed dropped in 1830 from 121,238 to 96,897, the Indians in the Company's service outnumbered

[1] N. K. Sinha, *The economic history of Bengal from the Plassey to Permanent Settlement*, Calcutta, 1956, Vol. 2, p. 230.
[2] India Office Library (I.O.L.) Mss Eur. F. 109, John Adam papers, Box e. Cf. India Office Records (I.O.R.) Bengal Public Consultations 11 Sept. 1819.
[3] R. Roy, *Petitions against Press Regulations*, in *The English works of Raja Rammohun Roy* (ed. by K. Nag and D. Burman), Calcutta, 1945–9, pt 4, p. 27.
[4] *P.P.H.C.* 1852–3, (25) XII, p. 373.

the Europeans by about 5 to 1. However, this was an army of petty clerks. The handful of Indians who were employed in more responsible posts were also in the Revenue and Judicial Departments. Figures now available for 1851 show that, of 2,910 Indians employed as unconvenanted servants, 2,762 were in the Revenue and Judicial Department.[1] Before 1828 there were only two grades of native judges, the *Sudder Ameens* and *Munsiffs*. In 1833 the office of Deputy Collector was created for the Indians, in 1837 that of *Principal Sudder* and in 1843 that of Deputy Magistrate. However, Indians still received miserable salaries. In 1827 no Indian employed in the Judicial or Revenue Department received more than Rs. 250 per month or £300 a year. The figures given in Table 3 show that out of 2,813 Indians employed in 1849 as unconvenanted servants only 493 received salaries above the £240 grade, while 2,320 were below that grade.

Table 3.[2] *Allowances received by Indians in 1849*

Received by	£ (per annum)
1	1,560
8	840–960
12	720–840
68	600–720
69	480–600
58	360–480
277	240–360
1,173	120–240
1,147	24–120
2,813	

It is clear from these figures that the British administration replaced the Indians, Hindus and Muslims in all responsible, high-salaried posts and created an administrative machinery which required a large army of clerks and junior administrators in some departments, especially in the Revenue and Judicial Departments. The education and the skill that was required was readily provided by the Hindus. The Muslim population in Bengal consisted largely of officers or 'nobility' (for want of a better term), who were almost invariably non-Bengali, and the Bengali peasantry. Neither of these two classes were interested or had skills for the jobs offered by the Company's government. There was undoubtedly a middle group which consisted of teachers. petty government officers, *vakils* and men in similar professions. This was never very large, not as large as the Hindus in a similar position (with the exception

[1] *P.P.H.C.* 1857–8, XLII (42), p. 153.
[2] *P.P.H.L.* 1852–3, (110C.) LXXI, 1, pp. 51–2.

of *vakils*) and played a marginal role in the social and political history of Bengal, unless they happened to be *vakils* at the *Sadr Dewani Adalat* like Maulavi Aminullah.

The statistics of the traditional educational system, imperfect as they are, confirm the view that the majority of the middle group were Hindus. In the province of Bengal (which included Bihar) the proportion of the Hindu population to the Muslim population was two or less than three to one. But the proportion of the educated Hindus to the educated Muslims was eighteen to one. What is more significant, the *kayasthas* dominated the schools where Persian was taught;[1] Muslim scholars formed a minority in these schools. William Adam noticed that there was no 'account or record of any private institutions for Mahomedan learning either in Calcutta or in the surrounding districts'.[2] According to Ward, in 1818 in Calcutta there were twenty-eight Hindu schools where 173 students received a free education. No rich Muslim community in Calcutta was willing to patronize traditional education nor was there a class eager to receive such education. The traditional educational system had a practical side; it taught, both at the elementary schools and at the higher centres of learning, rudimentary arithmetic, Persian, book-keeping and the Shastric or Koranic law, essential for trade, commerce, managing *zamindaris*, and for the junior posts in the administration. Neither the 'nobility' nor the peasantry had any interest in these professions. The British administrative reforms had helped to create a Hindu middle-income group.

III

It is not certain how many clerks and junior administrators lived in Calcutta, but it is reasonable to assume that since Calcutta was the centre of British-Indian administration in Bengal a large number of the clerks and some of the junior administrators settled in the city although a large number of the Indian unconvenanted servants appointed by the Revenue and Judicial Department would necessarily be stationed outside.

The coming of the British had also opened up new opportunities in many fields other than administration, not least in trade, commerce and in the ownership and management of land. Here too the Bengali Hindus had an advantage over the Muslims. Their role as brokers, financiers and agents was vital to the British-Indian economy. This was not so much because the Hindus had controlled the economy of the country during the Mughal rule; it has been estimated that nine-tenths of the total land was under their control. All large *zamindars*

---

[1] *Calcutta Review*, Vol. 2, Oct.–Dec. 1844, pp. 19–20.
[2] W. Adam, *Reports on the state of education in Bengal*, p. 23.

who paid over 50 per cent of the total land revenue in Bengal were Hindus, and almost all the bankers were also Hindu.[1] The bankers and *zamindars* have also been described as the 'junior anti-feudal ally of the British'.[2] But they were not the real gainers; the Jagat Setts, the Maharaja of Krishnagar and others who helped the British in 1757 either vanished from the scene or were reduced to insignificance before the end of the eighteenth century. If the British rule brought misery to the Muslim 'nobility' and the high-ranking Hindu officers, the misery was shared by the old *zamindars* and the old bankers.[3] The men who gained most in the New World were small traders, brokers and junior administrators, *pykars, dallals, gomasthas, munshis, banyans,* and *dewans.*

From the very beginning it was essential for the Company to have interpreters, brokers and other native agencies to conduct business with Indian producers. The brokers, like the Setts and Basaks, who were weavers by caste and whose traditional occupation was trade in cotton piece-goods, flourished in Calcutta under the Company's rule. The Setts controlled the broker's office in Calcutta until the end of the *dadni* system in 1753. By the beginning of the nineteenth century they had become *shroffs* (money-lenders) in Calcutta.[4] Their descendants helped the cause of the modernists in the 1820s and 1830s by establishing English schools, opening 'reading rooms' in their large houses for the 'educated youths of the metropolis' and acting as 'justices of peace' in the City. They also supplied the holy water for the idols of Somnath and Dwarkanath and established their family idol *Radhakanta Jew* in Calcutta.[5]

In the eighteenth century the British administration in Bengal, more particularly in Calcutta, was so organized that it had to depend on Indian junior administrators who worked more like speculators or contractors than as civil servants. The contractors-cum-administrators had a better chance of becoming prosperous in the revenue and commercial departments. Akrur Datta, a sloop contractor, Govinda Mitra 'the black collector' of Calcutta, Baranasi Ghosh, *dewan* of the Sheriff of Calcutta, Hidaram Banerjee, *ameen* to the Sheriff of Calcutta, amassed fortunes in this manner. Moreover, the system of 'farming out' (meaning letting out of a fluctuating source of revenue income for a

---

[1] N. K. Sinha, *The economic history of Bengal,* Vol. 2, p. 225. Cf. W. Hamilton, *The East India Gazetteer,* 1815, p. 131.

[2] B. B. Misra, *The Indian Middle Classes: their growth in modern times,* London, 1961, p. 78.

[3] W. Hamilton, *The East India Gazetteer,* 1815, p. 136.

[4] B. Ghosh, 'Some old family founders in eighteenth century Calcutta', *Bengal Past and Present (B.P.P.),* Vol. 79, 1960, pp. 42–55. For the role of the Indian traders see S. Bhattacharya, *The East India Company and the economy of Bengal from 1704–1740,* Calcutta, 1954, pp. 25–7, 218–25.

[5] L. N. Ghose, *The modern history of the Indian Chiefs, Rajas, Zamindars etc.,* Calcutta, 1879–81, Vol. 2, pp. 155–7.

more or less stable annual sum to the highest bidder) which was first used in Calcutta for collecting rents and duties, and later used extensively throughout the whole province, especially during the period between 1772 and 1777, created an unprecedented instability in the economy but allowed a large-scale circulation of money and gave new groups, *banyans* and *gomasthas*, the opportunity to control land and land-rent, thus replacing the 'ancient families'. Significantly, the 'new landed aristocracy' came into existence in areas where the British used their method of farming out first in Calcutta, The Twenty Four Parganas and Burdwan.[1]

However, it was in the private sector of the English trade in Asia that the Indian middlemen flourished. In the eighteenth century the trade between Asia and England was so organized that co-operation between the Company and various forms of private enterprise was essential for its development. While the Company clung to its monopoly of trade between Asia and Europe, it allowed private Englishmen, 'free merchants' and company servants to enjoy a large share in 'the Country Trade', trade in the Indian Ocean between Asian countries. The Indian financiers played a vital role in the private sector; they provided the capital which could not be raised in the absence of a modern joint stock banking system. The Indians also invested large sums in Calcutta, where there was a boom in building, especially during the 1760s and 1770s. Recently, Marshall has pointed out that case after case argued before the Calcutta Mayor's Court shows 'that Europeans traded on the capital of their *banyans* or Indian agents; or to be more exact the *banyans* traded on their masters' names and authority'.[2] Men like Nubkissen, Madan Datta, Dattaram Ghose, and later Ramdoolal Dey, invested money in this manner and amassed vast fortunes. Lack of capital, lack of knowledge of local products and restrictions imposed on the free application of European skill and capital especially in the *mofussil* areas made it necessary to work through the Indian agencies. It appears that the Indian commercial class did very well from trade. As early as 1802 their significance was noted by an English observer. 'The formerly timid Hindu now lends money at respondentia in distant voyages, engages in speculations to various parts of the world and works as an underwriter in the different insurance offices, erects indigo works in various parts of Bengal and is just as well acquainted with the principles of British laws respecting commerce as the generality of European merchants.'[3]

[1] N. K. Sinha, *The economic history of Bengal*, pp. 68–95, 31.
[2] P. J. Marshall, 'Private British investment in eighteenth century Bengal', *B.P.P.* Diamond Jubilee number, 1967, p. 55.
[3] *The Reporter of Internal Commerce of Bengal*, as quoted in N. K. Sinha, 'Indian business enterprise, its failure in Calcutta' (1800–1848), *B.P.P.* 1967, p. 115.

This commercial class had also invested large sums in land. The transfer of land from the 'ancient families' to the new groups continued throughout the eighteenth century, even after the Permanent Settlement. Darpanarayan Tagore, who acquired a large fortune working as a *dewan* of the French Company in Chandranagore, settled in Calcutta some time during the latter half of the eighteenth century and purchased a big *zamindari* in north Bengal which originally belonged to the 'ancient family' of Rajsahi.[1] After the Permanent Settlement the security of investment attracted Calcutta Hindu merchants like Dwarkanath Tagore and Motilal Seal to land. A large number of estates changed hands during the years immediately following the Permanent Settlement, when the government confiscated many *zamindaris* for revenue arrears and put them up to auction.[2]

There is evidence to show that a large number of Indians, rich and poor, moved into Calcutta during the period between 1742 and 1756.[3] But the vast majority of the Indians settled down in Calcutta during the 1860s and 1870s, when Calcutta was being transformed from a small European settlement into a prosperous commercial city. The opulent merchants and bankers were the first group of Indians to settle down in the city. They built large houses, established family deities, patronized Brahmins and *ghataks* (match-makers), entertained European officers and friends as a Mughal courtier would do, imitated the Europeans in architecture, furniture and in the nineteenth century, in the consumption of tea, wine and soda water.[4] These were the Bengali *abhijat* (aristocratic) families, Debs, Tagores, Deys, Ghoses, Mallicks, whose descendants claimed leadership in Calcutta society during the nineteenth century. They were the first urbanized social group in Bengal, who transformed their Calcutta *basas* (temporary residences) into *baris* (permanent homes) in the eighteenth century, long before any other social group.[5]

---

[1] L. N. Ghose, *The modern history of the Indian Chiefs*... Vol. 2, pp. 160–2.

[2] For an account of the ruin of the 'old landed families' see W. W. Hunter, *Annals of rural Bengal* (reprint), Calcutta (n.d.), pp. 56–8.

[3] Raja Binaya Krishna Deb, *The early history and growth of Calcutta*, Calcutta, 1905, p. 60.

[4] W. Hamilton, *The East India Gazetteer* (2nd ed.), London, 1828, Vol. 1, p. 324, as quoted in A. F. S. Ahmed, *Social ideas and social change in Bengal 1818–1835*, p. 13. European clothes became fashionable among the young undergraduates in the forties. Ralph Smyth, Bengal Artillery Revenue Surveyor, observed in 1851, 'a late introduction of pantaloons, stockings and patent leather shoes, in an attempt to Europeanize themselves, is to be seen amongst the young Bengalis in Calcutta, but it is unsuited to them, their own peculiar costume always obtains respect, which the innovation seldom does'. R. Smyth, *Statistical and geographical report of the 24 Pergunnahs district*, Calcutta, 1851, p. 17.

[5] This process of urbanization was slow to start among other classes, who even in the twentieth century used their Calcutta residences (*basa*) as temporary living quarters, while their real homes (*bari*) were in the villages where all the important family functions like *sradhs*, marriages and *pujas* took place. See P. Sinha, *Nineteenth century Bengal: Aspects of social history*, Calcutta, 1965, pp. 124–7.

Table 4 gives us a list of leading men in Calcutta, who were prominent in public affairs in the city during the period between 1815 and 1838. The table gives the caste, name and occupation of the 'family founder' (*paribar pratistatha*) and the area of Calcutta where the family house was situated. These were the established Calcutta *abhijats*, who considered themselves as 'natural leaders' of men,[1] and who according to Bishop Heber lived in 'very large, very fine, generally very dirty houses of Grecian architecture' built amidst the dingy bleak part of the black town.[2] They were the top group (*prathamadhara*) in Bhavanicharan Banerjee's list of *bhadralok*, who moved in large carriages and wore fine clothes, and were described as *dewans* and *mucchudis*.[3] The list is based on 'The accounts of all respectable and opulent natives of the Presidency', originally made by Radhakanta Deb for H. T. Prinsep in 1822, and on another list made in 1839.[4] It is interesting to note that Rammohun Roy was not included in the list. No doubt this was partly due to Deb's hostility towards the reformer, but I think largely because Rammohun was relatively a newcomer to Calcutta and he had yet to establish himself among the Calcutta *abhijats*. (Although Rammohun had business connexions with the city from the end of the eighteenth century, he did not settle down there until 1815.) It is equally significant to note that Deb did not think it was necessary to include any Muslim family. It seems that there was no Muslim family in Calcutta rich enough and strong enough to be involved in public affairs.

This list is not complete; it excludes Rammohun Roy and fails to mention many other prominent men like Baidyanath Mukherjee, Motilal Seal, Ramkamal Sen, Hidaram Banerjee's family, Biswnath Motilal, Bhavanicharan Banerjee, Brindaban Mitra, and Kalinath Munshi. In fact, in 1839 another list of 'eminent natives' was made to bring Deb's list up to date.[5] In the 1839 list Calcutta was divided into twenty wards (*pallis*) and the names of leading men in each ward were given separately. This list is fuller than Deb's list of 1822, for it gives most names which figure prominently in contemporary newspapers and other documents and mentions various branches of the Tagore and Mallick families separately. But the new list still excludes Rammohun Roy's family and the short family histories mentioned in Deb's list are missing. However, when we read these two lists together we get a

---

[1] *Dwijendranath Thakurer Smritikatha* (*Memoirs of Dwijendranath Tagore*), as published in B. B. Gupta, *Puratan Prasanga*, Vishbharati edition, Calcutta, 1373 (Bengali era), pp. 284–6.

[2] R. Heber, *Narrative of a journey through the upper provinces of India*, London, 1828, Vol. 3, p. 238.

[3] Bhavanicharan Banerjee, *Kalikata Kamalalaya*, Calcutta, 1823, as reprinted in 1343, pp. 8–9.

[4] Radhakanta Deb to W. H. MacNaughton, 9 Nov. 1835. Bengal Public Consultations, 25 Nov. 1835, as reprinted in B. N. Banerjee, 'Raja Radhakanta Deb's services to the country', *Indian Historical Records Commission* (*I.H.R.C.*), Vol. 9 (1926), pp. 105–9.

[5] *S.S.K.* (3rd. ed.), Vol. 2, pp. 157–8. I have not yet succeeded in locating the original copy of Deb's list which is now incorporated in the 1839 list (Sept. 1969).

Table 4[1]

	Name	Caste	Area	Family History
1	Babu Jagannath Prasad and Babu Kashi Prasad	Baidya	Shyambazar	Descendants of Maharaja Durlabhram; were related by marriage to Raja Rajballabh. Durlabhram and Rajballabh were revenue administrators during the Mughal rule and helped the British in 1757
2	Maharaja Rajkrishna Deb	Maulik Kayastha	Sobhabazar	Son of Raja Nubkissen Deb, *dewan* of Clive and Persian *Munshi* to the Company
3	Raja Gopimohun Deb	Maulik Kayastha	Sobhabazar	Gopimohun was adopted son and nephew of Nubkissen
4	Raja Ramchandra Roy	Subarnavanik	Pathuriaghata	Son of Raja Sukhamoy Roy, *dewan* of Sir Elijah Impey. Sukamoy's grandfather served as *baniyan* of Clive and other Governors of Bengal
5	Gaurcharan and Nimaicharan Mallick	Subarnavanik Kayastha	Jorasako and Burrabazar Jorasako (?)	Bankers and businessmen, long established in Calcutta
6	Babu Srinarayan Singha			Descendants of Dewan Ganga Govind Singha, *dewan* of the Board of Revenue during the time of Warren Hastings
7	Kali Sankar Ghoshal	Radi Kulin Brahmin	Khidirpur	Descendants of Gokulchandra Ghoshal, *dewan* of Verelest
8	Rajnarayan Roy and Taraknath Roy	Kayastha	Andul (outside Calcutta)	Descendants of Ram Charan Roy, *dewan* of Vansittart and General Smith
9	The Tagores	Pirali Brahmin (*Bhagna Kulin*)	Pathuriaghata, Jorasako and Mechuabazar	Descendants of Darpanarayan, who worked as *dewan* of the French Company
10	Gourcharan Sett and his kinsmen	Weaver	Burrabazar	*Shroffs* of Calcutta, established since the beginning of the eighteenth century
11	Radhakrishna Basak	Weaver	Pathuriaghata	He was born in the family of *shroffs* who were related by marriage with the Setts of Burrabazar. Radhakrishna was a *dewan* in the Sub-Treasurer's Office
12	Ramdoolal Dey	Kayastha	Simla	A shipping magnate started his career as a *sarkar* (bill collector) at the very low salary of Rs. 5 per month
13	Prankrishna and Jagomohun Biswas	Suri (?)	Barrackpore	Ramhari Biswas father of Prankrishna and Jagomohun, made money as *dewan* of the salt agent at Chittagang
14	Rajkrishna Singh and Sibkrishna Singh	Kayastha	Jorasako	Descendants of Santiram Singh, *dewan* of Sir Thomas Ramsbold and Middleton of Patna
15	Bhagabaticharan Mitra and Bhavanicharan Mitra	Kulin Kayastha	Bagbazar	Descendants of Govindaram Mitra, *dewan* of the *zamindari* office in Calcutta ('The black Collector of Calcutta')
16	Nabakrishna Mitra	Kulin Kayastha	Bagbazar	Descendants of Gokulchandra Mitra, who made money working as a contractor
17	Ganganarayan Sarkar	Kayastha (?)	Garanhata	He was a *dewan* of Palmer and Co.
18	Premchandra, Ratanchandra and Umeschandra Palchandhuri	Tili	?	Krishnachandra Palchandhuri, father of Premchandra and his brother made money working as *dewan* to the salt agent in Calcutta
19	Rajnarayan and Rupnarayan Sen	Kayastha	Jorbagan	Mothuramohun Sen, father of Rajnarayan and Rupnarayan, was a *shroff* of Calcutta
20	Radhamadhab and Gauricharan Banerjee	Radi Kulin Brahmin	Jorbagan	Descendants of Ramsundar Banerjee, who married into the wealthy family of Rajnarayan Misra and worked as *dewan* of the opium agent at Patna
21	Shibnarayan Ghosh	Kulin Kayastha	Pathuriaghata	Ram Gopal Ghosh, father of Shibnarayan, was a *sarkar* of Warren Hastings
22	Nilmani Mallick	Subarnavanik	Pathuriaghata	Descendant of Ramkrishna Mallick, a businessman
23	Rasiklal and Haralal Datta	Kayastha	Nimtala	Descendants of Madanmohun Datta, the shipping magnate of Calcutta

[1] 'Principal Hindu inhabitants of Calcutta', Foreign Dept. Misc. Records 1839, Vol. 131, pp. 316–36, as printed in B. N. Banerjee, *Sangbadapatre Sekaler Katha* (*S.S.K.*) (3rd ed.), Calcutta, 1356, Vol. 2, pp. 753–56.

shrewd idea about the origin and nature of the Calcutta *abhijat bhadralok* group, which confirms the points I have raised before. The nineteenth-century *abhijat bhadralok* were new men: not only did they move into the city during the second half of the eighteenth century, they rose to high social status in one or two generations. They were of humble origin, small traders, junior administrators and small landholders, who made money working as junior partners (*banyan* or *dewan*) of the English officers and free merchants.

No doubt some of them had already established themselves during the Mughal rule in Bengal, like the families of Rammohun Roy and Brindaban Mitra. Pitambar Mitra, father of Brindaban, was a *vakil* of the Nawab *vizier* of Oudh at the Court of Delhi. But there were many who rose from poverty to wealth. The great shipping magnate, Ramdoolal Dey, is a good example of this kind of vertical mobility. He was an orphan, who began his career as a *sarkar* (bill collector) at the very low salary of Rs. 5 a month at Madan Datta's office in Calcutta. With careful investment and good luck he became a millionaire in the nineteenth century. With the growth of 'consignment trade' and agency houses he got himself attached as *banyan* agent to Fairlie Fergusson and Company. But he also worked as an independent agent. Foreign traders, especially the Americans, found it more profitable to do business with Dey than with one of the established English houses since he charged them a commission of not more than 1 per cent.[1] He established contacts with the merchants in New York, Boston, Newberry Port, and Philadelphia. His American business friends named a ship after him and sent him a portrait of George Washington as a token of friendship. His name figures prominently in the shipping list of Calcutta port for the years 1817, 1820 and 1824.[2]

Motilal Seal is another example of this kind of vertical mobility. He was born in Calcutta of a small cloth merchant family. Seal started his career selling empty bottles and corks; by 1820 established himself as a leading merchant, working as *banyan* to various agency houses, investing in indigo plantations, in flour mills, and purchasing *zamindaris*.[3] In the 1830s, after 'the agency house crisis', he started working as 'general merchants and agents' in partnership with Europeans and opened Oswald and Seal and Company.[4]

---

[1] Mins. of Ev. 11, sec. com. H. C. 1831–2 (735. 11), p. 151. Cf. Grish Chunder Ghose, *A lecture on the life of Ramdoolal Dey, The Bengali Millionaire*, Belloore, 1868, p. 20.

[2] *The Bengal Almanac and Annual Directory for 1818*, Calcutta, 1818, pp. 153–5, and *The new annual Bengal Directory and general Register for 1820 and 1824* (India Office Library reference ST. 1216). There were two other Bengalis whose names appear in the shipping lists, Davy Persad Ghose and Rajkissen Dutt.

[3] *Mutylal Seal, being a lecture delivered by K. C. Mittra*, Calcutta, 1869, pp. 6–16.

[4] N. K. Sinha, *B.P.P.* 1967, p. 118.

Thus the administrative and economic changes created a new sub-servient capitalist class in Calcutta. They remained interested in commerce and trade throughout 1815 to 1838, even after they purchased large *zamindaris* and settled down in Calcutta. They flourished because they were still an important link in the British-Indian economic system. Of the 202 proprietors of the Union Bank in 1835, seventy-three were Indians. Of the seventy-three Indian proprietors, seventy were Bengali Hindus, two were Muslims and one was Parsi. There were four Indian directors of the Bank; of them, three were Bengali Hindus, Ashutosh Dey, son of Ramdoolal Dey, Radhamadhab Banerjee and Dwarkanath Tagore.[1]

This class was predominantly Hindu. No doubt there were many rich Muslim merchants, like Shaik Abdullah and Shaik Gulam Hosein, whose names appear in the shipping lists for 1815, 1817, 1820 and 1824, who donated regularly to the School Society and School Book Society and who signed various petitions.[2] But they were so-called 'Mughal merchants', a marginal social group, isolated from the vast majority of the Bengali Muslim masses and from the other non-Bengali Muslim groups in Calcutta. The Muslims failed to produce an administrative or commercial middle class, not because they were, as a group, averse to English education, nor because they were dispossessed as a community by the new administration (it only dispossessed a section of that community), nor because the British deliberately discouraged the introduction of English education amongst them,[3] but because the vast majority of Muslims had neither the inclination nor the skill required for the type of administrative posts open to the Indians, nor for the areas of economic activity which received a new impetus under the British and opened up opportunities for men to move up in the new world. As early as 1815, Walter Hamilton observed: 'The men of opulence now in Bengal are Hindu merchants, bankers, and *banyans* of Calcutta, with a few at the principal provincial stations. The greatest men formerly were the Mahommedan rulers whom the British have superseded and the Hindu zamindars. These two classes are now reduced to poverty and the lower classes look up to the official servants and domestics of the English gentlemen.'[4]

Below this *abhijat bhadralok* were the large shopkeepers, small traders,

<hr>

[1] *Bengal Directory*, 1858, Commercial.
[2] *The Bengal Almanac and Annual Directory*, 1815 and 1818, and *The New Annual Bengal Directory*, 1820 and 1824.
[3] Recently Professor Mallick has argued that the slow growth of English education among the Muslims can be attributed to the British Government's failure to introduce English education in the Calcutta Madrasa and other Muslim educational institutions. A. R. Mallick, *British policy and the Muslims in Bengal 1757–1858*, Dacca, 1961, pp. 166–93.
[4] W. Hamilton, *The East India Gazetteer*, 1828, p. 136.

4

small landholders and white-collar workers in commercial houses and government offices, teachers, 'native doctors', journalists and writers. These people formed the bulk of the middle group (*madhyabit*) in Bhavanicharan Banerjee's list. They were not rich but comfortable (*dhanadya nahen keval annajoge achen*)[1] and followed the leadership of the rich and imitated their life-style. Dwijendranath Tagore described them as *grihasthas* (householders), who formed the lower order of the *bhadralok* group and had accepted the leadership of the *abhijats*.[2] There are no reliable statistics to show how many people belonged to this middle income group. However, as we have already noticed the government appointed a large number of clerks, and since Calcutta was also growing as a commercial city, it is reasonable to suppose that the commercial houses provided a great deal of employment for clerks. We do not have the figures of the number of teachers employed in the city, but, if Adam's *Reports* are to be believed, then the number of teachers must have substantially increased during the period 1817 to 1838, when the schools, elementary and higher, multiplied so fast that Adam could not include them all in his list.[3] We do not know how many Indian doctors were practising in Calcutta, but we do know that, in 1822 when the School for Native Doctors was opened, twenty attended the institution, and by 1826 fifty had gone through the School.[4]

However, we know that the Indians found the press a useful and profitable profession. Although not all Calcutta newspapers were as rich as the *Bengal Hurkaru* (who paid Rs. 800 to its editor, employed seventy people as sub-editors and reporters and had a library and a reading room with gaslight for the use of the public),[5] many men like Nilratan Haldar, editor of *Bangadoot*, Bhavanicharan Banerjee, editor of *Samachar Chandrika*, made a living as editors of newspapers and periodicals and authors of books and pamphlets. There were others like Ganga Kissore Bhattacharjee, the editor of the *Bengal Gazetteer*, who 'conceived the idea of printing works in the current language as a means of acquiring wealth'.[6] He had his own newspapers and his own press, and wrote and published a number of books. Then there was Babooram, who had similar ideas and worked as H. T. Colebrook's pandit; he later took to printing and publishing and was said to have amassed a fortune of Rupees 1 lakh before he retired in Benaras.[7] It was estimated that some

[1] Bhavanicharan Banerjee, *Kalikata Kamalalaya*, pp. 8–9.

[2] *Dwijendranath Thakurer Smritikatha*, p. 185.

[3] W. Adam, *Reports on the state of education in Bengal*, pp. 9, 15–16, 46–9.

[4] *Samachar Darpan*, 6 July 1822, *S.S.K.* (2nd ed.), Calcutta 1344 (Bengali era), Vol. 1, pp. 35–6.

[5] 'Present state of the Indian Press', *Alexander's East India Magazine and Colonial and Commercial Journal*, London, Vol. 1, Dec. 1830 to June 1831, p. 48.

[6] *The Friend of India* (Quarterly series) (2nd ed.), Serampore, 1822, Vol. 1, pp. 134–5.

[7] *Op. cit.* p. 134.

15,000 Bengali books were sold in Calcutta in ten years between 1811 and 1821. The majority of the books were on Hindu mythology, erotic art and law, some with plates engraved by Harihar Banerjee, whose gods and goddesses were, according to the missionaries, 'stiff and uncouth' but 'tolerably accurate' and 'not discreditable for neatness'.[1]

There were many others employed in the press, or hired by the rich as legal agents, or *munshis*, or *gomasthas* (secretaries or managers). These people often lived on the ground floors of the large houses in Calcutta.[2]

IV

Throughout this essay I have referred to the *bhadralok* as a social class. Although it is now fashionable in the academic world[3] to discard the concept of class altogether I still find it a valuable intellectual tool in analysing the social and political development of modern India. Recently the *bhadralok* has been described as a 'status group', not a 'class'. It seems to me that to describe the *bhadralok* as a 'status group' or alternatively a 'mere category' is to ignore the economic changes and the social mobility in Bengal in the nineteenth century.[4]

A class can be described as a social group which holds a common position along some continuum of the economy. This continuum need not necessarily be of income or occupation. The position of a class should be understood, as Marx had suggested, in terms of its position in the process of production. Thus in a modern capitalist system there are two important classes, the capitalist, the owners of the means of production, and the proletariat, the producers who sell their labour to the capitalist class. But these are broad categories which helped Marx to ascertain the large groupings characteristic of a developed capitalist system.[5] On this point Weber agrees with Marx; to Weber property and the lack of property were 'the basic categories of all class situations'.[6] But within these broad categories, class situations are further differentiated, according to, as Weber put it, 'the kind of property that is usable for returns' and according to 'the kind of services that can be offered in the market'.[7] Marx himself recognized the existence of many

---

[1] *Op. cit.* pp. 137–8.   [2] Finch, *T.S.S.L.* Vol. 13, p. 173.

[3] P. H. M. van den Dungen, 'Changes in status and occupation in nineteenth century Panjab', in D. A. Low (ed.), *Soundings in Modern South Asian History*, London, 1968, p. 85.

[4] J. H. Broomfield, 'The Non-cooperation decision of 1920: a crisis in Bengal politics', in D. A. Low, *op. cit.*, pp. 231–6, 245–7 and 255–6. At the seminar during the discussion on this paper Mr R. Guha, of the University of Sussex, called the *bhadralok* 'a mere category not a class'.

[5] Karl Marx, *Capital* III, as quoted in T. B. Bottomore and Maximilien Rubel, *Karl Marx, Selected Writings in sociology and social philosophy.* London (Pelican), 1965, p. 186.

[6] Max Weber, *From Max Weber—essays in sociology* (ed. by H. H. Gerth and C. Wright Mills), London, 1947, p. 182.   [7] *Ibid.*

social classes which played important roles in history. In describing the political situation in France in 1848, Marx distinguished between the finance aristocracy, industrial bourgeoisie, petty bourgeoisie, proletariat, peasantry and lumpenproletariat.[1] The Marxist concept of class is inclusive: it assimilated economic power, market chances, occupational prestige and style of life into class. Weber, on the other hand, wanted to distinguish 'the class situation' (determined by market chances) from 'the status situation' (determined by 'a specific, positive or negative, social estimation of honor').[2] Moreover, to the Marxists, class is always a category for the purpose of the analysis of social conflicts.

In other words a social class is not formed just because a group of people hold a common position in a particular sector of the economy and enjoy a similar life-style but because its members are conscious of their existence as a group and are organized in opposition to other groups. As Marx said 'In so far as millions of families live under economic conditions of existence that separate their mode of life, their interests, and their culture from those of the other classes, and put them in hostile opposition to the latter, they form a class'.[3] Weber played down the importance of conflict in 'class situations'; he put an undue emphasis on 'communal actions', meaning not actions between members of the same class but actions between members of different classes.[4]

The term 'class' is used here to describe a *de facto* social group, which holds a common position along some continuum of the economy, enjoys a common style of life and is conscious of its existence as a class organized to further its ends. In contrast to caste society, a class society is an open system, in theory and, to some extent, in practice. We find that in a modern society, based on a money economy, the distinction between 'class situations' and 'status situations' is more theoretical than real. More often than not the rich enjoy high status in society. Thus 'honor', as Weber himself said, 'can be knit to a class situation'; the style of life and consumption of goods are linked with the acquisition of goods.

In Calcutta, in the nineteenth century, class was one dimension of social stratification which determined social relationships in the city. If we use Marxian class analysis then Indian society in Calcutta was divided into two classes. There was the *abhijat bhadralok*, the big *zamindars*, merchants and top administrators, who were the owners of land and

---

[1] Karl Marx, *The class struggles in France 1848 to 1850* in *Selected Works*, Moscow, 1950, Vol. 1, pp. 128–31.
[2] Max Weber, *op. cit.* p. 187.
[3] Karl Marx, *The Eighteenth Brumaire of Louis Bonaparte*, in *Selected Works*, Vol. 1, p. 303.
[4] Max Weber, *From Max Weber—essays in sociology*, p. 185.

capital (although as a capitalist class they were subservient to the British). Then there were the dockers, the builders, the workers, the domestics, the palankin bearers and other wage-earners—a large migrant labour force, some of whom came from Orissa and the Up Country, formed the class of producers. The relationship between these two classes was contractual and economic, and was not determined by caste or custom.

Between these two groups there was already growing, as we have noticed, a middle class, the *grihastha bhadralok*, whom in 1829 the *Bangadoot* referred to as *maddhyabitto sreni*.[1] The shopkeepers, small *zamindars*, small merchants and white-collar workers belonged to this group. However, this had not yet crystallized into a homogeneous social class. They accepted the leadership of the *abhijat* and imitated their life-style. They were dubbed together with the *abhijat* by the English officers as 'the educated natives' to distinguish them as a group from the old 'nobility' and the masses.[2] The line of demarcation between the *abhijat* and the *grihastha* is not very clear; after all, the rich *bhadralok* emerged from a new 'middle class', who were considered as 'upstarts' by many.[3] Although the *abhijats* were rich, enjoyed high status, and exercised considerable power in Calcutta, their subservience to the British and their imitation of the life-style of the colonial elite and the Mughal courtiers made all *bhadralok*, rich and of the middle-income group, in this sense, part of a 'new middle class'.

The class situation in Calcutta can be compared and contrasted with the class situation in England in the early nineteenth century. The Industrial Revolution brought about profound social and economic changes; the steam engine broke the eighteenth-century pyramidal structure of English society. England witnessed not only what Engels called the 'disintegration of society into individuals' but also the carving-out of classes.[4] Before the rise of a politically conscious working-class movement, a class struggle was waged by the middle class against 'aristocratic tyranny' and 'hereditary opulence'. In contrast, in Calcutta, there was no Industrial Revolution, no large-scale introduction of the steam engine to break down the old social structure completely. Yet the market in land, trade and commerce brought about a significant social change, and Bengal witnessed the rise of a new middle class. This class was less aggressive and less homogeneous than its English counterpart but it was equally articulate in politics.

---

[1] *Bangadoot*, 13 June 1829, as reprinted in *S.S.K.* Vol. I, p. 398.
[2] H. T. Prinsep, *Three generations in India 1770–1904*, I.O.L. MSS. Eur. C97/1, 1 and 3.
[3] 'Mookerjee's Magazine' as quoted in N. N. Ghose, *Memoirs of Maharaja Nubkissen Bahadur*, p. 171.
[4] Asa Briggs, 'The language of "class" in early nineteenth-century England', in Briggs and J. Saville, *Essays in labour history. In memory of G. D. H. Cole*, London, 1960, pp. 43–78.

There was in fact in Bengal no conflict between trade and the land, nor between the 'old *zamindars*' and the 'new *zamindars*'. No doubt many old *zamindaris* were bought off by the *abhijat bhadralok*, and there was some resentment against the *nouveaux riches* amongst the 'old aristocracy', but there was no class struggle between the *bhadralok* and the 'old aristocracy'. The tension between the family of Nubkissen and that of the Maharaja of Krishnagar, over the family idol, was a family feud not a class struggle.[1] In fact the 'ancient families' were respected by the *bhadralok*. It was Radhakanta Deb, grandson of Nubkissen, who in 1838 proposed that the Maharaja of Krishnagar should be asked to be the President of the *Zamindar Sabha*, since he came from the 'most ancient lineage' in Bengal.[2] In some areas the 'ancient families' still exercised considerable influence. If Ram Ram Bose is to be believed, the descendants of Raja Basanta Roy (uncle of Pratapaditya Roy, one of the Bengali chieftains who fought the Mughals in the seventeenth century) were still respected in Jessore, and were leaders (*Goshtipati*) of *Bangaja Kayasthas* in that district.[3]

Similarly the *bhadralok* had a deep respect for the Mughal nobility. In 1842 Radhakanta Deb went to pay his homage to the Nawab Nazim of Murshidabad on his way to Gaya.[4] Rammohun Roy proclaimed his allegiance to the family of Babar and accepted the title of Raja conferred upon him by Akbar II.

However, there was some hostility towards the lower orders, the dockers, palankin bearers and other wage-earners in Calcutta, and the tenants and the landless labourers in the rural area. The *bhadralok* attempted to resist the wage demands of the palankin bearers by various means, fair and foul, and complained in their newspapers that money was being drained out of Bengal by the Oriya palankin bearers.[5] Dwarkanath Tagore, 'a Hindoo of an enlarged mind, and a truly British spirit', as he was known to his English friends, did not hesitate in bullying a corrupt magistrate to break up an *ekjoti* (rent-strike) amongst his tenants.[6] Many were afraid that the spread of English education among the lower classes would hurt the interests of the *bhadralok*; they would demand higher wages, equality and even the jobs so dearly held by the *bhadralok*. *Samachar Chandrika* claimed that the demand for higher wages and the lack of washermen in Cal-

[1] N. N. Ghose, *Memoirs of Maharaja Nubkissen Bahadur*, p. 190.

[2] The Landholders' Society, *Rules and Regulations and Proceedings of the meetings held in B. S. 1244 and 1245*, Calcutta, 1838, p. 12. (I.O.L. ref. ver. Tract no. 1900.)

[3] Ram Ram Bose, *Raja Pratapaditya Charit*, Serampore, 1801, p. 156.

[4] *A rapid sketch of the life of Raja Radhakanta Deva Bahadur with some notices of his ancestors and testimonials of his character and learning*, Calcutta, 1859, p. 22.

[5] *Samachar Darpan* 21 August 1819, and 2 June 1827, *S.S.K.* (2nd ed.), Vol. 1, pp. 171, 344–5.

[6] R. M. Martin, *Statistics of the Colonies of the British Empire*... p. 289. Cf. K. C. Mittra, *Memoir of Dwarkanath Tagore*, Calcutta, 1870, pp. 16–19.

cutta were due to the spread of education among the lower classes.[1] Thus, although there was no sharp class struggle of the type England had witnessed under the impact of the Industrial Revolution, and the interrelationship between classes was not one of continuous conflict, many social conflicts and collective activities can only be understood in terms of class. Not all social relationships in Calcutta were determined by class; society as a whole was not just separated, as some of the missionaries thought, into two 'classes, the borrower and the usurer, the industrious though exhausted poor, and the fat and flourishing money-lender'.[2] The people were also separated into communities and castes. Nevertheless, the importance of class as one dimension of social stratification in Calcutta cannot be denied.

The caste structure in Bengal during the pre-colonial period was less rigid than it is supposed to have been in other parts of India. The Bengali Brahmins, though enjoying a very high ritual status, never had that exclusive high social and economic status which the Brahmins in South India had enjoyed in the past.[3] The Brahmins had to share the economic and social power with other castes. Traditionally, the Hindu community in Bengal was divided into two *varnas*, Brahmin and Shudra. The Shudras were further subdivided into three groups: clean, unclean and untouchable. All *jatis* in Bengal were fitted into these four broad categories, Brahmins, clean Shudras, unclean Shudras and untouchables; there were at least forty-one *jatis* in Bengal.[4]

Two caste groups, *Kayastha* and *Baidya*, enjoyed a very high social and political status along with the Brahmin, although their ritual status was rather low. They had the monopoly of the educational system, and held important administrative posts; being landowners they controlled the agrarian economy. According to Abu-ul-Fazl, the majority of the Bengali *zamindars* in the sixteenth century were *Kayasthas*.[5] By the eighteenth century large *zamindars* were almost invariably Brahmins. According to Hamilton a large number of the Brahmins were also employed as 'managers' of *zamindaris* belonging to other castes. They could obtain land leases on better terms and were exempted from 'various impositions and extortions to which the inferior classes are exposed'.[6] Thus in some parts of Bengal, in the eighteenth century, the Brahmins exercised considerable influence by combining

[1] *Samachar Chandrika*, 12 May 1830, pp. 144–5.
[2] *The Friend of India*, Vol. 1, p. 90.
[3] André Béteille, *Caste, Class and Power*, Berkeley, 1965, pp. 3–10 and 191–2.
[4] For a stimulating discussion on the caste structure in medieval Bengal see N. Ray, *Bangalir Itihas, Adi parva*, Calcutta, 1359, pp. 257–323. Cf. W. Ward, *A View of the history, literature and mythology of the Hindoos*, London, 1817–20, Vol. 3, pp. 94–143.
[5] Abul Fzal-i-Allami, *Ain-i-Akbari*, Vol. 2 (trans. H. S. Jarrett, Sir Jadunath Sarkar), Calcutta, 1949, p. 147.
[6] W. Hamilton, *The East India Gazetteer*, 1828, p. 135.

their high ritual status with political and economic power. However, the *Baidyas* and *Kayasthas* were equally important, the majority of the administrative posts were held by them, many small *zamindaris* were under their control, and, while the *Kayasthas* monopolized the vernacular educational system, the *Baidyas* shared the knowledge of Sanskrit with the Brahmins.[1] It would seem that the Brahmin, Baidya, and *Kayastha* together formed a sub-elite group in the power structure of the traditional society; all rulers of Bengal, the Palas, Senas, Pathans, and Mughals had to rely on their support.

Despite the social upheaval, the Brahmins, *Kayasthas* and *Baidyas* continued to exercise considerable power in Calcutta. At least eleven out of the twenty-three families mentioned in Table 4 were *Kayasthas*, three were Brahmins and one was *Baidya*. L. N. Ghose, writing during the second half of the century, gave a list of sixty eminent families of Calcutta, thirty-four of which were *Kayasthas*, eleven were Brahmins and one was *Baidya*.[2] Educational records of Bengal of this period also show that the majority of men who went for higher education came from these three castes. This factor has led many scholars, old and new, to believe that the *bhadralok* was a traditional elite, consisting of Brahmin, *Baidya* and *Kayastha*, which continued to enjoy high status and exercise power as junior administrators and landowners throughout the nineteenth century.[3] However, this view fails to recognize that, in contrast to caste, the *bhadralok* was an open *de facto* social group. Although the *bhadralok* was almost exclusively a Hindu group, caste had no part in the selection; men who held a similar economic position, enjoyed a similar style of living and received a similar education were considered as *bhadralok*. Men like Motilal Seal, a *Subarnavanik* (unclean Shudra), and Gaurchand Basak, a Weaver, although of very low ritual status, were leading *bhadralok* of Calcutta. In Table 4 we have the names of families belonging to such castes, *Subarnavanik*, Weaver, and *Suri*. Even L. N. Ghose included six *Subarnavaniks*, one Weaver, one Brazier, one *Sadgop*, one *Tili*, and one *Kaibartya* (not to mention the Parsee, Khetri and Muslim families) in his list of eminent men of Calcutta. The lives of the Bengali *abhijat bhadralok* proved, as the nineteenth-century biographer of Ramdoolal Dey put it, that 'there is an aristocracy which is not born but may be made'.[4] Those who could acquire enough wealth, English education, and high status through administrative service, belonged to this 'new aristocracy', and since a large number of Brah-

[1] Sir William Jones was taught Sanskrit by a *Baidya* teacher; see S. N. Mukherjee, *Sir William Jones*, p. 195.

[2] L. N. Ghose, *The modern history of the Indian Chiefs*... Vol. 2.

[3] D. A. Low, *Soundings in Modern South Asian History*, pp. 6 and 331. Cf. A. Seal, *The Emergence of Indian Nationalism*, Cambridge, 1968, pp. 36–57.

[4] Grish Chunder Ghose, *A lecture on the life of Ramdoolal Dey*, p. 62.

mins, *Baidyas* and *Kayasthas* had administrative skill, and economic incentives, they formed the bulk of the *bhadralok*. The majority of the Brahmins and *Kayasthas*, poor and illiterate, were not considered as *bhadralok*. According to Ward three-quarters of the total number of Brahmins in Calcutta and the Twenty-Four Parganas, were domestics.[1]

Despite the Brahminical laws, a caste in Bengal, at least since the eighteenth century, was not a hereditary occupational group. In 1795, Colebrook noticed that every profession, with few exceptions, was open to 'every description of persons'. 'Brahmins are often employed in the most servile office and the Sudras often elevated to situations of respectability and importance.'[2] In 1815, Hamilton confirmed this view, 'commerce and agriculture are universally permitted to all classes and under the general designation of servants to the other three tribes, the Sudras seem to be allowed to prosecute any manufacture. In this tribe are included not only the true Sudras, but also other castes...daily observation shews even Brahmins exercising the menial profession of a Sudra.'[3] Rickards also observed the diversity of castes among the workers in various industries. He noticed five or six different castes working as carpenters and as many different castes working as bricklayers often even employed to work on the same building.[4]

Social mobility in Bengal could be noticed even in the rural areas, in the traditional educational system. Adam's *Reports* show that teachers in vernacular elementary schools came chiefly from the *Kayastha* caste. In Bengal, however, castes both superior and inferior to the *Kayasthas* had invaded the profession. In contrast, in Bihar the monopoly of the *Kayasthas* had not been challenged. In the traditional society vernacular education was particularly suitable for the *Kayastha* caste, a fixed stratum somewhere in the middle of a relatively stable social pyramid. In Bengal, from the eighteenth ecntury, no stratum could be permanently fixed. William Adam himself considered this to be a sign of social change: 'Both the Bengal and Behar districts need an improved system of vernacular instruction; but the former appear to have undergone a social change, partaking the nature of a moral and intellectual discipline, which removes prejudices still to be met and provides facilities not yet to be found in the latter.'[5]

In Calcutta, professions old and new, high and low, were open to all

---

[1] W. Ward, *A view of the history...of the Hindoos*, p. 86 n.

[2] H. T. Colebrook, *Remarks on the present state of the husbandry and commerce of Bengal*, Calcutta, 1795, p. 133.

[3] W. Hamilton, *The East India Gazetteer*, 1828, p. 132.

[4] R. Rickards, *India: or facts submitted to illustrate the character and condition of the native inhabitants with suggestions for reforming the present system of government*, London, 1829–32, Vol. 1, p. 32.

[5] W. Adam, *Reports on the state of education in Bengal*, p. 249.

caste groups. The lists of *shroffs* (money-lenders) of Calcutta show that this old profession was not monopolized by any single caste group. The caste breakdown of the students of the Medical College given in Table 5 shows that only three out of fifty students in 1839 were *Baidyas* (whose traditional occupation was medicine).

Table 5.[1] *The students of Calcutta Medical College*

Brahmin	5	Goldsmith	2
Baidya	3	Bankers	8
Kayastha	15	Miscellaneous	10
Druggist	1		
Weaver	6	Total	50

If castes in Calcutta could not be regarded as hereditary occupational groups then the intercaste relationships and the caste hierarchical order were also undergoing profound changes. The taboos regarding food and pollution could not be enforced rigidly, where the Brahmin had to share the same civic amenities along with other castes—often living in the same street—and when they had to work in an office all day or conduct business at the docks. In about 1821, a book called *Karmalochan* was published, which listed the daily religious duties that a pious Hindu should perform. The publisher soon discovered that men in Calcutta were reluctant to purchase the work, 'as the instances of their religious omissions were so numerously recorded in it, that they were afraid of being reduced to beggary, by imposition of fines from the Brahmin on account of neglect of religious rites'.[2] In fact, it was widely believed outside Calcutta that the *bhadralok* had 'fallen from the approved usage' (*acharbhrasta*).[3] It would also seem that no particular area was allocated to any particular caste as it had been in the traditional village society. This is demonstrated in Table 4. In Pathurighata there were *Radi Kulin* Brahmins like Baidyanath Mukherjee, *Kayasthas* like Ramlochan Ghosh, *Pirali* Brahmins like Gopimohun Tagore, *Subarnavaniks* like Nilmani Mallick and Weavers like Radhakrishna Basak.[4] Pathuriaghata was no exception; all areas in the Indian part of the town was adorned with large houses of the multi-caste *abhijat bhadralok*.

In the new schools and colleges boys from different castes mixed freely. There was no caste privilege in the classrooms or in the playgrounds. In David Hare's school Ramtoonu Lahiri, a poor *Barendra Kulin* Brahmin pupil from Krishnagar used to be bullied by his class

[1] General committee of Public Instruction, *Report on the colleges and schools for Native education...
in Bengal for 1838–9*, Calcutta, 1840, p. 42.
[2] J. Long, *A descriptive catologue of Bengali works*, Calcutta, 1855, miscellaneous.
[3] Bhavanicharan Banerjee, *Kalikata Kamalalaya*, p. 8.
[4] *S.S.K.* Vol. 2, pp. 757–8.

monitor called Aditya, who was a Washerman by caste. This free mixing left a deep imprint, which had a far-reaching influence outside the school compounds. The *Enquirer*, the mouthpiece of young Bengal, observed, 'boys of different castes can never long remain on an equal footing in a class without forgetting and giving up their distinctions'.[1] Menfolk, like their sons, mixed freely at business, at school committees, at public meetings, in *sabhas*, and other public gatherings. The family functions of the *abhijat bhadralok*, marriages, *sradhs*, *pujas* were transformed into multi-caste social gatherings, and were celebrated with great pomp and splendour. The *barowaree*, or later the *sarvajanin pujas*, were invented in response to urban life. These *pujas* were not performed in temples or in family chapels but by 'subscription assemblies', annually formed for this purpose only.[2] By the end of the nineeenth century almost every area in Calcutta had such multi-caste 'subscription assemblies'.

Caste, however, remained important, as we shall see, in relation to marriage and inheritance. The rich members of ritually low caste started to establish horizontal links with caste brothers outside their regions and began movements to improve their ritual status. The *Baidyas* were the first caste to take steps in this direction. In the eighteenth century, under its leadership of Raja Rajballabh, some of them started wearing the 'sacred thread' and declared themselves 'twice born'.[3] Since 1822, there had been a continuous pamphlet warfare between the Brahmin and the *Baidya* pandits of Calcutta over the ritual status of the *Baidyas*.[4] In 1831, the *Baidya* doctors, under the leadership of Khudiram Bisharad, who was a teacher of medicine at the Sanskrit College, formed the *Baidya Samaj*, to defend their caste privileges. Although it was primarily for the *Baidya* medical practitioners, the leading members of the caste like Ramkamal Sen gave the new *Samaj* their full support.[5] The ritual status of the Brahmins was also challenged in Calcutta. In 1832, Dharma Sabha called a special meeting to discuss a crucial question concerning the Brahmin–Shudra relationship; they debated whether a Shudra (if he is a *Vaishnava*) can claim 'reverence' from the Brahmin.[6] But despite the evidence of caste consciousness and the importance of caste rules in marriage and inheri-

---

[1] Sivanath Shastri, *Ramtoonu Lahiri o Tatkalin Banga Samaj* (3rd ed.), Calcutta, 1909, p. 49. Cf. *The Enquirer*, Feb. 1835, p. 37.

[2] *The Friend of India*, May 1820, pp. 129–30, as reprinted in *S.S.K.* Vol. 1, p. 480.

[3] W. Ward, *A View of the history... of the Hindoos*, p. 95.

[4] J. Long, *A descriptive catalogue of Bengali Works*. Cf. *Samachar Darpan*, 4 Sept. 1830, in *S.S.K.* Vol. 2, pp. 149–50.

[5] *Samachar Darpan*, 6 Aug. 1831 and 13 Aug. 1831 as in *S.S.K.* Vol. 2, pp. 397–8.

[6] Bhavanicharan Banerjee, *Biprabhakti Chandrika*; cf. Bai[rava] Chandra Datta, *Sri Sri vaishnava bhakti kaumudi*. These two pamphlets are reprinted in N. N. Law, *Subarnavanik, Katha o Kirti*, Calcutta, 1940, Vol. 1, pp. 50–64.

tance, class consciousness, breaking down the caste barriers, is noticeable. Although the *bhadralok* had yet to evolve a class ideology, they were conscious of their existence as a social group and had every confidence in themselves as an agency for change. They increased in number and in strength during the 1820s. In 1829, Nilratan Haldar wrote that the rise of this 'new class' (*nutansreni*), whom he earlier referred to as *maddyabitto*, would bring 'economic prosperity' and 'political stability' in Bengal.[1]

A numerical study of the housing situation in Calcutta confirms the view that many new *bhadralok* moved into the city during the first four decades of the century. By and large the Indians lived in two types of houses, brick buildings for the higher classes and tiled huts and straw huts for the lower classes. It seems that there was a considerable decrease in the total number of houses in Calcutta, in each successive period since 1793, shown in Table 6. The reason for this decrease was not the depopulation of Calcutta but the erection of new and large houses by the wealthy classes, including the English, which meant the demolition of the huts. During the years between 1822 and 1827, while 6,000 huts disappeared, over 3,000 new brick buildings were built. The group inhabiting the brick buildings became larger and more prosperous.

Table 6[2]

Year	Total number of houses
1793	74,760
1822	67,511
1837	65,469

V

The class of *abhijat bhadralok* was undoubtedly one of the most important agencies for change in nineteenth-century Bengal. It would be true to say that it was their class interest which stirred them most; the economic issues such as stamp duties, house tax, the resumption of *la-ki-raj* (rent-free) land, and the general fear that the government might interfere with landed property forced all *abhijat bhadralok*, of all shades of opinion, into agitational movements. They organized public meet-

[1] *Bangadoot*, 13 June 1829, *S.S.K.* Vol. 1, pp. 398-9.
[2] This table is made from the list of houses printed in C. Finch, 'Vital statistics of Calcutta', p. 170. The process of replacing huts by large houses continued throughout the nineteenth century. This was no doubt partly due to the 1837 Municipal Regulation, which required all straw huts to be removed, but largely due to 'the increased trade and prosperity of the town'. See *Report of the Census of Calcutta*, pp. 13 and 25.

ings, wrote petitions and in 1838 founded the first political association in India, the Landholders' Society. Many of their other public activities were also economically motivated: they were eager to introduce modern banking, steam navigation and tea plantation. Many invested money and took an active interest in the scheme to colonize Saugar Island.[1] They were all in favour of the modernization and commercialization of the economy of Bengal. However, they were also inspired by ideas which reached them from Europe through books, through personal contacts with some of the more enlightened European officials, the missionaries and the free traders, men like Justice Hyde East, David Hare and James Silk Buckingham. The *bhadralok* had faith in reform and in their ability to change their destiny. In this sense they were all agents of 'modernity'; rising above local and parochial ties, they felt that they had commitments to larger communities. They organized meetings to raise funds to help famine-stricken Ireland, for flood-relief in Barishal or to help the sick migrant labourer in Calcutta.[2] Rammohun Roy went further than most in wanting to make common cause with the 'fighters' for 'liberty' everywhere in England, France, Spain and Latin America.[3]

They were all deeply interested in science and in 'useful knowledge'. Rammohun Roy implored the government 'to instruct the natives of India in Mathematics, Natural Philosophy, Chemistry, Anatomy and other useful sciences, which the Nations of Europe have carried to a degree of perfection that has raised them above the inhabitants of other parts of the world'.[4] Dwarkanath| Tagore was interested in the application of modern science to industry. He also donated large sums to Calcutta Medical College and gave scholarships for medical students.[5] He used to be present at the dissection room of the College to discourage prejudice against modern medicine. Radhakanta Deb was an active member of the Agricultural and Horticultural Society; for a time he served as its vice-president and wrote scholarly papers for it. He helped to introduce smallpox vaccination, attended regularly 'the experiments in the Medical College' and 'every lecture on Natural

[1] J. C. Bagal, *Radhakanta Deb* (5th ed.), Calcutta, 1364, in *Sahitya Sadhak Charitmala*, Vol. 2, p. 40. Cf. *Samachar Darpan*, 4 Sept. 1833, 22 Jan. 1834, *S.S.K.* pp. 343–5.

[2] *Samachar Darpan*, 29 June 1822, 12 Oct. 1822, 11 May 1833, 1 June 1833, 28 Sept. 1833 and 17 May 1834, *S.S.K.* Vol. 1, pp. 149–50, and Vol. 2, pp. 302–7.

[3] S. D. Collet, *The life and letters of Raja Rammohun Roy* (3rd ed.), D. K. Biswas and P. C. Ganguli (eds.), Calcutta, 1962, pp. 161–3.

[4] R. Roy, 'A letter to Lord Amherst on western education', as reprinted in Collet, *op. cit.* p. 458.

[5] K. C. Mittra, *Memoir of Dwarkanath Tagore*, pp. 29, 69 and 107. Cf. Shivanath Shastri, *Ramtoonu Lahiri o Tatkalin Banga Samaj*, p. 171. Four medical students, Bholanath Bose, Suryakumar Chakravarti, Dwarakanath Bose and Gopal Seal, accompanied Tagore to England in 1845. Tagore provided money for the education of Bose and Chakravarti. It was the very first group of Indian students to go to England for higher studies.

Philosophy at the houses of his European friends'.[1] Ramkamal Sen sat on a committee which recommended the foundation of Calcutta Medical College, and also in the Fever Hospital Committee which made a number of suggestions for improving the drainage and sanitation of the city.[2] They all helped to further the cause of English education.

The formal political aims of this class were very limited. Recognizing that their interests were tied to the colonial set-up, they all wanted to work within the framework of the British-Indian administration; no one wanted to rock the boat. No one, not even the young radical students, wanted to follow the American example; any leaning in that direction was sharply rebuked.[3] In 1838, when the Calcutta *bhadralok* made a membership drive for their Landholders' Society, in the *mofussil* areas, they were careful to mention that their activities had the support of the British government.[4] Almost all petitions, whether they were protests against the Press Regulation of 1823 or against the resumption of the *la-ki-raj* land in 1828 or about the right of the Indians to sit as jurors on the Grand and Petty juries, started with a preamble which listed the benefits that the natives of India had received from the Company's rule.[5] The Regulations of Cornwallis, particularly the one on the Permanent Settlement, formed the 'Magna Carta' of the *bhadralok*. They held their alien rulers to the promise of the 'rule of law' and 'the security of property' implied in the Cornwallis system. However 'the system' was not perfect for it deprived Indians of high administrative posts. Under the Company's government, the politically ambitious *bhadralok* could do little. He could not dream of getting elected or nominated to the Governor's legislative council as his descendants could during the second half of the century; he could not even be a corporation councillor, as local government was beyond the control of the *bhadralok*. Although the *bhadralok* wanted to work within the framework of the British-Indian administration, they also wanted minor readjustments of existing institutions, to give a better deal for Indians. Indians should be allowed to sit as jurors on the Grand and Petty juries, work as Justices of the Peace and have some say in the running of local government in Calcutta, to be selected as collectors of revenue or to be promoted to similar high posts in the district headquarters or in the Revenue and Judicial Department.[6]

[1] *A rapid sketch...* p. 30.
[2] P. C. Mittra, *Life of Dewan Ramcomul*, Calcutta, 1880, pp. 1–12. Cf. J. C. Bagal, *Ramkamal Sen and Krishnamohun Bandopadhaya* (2nd ed.), Calcutta, 1362, pp. 15–16 and 20–2.
[3] *The Enquirer*, Dec. 1834, pp. 25–7, and Jan. 1835, pp. 17–18.
[4] *The Landholders' Society*, Preface.
[5] For the texts of some of these petitions see Ahmed, *Social ideas and social change in Bengal, 1818–1835*, pp. 173–90.
[6] 'Political faith of educated Hindoos', *The Reformer*, July 1831, as quoted in J. K. Majumdar (ed.), *Indian speeches and documents on British rule 1821–1918*, Calcutta, 1937, p. 46.

To achieve these ends the *bhadralok* had to create a strong pressure of public opinion in India and Britain on the British government to concede to Indian demands. The medium through which this was done was new to India; it included the press, public meetings, petitions and associations. If the Indian elites, in the twentieth century, are steeped in the grammar of modern politics, then the *bhadralok* of Calcutta had started to learn its alphabet during the 1820s. They had yet to evolve a political programme and a political association. But through the process of trial and error, working as has been seen earlier in school committees, organizing public meetings, forming *sabhas* for social and educational purposes, or for religious movements like *Brahmo Samaj* and *Dharma Sabha*, organizing signature campaigns, waging pamphlet wars for some worthy and also some unworthy causes, the *bhadralok* learnt the techniques of modern politics. This was the beginning of what came to be known as the constitutional agitation.

Admittedly, some of the protest meetings and petitions were European-inspired, if not European-controlled. There was a deep division of opinion within the European community, especially between the free traders and the Company officials, on such issues as the restrictions on the free employment of European capital and skill in India. During the years immediately before the revival of Company's Charter in 1833, free traders mounted a strong agitation in India and in England against the Company. Many protest meetings were held in Calcutta during the late 1820s and in the 1830s, chiefly to petition to Parliament to meet the grievances of the free traders, on colonization, on the restriction of the press, or against the so-called Black Act.[1] They were organized by such men as Theodore Dickens and Thomas Turton, English merchants and lawyers in Calcutta. However, they were able to enlist the support of many *bhadralok* and other 'respectable natives' of the city.[2] The Company officials on their part also succeeded in stirring up Indian opinion against the unrestricted employment of European skill and capital in Bengal. On this issue, the *Samachar Chandrika* echoed *John Bull*, a pro-government English newspaper established in 1821.[3]

It would be wrong to think that the *bhadralok* followed their European friends and patrons passively. They took an active part in organizing such meetings. They spoke from the platforms, signed petitions and joined committees. They were aware that on many issues their interests were tied up with those of the Europeans. Dwarkanath Tagore,

[1] Ahmed, *Social ideas and social change in Bengal, 1818–1835*, pp. 9–10. The Act XI of 1836 of the Legislative Council was called 'The Black Act' by the Europeans for it deprived them of their rights to appeal to English Courts of law against the decisions of 'the Mofussil Tribunals'.
[2] Calcutta, *Meeting at the Town Hall on 5 January 1835* (a pamphlet issued by the editor of *Bengal Hurkaru*), Calcutta, 1835.
[3] *Alexander's East India Magazine*, Vol. 1, Dec. 1830 to June 1831, p. 50.

speaking at a public meeting held in protest against the 'Black Act', recognized this community of interest: 'we support not only their cause, which in gratitude we are bound to do, but our own'. The Indians, he claimed, suffered from similar Black Acts; in *mofussil* areas a man could be sent to prison for seven years without the right to appeal against such conviction. He urged his countrymen to help the Europeans, 'the mischief that has commenced will go on unless we all come forward and support each other to put a check on it'.[1]

Many protest meetings were organized, and many petitions were sent to Parliament, by the *bhadralok* independently of and sometimes against the interests of the European residents and the wishes of the Company officials. The Jury Act of 1826 failed to satisfy the *bhadralok* and other 'natives of wealth and talent in Calcutta'. This Act allowed 'all good and sufficient persons resident within the limits of the several towns of Calcutta, Madras and Bombay . . . [to] be deemed capable of serving as jurors on Grand or Petty Juries and upon all other inquests'.[2] However, it added another clause which stipulated 'that Grand Juries in all cases, and all juries for the trial of Persons professing the Christian Religion, shall consist wholly of persons professing the Christian Religion'. This successfully prevented Indians from sitting on the Grand juries and Petty juries for the trial of Europeans; the *bhadralok* complained against this racial discrimination in their newspapers and threatened not to serve in Petty juries if summoned to do so.[3] They collected two hundred and forty-four signatures to petition to Parliament to repeal this discriminatory clause from the Act and Rammohun Roy lobbied for them in England.[4] Finally, in 1832 Parliament passed a bill, which was initiated by Charles Grant, which not only repealed the objectionable clause but allowed Indians to work as Justices of the Peace. Many other petitions and agitational movements, like that against the resumption of the *la-ki-raj* land, were also conducted by the *bhadralok* independently. These examples show that they had already learnt to use the modern political idiom. H. T. Prinsep noticed the contrast between the Calcutta he left in 1843 and the Calcutta he found on his arrival in 1809. The most marked difference 'was observable

---

[1] Calcutta, *Report of a Public meeting held at the Town Hall, Calcutta, on 24 November 1838*, London, 1839, pp. 30 and 28–9.

[2] George IV 7, Cap. 37, in I.O.L. *Parliamentary Branch Collections*, no. 1, pp. 317–18. The petition against this Act was signed by 128 Hindus and 116 Muslims.

[3] *Samachar Darpan*, 3 Feb. 1827, and *Samachar Chandrika*, 16 June 1827. *S.S.K.* Vol. 1, pp. 201–3. But the *bhadralok* did not have the courage to carry out their threat; in 1828 three Bengalis were selected to serve on the Petty Juries; they were Bhavanicharan Banerjee, Krishnamohun Dey and Tarinicharan Mitra, and they carried out their duties without protest. *Samachar Darpan*, 19 Apr. 1828. *S.S.K.* Vol. 1, p. 202.

[4] R. Roy, 'Extracts from a letter on Grant's Jury Bill', *India Gazettee*, 22 Jan. 1833, as reprinted in *The English Works of Raja Rammohun Roy*, Calcutta, 1947, Pt. 4, p. 39–41.

amongst the natives of whom there were now large classes, who imitated the English in manners and rivalled them even in literary attainments. Their education was often superficial and they mostly over-estimated the advantage they derive from it; still they formed a separate public of their own, which had no existence at all when I arrived in 1809 and was daily increasing in influence.'[1]

It is important to remember that the 'native public opinion' which was so noticeable in 1843 began to make itself heard from the end of the 1820s. By then the *bhadralok* had gained at least ten years experience in journalism and in public work.

It has already been noticed how the press in Calcutta provided a livelihood for a number of editors, authors and printers. The *bhadralok* were quick to recognize the importance of the press as a weapon for agitational movements. In 1830 there were at least seven Bengali, Persian and Nagari weekly newspapers, of which five were owned and edited by the *bhadralok*. Two of these, *Sangbad Kaumudi* (founded in 1821) and *Samachar Chandrika* (founded in 1822), were well established, and competed with each other to gain more readers in Calcutta and in the *mofussil* towns. Many English weeklies like the *Bengal Herald* were controlled by the Bengalis; and some of them had also established a financial interest in some English daily newspapers, like the *Bengal Hurkaru*. In the early part of the 1830s there was a rush by the *bhadra-lok* to publish new newspapers or gain control over those already established.[2] Not suprisingly the *bhadralok* were as anxious to defend the free press as the European free traders.

In 1822, when some of the *abhijat bhadralok* gathered to draft a farewell address to the departing Governor General, the Marquis of Hastings, Gopimohun Deb and his son Radhakanta Deb suggested that a clause should be included in the address to congratulate Lord Hastings for abolishing the censorship of the press in Bengal.[3] In 1823, Rammohun Roy and his friends were most active in petitioning against new press regulations, introduced by John Adam.[4] In 1835, the Indians joined the Europeans in a large meeting held at the Calcutta Town Hall, to protest against the continued restrictions on the press. Among the ninety-three signatories seeking permission to hold the meeting were Rustomjee Cowasjee, a Parsee merchant, and eight *bhadralok*, Rasick Krishna Mullick, Dwarkanath Tagore, Kalinath Roy, Rassomoy Dutt, Radhamadab Banerjee, Ashutosh Dey, Promothonath Dey and Chandra Shekhar Deb.[5]

---

[1] H. T. Prinsep, 'Three generations in India'. p. 263.
[2] Ahmed, *Social ideas and social change in Bengal*, pp. 69–71, 95–7.
[3] *Samachar Darpan*, 28 Dec. 1822, *S.S.K.* Vol. 1, p. 233.
[4] R. Roy, 'Petitions against the Press Regulation', as reprinted in *The English Works of Raja Rammohun Roy*, Pt. 4, pp. 1–31.   [5] Calcutta, *Meeting at the Town Hall*, pp. 2–3.

The foundation of *Atmiya Sabha* in 1815, as the first organization for collective thinking, discussion, and reform, marks the beginning of the modern age in Calcutta. No doubt it had a far-reaching effect on the history of the social reform movement. However, the meetings of the *Atmiya Sabha* were informal gatherings of a small elite, who dared to denounce the orthodox religion.[1] There was no formal organization, no constitution, and no programme for action. It was in the field of education and 'public welfare', in the School Book Society and the School Society, in the Committee of Managers of Hindu College, that the *bhadralok* gained valuable organizational experience. They sat on committees which had to function according to a written set of rules, drawn up by the founders. They learnt the techniques of fund-raising, and, in the case of the School Book Society, of establishing contact in the *mofussil* areas through agents. They organized public examinations of school pupils under the management of the School Society, and launched a publicity campaign through the press. They also established contacts, no doubt through the Europeans, with similar societies in Bombay and in London.[2] It is interesting to note that many of their *sabhas*, like *Gauriya Samaj* in 1823 and *Dharma Sabha* in 1830, were modelled after the School Book Society and the School Society. They drew up a similar set of rules and regulations which governed the formal structures of their societies.[3]

It was important for the ambitious *bhadralok* to be on the school committees, and in the societies for public welfare and social reform. This area of public activity was not directly under the control of the government, here they could exercise considerable power, influencing the policies of institutions, appointing or sacking teachers, nominating students and controlling finance.[4] Men who wished to gain the leadership of Calcutta society had to be involved in these activities. The leading men would be invited to tea parties at the Bishop of Calcutta's

[1] For the history of *Atmiya Sabha* see *Tatvabodhini Patrika*, no. 50, Ashin 1769 (Saka era).

[2] The Calcutta School Book Society, *The Sixth Report* and *The Ninth Report*.

[3] For the history and the activities of the short-lived *Gauriya Samaj* see *Samachar Darpan*, 8 Mar. 1823, 28 Mar. 1823, 17 May 1823 and 3 July 1824, *S.S.K.* Vol. 1, pp. 10–13. For the rules and regulations of *Dharma Sabha* see *Samachar Darpan*, 23 Jan. 1830 and 6 Feb. 1830, *S.S.K.* Vol. 1, pp. 300–3 and 304–6.

[4] The Government of the College was vested in a committee of Managers consisting of Hereditable Governors ('contributors of 5,000 rupees and upward to the College Fund before the aggregate sum of a lakh and a half of sicca rupees may have been subscribed to that fund'), Governors for life (contributors of 5,000 rupees and upwards after the target of one and a half lakh of rupees had been reached), and Directors, annually elected by subscribers, whose joint or separate subscriptions to its college amounted to at least 5,000 rupees. The committee of managers consisted entirely of Hindu *bhadralok* who had complete power over the running of the college. Since 1824, however, the government had tried to control the policy of the college, through H. H. Wilson who was nominated as the Visitor of the college. Government of Bengal, Education Department, *Presidency College Register*, Calcutta, 1927, pp. 5–6.

house, or to the receptions at Government House, or at the end of the period would be nominated as jurors on the Grand jury or as Justices of the Peace or appointed to such semi-official bodies as the General Committee for Public Instruction. In short, the *abhijat bhadralok* who were active in educational and social reform were respected by their fellow countrymen, and the government accepted them as representatives of 'native opinion'. It was natural that there should be such keen competition to gain control of schools and other societies.[1]

There was a deep division of opinion and rivalry between groups within the *bhadralok* class. Although there was a wide spectrum of views, ranging from Bhavanicharan Banerjee to the young students of Hindu College, the *bhadralok* of Calcutta could be divided into two large groups, as we have already noticed, the 'liberals' led by Rammohun Roy and Dwarkanath Tagore and the 'conservatives' led by Gopimohun Deb and his son Radhakanta Deb.

However, these ideological labels had limited application. There was no deep division of opinion over any important political issue except on European colonization. But there are good reasons to believe that on this issue the 'conservatives' were largely influenced by some Company officials, who on their part supported the 'conservatives' on *sati*.[2] The liberal-nationalists and some Marxist historians have presented Rammohun Roy and his *Brahmo Samaj* movement as the only agents of modernity, who had to wage war against the orthodox party led by Deb. All too often, the contribution made by Deb, Sen, Seal and other 'conservatives' to the cause of modernity is glossed over. Some have even tried to discover a class basis for the ideological cleavage. Professor Ahmed suggested that the 'conservatives' 'had more links with land than with trade', whereas the 'liberals' were largely merchants.[3] This is rather too simple. It has already been noticed that the *bhadralok*, 'conservative' or 'liberal', was deeply interested in modernizing the economy, was involved in trade and had invested money in land. Radhamadhab Banerjee, a member of the orthodox *Dharma Sabha*, was a director of the Union Bank and Dwarkanath Tagore, the 'liberal', was a big landlord.

In fact in our analysis of the social and political development of Calcutta in the nineteenth century we should not look at modernity in opposition to tradition. The 'conservatives' were interested in English education, modern science, and in modernization of the economy. Radhakanta Deb, a director of Hindu College, a member of the Calcutta School Book Society and the native secretary of the

---

[1] In 1833 the Calcutta Supreme Court nominated seven Indians to the Grand jury.

[2] *Alexander's East India Magazine*, Vol. 1, Dec. 1830 to June 1831, p. 50.

[3] Ahmed, *Social ideas and social change in Bengal, 1818–1835*, pp. 169–70.

Calcutta School Society, did more than his 'liberal' opponents for the encouragement of English education. It was in his father's house that the Calcutta School Society held their annual examinations and prize-giving ceremonies.[1] They were as much interested as Rammohun Roy and Dwarkanath Tagore 'to raise the natives of India to a higher state of civilization and welfare'.[2] But if the 'conservatives' acted as the agents of modernity then the 'liberals' were not so alienated from tradition as they have often been presented to us.

Dwarkanath Tagore, despite his zeal for the vaidantic religion, did not hesitate to give a feast to the *Chaubeys* in Brindaban, and to feed over 50,000 Brahmins and others during the *sradh* ceremony of his mother.[3] Prassanakumar Tagore, another member of the *Brahmo Samaj*, performed the family *Durga Puja* with the pomp and splendour that befits an *abhijat bhadralok*, for which, however, he earned a nickname, the 'half-enlightened' reformer.[4] But this snide remark from the young radical students was unjustified, since 'the Father of Modern India' himself was unwilling to give up his 'sacred thread'. Also, through his *Brahmo Samaj*, Rammohun Roy ceremoniously donated to the Brahmins, every year, as a *bhadralok* should do. In England, although he accepted invitations to dine with Europeans, 'his food is solely vegetables or sweetmeats, as he conforms in every essential particular to the habits of his country'.[5] Others, like the Basaks, as we have already noticed, found no particular difficulty in following the traditional religion and being engaged in reform.

There was a difference of opinion dividing the *bhadralok*. Rammohun Roy believed that 'the organization of society' depended on religion. Since Hinduism had imposed unnecessary restrictions on the Hindus, which denied them 'social comfort' and disqualified them from entering into 'difficult enterprises', he insisted that some religious reform was essential at least 'for the sake of their [Indians'] political and social comfort'. When *sati* was abolished, he wrote to his friends in England, that since the Act had 'removed the odium from our character as a people...we now deserve every improvement temporal and spiritual'.[6]

[1] *The Calcutta Annual Register for the 1821*, Calcutta, 1823, pp. 79–80.
[2] Radhakanta Deb to H. H. MacNaghton, 9 Nov. 1835, in Banerjee, *I.H.R.C.* Vol. 9, p. 106.
[3] K. C. Mittra, *Memoir of Dwarkanath Tagore*, p. 36. Cf. *Samachar Darpan*, 31 Mar. 1838, *S.S.K.* Vol. 2, p. 543.
[4] *Samachar Darpan*, 10 Dec. 1831, and *Samachar Chadrika*, 12 Nov. 1831, *S.S.K.* Vol. 2, pp. 419 and 527–9.
[5] *Tatvabodhini Patrika* no. 50. Cf. *Alexander's East India Magazine*, Vol. 1, Dec. 1830 to June 1831, pp. 557–66.
[6] R. Roy, *Tuhfatul Muwahhiddin or a gift to deists* (ed. and trans. by Moulavi Obaidullah Obaide), reprint Calcutta, 1949, pp. 6–7. Cf. 'Letter to a friend', 14 July 1832, as published in 'Notes on the suttee and its abolition', in Benoy Ghosh, *Report of the Regional Records Survey Committee of West Bengal 1958–9*, Calcutta, 1959.

The 'conservatives', however, did not find any necessary connexion between 'political and social comfort' and religious reform. They were eager to separate their religion from secular activities. Rhadhakanta Deb agreed to work with the School Book Society, provided no 'religious matter' was introduced into their publications.[1] No religious instruction was allowed in Hindu College; when Derozio was suspected of encouraging his students to question the authority of Hinduism, he had to resign. In 1824, the managers of the College were forced to seek financial help from the government, and had to agree to share its management with a government nominee. However, they reminded the General Committee of Public Instruction that the College 'is a Hindu institution for the purpose of cultivating especially English literature and science alone, that the admission of persons likely to injure respectability and consequently, to contract the utility of the College will always be strictly prohibited, and that works directed against the character and principles of our countrymen will be also excluded'.[2] They protested against Bentinck's Regulation to abolish *sati*, for they considered such an act was a direct interference with Hindu religion and custom.[3]

The 'conservatives' kept firm control over Hindu College. Baidyanath Mukherjee, the Secretary of the College, was originally a member of Rammohun's *Atmiya Sabha*, but he broke his connexions with the Sabha soon after Rammohun launched an open campaign against Hindu orthodoxy. Lakshminarayan Mukherjee, Baidyanath's son, followed his father as the Secretary of the Hindu College, and he was a supporter of *Dharma Sabha* in 1830. Gopimohun Tagore and his sons Chandrakumar and Prassanakumar were the only supporters of Rammohun Roy to be connected with the management of the College. The 'liberals' were also in the minority on the committees of the School Book Society and the School Society; only Prassanakumar Tagore was associated with these societies. However, by 1832 the Committee of the School Book Society had included Dwarkanath Tagore and Radhprasad Roy (son of Rammohun).[4]

As we probe a little deeper we begin to realize the complexity of the situation. The caste analysis of the two contesting groups brings out an interesting pattern. Although Rammohun succeeded in bringing together men from all castes (there were *Kayasthas* like Kalinath Munshi, Brindaban Mitra, and Nandakisore Bose, and *Subarnavaniks* like Kasi Nath Mullick), most of his active supporters were Brahmins, *Radi*

---

[1] Deb to MacNaghton, *I.H.R.C.* Vol. 9, p. 109. [2] *Presidency College Register*, p. 6.
[3] See the Petition of the Hindus against the abolition of *sati* (Regulation XVII of 1829) as reprinted in Ahmed, *Social ideas and social change in Bengal, 1818–1835*, pp. 176–9.
[4] *The Ninth Report of the Calcutta School Book Society*, p. vii.

Kulins, like Kali Sankar Ghosal, Baidyanath Mukherjee, Ananda Banerjee, Braja Mohun Majumdar and Ramchandra Vidyabagish, or *Piralis (bhagna Kulin)*, like the Tagores, Dwarkanath, his brothers and cousins, or *Barendra Kulins*, like Tarachand Chakranarti.[1] The leading members of the *Dharma Sabha* group were non-Brahmins; only two out of thirteen committee members were Brahmins. The protectors of orthodox Brahmanism were *Maulik* (low grade) *Kayasthas* like the Debs, or *Subarnavaniks* like Motilal Seal or *Baidyas* like Ramkamal Sen.[2]

It is interesting to note that many writers, social reformers and politicians during the nineteenth century were *Radi Kulin* Brahmins. In fact four great Bengalis, Rammohun Roy, Iswar Chandra Vidyasagar, Sir Surendranath Banerjea, and Ranglal Banerjee, were descended from three branches of the same Bando–Ghoti family.[3]

Professor Benoy Ghosh attaches great significance to the fact that two great social reformers, Raja Rammohun Roy and Iswar Chandra Vidyasagar, came from the *Radi Kulin* Brahmin caste. He argues that social reforms were inaugurated by the *Radi Kulin* Brahmin to safeguard their own interests. The strict laws of endogamy, the prohibition of the remarriage of widows, kulinism and polygamy left many women of this caste childless, consequently the caste was decreasing in number. The social reforms concerning *sati*, the remarriage of widows and polygamy aimed at increasing the birth rate.[4] However, although it is generally acknowledged that the *Radi Kulin* Brahmins were numerically weak, there is no hard evidence to support Ghosh's thesis.

It is more fruitful to look at the two contesting groups as two leading *dals*. *Dals* were social factions, formed under the leadership of a rich man, a *dalapati*. Although a member of any caste could aspire to be a *dalapati*, the majority of the *dalapatis* in Calcutta were either Brahmin or *Kayastha*. Most *dals* were multi-caste bodies; *Baidyas, Kayasthas, Tilis, Kaibartyas, Sadgops*, Weavers, *Subarnavaniks* and Brahmins could belong to the same *dal* and the Brahmins in many *dals* accepted the leadership of other castes. There were, however, some castes, like the *Subarnavaniks*,

[1] Shivanath Shastri, *Ramtoonu Lahiri o Tatkalin Banga Samaj*, pp. 22–41 and 95–114. Cf. M. N. Ghosh, 'Friends and followers of Rammohun', in A. Home (ed.), *Rammohun Roy, the man and his works*, Calcutta, 1933, pp. 124–32.

[2] The following men were selected as the members of the *Dharma Sabha* Committee after the first meeting held at Calcutta Sanskrit College on 17 January 1830: Ramgopal Mallick, Gopimohun Deb, Radhakanta Deb, Tarinicharan Mitra, Ramkamal Sen, Harimohun Tagore, Kashinath Mallick, Maharaj Kalikrishna Bahadur, Ashutosh Sarkar, Gokolnath Mallick, Baisnavadas Mallick, Nilmani Dey and Bhavanicharan Banerjee (the Secretary); *Samachar Chandrika*, 23 Jan. 1830, *S.S.K.* Vol. 1, p. 301.

[3] N. N. Vasu, *Banger Jatiya Itihas, Brahman Kanda*, Calcutta, p. 256. Cf. Pandit Lalmohan Vidyanidhi, *Sambandha Nirnaya*, Vol. 1, Calcutta, 1874, Appendix.

[4] B. Ghosh, *Vidyasagar o Bangali Samaj*, Vol. 1 (2nd ed.), Calcutta, 1371, pp. 74–6.

who had their own caste *dal*. Most Calcutta *dalapatis* had followers in the rural areas, in their *zamindaris* and their ancestral villages.[1]

In the eighteenth century, all disputes concerning caste were decided at the *jatimala* or 'caste-cutcherries'; it would seem that such 'cutcherries' had some formal recognition and two *dals*, one led by Nubkissen and the other by Madan Datta, competed with each other to get the leadership of Bengali Hindu society in Calcutta.[2] As more rich Hindus moved into Calcutta during the latter part of the eighteenth century many new *dals* were formed. Since about the end of the eighteenth century all disputes concerning the caste rules on pollution, marriage, status within the *jatis* and sometimes even disputes over the inheritance of property, were settled at 'courts' held in *dalapatis'* houses. Dwijendranath Tagore recalled, in his *Memoirs*, the days when his grandfather Dwarkanath and his father Debendranath 'ruled the society' (*samaj sasan*) as *dalapatis* and settled many disputes between the members of the *dals* which would usually be decided, in the twentieth century, in a court of law.[3]

In the absence of a church, or of even the caste *panchayats*, or chieftains' or old *zamindars'* courts, the *dals* gave Hindu society in Bengal, as Ghosh put it, 'its coherence, its submission to discipline, its recognition of leaders, its respect for tradition'.[4] Even Dwijendranath Tagore, a *Brahmo* leader, praised the *dals*, for they curbed the 'evils of individualism' and provided the society with cohesion and authority, and through the *dals* the 'traditional culture' was able to continue despite the changes of the nineteenth century.[5] The *dalapatis*, like the old rajas, patronized Brahmin pandits, and *ghataks* (match-makers), who debated on knotty problems of Hindu theology, wrote eulogies for their patrons, prepared 'family histories' (*Kula Panjikas*) and gave *vyavasthas* (decrees) on problems concerning caste rules and customary laws.

The activities of the *dals* were not devoid of politics. This was an area of power over which the British govermnent had no control. While the British managed state affairs, the *dalapatis* 'ruled the society'. The *dalapatis* had considerable authority and influence over men in Calcutta and in the rural areas where some of the *dals* had links. The *dalapatis* enforced their *vyavasthas* on caste rules through the weapon of excommunication, and everyone feared excommunication. If a person were excommunicated, then he might not be able to marry his children off or obtain a priest to perform the family rites, he might not be invited to traditional social functions like *sradhs*, *pujas* and marriages and his

---

[1] Bhavanicharan Banerjee, *Kalikata Kamalalaya*, pp. 28–34. Cf. *Samachar Chandrika*, 5 Jan. 1833, *S.S.K.* Vol. 2, pp. 271–2.
[2] 'Memoirs of Maharaja Nubkissen', I.O.R. Home Miscellaneous Series, no. 773, pp. 237–9.
[3] *Dwijendranath Thakurer Smritikatha*, p. 285.   [4] N. N. Ghosh, *Nubkissen*, p. 191.
[5] *Dwijendranath Thakurer Smritikatha*, pp. 285–6.

invitations for such occasions might not be accepted. So all *bhadralok* felt the necessity of belonging to a *dal*. If a person fell out with his *dalapati*, he could move to another *dal* or if he was rich enough and influential enough he could form his own *dal*, or live as an outcaste. The protection of a *dal* was essential; Nilmani Mullick, and his family, as *dalapati* 'introduced several reforms amongst their kinsmen, and saved many from excommunication of caste or other social degradation'.[1] Nabakrishna Sinha saved a *Tili* family from excommunication despite the opposition from the other members of his *dal*.[2]

Caste grades and ranks were also decided by the *dals*. Although theoretically the Bengali Hindu society was divided into two *varnas* and forty-one *jatis*, no *jati* in Bengal was a homogeneous group. Each *jati* was subdivided into numerous groups, with strict marriage laws and hierarchical orders within it. *The Friend of India* observed that in Bengal every caste was subdivided into numerous classes, each given a certain rank or status by tradition.

Hence the station of every individual in Bengal is settled with nearly as much precision as that of the nobility of Europe...No family is lost in the crowd; there are always some beneath it, who view its right and dignity with feelings of respect; every individual therefore possesses an acknowledged and defined rank in this mighty aristocracy. These family distinctions may be tarnished by ignoble alliances, but they may be regained by a series of advantageous marriages.[3]

Thus marriage was an important area of human activity for men seeking higher rank. The *ghataks* played a key role in all important marriage alliances, they compiled and interpreted the *Kulapanjikas* (marriage registers or family histories) and decided on the suitability of marriages. The *dalapatis* who patronized the compilers of the *Kulapanjikas* were able to improve their own status and exercise authority over men. Nubkissen, although a *Maulik Kayastha*, managed to marry his grandson to the daughter of the celebrated *goshtipati* Gopikanta Sinha of Gopinagar through his *ghataks*, and thus 'constituted his grandson as the Thirteenth *Goshtipati* from Srimanta Raya'.[4] His descendants claimed, in the nineteenth century, the *Kulin* status. Tagores also had their own *ghataks* who wrote the 'family histories' of their patrons.[5] The *dalapatis* also helped their castes to move up in the ritual ladder; thus the *Baidyas* were helped by Rajballabh and were already claiming the status of 'the twice born'. The *Kayasthas* soon followed them, and the

[1] L. N. Ghose, *The Modern History of the Indian Chiefs*... p. 59.
[2] *Samachar Chandrika*, 24 Dec. 1831, *S.S.K.* Vol. 2, pp. 266–7.
[3] *The Friend of India*, Vol. 1, p. 84.
[4] *A rapid sketch of Raja Radhakanta Deb*, p. 17.
[5] *A Brief account of the Tagore family*, Calcutta, 1868, pp. 1–5. Cf. K. C. Mittra, *Memoir of Dwarkanath Tagore*, pp. 2–3.

Deb family and their *dal* played a prominent part in it.[1] Many rich men of very low ritual status started claiming the *Kayastha* status. The rich cousins of *Kaibartya* Rajendra Das were claiming such status in the 1830s but they could only be recognized as *Kayasthas* if their claim was supported by such *dalapati* as Deb.[2]

It was important for the *bhadralok* who wished to acquire authority and influence over men in Calcutta to be active in the *dals*. Thus the *bhadralok* who wanted to be a representative of 'native opinion' must be active in 'public welfare', in the colleges and societies; he should also be a *dalapati* or at least be a leading member of an influential *dal* in Calcutta. Through the *dals*, the leading men in Calcutta acquired high status and exercised considerable influence and authority over men in Calcutta and outside. In 1833, Ashutosh Dey, son of Ramdoolal, decided to break away from Madan Datta's *dal* and form his own *dal*. He was already an important figure in Calcutta; he was a son of the richest man in the city and a formidable businessman in his own right; he was active in the schools, in societies and a prominent member of the *Dharma Sabha* Committee. However, he still felt the need to have a *dal* of his own, which no doubt gave him even higher status than he already had and he exercised even more influence over men of all castes in Calcutta and outside, who accepted him as their leader.[3]

The traditional style of politics was largely concerned with caste status. It meant competition among the elites of Calcutta to gain status and power through the *dals*. There were many *dals* in Calcutta, but during our period some *dals* were more important than others. It seems that there were at least two leading *dals*; that of the Tagores and that of the Debs. It must be noted, however, that the Tagores were not united; Harimohun Tagore and Ladlimohun Tagore, step-brothers of Gopimohun Tagore and Umananda Tagore, another member of the Pathuriaghata branch of the family, were in Deb's *dal* and were active in the *Dharma Sabha*.[4] The Debs managed to bring together many *dala-patis* under their leadership in the *Dharma Sabha*, and a large majority of these *dalapatis* were non-Brahmins. Dwarkanath Tagore also succeeded in gaining the support of many *dalapatis* like Kalinath Munshi of Taki and individuals for Rammohun's *Brahmo Samaj*. Many contempories considered *Brahmo Samaj* and *Dharma Sabha* as two rival *dals*.[5]

---

[1] N. N. Ghosh, *Nubkissen*, pp. 169–91.

[2] *Samachar Darpan*, 5 Aug. 1837, *S.S.K.* Vol. 2, pp. 273–5.

[3] *Samachar Darpan*, 5 Jan. 1833, *S.S.K.* Vol. 2, pp. 271–2. Many new *dals* were formed during this period and it was considered important to publish their news in a separate periodical called *Dalabritanta* printed solely for that purpose. See *Samachar Chandrika*, 23 Sept. 1831 and 21 July 1832, *S.S.K.* Vol. 2, pp. 181–2.

[4] *Samachar Chandrika*, 13 Feb. 1830, *S.S.K.* Vol. 2, pp. 306–7.

[5] *Samachar Darpan*, 1 July 1837, *S.S.K.* Vol. 2, pp. 272–3.

In fact they were two rival groups, each an amalgam of many *dals* contesting for status and power

The activities of Rammohun Roy, who was a newcomer to Calcutta, who had no *dal* of his own and who insisted on conducting politics solely in the modern idiom, threatened, at least for a time, the power of the *dals*. The young students of the Hindu College who ate beef and drank wine also defied the authority of the *dals*. But even Rammohun had to enlist the support of some of the established families like the Tagores and had to patronize the Brahmins, both through his *Brahmo Samaj* and through his Vedanta College.[1] It is also doubtful whether the young Bengal would have been able to defy authority had they not had the indulgence of some of their elders, especially of Prassanakumar Tagore who sat on the Committee of Managers during the troubled years.

The successful leading men had to master the two languages of politics. They had to learn to bargain with their masters for a better deal for their class and compete with each other to gain control of areas of power open to them. Yet at another level they fought each other as *dals* to gain high status and power over men.[2] What is, however, more significant, the shrewd *bhadralok* was able to use the modern media of communication, like the press, to extend the authority of the *dals* and use the authority and the contacts of the *dalapatis* to strengthen the position of a modern association like the *Dharma Sabha*.

On 17 January 1830 the 'conservatives' formed the *Dharma Sabha* to agitate against Regulation XVII of 1829, which prohibited the practice of *sati*. This was at once a modern association and an amalgam of traditional *dals*. It worked as a modern association should, with a programme of action, a committee with a president, a treasurer and a secretary, and a set of rules which delimited the power of the committee. The secretary meticulously kept a book of minutes and an account of its funds. They opened 'branch' *sabhas* in Dacca, Murshidabad, Santipur, Benaras, Cuttak and in Bhawanipur. The *bhadralok*, the *zamindars*, lawyers, *tahsildars*, Brahmins, *Baidyas*, *Kayasthas* and others of the *mofussil* towns joined these 'branch *sabhas*', collected signatures for the petition against Bentinck's Regulation, got the local pandits to write *vyavasthas* in support of *sati* and collected subscriptions for the Calcutta *Dharma Sabha*. They appointed agents in England to lobby for their cause.[3] But the *Sabha* also worked as a *dal*, a 'caste tribunal', what

---

[1] Collet, *The life and letters of Raja Rammohun Roy*, pp. 189–92.

[2] *Daldali* (feuds among *dals*) was a part of the *abhijat bhadralok's* life in Calcutta throughout the nineteenth century. See *Dwijerdrnath Thakurer Smritikatha*, pp. 285–6.

[3] For activities of the *Dharma Sabha*, cf. *Samachar Darpan*, 23 Jan. 1830, 6 Feb. 1830 and *Samachar Chandrika*, 13 Feb. 1830, in *S.S.K.* Vol. 1, pp. 300–7, and *Samachar Chandrika*, 6 May 1830 (British Museum reference 141.33.G.6).

George Johnson called the 'black tribunal'.[1] The *Sabha* gave *vyavasthas* on caste rules, marriage and inheritance; and imposed their will by the threat of excommunication. The pages of *Samachar Chandrika* are full of references to such disputes on which the Pandits of *Dharma Sabha* gave their *vyavastha*. They decided, for instance, whether or not the second brother of a certain Navakumar Mukherjee of Jahanabad had forfeited his right to inherit ancestral property since he had been living with a *chandal* (untouchable) woman or whether a Shudra could act as a *guru* of a Brahmin. The *Sabha* also tried to excommunicate the *Satidvesis* (the abolitionists).[2]

The success of the *Dharma Sabha* as the first Calcutta society to mobilize men in and outside Calcutta to resist a government measure, is rather startling. Within the first five months of its existence the *Sabha* was able to establish most of its 'branches' and the organizers had already collected 1,146 signatures protesting against the abolition of *sati*, by 14 January 1830, three days before the formal launching of the *Sabha*.[3] The petition did not move Bentinck and the appeal was dismissed by the Privy Council.[4] However, the organizational experience was very valuable to the *bhadralok*. In the *Dharma Sabha* and in the agitation for *sati* the *bhadralok* learnt the techniques of using the traditional channels like the *dals* to mobilize men for modern agitational movements. The energy that was generated by such activities in the Calcutta *bhadralok* could well be used for agitation for their political and economic advancement. After 1832, when the Privy Council rejected the appeal from the 'conservatives', the 'Dharma Sabha' ceased to function as a modern society for social reform and agitation and became a mere 'caste tribunal'.[5] However, the leading members of *Dharma Sabha*, Ramkamal Sen, Maharaja Kali Krishna Bahadur and Rashakanta Deb, were able to use their organizational experience and to canalize the energy of their members to a secular cause. It was the *dalapatis* of *Dharma Sabha* who led the other *bhadralok*, the Muslim *zamindars* and the European free traders in founding the first political association in India in 1838.

[1] George H. Johnson, *The stranger in India or three years in Calcutta*, London, 1843, Vol. 2, p. 152.
[2] *Samachar Chandrika*, 5 July 1830 and 12 Oct. 1832. Cf. *Alexander's East India Magazine*, vol. 1 pp. 403–4. It was becoming increasingly difficult to impose the sanctions. In the case of Navakumar Mukherjee's brother, the *Dharma Sabha* decreed that a man 'who is given up to licentious pleasures' must not be allowed to inherit his father's estate. But they had no way to impose their sanction since the English courts would not recognize such a sanction. If, however, they had a powerful local *dal* they imposed strict excommunication.
[3] *Samachar Darpan*, 23 Jan. 1830, *S.S.K.* Vol. 1, pp. 292–3.
[4] J. C. Bagal, *Radhakanta Deb*, p. 39 n. Cf. Ahmed, *Social ideas and social change in Bengal, 1818–1835*, p. 125.
[5] *Sangbad Prabhakar*, 16 Apr. 1848, as published in Benoy Ghosh (ed.), *Samayikpatre Banglar Samajchitra (S.B.S.)*, Vol. 1, pp. 168–9.

Economic and political interests had brought all *bhadralok* together to organize protest meetings and sign petitions from time to time. In 1826 it was against the Jury Act, in 1827 against the stamp duties, in 1828 against the resumption of *la-ki-raj* land and again in 1835 for the free press.[1] But they had no secular political society to organize movements to further their cause. In 1833 it was suggested in a Bengali pamphlet issued by *The Reformer*, a liberal newspaper, that the Bengali *zamindars* should have such a society,[2] but nothing came of it. A similar attempt by Roy Kalinath Chaudhuri and Ramlochan Ghosh and some members of the *Brahmo Samaj* also failed. Their society, *Banga-bhasa Prakasika Sabha*, founded in December 1836, became a defunct body by January 1837.[3]

The first serious step towards the formation of a political association was taken in 1836, in the *Dharma Sabha*. It was conceived by H. H. Wilson, who put his ideas to Ramkamal Sen. Sen proposed at a meeting of the *Dharma Sabha* on 23 April 1836, that 'a branch society should be immediately formed, where matters affecting the public welfare such as *zamindaris* and agricultural disquisitions should be treated of, [*sic*] instead of those limited dull questions, which now occupy the society's attention'. This was approved by the president Maharaja Kalikrishna Bahadur, but was opposed by Bhavanicharan Banerjee, who saw a threat to orthodox religion in the formation of a secular *sabha*. Banerjee was out-voted and it was agreed that a special meeting should be held 'to consider the expediency of establishing a branch society for the purpose suggested'.[4]

There was, however, no special meeting of the *Dharma Sabha* to discuss the proposal, at least not in public. Instead, Ramkamal Sen and other leading members of the *Dharma Sabha* called a meeting of all the *zamindars* in Calcutta, in November 1837 at Hindu College, to consider the expediency of forming a society to protect landed property in Bengal. The meeting was attended by the 'liberals' as well as by the 'conservatives', and it was decided to form a committee, which consisted of Radhakanta Deb, Ramkamal Sen, Bhavanicharan Mitra (all connected with the *Dharma Sabha*) and Prasannakumar Tagore, to write a manifesto and the rules and regulations for the proposed society.[5]

---

[1] The Requisition for the meeting in the Calcutta Town Hall to protest against the Stamp Duty was signed by both Rammohun Roy and Radhakanta Deb. The meeting, however, was not allowed by the Sheriff of Calcutta and the organizer held the meeting at Calcutta Exchange Room. *Samachar Darpan*, 12 and 19 May 1827, *S.S.K.* Vol. 1, pp. 198–200.

[2] *Samachar Darpan*, 31 Aug. 1833, *S.S.K.* Vol. 2, p. 157.

[3] *Samachar Darpan*, 17 Dec., 31 Dec. 1836 and 7 Jan. 1837. *S.S.K.* Vol. 2, pp. 398–405.

[4] *Alexander's East India Magazine*, July–Dec. 1836, Vol. 12, p. 366. Cf. *Samachar Darpna*, 30 Apr. 1836, *S.S.K.* Vol. 2, pp. 595–6.

[5] *Samachar Darpan*, 12 Nov. 1837. *S.S.K.* Vol. 2, pp. 405–6.

In March 1838 the committee put its proposal to a large audience consisting of all leading *abhijat bhadralok* of Calcutta, Muslim *zamindars* like Munshi Mahammud Amir, Europeans like Prinsep, Hare and Dickens. The meeting decided to form the Landholders' Society, primarily to defend private property in land, and to achieve the extension of the Permanent Settlement to North-Western Province, repeal Regulation XII of 1828 and improve the position of the *zamindars*. All landholders, irrespective of caste, creed and colour, were allowed to join the Society, provided they paid Rs. 5 as admission fee and Rs. 20 as the yearly subscription. The meeting appointed the first committee of the Society, which consisted of 'liberals' like Dwarkanath Tagore, Prasannakumar Tagore, 'conservatives' like Ramkamal Sen and Radhakanta Deb, one Muslim *zamindar*, Munshi Muhammed Amir, and free traders like George Prinsep. It is significant to note that five out of the twelve members of the Committee were from the *Dharma Sabha*.[1]

The Society was never big (it is doubtful whether the membership was ever more than two hundred)[2] and it became a defunct body by the end of the 1840s. Nevertheless, it can claim to be the parent of all subsequent political associations in India in the nineteenth century. Its organization and its techniques of agitation were used by loyal Indian subjects, in the British-India Association, in the Indian Association and even in the Indian National Congress. They all wanted to work within the British-India system, had faith in British justice, wanted to create a pressure of public opinion in Britain and in India on the British government to make political concession to the Indians. The Landholders' Society, although formed primarily to protect the interest of the landholders, had wider political implications. It was interested in preventing the resumption of rent-free tenure, and in extending the Permanent Settlement to North-Western Province, and also in reforming the police system, and the Revenue and Judicial Department, in the free use of capital in Indian agriculture and in the humane treatment of the Indian coolies in Mauritius. It opened branches in various parts of the Provinces of Bengal, Bihar and Orissa, and appointed John Crawford as a regular agent in London.[3]

In the preceding pages I have argued that the economic and administrative changes in Bengal brought about a social erosion. The most significant change took place in Calcutta, which witnessed the rise of a new urban class. The economic and political interests of this class

[1] *The Landholders' Society, Rules and Regulations of*, pp. 6–10 and 27. The five *Dharma Sabha* members were Raja Rajnarayan Bahadur, Roy Kalikrishna Bahadur, Radhakanta Deb, Asutosh Dey and Ramkamal Sen.

[2] Ninety-four *zamindars* joined the Society after the first meeting, four of whom were Muslims. See *The Landholders' Society*, p. 33.

[3] *Op. cit.* p. 38. Cf. *Bengal Hurkaru*, 14 and 15 Dec. 1839.

forced the *bhadralok* into agitational movements and finally in 1838 they formed the first political association in India, not only to protect the landed interest but also to press for the political and economic advancement of the class. Men with economic power and high status formed the elite of this class (the *dalapatis*). But since status was still attached to caste, men seeking higher status had to work through the traditional *dals*. The *dalapatis* also used the *dals* for modern politics, for both horizontal and vertical mobilization, to establish contacts in the *mofussil* areas and to exert pressure on their followers for agitation. But if politics were conducted through traditional channels it was the end of the caste 'tradition'[1] and status society and the beginning of a market and competitive society.

[1] E. R. Leach (ed.), *Aspects of caste in South India, Ceylon and North-west Pakistan*: Cambridge papers in Social Anthropology, no. 2, Cambridge, 1960, pp. 4–9.

COMPETING ELITES IN BOMBAY CITY POLITICS IN THE MID-NINETEENTH CENTURY (1852–83)

CHRISTINE DOBBIN

I. 'SHETIAS' AND INTELLIGENTSIA

In the seventeenth and eighteenth centuries the geographical and economic position of Bombay city made it a centre of attraction for two of the major linguistic groups of western India—the speakers of Gujarati and related dialects such as Kutchi, and the speakers of Marathi and its close relation, Konkani. The leading Gujarati castes and communities of the city were engaged in trading and commercial pursuits which had occupied them for centuries, and which they carried on in partnership with one another and with the most recent intruders in the area, the British merchants. Gujarati mercantile and banking society in the city was in the seventeenth century dominated by the great Bania castes, particularly the Kapol Banias, who had long controlled trade and commerce in Kathiawad and Kutch. But other castes, such as the Bhatias and the Bhansalis, had over the centuries been able to move from agriculture to trade. As they rose in status and wealth in Kutch and Kathiawad, they migrated to the great commercial cities, and by the early nineteenth century they were recognized as important trading communities in Bombay. Similarly, Hindu trading castes which had been converted to Islam—the Bohras, Khojas and Memons—were attracted to Bombay in the eighteenth century and the early nineteenth century, and achieved considerable commercial success. Other communities, such as the Parsis, whose main occupation had long been agriculture, were also beginning to move into trade from the seventeenth century, and a number of them made immense fortunes in collaboration with the British. The commercial monopoly of these communities was challenged by only a handful of outsiders belonging in the main either to the Marathi-speaking artisan castes such as the Sonars (goldsmiths), the shipbuilding Konkani Muslims and one or two commercially minded Saraswat Brahmins.

The British in western India were impressed with the outstanding commercial abilities and the wealth of Bombay's leading merchants. By the middle of the nineteenth century the great *shetias* of the city included men such as the first Parsi baronet, Sir Jamshedji Jijibhai, Beramji Jijibhai and M. N. Banaji, Kapol Banias such as Mangaldas Nathubhai and Varjivandas Madhavdas, and the Sonar *shetia* Jagannath Shankarshet. In addition to their immense wealth, they dominated the affairs of their own castes and communities as caste *shets*, and their investments in house property in the city had enabled them to become extensive landlords. Successive governors of Bombay were concerned to gain *shetia* support and *shetias* such as the first Sir Jamshedji Jijibhai and Jagannath Shankarshet became confidential advisers to a number of the Presidency's Governors. The government also saw the advisability of associating prosperous merchants and bankers with the public life of the city, and in 1834 the practice was begun of appointing some of the leading *shetias* as J.P.s, which involved them in the municipal administration of Bombay. When Indians were appointed to the Governor's Council in 1862 it was to the *shetias* that the government again turned for representatives of Bombay city. The British were disappointed to find, however, that although their protégés were ready to accept titles and other marks of distinction at their hands they were not prepared to embrace the intellectual heritage with which the British wished to endow them. The great *shetia* families of the city—Hindu, Muslim and Parsi—remained conspicuously absent from all government and missionary institutions—particularly the Elphinstone Institution—purveying the new learning. Most were prepared to acquire a knowledge of English through private tutors for commercial purposes, but even as late as the 1870s they were strongly resisting attempts to turn them into 'cultivated Indian gentlemen'.[1] The great *shetias* of Bombay were willing during the greater part of the nineteenth century to partner the British in trade and administration, but they were unprepared to enter into an intellectual partnership.

Part of the reason for this was that British educational policy in western India was bedevilled by internal contradictions. Successive educators oscillated between the desire to create a class of 'Indian gentlemen' who would be the regenerators of their country, and the need to provide the Raj with competent clerks and lower civil servants. Among the Marathi-speaking population of the city were Chitpavan Brahmins, Saraswat Brahmins and Pathare Prabhus, members of those castes which had administered the Peshwas' empire in the eighteenth century. These castes, with their tradition of learning and government service, were ready to enter government schools and colleges as soon as they were established, in the hope of gaining both knowledge and employment in government administrative or educational departments.

[1] *Report of the Director of Public Instruction, Bombay*, 1857–8, p. 104.

The government, despite its hope that education would be the preserve of 'the wealthier classes',[1] was forced to admit that in traditional society the 'upper classes' and the 'educated classes' were different entities.[2] The intelligentsia of Bombay city in the early part of the nineteenth century comprised those who of necessity earned their living in government service, and who were dependent on the government for both education and livelihood. They were overwhelmingly members of the Marathi-speaking writing castes, although a small number of Gujarati Brahmins—a group for long not renowned for their learning—also entered the new colleges. An additional and important component of this intelligentsia was a growing number of poorer Parsis, whose community was gradually being pushed out of trade by competition at the lower levels, and whose drift from declining business to English education and governmental jobs was by the 1840s completely altering the community's commercial aspect. After the middle of the century a number of independent professions were laid open to the intelligentsia, which relieved some of them of the burden of poverty and gave them some independence. Several, while retaining government posts, became journalists. The legal profession attracted the most talented—men such as Visvanath Narayan Mandlik, Mahadev Govind Ranade and Kashinath Trimback Telang. Lawyers had by 1870 become the elite of the intelligentsia, especially those, such as Pherozeshah Mehta and Badruddin Tyabji, who had gone to England to be called to the Bar and whose family background in any case gave them considerable financial security. Other members of the intelligentsia, such as Dadabhai Naoroji, Sorabji Shapurji Bengali, Dinsha Wacha, and J. U. Yajnik, made careers for themselves in commerce and banking. Both groups formed an important connecting link between the *shetias* and the majority of the intelligentsia.

2. BOMBAY POLITICAL ASSOCIATIONS, 1852–69

In 1852 a group of ex-students of the government's Elphinstone Institution decided that Bombay required an association to encourage political activity in the city in general, and to discuss the approaching renewal of the East India Company's charter in particular. Chief among them were Dadabhai Naoroji, then an assistant professor at the Elphinstone Institution, Naoroji Furdunji and Narayan Dinanathji, both translators at the High Court, and Bhau Daji, one of the Presidency's first medical graduates. They also realized that it was impossible for them to establish such an association without the moral and financial

---

[1] *Report of the Board of Education*, Bombay, 1845, App. 1, p. 45.
[2] *Ibid.* 1850–1, pp. 10–13.

support of the city's *shetias*. Jagannath Shankarshet, the Sonar *shetia*, had both an interest in political questions and reasonable command of English. He agreed to accept the presidency of the association, and to persuade a number of liberal-minded *shetia* friends both to join it and to provide it with the necessary funds. The Bombay Association was inaugurated on 26 August 1852, with a managing committee of twenty-three—ten Parsis, seven Hindus, three Muslims, two Goans and one Jew. The committee was dominated by the *shetias* of the different communities—men such as the first Sir Jamshedji Jijibhai, F. N. Patel, the Baghdadi Jew David Sassoon, Varjivandas Madhavdas, who was the brother of the Kapol Bania *nagarshet*, and a member of the Konkani Muslim Roghay family. It was understood that the organizational work would be done by the secretaries, Shankarshet's own son and Bhau Daji and Naoroji Furdunji. Very soon, however, the activities of the latter in attempting to investigate the inadequacies of British rule in the *mofussil* alarmed a number of the *shetia* members of the managing committee. Headed by Sir Jamshedji Jijibhai, the *de facto* head of the Parsi community, several of them resigned in October, just a few weeks before the publication of the Association's first petition to Parliament. One of their supporters, the member of a *shetia* family whose fortunes had somewhat declined, later alleged that the Association's secretaries were not sufficiently appreciative of British rule and coined the epithet 'the Bombay Ass-ociation'.[1] He was subsequently taken to court for also suggesting that these same secretaries were 'a refined species of pick pockets'.[2]

Despite this early split in the Association, sufficient *shetia* support remained for it to continue its activities. But the public face presented by the Association was increasingly that of its *shetia* leaders, and it directed its attention chiefly to questions of interest to those engaged in trade. In 1856 the Association, which now had seventy-five members, described itself as comprising men 'mostly possessed of considerable property, and all deeply interested in the efficiency of those Departments of Government which are charged with the preservation of order, the protection of life and property, and the vindication of the Law'.[3] Since the intelligentsia's own particular interests—such as the Civil Service problem and education—were rarely aired by the Association, it is not surprising they ceased to work actively for it, and the Association itself appeared moribund. Late in 1859, however, the government of India attempted to introduce a Licence Tax on trades and professions,

[1] M. Cursetjee, *A Few Passing Ideas for the Benefit of India and the Indians. Addressed to the Bombay Association* (Bombay, 1853), p. 76.
[2] *Ibid.* p. 12.
[3] *Minutes of Proceedings of the Third Annual General Meeting of the Bombay Association, 14 April 1856* (Bombay, 1856), App. A, p. 22.

a measure which particularly affected the intelligentsia. Bhau Daji immediately prepared a memorial on the subject to be submitted to Parliament, but he was powerless to call a general meeting of the Association to discuss it. In the meantime, Jagannath Shankarshet, the Association's President, invited the leading *shetia* members of the Association to two meetings at his own house, at which Bhau Daji's petition was overruled. The outraged Bhau Daji called a much larger rival meeting of those who were prepared to fight against a tax which exempted property holders, and subsequently Jagannath Shankarshet and the *shetias* prepared their own memorial, which was more in the nature of a general attack on recent increases in taxation. Hence, when in January 1860 the first annual general meeting of the Association since 1856 was held, it was an exclusively *shetia* affair and not even the secretary, Naoroji Furdunji, was present to read out the reports.

Although the intelligentsia had virtually been driven out of the Bombay Association, they had already established their own vernacular newspapers, such as the Parsi *Rast Goftar* (est. 1851 by Dadabhai Naoroji, with funds from the Kamas), and the Anglo-Marathi papers *Indu Prakash* (est. 1862) and *Native Opinion* (est. 1864). These papers, which were originally concerned with checking social abuses, gradually added political columns which mirrored the frustration their writers felt at being robbed of the leadership of the city. *Rast Goftar*, a veteran of struggles inside the Parsi community, proclaimed that the demand of the intelligentsia in all areas of life was for 'the inauguration of a new era, showing that opinion has taken the precedence of mere hereditary authority'.[1] All three papers extolled the virtues and successes of 'the educated classes'.[2] Trained in school and college to believe that they were the regenerators of their country, they could not permit their own city to slip through their hands. The burden of their attack was that the most important *shetias* were totally unfit to provide political leadership for Bombay, both because of their lack of education and their lack of interest in anything outside their own commercial transactions. Certain *shetias* were castigated by name, though *Rast Goftar* reserved its choicest phrases for the Bombay Association, which was accused, in turn, of 'servile imbecility', of being 'a disgrace to the community' and 'the laughing stock of all thinking men', and of leading an 'imbecile existence'.[3]

The Bombay Association showed signs of life in 1865, and once the city's share mania had died down the organs of the intelligentsia, led by Visvanath Narayan Mandlik's *Native Opinion*, began to demand a

---

[1] *Rast Goftar*, 22 June 1862.
[2] See e.g. *Rast Goftar*, 1 May 1859; 31 July 1859; 9 June 1861.
[3] *Rast Goftar*, 4 Aug. 1861; 8 June 1862; 10 Apr. 1864.

political revival. The Association was re-established in December 1867 with a membership of eighty-seven—fifty-one Hindus, thirty-five Parsis and one Muslim—but it was more firmly under *shetia* control than before. Despite the membership of all the prominent new graduates of the government law classes, Chitpavans such as Mandlik and Ranade and Saraswats such as Bhandarkar and Wagle, on all public occasions it was the *shetias* of the Executive Committee, the second Sir Jamshedji Jijibhai and Beramji Jijibhai, the Kapol Bania banker Mangaldas Nathubhai and the Saraswat *shetias* Raghunath Narayan Khot and Narayan Vasudev Dabholkar, who dominated. The Association's chief concern continued to be questions of mercantile interest, and India's financial affairs in general. In May 1869, however, the Bombay intelligentsia struck out on their own with a political association intended specifically for themselves. This was the Bombay Branch of Dadabhai Naoroji's London-based East India Association. Dadabhai gave the intelligentsia a promise of political salvation. As an all-India class he urged them not to be confined by the limits of Bombay problems, but to regard the entire country as their political platform. Despite this advice, Dadabhai was himself forced to rely on important *shetias* to help in the establishment of the Association. Beramji Jijibhai provided the funds for Dadabhai's first lectures in the city, and all but two of the Association's ten vice-presidents were *shetias*. He was also forced to rely on the landed notables of western India, an idea canvassed in both Marathi and Gujarati newspapers. Although the Managing Committee was in the hands of Elphinstonians such as Mandlik, Ranade and Bhandarkar, the Association did very little apart from promoting a few lectures and it was soon pointed out that little could be expected of it in the future because the professional men on whom it relied had insufficient leisure from their own careers to attend to its affairs.

3. THE MUNICIPAL REFORM MOVEMENT

From 1865 the Bombay municipality was administered by an excessively extravagant Municipal Commissioner, and over three hundred timid and apathetic Justices of the Peace. Less than half of the Bench of Justices were Indians, chiefly rich Parsi and Gujarati merchants, whose education was rudimentary and who rarely attended meetings. By the late sixties the most prominent members of the intelligentsia were also represented on the Bench, but as they were too few to command a hearing in debates they resorted to their newspapers to attack the Commissioner's reckless extravagance and the increasing pressure of taxation in the city. On the question of taxation the leading *shetias* on the Bench might well have given a lead to the intelligentsia, but they preferred merely to attempt to divest themselves of some of the burden of taxation by shifting it to other shoulders. Most of the big *shetias* and their families had heavily invested in house property in the city, the rents of which provided them with enormous incomes. On the Bench their chief concern by the late sixties was the reduction of the maximum house rate, and the fact that a number of them were also members of the Governor's Council ensured that their views received a hearing. In September 1866, and again in October 1868, Mangaldas Nathubhai, one of the richest property owners in the city, moved a Bill in Council which would levy town duties as an alternative to increasing the house rate. In October the Governor of Bombay noted that the Bill's purpose was 'that a direct form of taxation chiefly affecting the richer classes, should be replaced by indirect taxes, affecting the masses of the population'.[1] Mangaldas alleged that his aim was to ensure that taxation was more evenly distributed over all classes.

The newspapers of the intelligentsia had by now arrived at an alternative solution to the municipality's woes. In the mid-1860s the idea of some form of representative government for India was already being canvassed among the English-educated. From December 1867 Mandlik's *Native Opinion* began to link the current financial crisis of the municipality with the representative government question. The paper argued that the gross mismanagement of the city's affairs could be attributed to the fact that the Bench of Justices was an irresponsible body, appointed haphazardly by government. Municipal woes could only be righted by the hammering out of some form of elective system.[2] But Mandlik, and other members of the intelligentsia such as Naoroji Furdunji, who had been appointed to the Bench, still found it impossible to persuade their fellow Justices that drastic action was called for.

The intelligentsia were handicapped because they had no real party following. Towards the end of 1870, however, there was slowly taking shape a popular movement of those who were increasingly feeling the weight of taxation, but who had no access to the Darbar Room of the town hall, or the Governor's council chamber. In the early sixties a group of ratepayers had been brought together to protest against the incidence of municipal taxation upon the vegetarian part of the community, ghee and oil being more heavily taxed than mutton and beef.[3] In November 1870 certain ratepayers, remembering their earlier success, addressed two petitions to the Bench of Justices complaining that, because of the Commissioner's wild extravagance, taxes had been

[1] *Proceedings of the Council of the Governor of Bombay*, 1868, vii, p. 47.
[2] *Native Opinion*, 1 Dec. 1867; 31 May 1868; 3 May 1868; 20 June 1869.
[3] *Indu Prakash*, 20 July 1885.

reimposed upon the commonest necessities of life.[1] This protest was
from those who felt that they provided the sinews for the municipal
administration: small businessmen, men who paid rates for their
cramped shop premises or godowns, or who hired out carriages in a
small way and therefore paid the wheel tax. A large number were
Banias and Bhatias, who were well versed in organization for caste
purposes. They were led by a few unorthodox and moderately prosperous merchants, including the Bhatia Mulji Thackersey, who had
visited England in the sixties, and the Bhandari Tukaram Tatya
Padval, who had also recently been to London on business. The ratepayers' agitation, which by June 1871 had reached the Governor, was
concerned not with representative government, but with the need for a
thorough investigation of municipal administration and finance.

By the end of June 1871, the Bench of Justices, roused from lethargy
by certain European Justices and members of the intelligentsia, met
to consider proposals which might ensure better financial control of the
affairs of the municipality. Popular representation was discussed for the
first time, but the only really practical scheme was that outlined by the
twenty-six-year-old barrister Pherozeshah Mehta, who had recently
returned from England and who now suggested a popular and responsible corporation elected by the ratepayers themselves, a consultative
town council elected out of it, with a responsible executive officer
appointed by government at its head.[2] Pherozeshah's main point, which
he developed later, was that the Commissioner himself had done
excellent work in developing and beautifying Bombay, and that the
real problem was not to weaken a strong executive, but ensure that the
executive be responsibly controlled.[3] While these reform debates were
taking place, popular feeling in the city was running high. The Gujarati
papers were particularly violent, and warned those Justices who did
not support the popular cause that thrashing, pelting and public disgrace awaited them.[4] By August the ratepayers' leaders had taken up
the demand of the intelligentsia that the future of the municipality
must lie in popular hands, and private meetings were organized by
caste and communal associations to explain the nature of representative
municipal institutions. Street demonstrations and liberal donations

[1] Most of the ratepayers' successive memorials can be found collected in a pamphlet, *The
Rate-payers' Memorial to the Secretary of State for India* (Bombay, 1873?). The originals are of
course all available in the Government of Maharashtra Secretariat Record Office (General
Department files).

[2] *Times of India*, 8 July 1871.

[3] C. Y. Chintamani (ed.): *Speeches and Writings of the Honourable Sir Pherozeshah M. Mehta,
K.C.I.E.* (Allahabad, 1905), pp. 81–115.

[4] For newspaper cuttings and other correspondence relating to municipal reform see n. 1,
above. The files concerned are G.D. 1871, vols. 37–8; 1872, vols. 40–1. See also the *Times of
India* and the *Bombay Gazette* of 1871 and 1872.

gave the ratepayers' leaders considerable proof of popular support, and they now proceeded to demonstrate the strength of the movement by organizing a large public meeting in the town hall on 7 November 1871, and appointing a committee to conduct their affairs. This meeting, although it was carried on without the intervention of Mandlik and other members of the intelligentsia, swung the whole movement into the intelligentsia's camp by stressing the need, not for fiscal reform, but for the management and control of municipal affairs by the ratepayers through their elected representatives.

During the July debates several *shetias* had indicated their opposition to the idea of elective institutions. Shortly afterwards, a group of *shetias*, headed by Mancherji Naoroji Banaji, the grandson of a leading China trader of the early nineteenth century, forwarded a letter to the Governor of Bombay. The letter condemned irresponsible newspaper editors for encouraging 'the idle, ignorant and designing to overwhelm a laudable attempt at municipal reform with meaningless agitation, in which the powers of the Justices were gravely threatened'.[1] Banaji and the other house-owning *shetias* revealed their own attitude to reform by stating that the crucial point of the agitation was the desire for an overhauling of the municipal fiscal system, so that the owners of house property could be relieved of what was alleged to be grievously burdensome taxation. This achieved, Banaji stated, the Justices must be left firmly in control of municipal affairs. Pherozeshah Mehta, temporarily at odds with the intelligentsia because of his defence of a strong executive, and despite his advocacy of elective institutions, decided to align himself with the *shetias* at this time, a fact of importance later on.[2]

From March 1872, when the Bombay Municipal Bill was introduced into the Bombay Legislative Council, the supporters and opponents of municipal reform in the city marshalled their forces.[3] The *shetias* concentrated their onslaught on the principle of ratepayers' elections, and coupled with it an attempt to lower taxation on house property. The *shetia* leadership was in a strong position because it was strongly represented on the Governor's Council. Apart from a Maratha Sardar, the three Indian members of the Council in September 1872 were all merchant princes—the second Sir Jamshedji Jijibhai, Mangaldas Nathubhai, and Narayan Vasudev Dabholkar. During the second reading of the Bill, Dabholkar insisted that the government had misunderstood the whole nature of the recent agitation. He declared that the desire

---

[1] Letter to Sir R. W. Seymour Fitzgerald from Muncherjee Nowrojee Banajee, 2 Aug. 1871, in G.D. 1871/37, C. 508, p. 149.

[2] *Times of India*, 1 Dec. 1871; *Native Opinion*, 3 Dec. 1871.

[3] The relevant protracted debates are recorded in *Proceedings of the Council of the Governor of Bombay*, 1872, xi, 37–9; 59–258; 261–358.

was not for representative government at all, but for a relief of certain tax burdens. Since, according to Dabholkar, the few house-owners of the municipality were bearing two-thirds of the entire municipal taxation because they were paying rates which would normally be paid by occupiers, it was their tax burdens which must first be attended to. This was especially vital, considering the effects of the share mania, although he did also throw in a sop to the poorer owners. Success for the house-owners, of course, implied a shifting of taxation to other shoulders. Dabholkar's suggestions were a small levy of duties on articles of local consumption, a clear blow at the poorer classes; or a small Municipal Licence or Certificate Tax on all incomes above Rs. 200 a month, a blow at the professional classes. This scheme was continually pressed in Council, and even the unmilitant Sir Jamshedji Jijibhai entered the lists at the third reading of the Bill to insist that relief from the pressure of taxation was far more important than electoral representation.

Outside Council, vested interests had also been rallying. The control of the ratepayers' movement, now that the Bill was before Council, slipped from the hands of its Bania, Bhatia and Parsi founders into those of the intelligentsia. The need now was for expert opinion, and only men such as Dadabhai Naoroji, Kashinath Trimback Telang, and others were equipped to deal with the constitutional and political principals involved. The entire ratepayers' movement had now become a demand for acceptance of the principle of representation which, as Telang urged, was 'a demand from the whole educated native community of Bombay to which the government ought to pay deference'.[1] The Governor of Bombay was advised by 'the Residents and Ratepayers of Bombay' that the Bench of Justices must *not* be retained as the dominant factor in any new municipal corporation, if only because of the fact that of the 110 existing Indian Justices only about one-third had sufficient knowledge of English to take an intelligent part in discussion. It was also pointed out for the first time that it would not be enough to give the vote for an elected corporation to a few ratepayers. If this were done, the intelligentsia would suffer, comprising as they did a class 'who though owning little or no immoveable property, are, nevertheless, intelligent, and of business-like habits, and evince a lively interest in, and fitness for the administration of Municipal affairs'.[2] If the franchise for the new corporation were given only to a few rich ratepayers, it was apparent that the intelligentsia would be no better off than before. Few would qualify for the franchise themselves. They could only hope to gain influence in the corporation through manipu-

---

[1] *Bombay Gazette*, 23 May 1872.
[2] *The Rate-Payers' Memorial...* App. M (unpaginated).

lation of the enfranchised ratepayers, and they appear to have hoped that a lower qualification for the franchise would give them a chance to persuade the poorer ratepayers to use their vote to support the intelligentsia in future elections.

The *shetias* and their supporters were also rallying outside Council. As well as Pherozeshah Mehta they had managed to win over another talented lawyer, Shantaram Narayan, who appears to have wished to advance his career by association with the two Saraswat *shetias*, Dabholkar and Raghunath Narayan Khote. It was they who drew up a memorial to the Governor of Bombay requesting the abolition of occupiers' rates and perhaps the house tax, and the enactment of municipal income and licence taxes. This memorial was discussed on 9 October 1872 at a meeting at Shankarshet House in Girgaum, and, although the gathering was of course called by the house-owning faction, it was penetrated by a number of the leading reformist members of the intelligentsia. The notion of requesting a re-imposition of the income tax, which had been opposed by the *shetias* themselves in May 1870, was anathema to professional men such as Mandlik, Wagle, Bhandarkar and Naoroji Furdunji. The debate between the two sides became so heated that the meeting was forced to break up in confusion[1] and on the following day the 'Girgaum Memorial' was adopted in the absence of the reformers. Only Naoroji Furdunji attended to read a protest against the income tax suggestion signed by himself, Mandlik and others.[2] It should be noted that a few of the important *shetias*, including F. N. Patel, Varjivandas Madhavdas and D. M. Petit, apostatized, either for personal reasons, or through friendship with the reformers.[3] The newspapers of the intelligentsia were extremely bitter about the 'Girgaum Memorial'. *Native Opinion* had nothing but contempt for what it called 'the landlord's movement', and began to do its own research on the whole question of house property. It was able to produce statistics concerning a variety of houses and *chawls*, including some of V. J. Shankarshet's own houses. Naoroji Furdunji, for example, alleged that his rent for one floor of a four-storied house had increased in recent years from Rs. 25 to Rs. 45 a month.[4]

The Bombay Municipal Act was finally passed on 17 October 1872. It provided for a municipal corporation of sixty-four, thirty-two of whom were to be elected by the ratepayers, sixteen elected by the Justices and sixteen nominated by the Government. Out of this was to be elected a town council of twelve members, eight to be elected by members of the corporation, the chairman and three others to be appointed by the Government. The qualification for membership of

---

[1] *Times of India*, 11 Oct. 1872.
[2] *Ibid.* 12 Oct. 1872.
[3] *Ibid.* 14 Oct. 1872.
[4] *Native Opinion*, 27 Oct. 1872; 3 Nov. 1872.

the corporation was settled at the payment of Rs. 50 per annum in municipal rates and taxes, and those enfranchised would be persons paying Rs. 50 per annum towards municipal revenues in respect of house, lighting and police rates. Certain clauses gave the Government considerable residual powers to control the corporation. Even at the final reading of the Bill the debate on the pressures upon house-owners was protracted. The member of Council responsible for the Bill, after receiving the Girgaum Memorial, complained that it should have been stated much earlier that what the town wanted was not representative institutions but merely a diminution and redistribution of taxation. He agreed as a final compromise to reduce the minimum house rate to 4 per cent and the maximum to 7 per cent, but went on to stress that he had always thought that it was representation that the reformers had been clamouring for, and not revision of the fiscal system. The complaint of the intelligentsia that reliance on a ratepaying qualification would be of little help to them was now partially dealt with by the compromise that Fellows of Bombay University could be given the vote and the right to stand for election to the corporation. In the midst of claim and counterclaim sat the new Governor of Bombay, Sir Phillip Wodehouse, complaining that he had always understood that the point of the Bill was to grant the citizens of Bombay as much power as could safely be given them, and this he had endeavoured to do. 'Nothing has been more remarkable in the course of these debates', he announced, 'than the distrust of each other evinced by the different sections of the community as represented here. I think it is fortunate that there is a government to arbitrate between them.'[1]

4. BOMBAY POLITICS AND MUNICIPAL ELECTIONS, 1873–83

The *shetias* of Bombay city had won several important concessions during the passing of the Bombay Municipal Act, yet through lack of timely organization they had failed to see the representative principle thrown out. The intelligentsia, by diverting the ratepayers' cause into their own channels, had obtained the principle, only to find that the high franchise qualification might deprive them of the reality. It would be difficult to use the elective principle to begin their own journey to power if they themselves were neither qualified to vote or stand for election, or if they could not find sufficient electoral support. A monster protest meeting was organized for 5 November 1872, when 3,000 Bombayites marched to the Framji Kavasji Hall accompanied by brass bands, bearing immense placards written in Gujarati and festooned

[1] *Proceedings of the Council of the Governor of Bombay*, 1872, xi, pp. 276–7.

with streamers and flags.[1] There they listened to speeches from both members of the Ratepayers' Committee, and from young professional men such as Telang and Kaikhusru Naoroji Kabraji, editor of the Parsi reformers' paper *Rast Goftar*. The theme of the meeting was the microscopic minority—then estimated at 4,000—who were to get the franchise. Telang pointed out that no tenant—a category comprising most of Bombay's professional men—would get the vote. But the bitterest speech of the meeting came from Kabraji, who had been educated at Sir Jamshedji Jijibhai's Parsi Benevolent Institution for poor Parsi boys. He declared:

These four thousand will comprise most of the richer or houseowning classes, and the other classes are denied their rights simply because they are not rich. (Hear, hear.) But, Sir, we have had enough of the tyranny of landlordism, if I may so call it. The rich have had their sway, and now the time has come for all classes of the inhabitants to have their rights granted them. There is no shame, Sir, to acknowledge that we are poor. (Hear, hear.) Poverty is no offence. (Applause.) Then why this punishment?[2]

There was further punishment to come. The municipal reform agitation destroyed any effective political organization in Bombay until 1885. The Bombay Association was severely affected by the resignation of prominent *shetias* such as Dabholkar, V. J. Shankarshet, Raghunath Narayan Khote and Beramji Jijibhai.[3] With the aid of Mancherji Naoroji Banaji and other anti-reform *shetias* they decided to form their own Association of Western India in May 1873. Once again, they were able to rely on Pherozeshah Mehta and Shantaram Narayan for organizational purposes,[4] but the Association swiftly collapsed. Its collapse was attributable not only to the sudden deaths of V. J. Shankarshet and Dabholkar, but also to the fact that it was, in the words of *Gujarat Mitra*, largely composed of 'illiterate fools'.[5] The Bombay Association, after having the satisfaction of witnessing the collapse of its rival, declined and revived intermittently during the 1870s according to whichever *shetia* could be persuaded to take on its chairmanship. By 1879, however, it was declared dormant, if not dead.[6] The Bombay Branch of the East India Association did not fare much better, due largely to the preoccupation of its members with their own professions or with religious and social issues, on which they were often divided or which affected only their own communities. The one exception was the development by certain members of the Association with mercantile experience, particularly Dadabhai Naoroji, of an important contribution to contemporary Indian political ideology, the theory of 'the

[1] *The Rate-Payers' Memorial...* p. 19.
[2] *Bombay Gazette*, 7 Nov. 1872.
[3] *Native Opinion*, 13 Apr. 1873.
[4] *Bombay Gazette*, 14 May 1873.
[5] Quoted in *Times of India*, 22 Apr. 1873.
[6] *Times of India*, 5 May 1879.

drain of wealth'. Despite the lack of activism in the political associations in the 1870s, the intelligentsia found an outlet for their views in their newspapers in which it was obvious that the leaders of the mercantile and English-educated communities were as far apart in their political views as they had been thirty years earlier.

Table 1. *Results of Bombay Municipal Elections, 1873–83, by the Community of Winning Candidates*

Year	Maharashtrian Hindus	Gujarati Hindus			Parsis	Muslims		Europeans	Goans
		Kapol Banias	Others			Khojas	Others		
1873	8	2	4	10	1	2	4	1	
1875	4	2	4	14	3	2	3	–	
1878	6	3	4	13	4	–	2	–	
1880	3	3	6	13	4	–	2	1	
1883	4	3	5	12	3	1	3	1	

SOURCE: Govt. of Maharashtra Secretariat Record Office, G.D. files for the relevant years.

There were, however, certain points of convergence, and when these were reached, Bombay public life continued in the form of large public meetings on behalf of causes on which both leadership groups and their followers could agree. The primary example of this was the agitation over cotton duties in the late 1870s, first promoted by the early Maharashtrian Brahmin *swadeshi* militants such as the journalists on *Native Opinion* and *Indu Prakash*. They joined forces with former Elphinstonians who had originally come from Parsi mercantile backgrounds and had returned to mercantile life in collaboration with certain *shetias*, men such as Sorabji Shapurji Bengali, and Dadabhai Naoroji. Not only were men like Bengali collaborating in *shetia* mercantile transactions; the leadership of the intelligentsia was now firmly in the hands of lawyers from prosperous families, such as Pherozeshah Mehta and Badruddin Tyabji, and lawyers of discretion such as Kashinath Trimback Telang. Pherozeshah Mehta approached a number of prominent *shetias*[1] who as Gujaratis had long had constant contact with cotton-growing districts and who had by now invested heavily in the mill industry. On 3 May 1879 a large public meeting, chaired by Sir Mangaldas Nathubhai, was held to discuss the cotton duties issue. It was the first time that Telang, Mehta and Tyabji, later styled 'the

[1] Pherozeshah Mehta Papers, Microfilm Reel I: N.B. Jejeebhoy to Mehta, undated, 1879.

three political muses of Bombay',[1] had appeared together on a public platform, and the sentiments they echoed were identical with those of the big mill-owners.[2] This was the high watermark of co-operation in Bombay politics. The year 1883 and the Ilbert Bill marked the high tide. The flood was to come in 1885, but before that time an ark had been found by Bombay's lawyers and journalists in the form of co-operation outside the city with similarly stranded lawyers and journalists in other parts of the country.

Meanwhile, between 1873 and 1883, five Municipal elections took place in Bombay city (Table 1). It is interesting to note that Bombay's three 'political muses' stood well outside the electoral conflict, or retreated early from it, and gained seats on the Town Council partly by nomination and partly by election from the corporation. However, the elections opened up a new field of rivalry between the politically active *shetias* and the intelligentsia. It was difficult for most members of the intelligentsia to rally enough support to win votes, not only because of their paucity of numbers, but because their potential supporters were too poor to qualify for the franchise. Although, after agitation in *Rast Goftar*, franchise provisions were slightly modified in favour of poorer ratepayers in 1878, this in fact only made things more difficult for those members of the intelligentsia who were seeking power through the ballot box. It was with increasing frustration that the members of the growing professional classes saw themselves robbed of the fruits of their reform agitation and their hope for leadership of their city, just as they were beginning to move on to the all-India stage. After 1875 it appeared as if the Gujarati-speaking *shetias* were destined to sweep all before them. The Marathi-speaking intelligentsia felt their successive electoral defeats all the more keenly because the city's population was becoming increasingly Maharashtrian in composition, due to the continuous influx of Maratha labourers.

The months before the 1880 elections were filled with journalistic warfare against *shetia* candidates. It was alleged that men were elected because they possessed a fine carriage or a stud of horses, or because they were the relatives of *shetias*.[3] *Shetia* members of the corporation were accused of being 'quasi-officials',[4] of showing real antagonism to the cause of the people,[5] and of having no more knowledge of municipal affairs than bullocks.[6] The Maharashtrian intelligentsia required even stronger epithets to face the results of the elections. Only three Maharashtrians were elected to the corporation in 1880 and, of these, two were

---

[1] *Indu Prakash*, 2 Feb. 1885.   [2] *Times of India*, 5 May 1879.
[3] *Native Opinion*, 29 Aug. 1880; 28 Nov. 1880.   [4] *Ibid.* 9 Jan. 1881.
[5] *Ibid.* 29 Aug. 1880.   [6] *Jame Jamshed* quoted in *ibid.* 14 Nov. 1880.

the Saraswat *shetias*, Raghunath Narayan Khote and his son. Visvanath Narayan Mandlik, for long the star of the city's Maharashtrian intelligentsia, was defeated in his ward by three Gujaratis and a European. In general Khoja and Kapol Bania *shetias* predominated, though the Parsi community had by this time managed to strike a fairly even balance between wealth and learning. The 1883 elections were even more disastrous for the Maharashtrian intelligentsia. The four Maharashtrians elected were all *shetias* or their supporters. Mandlik did not bother to stand, and Kashinath Trimback Telang, standing for the first time, had no success. Again Khoja and Kapol Bania *shets*, their carriages and their supporters figured prominently, their success being attributed to 'the whole hosts of unintelligent voters...that were to be seen driven to the polling station on the last occasion like so many slaves'.[1] By this time reform of the entire electoral system was already being advocated in the columns of *Indu Prakash* and *Native Opinion*. The intelligentsia realized that they would win electoral victories only if the system could be reorganized to give more weight to the fellows and graduates of Bombay University, and to men with professional qualifications. This, together with a more realistic organization of the ratepayers, was the cry from 1883.

But, if Bombay was an electoral wilderness, Mandlik, Dadabhai Naoroji, Pherozeshah Mehta, Telang and Tyabji had already begun to find plenty in the all-India garden. Though they were becoming prominent in subcontinental and international affairs, they had yet to prove they could capture their own city.[2]

[1] *Indu Prakash*, 15 Oct. 1883.
[2] I have not encumbered this article, paricularly Pts 1 and 2, with a plethora of footnotes. Material for Pt 1 is derived *inter alia* from the three censuses of Bombay city taken during the period, the 1909 City Gazetteer, the large number of biographies of Bombay merchants available for the period and the annual reports issued by the Bombay Department of Public Instruction. Material for Pt 2 comes *inter alia* from the reports and minutes published at irregular intervals by the Bombay Association and from the *Journal of the East India Association*. All, except a few biographies, are available in the India Office Library. The period has also been dealt with in an unpublished Bombay University Ph.D. thesis by J. Masselos, entitled 'Liberal Consciousness, Leadership and Political Organisation in Bombay and Poona: 1867–1895'. The theme is the differences in political styles exhibited by Bombay and Poona. Because two cities are investigated, this work neglects source material crucial for an understanding of Bombay politics, including *Rast Goftar*, the leading newspaper of the reformist intelligentsia; the files in the Maharashtra Secretariat Record Office on the Municipal elections and the Maharashtrian millworkers; and *Proceedings of the Council of the Governor of Bombay*, 1872.

CHITPAVAN BRAHMINS AND POLITICS IN WESTERN INDIA IN THE LATE NINETEENTH AND EARLY TWENTIETH CENTURIES[1]

GORDON JOHNSON

During the last hundred years the fifth of the world's population living on the Indian sub-continent has become aware of the uses of political power. The country has not only thrown off foreign rule but it has developed, and continues to evolve, nationalisms which have little of the common language, religious solidarity, racial integrity, unified culture or centralized economy associated with the nation-states of Europe. The heterogeneity of provinces and communities accounts for many of the strains in Indian politics. The most striking feature of the changes that have taken place is that not all parts of the sub-continent have become active at the same time, and that political consciousness has spread unevenly among the people. The first Indian nationalists came from small well-defined social groups occupying privileged positions within their own provinces. Although different from each other in many ways, these provincial elites were drawn into continental politics by shared interests in British rule. Maharashtra was one of the first regions to become active. Chitpavan Brahmins exercised a disproportionate share of influence in Maharashtrian politics, education, social reform, journalism and literature, and, in the persons of Ranade, Gokhale and Tilak, Chitpavan leadership achieved recognition throughout India. This essay tries to analyse the reasons for Chitpavan pre-eminence in the late nineteenth and early twentieth centuries, and it investigates the distinctive contribution Chitpavan Brahmins made to Indian political life.

Maharashtra extends across western India from the Arabian Sea to the Bastar highlands and stretches from the Satpura mountains in the north to the plains of Andhra and Karnatak in the south. The area is characterized by a distinctive social structure and cultural tradition.[2]

[1] I wish to thank Miss M. L. P. Patterson for her advice while writing this paper and Miss L. Breglia for tracing the map. I am greatly indebted to all the people who contributed to the discussion of this paper, especially to Dr S. N. Mukherjee, Dr T. G. P. Spear and Professor E. T. Stokes, whose comments have been of particular help in revising it.
[2] I. Karve and V. M. Dandekar, *Anthropometric Measurements of Maharashtra* (Poona, 1951), pp. 1–12.

Marathi is spoken throughout the region, giving way to Gujarati in the north-west, Hindi in the east, and Kanarese in the south. (Map 2 *at the end of the the volume* shows those districts in western India which were recorded as predominantly Marathi-speaking at the 1901 *Census*, and Table 1 shows the languages spoken in districts adjacent to them.) During the nineteenth century, and for much of the twentieth, Maharashtra was divided between Bombay Presidency, Hyderabad, Central Provinces and Berar. This political fragmentation had some effects on the development of the region, and much of what follows mainly concerns the Marathi-speaking districts of Bombay Presidency, where Poona, 'the hub of Maharashtra',[1] was situated.

Table 1. *Language in western India. Districts adjacent to the Marathi-speaking region (per cent)*

District	Marathi	Kanarese	Telegu	Urdu	Hindi	Gondi	Rajasthani	Gujarati
Belgaum ⎫ Bijapur ⎪ Akalkot ⎬ Gulbarga ⎭	—	Predominant	—	—	—	—	—	—
Bidar	33·0	35·0	16·0	14·0	—	—	—	—
Nizamabad	—	—	Predominant	—	—	—	—	—
Adilabad	27·8	—	44·0	6·4	—	—	—	—
Balaghat ⎫ Seoni ⎬ Hoshangabad ⎭	—	—	—	—	Predominant	—	—	—
Chhindwara	19·0	—	—	—	46·6	25·5	—	—
Betul	23·0	—	—	—	—	28·6	39·8	—
Nimar	—	—	—	—	—	—	Predominant	—
Baroda ⎫ Surat ⎬	—	—	—	—	—	—	—	Predominant

SOURCE: *Census...1901*, VIII, i, p. 147; IX, i, p. 158, and ii, table X; XIII, i, p. 75; XXII, ii, table X.

The people of Maharashtra were almost all Hindus.[2] The caste-structure of the region was characterized by its comparative simplicity. Castes of intermediate ritual standing, of whom 40 per cent were Marathas, formed the bulk of the population, imparting to it a cohesion lacking in the social structures of some other parts of India.[3] There were some large out-castes, probably remnants of the aboriginal people of the region, like the Mahars who alone numbered 709,555 in the Marathi-speaking districts of Bombay,[4] but untouchables did not suffer

[1] *Census...1921*, VIII, i, p. 75. Throughout, references to the *Census of India* are abbreviated as *Census*...[year], [volume number], [part], [page reference or table number].

[2] Out of the total population of 17,368,078 some 15,353,967—or 88·5 per cent—were Hindus. *Census...1901*, VIII, ii, table VI; *ibid.* IX-A, ii, table VI; *ibid.* XIII, ii, table VI; *ibid.* XXII-A, ii, table VI.

[3] I. Karve, *Hindu Society—An Interpretation* (Poona, 1961), pp. 15–49. In the Marathi-speaking districts of Bombay Presidency there were 8,353,513 Hindus. Of these 2,533,984 belonged to the Maratha caste-cluster. *Census...1901*, IX-A, table XIII.

[4] *Census...1901*, IX-A, table XIII.

the same rigorous disabilities as did similar castes in south India. Brahmin castes accounted for 4·5 per cent of the population.[1] This minority dominated the social and religious life of Maharashtra, enabling it to wield considerable influence in the region. In the south, where Maharashtra overlapped into the Karnatak, Jains and Lingayats vied with Brahmin influence in the districts.

As in any pre-industrial society, those who controlled the land and its produce exercised a dominating role, at least at village level, in nineteenth-century Maharashtra. Unfortunately, very little is known at present about the distribution of power in the Deccan villages. At the end of the eighteenth century there was great mobility in the control of land, and many families who held the best plots in the villages had done so from relatively recent times.[2] Further, there were considerable social and economic cleavages within the villages, based on the type of land-tenure and on the size of holdings.[3] The British made a *raiyatwari* settlement in the Deccan resulting in about five-sixths of the land being held by cultivators direct from the government. The average size of holdings varied from 20 to 30 acres in the west Deccan to 30 to 50 acres in the east.[4] However, variations in size and quality of estates remained, and probably changes in revenue policy and fluctuations in economic opportunity during the nineteenth century served only to increase the gap between the few relatively prosperous families in a village, holding a high proportion of good land, and the majority of villagers, who were indebted because their small-holdings were not viable economic units.[5] Who the landholders were depended on the distribution of castes within highly localized areas. Most cultivators, and many of the more prosperous, were Marathas because they were the most common caste-cluster. But in the south, Jains and Lingayats held significant proportions of the land,[6] and during the nineteenth century Brahmins everywhere came to have increasing influence in the village economy.[7]

[1] *Ibid.*
[2] W. H. Sykes, 'Report on the Land Tenures of the Dekkan', *P.P.* 1866, LII, pp. 311–13. [*P.P. = Parliamentary Papers.*]
[3] *Ibid.* pp. 314–15; R. Kumar, 'The Rich Peasants in Western India', D. A. Low (ed.), *Soundings in Modern South Asian History* (London, 1968), pp. 26–9. Kumar argues that there were no serious economic divisions in a village, only social ones, but his own evidence seems to refute this—*ibid.* p. 30.
[4] G. Keatinge, *Rural Economy in the Bombay Deccan* (London, 1912), p. 37.
[5] R. Kumar, *Western India in the Nineteenth Century: A Study in the Social History of Maharashtra* (London, 1968), pp. 298–303. See also: Keatinge, *Rural Economy*; H. H. Mann, *Land and Labour in a Deccan Village* (London and Bombay, 1917), and *idem, Land and Labour in a Deccan Village: Study No. 2* (London, 1921).
[6] *B.G.* XXI, p. 235; *ibid.* XXII, pp. 252–3; *ibid.* XXIII, p. 307. [Throughout, references to the *Gazetteer of the Bombay Presidency* are abbreviated *B.G.* [volume number], [part], [page].]
[7] Most village accountants in Maharashtra were Brahmins. During the course of the nine-

Table 2. *Distribution of certain castes in the Marathi-speaking districts of the Bombay Presidency*

District	Hindus	Brahmins	Chitpavan Brahmins	Deshastha Brahmins	Marathas	Mahars	Lingayats
Thana	724,418	23,094	5,812	3,581	107,505	44,039	1,359
Ahmadnagar	756,572	33,146	1,694	27,344	326,662	64,936	4,765
Khandesh	1,282,109	50,384	2,890	32,546	93,681	107,242	5,945
Nasik	761,471	27,493	3,191	20,525	162,617	72,994	2,337
Poona	920,885	50,274	13,742	30,119	332,786	82,182	7,607
Satara	1,085,398	45,669	8,229	31,019	584,195	92,306	28,502
Sholapur	665,691	29,351	1,820	24,165	220,480	66,010	51,082
Kolaba	570,661	23,532	13,609	3,808	196,513	43,168	3,037
Ratnagiri	1,077,745	68,270	31,059	890	287,473	89,882	5,801

SOURCE: *Census...1901*, IX-B, iii, table XIII.

Almost half Maharashtrian Brahmins were Deshastha Brahmins.[1] They were found throughout the province, but particularly on the Deccan plateau (see Table 2). As the original Brahmin inhabitants of Maharashtra they were held in greatest esteem and considered themselves superior to other Brahmins.[2] Yet although Deshastha Brahmins composed the traditional religious and social elite of Maharashtra, they have not featured so prominently in recent Indian history as Chitpavan Brahmins. Hardly anything is known about the Chitpavans before the eighteenth century. Mythical accounts of their origin, their fair complexions, and their large settlements along the coast, particularly in Ratnagiri, suggest that the Chitpavans may have come to Maharashtra by sea, possibly from northern India.[3] The Chitpavans account for one-fifth of all Maharashtrian Brahmins.[4] In 1901 there were 113,605 of them in

teenth century their literacy enabled them to work to their advantage the new land-revenue laws, and Brahmins often found profit in money-lending. Thus, although the village headman was usually a Maratha, the Brahmin accountant came to wield most power. M. L. P. Patterson, 'A Preliminary Study of the Brahman versus Non-Brahman Conflict in Maharashtra' (M.A. thesis, Pennsylvania, 1952), p. 84.

[1] Out of 638,629 Brahmins living in the Marathi and Kanarese-speaking districts of Bombay, 287,477, or 45 per cent, were Deshastha Brahmins. *Census...1901*, IX-B, table XIII.
[2] J. Grant Duff, *History of the Mahrattas* (Indian reprint, Bombay, 1863), I, p. 8; *B.G.* XVIII, i, p. 101; R. E. Enthoven, *The Tribes and Castes of Bombay* (Bombay, 1920), I, pp. 244–5.
[3] V. N. Mandlik, 'Preliminary observations on a Document giving an Account of the Establishment of a New Village named Maruda, in Southern Konkana', *J.B.B.R.A.S.* VIII, 1864–66, p. 3 [*J.B.B.R.A.S.=Journal of the Bombay Branch of the Royal Asiatic Society*]; J. Wilson, *Indian Caste* (Bombay, Edinburgh and London, 1877), II, pp. 20–1; I. Karve, 'The Parasurama Myth', *J.U.B.* I, i, July 1932, pp. 115–39 [*J.U.B.=Journal of the University of Bombay*]; idem, 'Ethnic Affinities of Chitpavans', *ibid.* I, iv, Jan. 1933, pp. 383–400; idem, 'Ethnic Affinities of Chitpavans (II)', *ibid.* II, i, July 1933, pp. 132–58.
[4] Out of the 638,629 Brahmins enumerated in the Marathi and Kanarese-speaking districts of Bombay Presidency, 112,913 or 17·6 per cent were Chitpavans. *Census...1901*, IX-B, table XIII.

Table 3. *Distribution of Chitpavan Brahmins in the Bombay Presidency*

District	Number	Percentage of caste
Ratnagiri	31,059	27·4
Poona	13,742	12·1
Kolaba	13,609	12·0
South Maratha Jaghirs	10,924	9·7
Satara	8,229	7·3
Thana	5,812	5·1
Kolhapur	5,092	4·5
Bombay	3,776	3·3
Nasik	3,191	2·8
Khandesh	2,890	2·5
Dharwar	2,266	2·0
Savantvadi	1,968	1·7
Belgaum	1,821	1·6
Sholapur	1,820	1·6
Bhor	1,703	1·5
Ahmadnagar	1,694	1·5
Janjira	1,144	1·0
Kanara	762	0·7
Bijapur	683	0·5
Other districts	1,420	2·5
	113,605	

SOURCE: *Census...1901*, IX-A, ii, table XIII.

Bombay Presidency. 84·8 per cent of the caste lived in the Marathi-speaking area. 42 per cent of all Chitpavans lived in the Konkan (see Table 3). However, the Chitpavans had settled the least fertile part of the coast and from the first, while preserving their connexion with the Konkan, they migrated eastwards, spreading 'sparsely perhaps but effectively over the best part of Western India'.[1] Proverbially 'a very frugal, pushing, active, intelligent, well-taught, astute, self-confident, and overbearing class', Chitpavans followed 'almost all callings and generally with success'.[2] In the Konkan, the Chitpavans were cultivators, priests and traders. Those who migrated to the Desh did so to become administrators, diplomats and soldiers. Consequently, in contrast to their caste-fellows on the coast, and unlike the Deshastha Brahmins on the Desh, Chitpavan Brahmins in the Deccan were concentrated in towns. Almost 80 per cent of those living in Poona

[1] Temple to Lytton, 9 July 1879. G. R. G. Hambly, 'Mahratta Nationalism before Tilak: Two unpublished letters of Sir Richard Temple on the State of the Bombay Deccan, 1879', *J.R.C.A.S.* XLIX, 1962, p. 154 [*J.R.C.A.S.*=*Journal of the Royal Central Asian Society*].
[2] *B.G.* X, p. 112.

district lived in the sub-division containing Poona city, and the same pattern of settlement occurs throughout the Desh.[1]

Chitpavan Brahmins were conscious of a common bond. Partly this sprang from a recognition of their superior status in society, and partly from their ties of kinship. The caste was divided into fourteen exogamous patrilineal sibships called *gotras*. Thirteen of these *gotras* were grouped into six *gatas* or *ganas*, five of two *gotras* each and one with three *gotras*. Families belonging to *gotras* within the same *gata* were not permitted to intermarry, but families belonging to the fourteenth *gotra* were allowed to marry into any of the other *gotras*, thus knitting together the entire caste.[2] However, despite this feeling of solidarity, individual Chitpavans did not scruple to struggle towards success in bitter competition with caste-fellows and kin. The quarrels between the Patwardhans during the early nineteenth century were notorious,[3] and a fierce independence of opinion and action was a characteristic Chitpavan attribute.[4] There was no recognized Chitpavan aristocracy to dictate the way in which the caste should behave. No family, or group of families, wielded either hereditary or elected power within the caste. Unlike the Gujarati trading castes, or some of the lower Maharashtrian castes, the Chitpavans had no caste *panchayats* or formal system of organized interference in domestic matters. Their chief authority was the Shankaracharya of Sankeshwar, who deputed agents in each town to settle caste disputes. However, such disputes were dealt with at a public meeting, which could be called by any adult Brahmin, and the decision was determined, subject to an appeal to the Shankaracharya, by a majority of the votes of those present.[5] Such a caste organization left a wide area of discretion open to individual members.

Chitpavan Brahmins became powerful in western India with the rise of the Mahratta empire. In the late seventeenth century Chitpavans were employed as messengers and spies by the Mahratta chiefs.[6] The

[1] In Ahmadnagar 62 per cent lived in the Nagar sub-division; in Nasik 60·5 per cent lived in Nasik sub-division; 41 per cent lived in Sholapur sub-division; 30 per cent lived in Alibag in Kolaba district; in Satara district 27 per cent lived in Wai sub-division, 27 per cent in Satara, and 12·9 per cent in Tasgaon. *Census...1901*, IX-B, table XIII.

[2] M. L. P. Patterson, 'Chitpavan Brahman Family Histories: Sources for a Study of Social Structure and Social Change in Maharashtra', M. Singer & B. S. Cohn (ed.), *Structure and Change in Indian Society* (Chicago, 1968), pp. 407–9; I. Karve, 'What is Caste? (I)', *Economic Weekly*, X, 1958, p. 135.

[3] K. Ballhatchet, *Social Policy and Social Change in Western India 1817–1830* (London, 1957), pp. 52, 56.

[4] The quarrelsome and suspicious nature of Chitpavan Brahmins was one of the characteristics of the caste that mythical accounts of their origin sought to explain. Karve, 'Parasurama Myth', *J.U.B.* I, i, July 1932, p. 118–19.

[5] *Census...1911*, VII, i, p. 245; A. Steele, *The Law and Custom of Hindoo Castes within the Dekhun Provinces...* (new ed., London, 1868), pp. 82–3.

[6] Grant Duff, *History of the Mahrattas*, I, p. 8.

success of their patrons brought out their keen cleverness, good sense, tact and management; and from the appointment in 1713 of Balaji Vishvanath Bhat as Peshwa, Chitpavan Brahmins found their way into all departments of government. They settled in Poona and Satara, they followed Mahratta princes to Nagpur, Baroda and Indore. In the south, bordering on the Karnatak, the Patwardhans, a Chitpavan family, established themselves in Sangli, Miraj, Kurundvad and Jam-khandi.[1] As Poona under the Peshwa became the mainspring of the Mahratta federation, Chitpavan Brahmins used political influence to strengthen their position in the Deccan. The Peshwa rewarded his kin and followers with tax-reliefs and grants of land.[2]

The defeat of the Peshwa by the British altered the situation in the Deccan. Although Elphinstone made generous settlements with the old rulers of the country, their political collapse was complete. Moreover, while the new government necessarily worked within the framework of the old, several major changes took place which materially affected the Brahmins' position in the state and administration. The British continued to recognize the importance of Brahmins as the moral and intellectual guardians of Hindu society, but they were not prepared to subsidize them on the same scale as the Peshwa had done.[3] Within the administration not only did British officers hold the principal posts but Indians from outside Maharashtra were appointed to assist them.[4] The British significantly reduced the pay and power of *mamlatdars*, hitherto the most important government officers.[5] However, Elphin-stone's policies were sufficiently conciliatory to ensure acceptance of British rule, and indeed it soon became apparent that the new regime offered as many opportunities for advancement and power as had the old. The Chitpavans had first made their mark in Maharashtra by their adaptability, particularly in employment, and by applying learn-ing to administrative skills. Their literacy continued throughout the nineteenth century to be their most powerful asset, and it enabled them to retain their dominance over Maharashtrian society.

To begin with, the British supported classical learning in Maha-rashtra, but by the middle of the nineteenth century, partly because of growing disenchantment with orthodoxy and partly in response to the demand for western learning from Brahmins themselves, the govern-

[1] *B.G.* XXIV, p. 324.   [2] Patterson, 'Brahman versus Non-Brahman', p. 82.

[3] Elphinstone calculated that the Peshwa's annual expenditure on religious charities amounted to 15 lakhs of rupees. The British proposed to spend 2 lakhs. For example, at the annual Dakshina festival the Peshwa used to distribute up to 5 lakhs of rupees amongst scholarly Brahmins. In the first year of British rule, only Rs. 50,000 were so given. Ball-hatchet, *Social Policy*, p. 86.

[4] Indians from the Madras service were appointed to senior positions. Ballhatchet, *Social Policy*, pp. 91–3.

[5] *Ibid.* pp. 96–100, 106.

ment diverted its resources to high schools and colleges teaching English.[1] Consequently, although the Gujarati-speaking districts of Bombay Presidency were more literate than the Marathi-speaking districts in vernacular languages, Maharashtra led western India in its knowledge of English.[2] Parsis and Prabhus were proportionately the best-educated communities, but their overall numbers were small and they lived mainly in Bombay city. Maharashtrian Brahmins dominated the schools and colleges of Poona, and even those in Bombay city.[3] Table 4 compares the literacy of Deccan Brahmins with other Maharashtrian castes. Chitpavan Brahmins were particularly notable for their facility in English. Those who went to school, especially those who stayed to learn English and tried to graduate from the university, usually came from the less affluent families: three-quarters of the parents of children attending government institutions in Bombay Presidency in the 1880s were reckoned to have limited incomes, and the proportion was higher in private schools.[4]

Table 4. *Male literacy among certain castes in Bombay Presidency*

	Percentage literate	Percentage English literate
Chitpavan Brahmins	63·0	19·03
Deshastha Brahmins	61·5	10·22
Saraswat Brahmins	54·0	10·77
Marathas	4·6	0·22
Kunbis	9·4	0·27
Malis	3·9	0·46
Lingayats	13·6	0·30
Mahars	1·0	0·01

SOURCE: *Census...1911*, VIII, i, p. 148.

Because education opened up opportunities for poorer members of the literate castes, it was from amongst them that private enterprise in education found most support. In Poona, the New English School, and

[1] R. Kumar, 'The New Brahmans of Maharashtra', Low (ed.), *Soundings*, pp. 102–7.
[2] A. Basu, 'Indian Education and Politics 1898–1920' (Ph.D. thesis, Cambridge, 1967), pp. 201–3.
[3] *E.C. (Bombay)*, I, p. 137 [*E.C. (Bombay)* = *Report of the Bombay Provincial Committee*. Education Commision, 1882 (2 vols., Calcutta, 1884)]. Bhandarkar noted that, of the Hindu graduates of Bombay University 1862–80, 193 were Maharashtrians and only 40 were Gujaratis. Quoted in C. Dobbin, 'The Growth of Urban Leadership in Western India, with Special Reference to Bombay City, 1840–85' (D.Phil. thesis, Oxford, 1967), p. 287.
[4] '...except in Bombay, Government colleges and schools of the higher class are attended by children of people whose average monthly income is about Rs. 30 or 40 in the case of schools, and about Rs. 75 or 100 in the case of colleges.' *E.C. (Bombay)*, II, p. 424. At Poona's New English School nearly half the boys' parents earned less than Rs. 25 a month. *Ibid.* p. 234.

later Fergusson College (both controlled by the Deccan Education Society), were started to encourage the spread of literacy. The school was an instant success (see Table 5). Most of its pupils came from Poona itself, but the school excited interest in Brahmin centres throughout Maharashtra (see Table 6).[1] Similarly the college, which like the school undercut the fees in government institutions,[2] not only provided places to cope with the existing demand for education but stimulated its growth.[3] As the regional and caste distributions of pupils at the New English School and Fergusson College show, the main beneficiaries of the institutions were Poona Brahmins (see Tables 6 and 7). However, as the nineteenth century came to a close, efforts were being made in other Deccan towns, like Amraoti, to expand educational facilities by private initiative.

Table 5. *Total number of pupils attending the New English School, Poona, and Fergusson College, Poona, 1880–1900*

Year	New English School	Fergusson College	Year	New English School	Fergusson College
1880	336	—	1891	1108	199
1881	501	—	1892	1029	243
1882	593	—	1893	901	276
1883	732	—	1894	891	281
1884	1009	—	1895	889	292
1885	955	99	1896	990	213
1886	1072	133	1897	316	348
1887	1027	94	1898	180	149
1888	939	116	1899	227	282
1889	995	150	1900	389	243
1890	1056	240			

SOURCE: P. M. Limaye, *The History of the Deccan Education Society (1880–1935)* (Poona, 1935), Appendix XXVII. Attendance figures at the New English School were affected by the plague epidemic in the years following 1897, although numbers rose again after 1904.

Chitpavan Brahmins were to be found in every walk of life. It was estimated at the 1911 census that 12·3 per cent of Chitpavans in Bombay Presidency followed religious vocations. As many as 25·6 per cent were cultivators, and a further 20·5 per cent supported by income from the

[1] Berar raised Rs. 200 for the school in 1882, mainly from Agarkar's relations. Bhagwat to Agarkar, 19 November 1882. Agarkar Papers.
[2] *Report of the Deccan Education Society Poona for 1885* (Poona, 1886), p. 43. The fees at the New English School were three-quarters that of those at the government school in the first five standards, and two-thirds in the upper standards. 15 per cent of the places at the New English School were free, compared with 5 per cent at the government High School. P. M. Limaye, *The History of the Deccan Education Society* (Poona, 1935), p. 11, Appendix XXXIII-A.
[3] *Report...Deccan Education Society*, p. 43.

Table 6. *Regional distribution of pupils at Fergusson College, Poona*

Place	1885	1910	Place	1885	1910
Poona	48	192	Dharwar	1	29
Satara	6	44	Kanara	0	14
Sholapur	1	19	Bijapur	0	20
Ahmadnagar	1	26	South Maratha Jaghirs	6	72
Nasik	6	15	Berar	2	8
Khandesh	3	18	Gujarat, Baroda and		
Thana	1	10	Kathiawar	4	10
Kolaba	0	20	Mysore and Madras	0	11
Ratnagiri	3	33	Hyderabad	0	15
Bombay	1	5	Sindh	0	7
Belgaum	16	38	Elsewhere	0	4
				99	610

SOURCE: P. M. Limaye, *History of the Deccan Education Society*, Appendix XXIX.

rent of land.[1] The Chitpavans also featured in the commerce and money-lending of western India, although much less prominently than the Parsis, Marwaris and Gujaratis.[2] However, it was in the professions, for which the Chitpavans were well qualified by their education, that the greatest opportunities for advancement occurred. In every district, as the century progressed, the number of lawyers, teachers, doctors and civil servants increased. In 1911 as many as 13·6 per cent of Chitpavan Brahmins were dependent upon incomes from the professions.[3] Brahmins controlled the administration of western India, even in the Kanarese-speaking districts[4] and Gujarat, besides the Mahratta states. The Public Service Commission found that in Bombay Presidency

[1] *Census...1911*, VII, p. 338. In Ratnagiri the Chitpavans held many of the privileged *khoti* tenures. So well entrenched were they in landholding that the anti-landlord movement of the 1920s was synonymous in Ratnagiri with the anti-Brahmin movement. *I.S.C.* VII, p. 229 [*I.S.C.= Indian Statutory Commission*]. Elsewhere, Chitpavans were buying land: 'Professional classes have a marked fondness for land investment. Few successful pleaders, Government servants, or even priests, religious mendicants, and the like will be found who do not own some land. The fondness for land investment has undoubtedly increased under British rule.' *B.G.* XIX, p. 180.

[2] 7·4 per cent of the caste were dependent on trade for their living. *Census...1911*, VII, p. 338. The *Gazetteer* recorded for Poona that 'Brahman capitalists who belong to the district are mostly Konkanasth Brahmans [Chitpavans] in towns and Deshasth Brahmans in villages'. *B.G.* XVIII, ii, pp. 99–100.

[3] *Census...1911*, VII, p. 338.

[4] In the Revenue, Agricultural, Registration and Judicial departments in Belgaum, Dharwar and Kanara districts, Brahmins held 722 appointments against 98 held by non-Brahmins. *P.S.C.* (*Bombay*), IV, section iii, C, p. 202 [*P.S.C.* (*Bombay*)= *Report of the Public Service Commission. Proceedings relating to the Bombay Presidency (including Sind)* (Calcutta, 1887)]. Of course these need not all have been Maharashtrian Brahmins, but Kanarese-speaking Brahmins were less well educated than the Maharashtrian castes.

Table 7. *Caste of pupils at Fergusson College, 1910*

Chitpavan Brahmins	256
Deshastha Brahmins	197
Karhada Brahmins	57
Saraswat Brahmins	16
Total Brahmins	526
Prabhus	13
Marathas	11
Gujaratis	6
Sindhis	7
Other Hindus	23
Lingayats	13
Muslims	7
Christians	4
Grand total	610

SOURCE: P. M. Limaye, *History of the Deccan Education Society*, Appendix XXX.

41·25 per cent of the deputy collectors were Brahmins, as were 75·5 per cent of the *mamlatdars*; and seventy out of one hundred and four subordinate judges were Brahmins.[1] Deshastha Brahmins, being more numerous, held most appointments, but the Chitpavans had, during the nineteenth century, made the posts requiring knowledge of English in the lower administration their own preserve.[2] Moreover, the superiority the Chitpavans derived from their knowledge of English showed in the higher ranks: thirty-three of the seventy Brahmin subordinate judges in the Presidency were Chitpavans.[3]

English literacy gave Chitpavan Brahmins a strong position in the administration and professions, but literacy in the vernacular gave them a virtual monopoly of the new methods of communication in Maharashtra. The growth of Marathi literature (see Table 8), and in particular the growth of Marathi journalism (see Table 9), had the effect of knitting together the centres of the Marathi-speaking country in a way which had not been possible when the oral rather than the printed word was the main means of communication. By the late nineteenth century, 'access to the flow of information in the rural areas was no longer completely dependent upon participation in personal networks of relationships. New formal communicative institutions provided opportunities for new social, intellectual and economic ties between literate

[1] *P.S.C.* (*Bombay*), IV, section i, B, pp. 71, 91.
[2] E. E. McDonald, 'The Modernizing of Communication: Vernacular Publishing in Nineteenth Century Maharashtra', *Asian Survey*, VIII, 7 July 1968, p. 596.
[3] *P.S.C.* (*Bombay*), IV, i, B, p. 91.

Table 8. *Growth in numbers of authors writing in Marathi, 1800–1918*

	1800–18	1818–36	1836–56	1856–66	1866–76	1876–96	1896–1912	1912–18
Poets	2	0	1	3	11	41	41	45
Dramatists	0	0	2	3	5	68	36	45
Novelists	0	0	0	0	18	50	19	74
Prose writers	3	6	7	17	25	88	167	162
Christian writers	2	0	3	2	9	13	2	2
Totals	7	6	13	25	68	260	265	328

SOURCE: G. C. Bhate, *A History of Modern Marathi Literature*, p. 512.

Table 9. *Growth of Marathi and English–Marathi newspapers in the Bombay Presidency*

	Marathi		English–Marathi	
Year	Number	Circulation	Number	Circulation
1887	58	19,696	10	7,775
1892	59	26,875	12	10,565
1897	82	48,960	14	16,250
1902	60	53,004	12	11,355
1907	67	63,937	13	15,610
1912	48	48,457	6	8,850
1917	34	58,293	8	9,050
1921	64	110,415	9	10,350

SOURCE: Calculated from lists of newspapers, R.N.P. (Bombay), January 1887, 1892, 1897, 1902, 1907, 1912, 1917, October 1921.

groups in the regional centers and scattered throughout the hinterland.'[1] At first these structural changes in communication worked to the advantage of those already literate: the old literate castes manned the new printing presses. Out of 128 nineteenth-century Marathi authors listed by G. C. Bhate in his *History of Modern Marathi Literature*, 114 were Brahmins and 10 were Prabhus. Only four came from outside the traditionally literate groups.[2] Of the Brahmins, some seventy-five were Chitpavans.[3] The Bombay government's caste-analysis of newspaper editors reveals a similar picture. Brahmins accounted for about two-thirds of all editors listed between 1901 and 1921, and throughout these

[1] McDonald, *Asian Survey*, VIII, 7 July 1968, p. 606.
[2] *Ibid*. p. 604.   [3] *Ibid*.

Table 10. *Caste of editors of Marathi newspapers in the Bombay Presidency*

(a) *Caste of editors of Marathi newspapers*

Caste	1902 No.	1902 %	1907 No.	1907 %	1912 No.	1912 %	1917 No.	1917 %	1921 No.	1921 %
Chitpavans	23	38·3	29	41·4	16	32·7	12	35·2	19	29·7
Other Brahmins	26	43·3	30	42·9	19	38·8	14	41·2	22	34·4
Total Brahmins	49	81·6	59	84·3	35	71·5	26	76·4	41	64·1
Non-Brahmins	11	18·4	11	15·7	14	28·5	8	23·6	23	35·9
Total editors	60	100	70	100	49	100	34	100	64	100

(b) *Proportion of circulation of Marathi newspapers controlled by different castes*

	1902 Circulation	1902 %	1912 Circulation	1912 %	1921 Circulation	1921 %
Chitpavans	32,900	62·1	25,807	53·3	57,685	52·2
Other Brahmins	17,779	33·5	8,500	17·5	28,655	26·0
Total Brahmins	50,679	95·6	34,307	70·8	86,340	78·2
Non-Brahmins	2,325	4·4	14,150	29·2	24,075	21·8
Total circulation	53,004	100	48,457	100	110,415	100

SOURCE: Calculated from list of newspapers, R.N.P. (Bombay), January 1902, 1907, 1912, 1917, October 1921.

years Chitpavan Brahmins never accounted for less than a quarter of vernacular editors and they usually made up a third or more (see Table 10).[1]

The coming of British rule had not deprived Brahmins of their predominance in Maharashtra. It left their religious and social status untouched, and, by administrative reform and the creation of new educational and professional opportunities, it probably increased their economic power. But foreign rule cramped the Chitpavans' political ambition. Sir Richard Temple, carefully distinguishing between Chitpavan and other Brahmins, wrote to Lytton:

They are inspired with national sentiment and with an ambition bounded only with the bounds of India itself...nothing that we do now, by way of

[1] McDonald, *Asian Survey*, VIII, 7 July 1968, p. 604. In fact Chitpavan influence was even greater than the number of Chitpavan editors suggests, since the newspapers they edited accounted for more than half the circulations of Marathi papers throughout the period 1901–21.

education, emolument, or advancement in the public service, at all *satisfies* the Chitpawuns. They will never be satisfied till they regain their ascendancy in the country, as they had it during the last century. And British rule is the one thing which is an absolute bar to their aspirations. Whether as British rule becomes consolidated continuously more and more, this ambition of theirs will dwindle and die out, no man can say. But that such ambition exists in this generation of Chitpawuns, and will continue during the next generation at least, may be taken for certain.[1]

Temple's observations came in the wake of a minor uprising in the Deccan. Wasudeo Balwant Phadke, a Chitpavan Brahmin and former government clerk, proclaimed a revolt against the British and emulated his seventeenth-century predecessors by disturbing the Deccan with raids and sorties from hill retreats.[2]

But by the late nineteenth century such movements as Phadke's revolt were out of date, and his call met with little response except from amongst the Ramoshis, a semi-aboriginal tribe. The British could no longer be driven from India by force of arms. However, British rule had wrought important changes, one of which, as Sir Henry Cotton perceived, was the emergence of 'able and energetic Indians, enlightened and educated by ourselves, expanding with new ideas and fired by an ambition to which English education has given birth, making demands which are continually more and more reasonable and more irresistible'.[3] These Indians, who were lawyers, civil servants, teachers, doctors and jounalists, brought India across the threshold of modern politics. They formed political associations which worked within the constitutional framework of the raj. They scrutinized every change in government policy, and made their opinions felt through petitions and the columns of newspapers. In Maharashtra such people were Chitpavan Brahmins, and some of them began to find an outlet for their aspirations in modern political activity.

The leading association of western India was the Poona Sarvajanik Sabha. It was formed in 1870 by amalgamating a previous district association with a committee of Brahmins responsible for the administration of the revenues of the temple of Parvati. Under Ranade's influence the Poona Sarvajanik Sabha became one of the most active and energetic political associations in India. The Sabha claimed to voice 'the wants and wishes of the inhabitants of the Deccan' and its members were required to show that they held a mandate from at least fifty adult men 'from any caste or community'.[4] The association comprised

[1] Temple to Lytton, 3 July 1879. Hambly, J.R.C.A., XLIX, pp. 154–5.
[2] *Source Material for A History of the Freedom Movement in India (Collected from Bombay Government Records)*, Vol. 1, 1818–85 (Bombay, 1957), pp. 73–129.
[3] H. J. S. Cotton, *New India* (new and revised edition, London, 1904), pp. v and vi.
[4] *The Constitution of the Poona 'Sarvajanik Sabha', And Its Rules* (Poona, 1884), pp. 1, 6.

'Sirdars, Land-holders, Sowcars, and other representatives of the people',[1] and most of its members were Poona lawyers, teachers, government servants and journalists.[2] Inevitably the Sabha was almost entirely Hindu, and the dominance of Brahmins in the professions meant that they were its most prominent members.[3] Indeed, two out of every three of the 125 people who served on the Sabha's managing committee between 1878 and 1897 were Chitpavan Brahmins (see Table 11).[4]

Table 11. *Caste composition of the Managing Committee of the Poona Sarvajanik Sabha for the years 1878/9 to 1896/7*

Year	Chitpavan Brahmin	Deshastha Brahmin	Karhada Brahmin	Other Brahmin	Maratha	Muslim	Parsi	Gujarati Marwari	Not known	Total
1878/9	23	3	0	1	1	1	1	1	4	35
1879/80	22	3	0	1	1	1	1	1	4	34
1880/1	19	1	0	1	1	1	2	1	6	32
1881/2	19	1	0	1	1	1	2	1	6	32
1882/3	17	1	0	1	1	1	2	1	6	30
1883/4	18	0	2	1	1	0	2	2	7	33
1884/5	18	0	1	1	2	0	2	2	7	33
1885/6	19	0	0	1	2	0	2	2	6	32
1886/7	20	0	0	1	2	0	2	2	6	33
1887/8	20	0	0	1	2	0	2	2	6	33
1888/9	20	0	0	1	2	0	2	2	6	33
1889/90	21	2	0	0	2	2	2	1	4	34
1890/1	21	2	0	0	2	2	2	1	4	34
1891/2	24	1	0	0	1	1	2	2	5	36
1892/3	27	1	0	0	1	1	1	2	3	36
1893/4	26	0	0	0	1	1	1	2	3	34
1894/5	26	2	1	0	2	1	1	0	4	37
1895/6	27	2	0	0	0	1	0	2	3	35
1896/7	26	1	1	0	0	1	2	1	4	36

SOURCE: List of office-bearers given on inside cover of the first number of each volume of the *Quarterly Journal of the Poona Sarvajanik Sabha*, 1879–97. Regular family surnames characteristic of Brahmin castes were well established in Maharashtra. For lists of Chitpavan names see *B.G.* X, p. 111; XIII, i, p. 76; XVIII, i, p. 101. I have corresponded with Miss M. L. P. Patterson on this point, and she has been able to confirm and correct my original findings and to identify some of the other names.

The Poona Sarvajanik Sabha's main concern was with government policy as it affected education, taxation, land-revenue and public employment. The Sabha petitioned and agitated on a wide range of subjects: it organized meetings against Lytton's Vernacular Press Act, it campaigned against the Bombay Forest Regulations, the Licence Tax, famine policy and the government's threatened withdrawal of subsidies from higher education. The Sabha supported the Ilbert Bill, it pressed for an extension of local self-government, it proposed reform of the legislative councils and of recruitment to the civil service.[5] Some

[1] Address of Welcome to Lord Ripon, 19 June 1880. *Quarterly Journal of the Poona Sarvajanik Sabha*, Vol. III, No. 2, p. 29.

[2] *B.G.* XVIII, iii, p. 64.

[3] In 1894 the Sabha informed the Government that its elected delegates comprised 152 Hindus, two Muslims and four Parsis. *Journal*, Vol. XVII, No. 3, p. 43.

[4] Probably eighty-three of the 125 were Chitpavan Brahmins.

[5] *Journal, passim*; cf. A. Seal, *The Emergence of Indian Nationalism: Competition and Collaboration in the later Nineteenth Century* (Cambridge, 1968), p. 236; B. B. Majumdar, *Indian Political Associations and Reform of Legislature (1818–1917)* (Calcutta, 1965), pp. 106–30.

of these questions interested politicians in other parts of India, particularly the English-speaking elites in Bengal and Madras who had founded associations similar to the Sarvajanik Sabha. Touched equally by the policies of the British, these Indians began to consider joint action and the possibility of laying an all-India case before Parliament. In 1876–7 delegates from the Sabha conferred with other politicians about methods of achieving unity,[1] and in 1880 the Sabha joined the Calcutta Indian Association in sending an appeal to the British public on the eve of the general election.[2] From such alliances, which cut across some of the regional and social divisions of India, grew the Indian National Congress, and the Poona Sarvajanik Sabha played a leading role during the 1880s and 1890s in establishing the Congress and its associated Provincial Conferences.[3]

While the Sarvajanik Sabha was well suited to the politics of late-nineteenth century India, it was unable to contain the intense rivalries of Poona politicians. Although the most prominent men in western India were Chitpavan Brahmins they were, nevertheless, unable to work together in concert. The history of Poona during these years is one of angry dissensions, and both the Sabha and the Congress fell victim to them. The Chitpavans urged such a variety of programmes and tactics and each was so much an individualist, that disunity rather than cohesion was the characteristic result of their endeavours. Men like Tilak thought that Maharashtra could be rejuvenated by a return to strict orthodoxy in religious and social matters, allied to openly anti-British politics made effective by mass support under Brahminical leadership. Such an attitude suggested to the government that Chitpavans remained a dangerous and seditious caste, an outlook that seemed justified when the Chapekar brothers murdered two British officers in 1897. Other Chitpavans believed that the best hope for Maharashtra lay in social reforms and in the exploitation of the possibilities of British rule by constitutional politics. Gokhale was the foremost exponent of this course. His genuine concern for social reform and his insistence on secular politics made it easier for him than for Tilak to appeal beyond his caste. Gokhale formed strong alliances with other parts of the country and he was respected by the government: two factors which made him a formidable opponent to Tilak in continental politics.

The personal enmity between Poona leaders was fundamental in exacerbating these differences in outlook. Of particular consequence

[1] J. C. Masselos, 'Lytton's Great Tomasha and Indian Unity', *Journal of Indian History*, Vol. XLIV, No. III (December 1966), pp. 743–8.

[2] Seal, *Indian Nationalism*, p. 236.

[3] The first four Provincial Conferences in Bombay were little more than open meetings of the Poona Sarvajanik Sabha, which published the proceedings of the 1888 and 1889 sessions in its *Journal*.

was the hostility between Tilak on the one hand and Agarkar, Ranade and Gokhale on the other. The disputes began in the Deccan Education Society when Agarkar and Tilak competed with each other for leadership after the death of Vishnu Krishna Chiplonkar. Tilak was forced to resign in 1890 because quarrels with his colleagues about status and money aggravated differences of opinion about social reform and inflamed relatively minor disagreements about how the New English School and Fergusson College should be managed.[1] The occasion of Tilak's resignation was the appointment of Gokhale as secretary to the Poona Sarvajanik Sabha. Tilak claimed that the post involved two or three hours of work a day and was therefore incompatible with Gokhale's teaching responsibilities at Fergusson College. At a stormy meeting of the Deccan Education Society's Council, Tilak succeeded in passing a resolution against Gokhale in this matter, but it was countered by Agarkar, who moved, equally successfully, that the outside interests of himself, Tilak, and some other members, were similarly incompatible with the full discharge of their educational work.[2] The wrangling within the Deccan Education Society in the 1880s gave to Poona affairs a bitter edge which they subsequently never lost.

Tilak spared no effort to be revenged on his former colleagues, and during the 1890s he set out to undermine the positions of Ranade and Gokhale in Maharashtra. He used his newspapers, the *Mahratta* and *Kesari*, to rally support amongst the more orthodox Chitpavans for a campaign against the social reformers. Tilak won popularity from his stand aginst the government's intentions to legislate about Hindu marriage in 1892; and in 1894 he was responsible for persuading the Sarvajanik Sabha to deviate from its policy of religious neutrality.[3] In July 1895 he brought his campaign to its peak when, at the annual election of office-holders in the Sarvajanik Sabha, he managed to replace almost the entire committee with his supporters.[4] Among the ten members of the old committee who were re-elected was Gokhale. However, he could not see himself working for Tilak's friends, and took six months' leave as secretary before finally resigning.[5]

Because the 1895 Congress session was to be held in Poona, Tilak was

---

[1] G. Johnson, 'Indian Politics 1888–1908' (Ph.D. thesis, Cambridge, 1967), pp. 50–64.

[2] P. M. Limaye, *The History of the Deccan Education Society*, pp. 118–19.

[3] S. A. Wolpert, *Tilak and Gokhale: Revolution and Reform in the Making of Modern India* (Berkeley and Los Angeles, 1962), p. 70. The Sabha petitioned the government about the regulations concerning the playing of music in processions which could only be construed as hostile to Muslim interests. *Ibid.*

[4] Johnson, 'Indian Politics', pp. 127–9.

[5] Gokhale to Joshi, 8 February 1896. Gokhale Papers, Reel 5. Gokhale wished 'to wash my hands of all political work in Poona. There is so much that is selfish and ignoble here that I would fly from it to the furthest extremities of the world.' *Ibid.*

able to transfer his local vendetta to all-India politics. In previous years, after the Congress had closed, the same tent was used for the National Social Conference, a meeting of social reformers from all parts of India. Although Ranade's official position prevented him from participating fully in the Congress, he dominated the Social Conference. Tilak, to reduce Ranade's prestige beyond Poona, agitated for the total separation of the Congress and Conference. He stirred up local feeling against the Conference in his newspapers. 'Poona is essentially a conservative town', he wrote, 'and it is but natural that public opinion should not be in favour of the Social Conference.'[1] The association of Congress and Conference, he argued, 'kept back the masses from joining the Congress' and he urged that 'this defect should be removed at the Poona sitting'.[2] Throughout October and November Tilak and his friends agitated Poona to such an extent that Ranade eventually thought it would be impolitic to ask for the Congress pandal for the Social Conference. His capitulation was accepted by his supporters, and Congress preparations were resumed in Poona.

Although the 1895 Congress turned out to be 'a greater success than what even the most sanguine expected',[3] Tilak's activities had fluttered the dovecots. By intruding his local quarrel into the Congress, he had shaken the confidence of other Indian leaders in Poona. Significantly the Congress never met in Poona again during this period, nor was Tilak ever president. The Sarvajanik Sabha, having for twenty-five years discharged the function of giving 'adequate expression to the spirit of moderate liberalism which animates the more thoughtful leaders of public opinion on this side of India',[4] became moribund. Those who had joined the Sabha to help Tilak wrest it from Ranade's control proved to be men who were 'unable to understand—and who have never cared to take—interest in politics'.[5] As a result Gokhale and Ranade founded the Deccan Sabha to carry on the traditions of the Poona Sarvajanik Sabha. But activity in Poona was soon to be damped. For the next decade a recurring plague epidemic ravaged the city, and, after the Chapekar assassinations, the government imposed a punitive police force on the town. Poona itself ceased to be the backcloth for the rivalries of its politicians. The twentieth century brought renewed interest in the Congress, and Gokhale, the heir of Agarkar and Ranade, locked with Tilak in a struggle for political power which culminated in the split in the Congress at Surat in 1907.

The Poona Chitpavans found difficulty in working together and

[1] *Mahratta*, 29 September 1895.   [2] *Ibid.* 13 October 1895.
[3] Wacha to Naoroji, 4 January 1896. Naoroji Papers.
[4] Advertisement for 'The Deccan Sabha'. Copy in the Tilak Papers.
[5] Gokhale to Joshi, 8 February 1896. Gokhale Papers, Reel 5.

they encountered equal difficulty in attracting non-Brahmin support. Tilak courted popularity more overtly than his colleagues and he appealed imaginatively to indigenous religious and political traditions. His success was reflected in his title *Lokhmanya*—loved by the people— and in the exaggerated fear the British had of him, which led twice to his imprisonment. Tilak's most ostentatious bid for support came in the Ganpati and Shivaji festivals which were organized in Poona and some other Deccan towns in the 1890s. Certainly his championship of Indian traditions enabled him to score over his more westernized rivals, yet the two festivals did not succeed in bringing non-Brahmin castes to Tilak's side. The worship of Ganpati was particularly associated with Chitpavan Brahmins, and the main effect of the festival was to turn what had been a family event among Chitpavans into a public occasion.[1] While non-Brahmins were prepared to enjoy the Ganpati holiday they remained as uncommitted to Brahmin leadership as their previous participation in the Moharram had left them uncommitted to Islam.

With the Shivaji festival, Tilak tried to win the support of the Maratha descendants of the great seventeenth-century chieftain, and he tried to symbolize in Shivaji's achievements the political aspirations of Maharashtra and India. Despite a small government grant for its restoration, Shivaji's fort at Raigarh was in a lamentable state. In 1895 Tilak began to campaign for funds to repair the ruins, to build a memorial to Shivaji, and to celebrate annually the death of the Mahratta hero.[2] The festival was inaugurated on 15 April 1896 at Raigarh, Poona, and 'at Brahmin centres' in the Deccan.[3] Yet despite the initial enthusiasm the 40,000 rupees necessary for building the monument were not forthcoming. Despite appeals to Indian princes, and a committee in Bombay—usually 'not an amenable city'[4] from Poona's point of view—the figure of November 1895 had barely been doubled by July 1899, and the work was not completed until after Tilak's death.[5]

The movement turned out to be a disappointment because the

---

[1] G. S. Ghurye, *Gods and Men* (Bombay, 1962), pp. 114–39; V. Barnouw, 'The Changing Character of a Hindu Festival', *American Anthropologist*, Vol. 56, No. 1, pp. 74–86. Ghurye argues that 'Ganapati having so few temples in so few villages in a community, in which the two most important centres of Ganapati worship almost enclose the east–west axis of it, demonstrates His relatively late enthronement and comparative absence of support from the non-elite'. G. S. Ghurye, *Anatomy of a Rururban Community* (Bombay, 1963), p. 185.

[2] *Mahratta*, 2 June 1895.

[3] Inspector-General of Police to Govt. Bombay, 15 July 1899. Enclosure 2 to Govt. Bombay to Govt. India, 25 August 1899. Home Public A Proceedings, September 1899, 5.

[4] N. C. Kelkar, *The Life and Times of Lokhmanya Tilak* (trans. D. V. Divekar, Madras, 1928), p. 290.

[5] *Ibid.* p. 295.

Marathas were suspicious of its Brahmin leaders. The Maharaja of Kolhapur, the only living ruling descendant of Shivaji, could easily have met the cost of the memorial. Yet he refused to do so: 'The Shivaji movement of Poona had his full sympathies in the beginning. A deputation including Mr. B. G. Tilak waited upon him and secured assurance of his support. But the political turn which the movement took under Mr Tilak's lead compelled His Highness to leave it alone.'[1] By 'political turn' the writer primarily meant the connexion which was held to exist between Shivaji festivals and Brahmin terrorist clubs. Yet the restoration of Shivaji in Maharashtra was accompanied by other propaganda which was acceptable to neither the Maharaja of Kolhapur nor Marathas at large. Shivaji festivals not only urged Maharashtrians 'to be up and doing', and to imitate 'Shivaji's methods, his prowess and success against a superior power', but they also reminded the people of Shivaji's 'implicit deference to Brahmins'.[2] Symbolizing the joint political and religious character of the occasion, the first festival at Raigarh began with portraits of Shivaji and his Brahmin *guru* Ramdas being carried in procession up the mountain,[3] and came to a close 'amid cries of Jai to Shivaji, Ramdas and Queen Victoria'.[4]

If Queen Victoria was added to convince the rulers that the celebration was not disloyal, the prominence of Ramdas could not but cut support from under Tilak's feet, for 'with Ramdas we come upon one of the key men in the whole history of the Brahman versus non-Brahman movement in Maharashtra'.[5] Deccan Brahmins claimed that, without the spiritual guidance of Ramdas, Shivaji would have had no success at all. Brahmins also denied Shivaji and his descendants full Kshatriya status. Shivaji 'was a brave man', but 'All his bravery did not give him a right to a status which very nearly approached that of a Brahmin. If Shivaji worshipped the Brahmin, it was as a Sudra he did it—as a Sudra, the servant, if not the slave of the Brahmin.'[6] Whatever may have been the historical truth of the dispute, there was no doubt that at the end of the nineteenth century Brahmins refused to acknowledge

[1] A. B. Latthe, *Memoirs of His Highness Shri Shahu Chhatrapati, Maharaja of Kolhapur* (Bombay, 1924), Vol. I, p. 129.

[2] Ollivant to Peile, 3 November 1897. Enclosure to Hamilton to Elgin, 21 Jan. 1898. Elgin Papers, India Office Library, MSS. Eur. F. 84. 16. The smaller Shivaji festivals always had a strong religious overtone. For example, at the festival held in Poona on 12 June 1908 at the temple of Vithoba, a student from Fergusson College read a paper in which he said 'the Goddess of Independence must be installed on the pedestal of religion and religion alone'. Weekly Report of the Director of Criminal Intelligence, 27 June 1908. Home Political B Proceedings, July 1908, 80.

[3] Wolpert, *Tilak and Gokhale*, p. 81.

[4] T. V. Parvate, *Bal Gangadhar Tilak* (Ahmedabad, 1958), p. 133.

[5] Patterson, 'Brahman versus Non-Brahman Movement', p. 56.

[6] Latthe, *Chhatrapati*, Vol. I, p. 175.

the Marathas' right to Kshatriya status and full Vedic ceremonies, and consequently the non-Brahmin castes were unlikely to support a movement which so bluntly asserted Brahmin superiority.

In many ways the more liberal element in Poona was better placed to attract non-Brahmin support. Secular politics and social reform need not have been exclusively Brahmin preserves. Non-Brahmins were prepared to support educational and social work. The Maharaja of Kolhapur was President of the Deccan Education Society, and much admired the work of Ranade and Gokhale.[1] But non-Brahmins found that even the most liberal social reformers 'with all their intellectual recognition of the goodness of the cause...showed the same lack of active sympathy and readiness to go the whole length which charaterized all leaders from out-side the Backward Communities themselves'.[2] Besides, much of the work of Brahmin social reformers was to do with marriage customs and the education of women rather than with radical alterations to the hierarchies of Hindu society. Further, there was little doubt that among the Brahmins it was Tilak who was the most popular, and his brand of revivalism was completely unacceptable to the non-Brahmin castes.

Some of the most important policies of the Poona Sarvajanik Sabha worked against non-Brahmin interests. The Sabha had made more attempts than other provincial associations to unravel the problems of agrarian poverty, but its solutions were hardly calculated to bring the Maratha peasantry flocking behind its banner. When in 1875 the bankrupt peasantry of Poona and Ahmadnagar attacked the property, and in some cases the lives, of their Bania and Brahmin creditors, the Sabha laid detailed proposals before the government. Its reforms aimed to revitalize the Deccan economy by encouraging a class of improving landlords. If the government made a permanent settlement of land-revenue, then investment would be attracted to land and 'in course of time the provident and thrifty classes [would] succeed to the ownership of land, and a class of landlords would spring up all over the country, whose interests it [would] be to make the most of the resources of the soil, and of the great public works constructed by Government'.[3] The Sabha accepted as natural that the new landlords would be the old money-lending classes, and it disparaged the spirit of the Bombay government's land legislation which attempted to restrict the transfer of real property.[4]

---

[1] Limaye, *Deccan Education Society*, Appendix II; Latthe, *Chhatrapati*, Vol. I, p. 137.
[2] *Ibid.*
[3] 'The Agrarian Problem and its Solution', *Journal of the Poona Sarvajanik Sabha*, Vol. II, No. 1, p. 17.
[4] When proposals were made to adjust the relationship between landlord and tenan in favour of the latter in Ratnagiri district, an article appeared in the Sabha's *Journal* claiming:

Although Elphinstone's policies of the 1820s had helped to maintain Brahmin predominance in Maharashtra and the surrounding districts, by the end of the century non-Brahmin castes were beginning to see that they too could exploit the advantages of British rule, and possibly break the power of the Brahmins in the region. Jotirao Phooley, a Mali by caste, began anti-Brahmin propaganda in Poona, the centre of Brahmin power, in the mid-nineteenth century. He founded the Satya Shodhak Samaj in 1873 to campaign against Brahmin supremacy. He sought to prove from Hindu scriptures the equality of mankind and that there was no need for priestly mediation between man and God.[1] Above all he sought to educate non-Brahmins so that they would be able to compete with Brahmins on their own terms. He exhorted the Education Commission: 'Let there be schools for Sudras in every village; but away with all Brahmin schoolmasters! The Sudras are the life and sinews of the country, and it is to them alone, and not to the Brahmins, that the Goverment must ever look to tide them over their difficulties, financial as well as political.'[2]

As the Brahmin monopoly of higher education began to show signs of breaking, the non-Brahmins began to agitate for an increasing share of public patronage. The editor of *Dinbandhu* told the Public Service Commission that so far their control of English education had enabled Brahmins to monopolize all goverment offices:

Their chief object is to keep the masses in ignorance, and impart to their own people the fruits of Western liberality. In a large town like Bombay, it is not possible to know the oppression they exercise over other castes, but I have no hesitation in saying that to their machinations is to be attributed solely the backwardness of the other people. My object in making this observation is that the Commission, whose object is to gauge the aspiration and make themselves acquainted with the condition of the people, will see their way to bring this state of things to the notice of Government and recommend measures to remedy the evils complained of.[3]

The remedies could take a very precise form: non-Brahmins in the Kanarese-speaking area urged 'that strict orders may be passed directing that henceforth...we non-Brahmans alone may be employed till the number of Brahman and non-Brahman employès becomes equal'.[4]

'Misguided philanthropy at the expense of others is, however, one of the besetting sins of the Indian Bureaucracy. The members of the Indian Services belong chiefly to the landless classes in their own country, and nothing is so easy as to secure their adherence to all manner of socialist experiments in India.' 'A Vindication of the Khoti Settlement of 1880', *Journal*, Vol. V, No. 3, p. 20.
[1] *I.S.C.*, Vol. VII, p. 227. D. Keer, *Mahatma Jotirao Phooley: Father of our Social Revolution* (Bombay, 1964), p. 126.
[2] *E.C. (Bombay)*, II, pp. 141–2.
[3] *P.S.C. (Bombay)*, IV, section iii, B, p. 107.
[4] *P.S.C. (Bombay)*, IV, section iii, C, p. 200.

And in Kolhapur the Maharaja pursued such a policy from 1902.[1] Although not strong enough to shake the Brahmins' position, the stirrings of non-Brahmins were sufficient to cause comment. More of them gained entrance to colleges[2] and their political aspirations grew. The submerged groups came to look towards the raj for fair dealing and for a greater share in the wealth and power of the community. Events were taking place which ensured that freedom from alien rule in western India was not to be a case of the Peshwai revisited.

Maharashtra, like Bengal and Madras, became politically active in the second half of the nineteenth century because British rule initially had most impact upon the maritime provinces. Maharashtra had been dominated socially, economically and politically by Brahmins, particularly by Chitpavan Brahmins. This caste had risen to prominence in relatively recent times. Enterprising individuals from the caste migrated eastwards to take service in the Mahratta states. The appointment of Balaji Vishvanath as Peshwa helped to establish Chitpavans in the region. However, the majority of the caste continued to live a modest existence as cultivators in the Konkan, or as minor clerks, religious mendicants, petty traders and money-lenders, or as servants to more successful kin. When the Peshwa lost Maharashtra to the British, the Chitpavans' literacy, and their lack of commitment to any particular employment, allowed them to respond quickly to the changed situation. Indeed, British rule opened new opportunities in the bureaucracy and professions, and the second half of the nineteenth century saw Chitpavans turn eagerly to English education in the schools of Bombay, Poona and the Deccan towns.

Literacy in English, besides providing a pass to employment, also qualified Chitpavans to take the lead in modern Indian politics. They shared interests in British rule with social groups in other parts of India, and, through newspapers, associations and the Congress, they were prominent in continental politics. However, their influence did

---

[1] Latthe, *Chhatrapati*, Vol. I, pp. 152, 220–1.
[2] Male Brahmin and non-Brahmin Hindu students attending Arts Colleges in Bombay Presidency 1901–22:

Years	Brahmin pupils	Non-Brahmin pupils
1901–2	902	598
1906–7	1,172	937
1911–12	1,692	1,211
1916–17	2,303	1,635
1921–2	2,141	1,558

Basu, 'Indian Education', table 29.

not depend upon their ability to organize their caste for politics (significantly it was in Poona and the Deccan towns, not in Ratnagiri, that Chitpavans were politically active), or upon their ability to lead the Maharashtrian peasantry. It derived from their position as an educated elite which skilfully exploited the constitutional framework of British rule. Their failure to persuade the much larger non-Brahmin castes to accept their leadership—whether in politics, education, or social reform—was to prove their undoing in the twentieth century. Indeed, a desire to end Brahmin domination provided the main stimulus for the intermediate castes to enter politics. Unable either to control or even to intrigue in mass politics, the Chitpavan Brahmins abdicated their political role. Power moved from the one loved by the people to the people themselves, and the inheritors of modern Maharashtra proved to be not the Tilaks and Gokhales but the Chavans and Naiks.

THE LANDED GENTRY OF THE TELENGANA, ANDHRA PRADESH

HUGH GRAY

The landed gentry are an elite who operate at every level: in the villages where they are based, on local government bodies, at district and state levels, and at the seat of the central government in Delhi.

In order to maintain power in their villages and zones of overlapping economic and territorial interests, the ruling village families, as a dominant class of dominant castes, have sent their educated members into the new battlefields provided by the institutions of parliamentary democracy. This elite of rural leaders has joined political parties, become members of the Legislative Assembly, chairmen of *Zilla Parishads*, presidents of *Panchayat Samithis*, and *sarpanches* of village *panchayats*. A number of *sarpanches* have entered politics merely to prevent interference in their villages without any further political ambitions, although these sometimes develop under the stimulus of political activities.

There is often a division of labour within landowning families that allows them to remain effective in both traditional and modern roles. If a family has four sons it might try to cover the field by having one in local politics, one as an M.L.A., another in a profession, and the fourth as manager of the land. The members of these families, the ruling elite, are known in the Telengana as *doras*.

The word *dora* is Telegu and means sir, master, lord of the village. The British too were referred to as, and called themselves, *dora* (e.g. Brown Doravaru, the author of a nineteenth-century book). To qualify for the title a man must have control over men or property: generally he wields authority by right of birth. He is a country gentleman and a member of one of the dominant landowning castes (although occasionally the status can be achieved and I have heard a man spoken of as 'a *dora* by education'). A *dora* is often an ex-*Jagidar* or *Deshmukh*,[1] although the term is also used of the newly rich Reddi who owns most of the land in a village.

Traditional services are rendered by villagers to their *dora* and to village officers, which are sometimes paid for in cash or kind, or extracted free.

The *dora* is a combination of a landlord, moneylender, village official, government representative and politician. He is the link between government officials and the villagers. When a government official

---

[1] Revenue-collecting officer of profit in the time of the Nizam of Hyderabad.

visits a village where there is a *dora* he first calls on him, as he controls the power structure of the village through village officials, caste elders and *Gram Panchayat* members. Since the introduction of *Panchayat Raj* the *dora* must be a politician, otherwise an alternative bridge between people and government will emerge, and his power would diminish and his economic interests be damaged.

In the past there were few public works department contracts available at *taluk* and district levels. With *Panchayat Raj* came not only the decentralization of democracy but also the placing of contracts. In the past there were only one or two contractors in a district, now there are many. *Doras* have become contractors and this is another reason why it is essential for them to have political influence—so that contracts are appropriately placed. The spreading outwards of a *dora*'s economic as well as political interests has taken him out of the village.

Moneylending

In most cases the *doras* themselves are the moneylenders. Banyas are not found in all villages and are excluded from some *dora*-dominated villages, or they may be allowed by the *dora* to trade but not to lend money. They may also be forced by *doras* to act as middlemen in marketing produce. In one village the *dora* instead of lending money directly to the villagers himself advanced money to a Banya at an interest of 12 to 15 per cent and allowed him to lend it at 18 to 36 per cent interest.

The Banyas are moneylenders, businessmen and in some cases landowners. Sometimes the roles are reversed and, if a *dora* is heavily in debt to a Banya, the Banya may use the *dora* as his agent. The most usual arrangement is that a *dora* permits a Banya to lend money to his villagers and the Banya markets the *dora*'s produce for him. Where the *dora* has the upper hand he may force the Banya to accept more money than he needs, at a high rate of interest. If there is conflict between a Banya and his client, the *dora* will support the Banya if they are in business together.[1]

In a village without a *dora*, a Banya may become *sarpanch*, reinforce political power by moneylending, and become president of the local Mandal Congress Committee. The power of a Banya rests on moneylending and wealth, not social status; on manipulative ability, not a traditionally honoured place in society. But Banyas are threats to the power of the *doras*, particularly in big villages.

When there is a dispute between a *dora* and a Banya, the latter will hesitate to go to court, because of the high interest he charges, or because he may not be in possession of the necessary official licence to

---

[1] On the other hand people often say that when Reddis and Brahmins fall out, it is the Banyas who come to power.

lend money. And if he goes to court against a *dora* he may have difficulty in finding witnesses.

A *dora* often acts as a paid arbitrator. I was told of a case in which a debtor and a Banya had agreed to the arbitration of a certain *dora*. The debtor had borrowed money from the Banya, depositing gold with him as security. The *dora* demanded the gold from the Banya and Rs. 20,000 from the debtor, pending a decision. The gold and money were handed over to the *dora*. The case dragged on for twelve years and both parties died. The *dora* kept the gold and the money.

In one village there were no resident Banyas. The *dora* of this village was a *Samithi* President and one of the most powerful men in the area. At the time of the General Election of 1962 he backed an Independent (a dissident Congressman) against the official Congress candidate. From a nearby village a less powerful *dora* backed the Congress candidate. The *Samithi* President could not influence the other *dora* but he threatened the Banyas, whom he allowed to come and work in his village, that unless they used their influence to oppose the Congress candidate he would exclude them from his village in future, so they worked against the Congress candidate and between 20 and 30 per cent of the votes from the lesser *dora*'s village were given to the Independent candidate.

The Role of the 'Dora'

The interests of businessmen living in *taluk* or district towns are often intertwined with those of the rural *doras* with whom they have alliances. Excise contracts are auctioned and on obtaining one the *dora* can either allot trees to tappers, or employ tappers to do the work.

Forest and fishery contracts are also auctioned and in some areas contracts for bidi leaves. If more than one person bids, there is a clash of interests, but generally a ring is formed of *doras* who keep out of each other's zones of interest and do not bid against each other. It is not only a question of economic profit, which may sometimes be small, but also of prestige and power. Clashes on economic questions generally have political consequences.

If people from two villages quarrel their *doras* meet and decide what shall be done and who shall be called in to arbitrate. Conflicts between two villages, or between two parties belonging to different villages who are not from the same caste, may be settled between the *doras* concerned or, if there are no *doras*, an inter-village *ad hoc panchayat* may be set up on which the elders of the two villages that are parties to the dispute, as well as elders from neutral villages who are invited, sit and hear the dispute, and give a verdict. If there are *doras* and they have agreed to such a *panchayat*, they will enforce the verdict.

A *dora* also has to be careful which cases he takes himself and which he leaves to others. For example, a girl was raped in the woods by a *dora*'s bodyguard. The villagers from the girl's village (who were without a *dora*) came to see the man's *dora* and asked for justice. The man denied that he had raped the girl. The *dora* decided that it would be better if he did not hear the case himself, and he referred the dispute to a caste elder who found the man guilty and fined him Rs. 50. The fine was in fact paid for the man by the *dora*, who knew the man was guilty but to whom he was useful.

A 'Dora's' Power

A *dora* has many servants and some are used as strong-arm men to enforce his wishes and deal with the recalcitrant. *Doras* are occasionally murdered, but it is more likely for a village to boycott a *dora* by refusing services. When there is such collective action by a village negotiations must follow and a settlement will be reached.

A *dora* can also coerce by litigation. He may file cases against a man in different places: the *taluk* town, the district town, the city; and his opponent will be forced to give in because of the expense involved. Criminal as well as civil cases may be brought. A *dora*'s servant will say that a man attacked him and bring assault charges.

A *dora* controls immigration into his village, and only with his permission can land be bought and sold.

Traditionally in the Telengana power has always brought economic gains. In the time of the Nizams of Hyderabad any number of *watands*[1] might be held by the same man (e.g. Shri Kisham Rao, a Brahmin of Karimnagar District, is said to have held between fifty and sixty such offices). When Hyderabad was incorporated in India, the economic status as well as the power status of the *doras* was threatened, so they took up new forms of enrichment like public works contracts, excise and forest contracts, etc. The coming of democracy forced the *dora* to enlarge his sphere of operations.

Many outside influences threaten the power of a *dora*. He may have to suffer intrusions from politicians, officials, schoolmasters, postmasters, village-level workers, contractors, excise and forest inspectors, mining or special business interests. Apart from political parties he may have to deal with co-operative societies of weavers, tanners, toddy tappers, etc. Missions, particularly if they establish schools, clinics or hospitals, are particular threats to a *dora*'s influence.

Many *doras* provide elementary welfare services for villages. They dispense medicines, and help individuals and groups in times of diffi-

[1] Village offices.

culty and disaster, by providing food and transport. Many *doras* inspire loyalty and affection as well as fear.

Gram Panchayat politics are a new source of power, and a *sarpanch* is on a line of political communication reaching to the State level. With the introduction of *Panchayat Raj* in 1959, a *dora*'s first step was to ensure that the new office of *sarpanch* was in his own hands or that of his opposition. His power problem is to maintain the dominating position of his family. Village feuds are to his advantage, if the feuding parties do not bring in outside forces which might stay on and upset his balance of power. In the new conditions of today, with the political parties pushing downwards into the villages, he or one of his brothers must enter the political arena and limit intrusions into the family's sphere of influence from outside, as well as extend its economic and political power. As an ex-*Jagirdar* said 'a man cannot rule in his own village today unless he is in politics'.

THE VILLAGE 'DORA': A CASE STUDY

The Family History

The male members of this Kamma family say that their ancestors came to the Telengana from Andhra between one hundred and two hundred years ago, and were given the *Jagirs* of fourteen villages, seven in one district and seven in another. They maintained law and order in their villages with the help of 500 armed men and they were responsible for guarding the *gundia* (passages through the forest) and protecting travellers from *dacoits*. About fifty years ago the family relinquished the titles to all seven villages in one district but retained the seven villages in the other district, where they still live. The family house was in one of these villages. In 1901 the property was divided up between brothers, and the father of the present *dora* received as his share one village and some land around other villages. He considered the income small and took to agriculture. Before he settled in his village he had only visited it to collect revenue and the cultivable area was negligible. Under his direction forest lands were cleared, the village tank was repaired, and the area of land under wet cultivation greatly increased. The village population grew, perhaps by 40 per cent, and he persuaded people to settle there by giving them land, a house site and bullocks. The present village population is 787, and there are 165 families (269 males, 277 females and 241 children). As there was no Brahmin in the village, he settled an Ayyavaru family there to officiate at *pujas* and other religious ceremonies. He also settled a theatre group of 'Bhagotham' families on the outskirts of the village to enhance his prestige. He retained ownership of about 75 per cent of the village land, and 50 per cent of the houses and land in the village.

After he became rich he started moneylending and had clients from ten to fifteen villages around his own. According to his son he lent out as much as Rs. 150,000 in this way, charging up to 50 per cent interest. He also made loans in kind (called *pechulu*). In this way he extended and consolidated the power and wealth he had inherited.

When he died he left a widow and four sons. A family council, consisting of the widow, her father, and the two elder sons who were students, was called. The eldest son was unwilling to leave his studies, but the second son was anxious to do so, and gave them up to manage the family estate. The eldest son continued at Osmania University, and after taking a B.A. stayed on to study for a higher degree, but he left the University in the 'quit college' movement of 1948. For a time he was active in Congress Party politics, then went into business in Hyderabad but was unsuccessful and has since lived on his share of the income from the estate.

The second son did not play an active role in politics until 1957 when he became President of the *Taluk* Congress Committee. In 1961 he became the first president of the new *Panchayat Samithi* in which his village was situated.

Meanwhile the third son had graduated and it was decided that, as the second son had now gone in for politics, the third son should take over management of the family estate from the second son.

The fourth son (in 1962) was still studying for a medical degree and did not intend to return to the village.

In the division of labour between the brothers, the eldest, who is well known in the city of Hyderabad, looks after external affairs and handles all matters that concern government departments. Although he is no longer politically active he has many friends from before Police Action days, and can sometimes approach and influence politicians who are not accessible to his brother in the same personal way.

Since the introduction of Land Ceiling Legislation the landholding of the family, which is now concentrated in three villages, has been divided *de jure*, but not *de facto*, as the brothers are close friends and wish to continue as a joint family.

Style of Living

This *dora* joint family lives in a large brick and tile-roofed house, in the middle of the village, surrounded by high walls and entered by massive double wooden gates which give on to a large courtyard in front of the house. There are a number of rooms in two wings of the house, extending down two sides of the courtyard towards the gate. In these visitors are entertained. On important occasions, as on Dassara, when a *puja* is performed and a goat sacrificed, or when important visitors are staying the night, theatrical entertainments are staged in the courtyard and the whole village attends.

There are many servants, among them families of the 'Dasi' class. In the past it was customary for a bride to bring maidservants with her into her husband's household. Children were also purchased. Female Dasis were not allowed to marry but became the mistresses of male members of the *dora* family or household, or with the *dora*'s permission contracted relationships with men in the village. The institution of Dasis is described as a dying one and 'part of a disappearing feudal system'.

As a consequence of past Muslim domination the members of the Hindu-dominant agricultural castes have taken on many Muslim habits. The female members of the *dora*'s family, when in the village, live in purdah. The eldest brother of this family told me that he had not seen his brother's wife, although they reside in the same house, since her wedding day.

This *dora* family did not have a motor car, as the family had the use of the *Samithi* President's jeep (the second brother was the President), but they possessed a tractor, a high status symbol in the Telengana rural districts. The eldest brother had a small rented house in the centre of Hyderabad which was also used by the other male members of the family when visiting the city. Foodstuffs, particularly rice, were always dispatched to him regularly in Hyderabad from the family estate.

It is said that *doras* are much more generous with gifts of kind than with money, and it is always easier to raise a contribution for a political cause in rice or chillies than in money.

The Ranking of the Family in Relation to other 'Dora' Families

There are four or five Kamma families in the district with whom this *dora*'s family are grouped. None of these are in the top landlord class. The district has four Velama families, two Reddi families and two Brahmin families in the top landlord class. All members of the *dora* class dine with, and take water from, each other; except the Brahmins, who only do so on political occasions. But those of different castes do not intermarry. The *dora* family I have described rates below the top class economically, but socially are on the same level as all well-off *dora* families. Ritually of course the Brahmins claim precedence, they are strict vegetarians and refer to Velamas, Reddis and Kammas as 'Shudras', jeering privately at their claim to Ksatriya status. The

Velamas, Reddis and Kammas retort by referring to Brahmins as their servants, and distinguish socially between Brahmins who are landlords and holders of *watands* (that is, the *doras*) and others.

The Village Political Situation

There is a maximum concentration of authority in this *dora* family. All three *watands*—*patwari, mali patel* and police *patel*—are in the name of the eldest son. The second son, the *Panchayat Samithi* President, is also the village *sarpanch*.

For *Gram Panchayat* elections the *dora*'s village is grouped with another village two miles away. This village is without a *dora* and sends a Banya representative to the *Gram Panchayat*. There is no overt opposition in this village. There was no contested election for the *Gram Panchayat* and the members of it were elected unanimously, after the *dora* had consulted with the village leaders. The *Gram Panchayat* consists of six *panchas*. These are the *Sarpanch* (Kamma), a Gudeti Kapu (a peasant owning a little land), a Golla (a shepherd with sheep as well as a little land), two Harijans and the Banya from the other village.

Formerly every caste represented in the village had an elder (*pedda*). If at any time the *dora* found that a caste elder was not carrying out his orders he would either remove him directly, or prompt his enemies in the caste to call for his removal. The new man appointed would be formally approved by his fellow caste members.

Since the formation of the *Gram Panchayat*, the *dora* consults its members as well as the caste elders. Their views seldom influence his actions, and they generally ratify his action as *sarpanch* without question.

The 'Dora's' Village Associates

Among the *dora*'s close associates are a Gone Kapu, a peasant farmer who owns twenty-seven acres of land, who was in the service of the *dora*'s father and with his help became a small independent farmer. In the village he is called *patel* and people say that an ancestor of his may have held such an office although he is probably called *patel* from having worked as a *gumastha* in the *dora*'s service. Although not directly employed by the *dora* he spends much of his time carrying out the *dora*'s orders and he runs the *dora*'s village intelligence service. A *dora* never enters villagers' houses and must work through agents. This Gone Kapu was married in childhood but never brought his wife home. He lives with another women, a Dasi from the *dora*'s household, and has a son and daughter by her. This has lowered his prestige in the village and he depends on the *dora*'s support to maintain his position. If the *dora*'s patronage were withdrawn his caste fellows would take disciplinary action against him, as his behaviour would not normally be tolerated. He has failed to arrange marriages for his children with members of his own caste and they will have to find marriage partners from among similarly mixed offspring. When villagers wish to approach the *dora* they often do so through him, and he carries the *dora*'s instructions to them.

A second close associate of the *dora* is the only potter in the village. He only owns seven acres of land but is said to be well-off. His sons do all the agricultural work and he has much leisure. People think well of him in the village and he always carries out the *dora*'s wishes. If a villager's interests are damaged by some action the *dora* is taking, the *dora* will often say that it is this man's opinion that the action should be taken, and it is thus made more acceptable to public opinion.

As in most villages in this district the Kapu group is numerically strong, and the *dora* used to consult its caste elder; but he is now 74 years old and the *dora* has turned to another member of the caste, who is on the *Gram Panchayat*.

In the hamlet of the village the important person is a Yellapu by caste, who owns nine acres of land and is a moneylender in a small way. He is opposed to the Gone Kapu who is close to the *dora*, and the *dora* plays them off one against the other and, if he is displeased with the Gone Kapu, moves closer to the Yellapu.

This *dora* has kept off the *Gram Panchayat* the two strongest men in the village, the Gone Kapu and the Yellapu. Both men are pleased at the exclusion of the other.

The Harijans are all subservient to the *dora* and they are mainly dependent on him for their livelihood. Approximately forty families of Malas, Madigas and Gollas (shepherds) are directly dependent economically on the *dora*.

The relations between the *dora* family and the villagers are cordial, because after the passage of Land Legislation in 1954 the *dora* sold more than 3,000 acres of land to them at prices below those prevailing on the market. This was done to avoid the intrusion of strangers into the village. Recently when three brothers of Ayyavaru caste, who go out of the village to work, wished to rent out their land and could not find tenants from the village, the *dora* took it on rather than let somebody from outside move into the village.

Inside the village the number of tenants has decreased and the number of peasant proprietors has increased since the Police Action, as a result of land legislation and the conscious policy pursued by the *dora* family. The *dora* family has also discontinued large-scale money-lending, and now only lends when it is a question of keeping strange Banyas away from the village. Only two Banyas, from a nearby village, are authorized by him to make loans. Villagers also get credit from *taccavi* loans and from commission agents in towns who lend peasants money against the sale of their produce after the harvest, when it is sold through them.

The villagers see their *dora* as the man who deals with the government. They say that villagers without *doras* have to entertain visiting officials and provide them with bullock carts. They are saved this inconvenience and, provided that others do not outweigh them, *doras* can be popular in their paternalistic roles.

General Elections as Seen from the ' Dora's ' Village

In the three general elections of 1952, 1957 and 1962 the villagers voted for the *dora*'s candidate. In 1952 the *dora* supported the official Congress Party candidate, and in 1957 the same man standing as an Independent again had his support. On both occasions all but about ten votes were given in the *dora*'s candidate's favour. In 1962, out of 324 votes 29 were cast for the official Congress Party candidate and the rebel Congressman, supported by the *dora*, received the remainder. The *dora* held an enquiry after the election into these unexpected defections.

Before the election the *dora* had seen all the village elders individually, and the members of the *Gram Panchayat*. They were told that if they used their influence against the *dora*'s candidate this would become known and they would be suitably penalized. Then the *dora* heard that a certain Ayyavaru, who was employed outside the village by a supporter of the Congress Party candidate, was speaking against the Independent who had the *dora*'s support. The young man was called and asked to explain his conduct. After discussion, they reached an agreement that the young man should be allowed to vote as his employer wished but that he would not canvas or discuss the matter in his, the *dora*'s, village. The young man took an oath (*pramanam*) holding rice above his head, and was allowed to go.

The post-mortem showed that the village schoolmaster had secretly canvassed for the Congress Party candidate. He was transferred away from the village shortly afterwards—the *Panchayat Samithi* being responsible for the postings of primary school teachers. It was also alleged that a Gone Kapu, jealous of his relative's (the *dora*'s right-hand man) influence over the *dora*, had also voted against the *dora*'s candidate with his family members and five associates from his caste, making a total of ten or eleven votes. This was noted by the *dora* for future account, although the man himself denied the charge. It was assumed that the other votes were cast by mistake, due to blindness, old age or stupidity.

The Village

Total population:	787	(269 males; 277 females; 241 children)
Total no. of households:	165	(86 huts; 78 houses with tiled roofs; 1 'bungalow', the *dora*'s house)
Land ownership:		60 to 80 people are in the service of the *dora*; 20 to 30 people are occasionally employed by the *dora*
500 acres	1	
20 to 30 acres	2	
10 to 20 acres	14	
5 to 10 acres	19	
1 to 5 acres	49	
Less than 1 acre	47	
Landless	33	
Total	165	

Breakdown of Village by Caste

Kammas	13	(The *dora* family)
Ayyavarus	8	(Priests)
Gudeti Kapus	52	(Note: in this village the Gudeti Kapus do not claim to be a Reddi sub-caste)
Munur Kapus	40	(A caste of peasants and agricultural labourers; no claim to Reddi status)
Yellapus	17	
Gollas	93	(Shepherds)
Weavers	55	
Bhagotham	41	(A caste of actors and musicians)
Potters	6	
Carpenters	18	
Goldsmiths	11	
Blacksmiths	16	
Tappers	39	
Washermen	44	
Tenegu	7	(A caste of peasants and agricultural labourers: unlike Harijans, but like Munur Kapus, they are allowed to enter Reddi houses)
Barber	8	
Muslims	22	
Malas	160	
Madigas	91	
Sonnaila	4	
Ladaf	4	(A caste of poor Muslims, inferior to Muslims in status although their co-religionists)
Dasis	16	(Unmarried female servants in *dora*'s household)
Total	787	

The Village Population

The Ayyavarus are Vyshnavites and non-vegetarians. They claim to be a sub-caste of Brahmins, but are not recognized by Brahmins as such. They were brought to the village by the present *dora*'s father. On Dassara and similar occasions the priest from this family performs the *pujas* and a procession for Lord Garudvahana is taken round the village. On Ogadi (Telegu New Year's Day) he predicts the good and evil features of the coming year and the fortunes of individuals are told. Their position in the caste structure is ambiguous. Most people seemed to place them below the *doras* but above the other castes.

Broadly speaking, the castes of the village fall into five named groups:

(1)   The Kammas (the *dora*'s family);
(2)   The Ayyavarus;
(3)   The Gudeti Kapus, the Gone Kapus, the Munur Kapus, the Yellapu;
(4)   The Gollas, Weavers, Bhogotham, Potters, Carpenters, Goldsmiths, Blacksmiths, Tappers, Washermen, Tenegus, Barbers;
(5)   The Muslims, Malas, Madigas, Ladaf, Dasis and Sonnaila.

There is no intermarriage between the members of any of these castes. No one will take water from Muslims except the Malas and the Madigas. None of the artisan castes in the fourth group will take water from the barbers and washermen. All the Kapu castes inter-dine. The Gollas, Weavers, Bhogotham and Potters inter-dine. None of the other artisan castes will take water from the Goldsmiths. The Malas will not take water from the Madigas.

About 25 per cent of marriages are inside the village. Most people marry from within a range of four to six miles, but some villagers have brides from villages further away, the furthest twenty-five miles. The *dora*'s family marry over a more extensive area, and the eldest son's bride came from over forty miles away.

There are no cases of adoption in this village, but a few cases of *illutam* (getting sons-in-law). Among Kapu families when this occurs and the son-in-law comes to live with the wife's parents, he inherits an equal share of the father-in-law's property with the father's sons. In other castes *illutam* is also practised, but only when there is no male heir.

In-laws visit at least once a year but generally as much as between four to thirteen times a year. When the villages are near each other families related by marriage help each other at harvest time. This reciprocal aid is common between fathers-in-law and sons-in-law, and brothers-in-law, particularly in Kapu and artisan families. However, there is a feud with an adjacent village over tank-bed lands and, although many of the Kapu families from these two villages are related, they line up with their village, not their relatives, in time of conflict.

Travel

There are two markets to which the villagers regularly go. One is in the *taluk* town, six miles away, and half the population goes there at least four times a year. The *dora*'s male family members go to the *taluk* town about once every three days. Villagers go there mostly to the market, a few to work, and others to the cinema.

The other market is at the nearest railway station, thirty-two miles away, and villagers go there only once or twice a year. There is an important chilli market there and chillies are the main cash crop of the village.

Once a year there is an important *mela* (fair) in a village one mile away. On this occasion all the villagers attend dressed in their finest clothes. The fair is called 'Mallana Jatra'.

Crime

There is little crime in the village. Disputes are always referred to the *dora*, who adjudicates himself, or refers them to the village elders, and for many years no case has gone outside the village.

Crops

The soil is above average in fertility. Paddy is grown on wet land and chillies are the main cash crop. Jawar, castor, towsar and pesal are also grown, maize as well. There are no gardens, except those of the *dora*, who grows some mangoes and guavas. The average standard of living is only just above subsistence level.

Education

In the *dora*'s family there are three graduates and the *dora* himself is educated to matriculation standard. A member of one Kapu family also studied to matriculation level, and two others from the village completed their primary education but none of these have remained in the village. Perhaps ten or twelve families have members who can read or write. Not more than fifty people from the village can sign their names.

Conclusion

The whole of life in this village revolves around the *dora* and his family. They forcibly integrate and govern the village, consciously excluding, eliminating and controlling threats to their power. They successfully divide and rule. Villagers take pride in the fact that their *dora* is *Panchayat Samithi* President. Although there is latent opposition in the village, as is shown by the twenty-nine dissident voters at the General Election, there is no imminent threat to the *dora*'s power. He is the Congress Party as well as the *dora* in his village and there are no Communist challengers of his authority.

CASE STUDY OF A 'PANCHAYAT SAMITHI'

The Community Development Block in which this *Samithi* was situated consisted of sixty-one villages and hamlets grouped on a population basis to elect thirty-eight *Gram Panchayats*. (The *Samithi* headquarters was in a village on the Godvari river, a place of pilgrimage, but is now elsewhere; and the frontiers of the Community Development Block have been changed.)

Table 1. *List of members of 'Panchayat Samithi' (as on 21.1.1962)*

Serial no.	Name	Village of which *Sarpanch*	Caste	Land holding	Age (years)	Education
1	Dharma Rao	Venglapur	Kamma	LA	35	Matric.
2	Narayan Rao	Rapalle	Velama	LC	39	Primary
3	Murahari	Polas	Brahmin	LC	36	Primary
4	G. Chandriah	Shakalla	Velama	LC	30	Can read and write
5	Ganga Rao	Kalleda	Velama	LC	30	Middle School
6	Purshotham Rao	Tungur	Velama	LC	30	Primary
7	Raja Ram	Laxmipur	Gudeti Kapu	LD	50	Just literate
8	Rango Rao	Stambampalli	Velama	LC	42	Middle School
9	Malliah	Jabitapuram	Gudeti Kapu	LD	48	Illiterate
10	Venkat Reddy	Habshipuram	Reddi	LC	36	Middle School
11	Malliah	Anantaram	Vysya	LD	45	Can read and write
12	Raj Reddy	Arpapalli	Reddi	LC	36	Middle School
13	Kamalaka Rao	Timmapur	Velama	LB	37	High School
14	B. Narsiah	Gopalapuram	Munur Kapu	P	45	Illiterate
15	Mutyam Rao	Chandoli	Velama	LC	40	Just literate
16	Hanmanth Rao	Sirkonda	Velama	LB	30	Middle School
17	S. Lachanna	Buggaram	Munur Kapu	P	40	Illiterate
18	Rajeshwa Rao	Maddnur	Velama	LA	—	High School
19	Egi Reddi	Jaina	Reddi	LD	30	Can read and write
20	Malla Reddy	Sarangadur	Reddi	LC	30	Middle School
21	Yella Reddy	Mallanapet	Reddi	LC	30	Primary
22	Narsiah	Narsimlapalli	Golla	P	40	Can sign name

Table 1 (*cont.*)

Serial no.	Name	Village of which *Sarpanch*	Caste	Land holding	Age (years)	Education
23	S. Jaivardhan Rao	Nerella	Velama	LA	30	High School
24	Gopal Rao	Welgonda	Velama	LC	30	Middle School
25	Ch Raja Ram	Municipality Dharamapuri	Munur Kapu	LC	50	Can read and write
26	B. Malliah	Kamalapur	Munur Kapu	P	40	Can read and write
27	Ram Kishtian	Velgatur	Weaver	Nil	40	Can read and write
28	Malla Reddi	Kondapur	Reddi	LC	36	Just literate
29	Jagannath Rao	Fonthapur	Velama	LC	30	Middle School
30	Vasudev Rao	Donur	Velama	LB	40	Middle School
31	Venkat Murali	Chilwakodur	Yellapu	LB	40	Primary
32	Prabhaka Rao	Birdur	Velama	LB	35	Middle School
33	R. Narayan Rao	Koluai	Velama	LB	35	Middle School
34	Rajna Sing Rao	Ibrahimpatam	Velama	LB	30	High School
35	Maruthy Rao	Velugmatla	Weaver	LC	30	High School
36	G. Bheemiah	Raipatam	Peraka	Nil	40	Illiterate
37	Rajiah	Jagdevpet	Vysya	LC	40	Just literate
38	Narsing Rao	Rajaram	Velama	LC	40	Can read and write
		Co-opted Members				
39	Bhavan Rao	—	Velama	LB	40	College
40	Meena Rao	—	Velama	LB	35	High School
41	Sowbhagya-vati	—	Harijan	Nil	30	VI Standard
42	B. Laxmi Devi	—	Brahmin	—	—	—
43	G. Yelliah	—	Harijan	Nil	?	Illiterate
44	O. Ramiah	—	Harijan	Nil	?	Illiterate

NOTE: The government of Andhra Pradesh has declared that for each individual the land-holding ceiling should be land yielding an income of Rs. 5,400 per annum.

KEY: LA equals more than land ceiling. LB equals the land ceiling. LC equals half the land ceiling to the land ceiling. LD equals one quarter to one half of the land ceiling. P equals less than one quarter of the land ceiling: a peasant proprietor.

Analysis of 'Samithi' Members' Landholdings

LA	3	(nos. 1, 18, 23)	Nil	5
LB	9		?	1
LC	18			—
LD	4		Total	44
P	4			—

The three members of the *Samithi* owning most land are its dominant members. They are also the only members who own tractors; nos. 29, 39 and 40 own jeeps. The President has the use of the *Samithi* jeep, and he also owns a tractor, as do nos. 18 and 23.

Nos. 1, 18 and 23 have decided that the *Panchayat Samithi* Presidency should always be filled by one of them. They come from families which in the past owned and controlled many villages and, as ex-*Jagidars*, they tend to look down on other *doras* as 'village officer class' although like them they control hereditary village offices. On this *Samithi* the class factor is dominant.

The other *doras* on the *Samithi* are nos. 5, 6, 13, 24, 29, 30, 32, 33, 34, 35, 39 and 40. No. 35, although a Weaver, owns a little land and was described to me as a '*dora* by education'.

Nos. 7, 17, 2 and 27 represent *doras* who do not wish to be on the *Samithi* themselves. No. 7, a Kapu, represents a Velama *dora*; 17, also a Kapu, represents a Brahmin. No. 2, a Velama, represents another Velama who opposes the ruling triumvirate from outside the *Samithi*. His prestige was diminished by the failure of the Congress candidate, backed by him at the general election, and the success of the Independent backed by the President and his two friends.

Unless nos. 1, 18 and 23 fall out, there is unlikely to be any change in the political situation of the *Samithi*, which is extremely stable. The Vice-President of the *Samithi* (no. 39) belongs to a family which moved into the district from Andhra and it is considered that he has been there too short a time ever to be in a position to bid for the Presidency.

Outside the *Samithi* there is a bitter feud between a group of Velama families (nos. 18, 23 and 39) and a wealthy Brahmin, who is not on the *Samithi* himself but is represented by no. 17, who has instructions always to oppose and vote against nos. 18, 23 and 39.

Election of the 'Panchayat Samithi' President

The Community Development Block representative on the *Zilla Parishad*, before the *Samithi* was formed, was no. 23.

The dominant leaders, who were *ex-officio* members of the *Samithi* (*sarpanches* of their villages), were nos. 1, 18 and 23—all members of the *Zilla Parishad* Chairman's group within the Congress Party at district level. They and their followers decided to put up no. 1 as their candidate. The members of the *Samithi* opposed to the candidature of no. 1 decided that they would support a Velama, from outside the *Samithi*, who would have to be co-opted. From among the *Samithi*'s thirty-eight members, no. 1 had twenty-two apparent supporters before co-options.

When voting took place on the first co-option to be filled (two candidates), there were defections from no. 1's group and the voting was 19–19. A coin was tossed to decide the winner and the no. 1 group candidate won. The opposition group did not contest the remaining co-options, once their presidential candidate had failed to get co-opted, and those put forward by the group led by nos. 1, 18 and 23 were all elected.

Before the election of the President took place no. 10 (the only non-Congress member and thought to be a Communist sympathizer) approached no. 1 and tried to persuade him to leave his group, saying that all other castes should form an anti-Velama front and 'teach the Velama despots a lesson'. This no. 1 refused to do.

APPENDIX

Analysis of the 106 Members of the Legislative Assembly for the Telengana (1962)

By caste:

Reddis	40
Kammas	2
Velamas	8
Brahmins	11
Vysyas	4
Backward Classes	13
Scheduled Castes and Scheduled Tribes	20
Muslims	7
Parsis	1
Total	**106**

By landownership:

In landowning category LA	12
,, ,, ,, LB	32
,, ,, ,, LC	17
,, ,, ,, LD	0
,, ,, ,, P	4
,, ,, ,, L?	12
No land owned	16
Not known whether landowners	13
Total	**106**

By education:

Graduates	50
Intermediate	8
Matric.	39
Middle School	5
Primary	6
Literate	11
Illiterate	1
Not known	6
Total	**106**

CANDIDATES FOR THE 1967 GENERAL ELECTIONS IN HYDERABAD, ANDHRA PRADESH

DAGMAR BERNSTORFF

Compared with electoral politics in western countries the candidates—their personality, their organizing skill, and their communal and caste backgrounds—determine to a far more decisive degree the outcome of elections in India. Most Indian parties, with the exception of the Jan Sangh, do not have strong permanent local party organizations with professional full-time staff which could serve as a basis for an election campaign. Few parties develop regional or national campaign strategies or give their candidates binding directions as to the ideological or factual content of their speeches. Candidates often have to build up their own organization in the constituency and choose the themes and techniques of their campaigns. Moreover, during the 1967 campaign the Indian parties did not designate their prospective candidates for the Prime Ministership or the Chief Ministerships; thus the success or the failure of the candidates depended to a lesser degree on the personal impact of their national leaders than in the west or even during previous election campaigns in India, when Jawaharlal Nehru was the Congress Party's undisputed designee for the next Prime Ministership. Personal contact with the voters or with group-leaders is essential in a society with a low literacy rate, underdeveloped media of mass communication and little ideological awareness.

Although candidates are given such a wide scope in the shaping of a crucial stage in the Indian political process it can be argued that they are not yet elites but aspiring to become members of the political elite. However candidates have been selected by their parties to contest the elections on their behalf or—in the case of Independent candidates—have to have the backing of a strong group in the constituency to be at least moderately successful.[1]

Analyses of political elites—the term is used in a strictly neutral and positional sense—distinguish between the minority which actually rules and takes part in political decision-making and a group from

---

[1] Some Independent candidates contest only in order to split some other candidate's votes, a few are adventurers who file their nominations expecting to be bribed by some other candidate to withdraw.

which these politicians are drawn and into which they return, if out of office. Bottomore[1] terms the first group 'political elites' or 'ruling elites' and the second group, following Mosca, 'political class'. I propose to consider candidates contesting a general election as belonging to the second category and prefer to call this group 'political elite', whereas I use the term 'ruling elite' for the first category. Some candidates are of course already members of the ruling elite, namely M.L.A.s and ministers who seek re-election.[2]

The following analysis is based on a case-study of seven Legislative Assembly constituencies of Hyderabad, Andhra Pradesh,[3] where thirty-four candidates contested the 1967 general elections. The sample is small and the results are not even typical for other cities of Andhra Pradesh; a comparison with samples drawn from other parts of India would be necessary to know more about political recruitment in the whole of India. Yet the analysis even of a small sample seems worthwhile in view of the fact that the discussion of elites in the new states is largely based on speculation rather than on empirical observation.

Some authors see the process of social and political change in developing societies as a conflict between 'old' elites with ascribed status and 'new' elites with achieved status. Richard Behrendt[4] even suggests that only elites risen from the lower strata of society can be dynamic and introduce structural change. The social origins, however, of the 'new' elites of politicians, administrators, and technocrats are largely unknown to us. A number of examples suggest that the 'old' and the 'new' elites are often closely interconnected.

The questions to be discussed here therefore are:

1. What are the social and educational origins of these candidates?

2. Do these members of the political elite represent a new elite or are they part of an established elite?

3. Do politics provide a channel for social mobility?

Hyderabad, having been the capital of a Muslim dynasty ruling over a largely non-Muslim population for two hundred years, has retained a peculiar social structure, very different from the rest of Andhra Pradesh. A striking characteristic is the religious composition of the population. Almost every second inhabitant of Hyderabad–Secunderabad is a

---

[1] T. B. Bottomore, *Elite und Gesellschaft*, München 1966, p. 15.

[2] Professor Morris-Jones suggested that it is necessary to study the level below the nomination-stage: from where do candidates emerge and what are their activities before they are nominated?

[3] The general elections 1967 were studied in several constituencies in Hyderabad and in Nalgonda district, Andhra Pradesh, by Rafi A. Khan, Alam S. Khundmiri, Eckehard Kulke, Jagan Madava and the author, under the auspices of the Arnold Bergstraesser Institute, Freiburg i.B. I am indebted to my colleagues for the collection of some of the data used for this article. The responsibility for the analysis rests entirely with me.

[4] Richard F. Behrendt, *Soziale Strategie für Entwicklungsländer*, Frankfurt a.M. 1965, p. 215.

Table 1. *Candidates and constituencies*

Candidates	Party	Votes polled
205 MUSHEERABAD		
1 Anjayya T.	Congress	16,811
2 Adam C. A.	Independent	560
3 Krishna Naidu N. T. retired in favour of T. Anjayya		655
4 Ram Moorty Naidu	Independent	1,831
5 Rama Rao T. S.	Jan Sangh	4,202
6 Satyanarayan Reddy N.	Communist	13,011
Electorate 73,383; Rejected votes 1,192; Total votes 38,262		
207 MAHARAJGANJ		
1 Aminur Rab Ansari Gandhi	Independent	230
2 Osman Bin Saleh	Independent	1,341
3 Govinda Chari M.	Independent	1,026
4 Jahangir Ali Ansari	Independent	392
5 Badri Vishal Pitti	S.S.P.	19,077
6 Seethiah Gupta K.	Congress	13,021
7 Hanumanth Rao Moyya	Jan Sangh	6,077
Electorate 71,871; Rejected votes 1,318; Total votes 42,282		
209 ASIFNAGAR		
1 Ismail Zabhi	Independent (Majlis)	11,762
2 Srihari	Jan Sangh	3,889
3 Sudershan Singh	Swatantra	644
4 Hashim M. M.	Congress	15,010
Electorate 64,148; Rejected votes 759; Total votes 32,064		
210 SITARAMBAGH		
1 Akbar Ali Nasiri Mir	Congress	8,928
2 Ahmed Hussain	Independent (Majlis)	17,478
3 Devenderpuri Goswamy	S.S.P.	10,824
4 Permishwer Rao B. retired in favour of Goswamy	Independent	757
5 Bal Reddy retired in favour of Goswamy	Independent	378
6 Raheem Faryadee	Independent	329
Electorate 76,332; Rejected votes 1,179; Total votes 39,873		
211 MALAKPET		
1 Abdul Rahman	Independent (Majlis)	8,692
2 Rangacharlu T. K.	Swatantra	943
3 Raja Reddy Baddam retired in favour of S. P. Reddy	Independent	1,356
4 Shankariah Bajaru	Independent	6,991
5 Sarojini Pully Reddy B.	Congress	17,662
Electorate 66,846; Rejected votes 1,415; Total votes 37,059		

Table 1 (cont.)

	Candidates	Party	Votes polled
	212 YAKUTPURA		
1	Khaja Nizamuddin	Independent (Majlis)	17,543
2	Gurunath Pershad Saxena	Independent	997
3	Nazeerunnisa Begum	Swatantra	338
4	Mohd. Taskeen	Independent	370
5	Raghuveer Rao S.	Jan Sangh	7,636
6	Rasheed M. A.	Congress	5,354

Electorate 61,339; Rejected votes 1,054; Total votes 33,242

	Candidates	Party	Votes polled
	213 CHARMINAR		
1	Om Prakash Nirmal	S.S.P.	333
2	Changanlal Meghraj	Jan Sangh	10,402
3	Mir Ahmed Ali Khan	Congress	6,732
4	Syed Ali Mohd. Hussain retired in favour of Ahmed Ali Khan	Independent	220
5	Sultan Salahuddin Owaisi	Independent (Majlis)	17,902

Electorate 62,501; Rejected votes 1,186; Total votes 36,775

The Majlis Ittehad-ul-Muslimin is not recognized as a party by the Election Commission. Therefore the Majlis candidates are officially listed as Independent candidates.

Muslim: 451,000 in a population of 1,251,119;[1] they constitute about one-fifth of the Muslim population of the state of Andhra Pradesh.

This pattern had a strong impact on electoral politics during the 1967 campaign, resulting in an unusually large number of Muslim candidates, the rise of a local Muslim party, the Majlis Ittehad-ul-Muslimin, and the prominence of communal issues.

The seven constituencies to be analysed here (see Table 1) cover the old town of Hyderabad south of the river Musi (Charminar, Yakutpura, Malakpet, Sitarambagh) and the city's commercial centres (Maharajganj, and a part of Charminar). The Asifnagar constituency comprises an upper class residential area and two densely populated, predominantly Muslim wards; the Musheerabad constituency is in a newly developed region which includes an industrial area as well as the campus of Osmania University. In five of these constituencies (in all except

[1] For a more detailed discussion of the socio-economic structure of Hyderabad see: R. A. Khan, 'Social and economic features of Hyderabad', manuscript to be published within the research project mentioned on p. 137, n. 3); G. Haberland, *Gross-Haiderabad, Wachstum und Wandel einer indischen Stadt*, Hamburg 1960, particularly pp. 76–8; Shah Manzoor Alam, *Hyderabad-Secunderabad (twin-cities), A study in urban geography*, Bombay 1965, particularly chapters 1 and 5.

Musheerabad and Malakpet) the percentage of the Muslim population is above average, between 50 and 60 per cent, in one ward (no. 17 of the Yakutpura constituency) even 73 per cent. Three constituencies include rural areas: Malakpet, Sitarambagh, and Asifnagar. 452,562 voters are registered in these seven constituencies, about two-thirds of the voters of Hyderabad-Secunderabad.[1]

Six parties and a number of Independent candidates contested for one or several of these seven seats. Only the Congress Party nominated candidates in all the seven constituencies. At the previous elections the Congress Party had won all but one seat in Hyderabad-Secunderabad and the aim of this party for the 1967 general elections was to win in all the eleven constituencies. However factional strife shook the Congress Party on the eve of the general elections 1967. A dramatic regrouping of the factions had taken place in the summer of 1966, from which a 'dissident' faction emerged under the leadership of N. Sanjivah Reddy, the former Chief Minister (then minister in the Central Cabinet, later Speaker of the *Lokh Sabha*), and his former enemy Sanjiviah, the Harijan leader (then also a minister in the Central Cabinet), against a 'ministerialist' faction around Sanjivah Reddy's former friend and protégé Brahmananda Reddy, the Chief Minister of Andhra Pradesh. The split not only affected the candidates but cut across the party organization in the town, blocking all efforts to conduct a planned and co-ordinated campaign throughout the city. The candidates could not always rely on local party leaders in their constituencies for loyal support. Four candidates (Asifnagar, Malakpet, Musheerabad, Yakutpura) were 'ministerialists' and three 'dissidents' (Charminar, Sitarambagh, and Maharajganj). The president of the City Congress Committee was a 'dissident'. Far from winning in all the seven constituencies, the Congress Party lost four, three to the Majlis and one to the S.S.P.

The Communist Party (Right) contested for only one seat in the city (two in 1962). Musheerabad. Here the Secretary General of the Andhra Pradesh Trade Union Congress, Satyanarayan Reddy, tried—unsuccessfully—to defeat the sitting M.L.A. and Secretary of the Congress-controlled Trade Union Congress (I.N.T.U.C.) in the state. The Left Communist Party decided not to nominate a candidate in Hyderabad.

The Jan Sangh Party, who had never won a seat in Andhra Pradesh before (it polled 1·04 per cent of the votes in 1962) nominated a strikingly large number of candidates in the state—eighty—and contested for five seats in Hyderabad. The five candidates were highly optimistic and expected to win at least three to four of these seats.

---

[1] Two of the four remaining constituencies of the 'twin-cities' are in Secunderabad, the former British cantonment, and two in a residential and in an industrial area.

Party leaders however admitted that the party's aim in nominating so many candidates was to build up and test its organization and to make the Jan Sangh better known in this part of Southern India. Unlike the Congress Party, the Jan Sangh ran a well-planned campaign through-out Hyderabad. Their candidates had been given a training in cam-paigning techniques and in the discussion of ideological and political issues. A city organizer kept in daily contact with all five candidates, and their public meetings and processions were co-ordinated. The Jan Sangh did not win a seat in Hyderabad, but improved its percentage of the votes considerably.

The Majlis Ittehad-ul-Muslimin[1] is a Muslim Party confined to Hyderabad. It was founded as a cultural-religious organization in 1926; its offspring, the Razakar movement, opposed the Communists during the Telengana uprisings and the Indian Army at the time of the Police Action. Only in 1960 was the movement reformed into a political party and it succeeded in winning one seat at the 1962 general elections. In 1967 it contested for the five constituencies with a majority of Muslim population and won three, two more than in 1962. It is remarkable that this party was successful without massive financial support.

The S.S.P. has little strength in Hyderabad and Andhra Pradesh; it contested for three constituencies and won the Maharajganj seat in the business centre of Hyderabad. This was considered to be a personal success of the candidate rather than of the party.

Representatives of the Swatantra Party admitted that their party had not yet started to spread in Hyderabad. It nominated three candi-dates—some of whom had joined the party only just before the elec-tions—who all lost their deposits.

These six parties nominated between them twenty-four candidates; ten candidates contested as Independents.

I. AGE (see Table 2)

An analysis of the ages of these thirty-four candidates shows that none of them is below thirty, although politicians enter political life often at a much younger age. But there is also no candidate above the age of sixty; three are just sixty. Only four are in their fifties. The largest number of candidates are in their thirties, and among them ten are between thirty-five and forty, almost one-third of our sample. While these ten are fairly evenly distributed among all the parties and the

[1] H. Gray, 'Power and politics in Hyderabad', Ph.D. thesis, London 1965, pp. 23–5; Alam S. Khundmiri, 'The Majlis Ittehad-ul-Muslimin', manuscript to be published within the research project mentioned on p. 137, n. 3), Theodore P. Wright, Jr., 'Revival of the Majlis Ittehad-ul-Muslimin', *The Muslim World*, vol. 53, no. 3, 1963.

Independents, it is striking that there is no Congress candidate among the group between thirty and thirty-five years of age. Two of the four candidates in the age-group thirty to thirty-five belong to the Jan Sangh, one to the Majlis, and one is an Independent. Four of the five Jan Sangh candidates are below forty, whereas four of the seven Congress candidates are above forty-five. This may indicate that it takes a young man longer in the Congress Party to reach the stage when he is given a ticket than in other parties. The fact that the Jan Sangh put up mainly young candidates supports an observation made all over India that this traditionalist party tries to and does appeal not only to the older but to the younger generation as well.

Table 2. *Ages of the candidates*

	Total	Congr.	C.P.I.	J.S.	Majlis	Swat.	S.S.P.	Indep.
Under 30	—	—	—	—	—	—	—	—
30–34	4	—	—	2	1	—	—	1
35–39	10	3	1	2	1	—	2	1
40–44	4	—	—	—	1	—	—	3
45–49	8	1	—	—	1	1	1	4
50–59	4	2	—	—	—	1	—	1
60	3	1	—	1	1	—	—	—
Over 60	—	—	—	—	—	—	—	—
No information	1	—	—	—	—	1	—	—
Total no. of candidates	34	7	1	5	5	3	3	10

It is remarkable that eight of the ten Independent candidates are above forty. A look at their political biographies reveals that most of them have been members of a political party and left it. These defections are not confined to the Congress Party, but this group contains disgruntled former members of the S.S.P. and the Majlis Ittehad-ul-Muslimin as well. On the other hand it is unlikely that a young man could have enough personal following to be a successful Independent candidate.

2. RELIGION (see Table 3)

In view of the religious composition of these seven constituencies it is not surprising that only half of the candidates (seventeen) are Hindus and half non-Hindus, namely fifteen Muslims (four Shias and eleven Sunnis), one Christian and one Sikh. Muslim candidates are the obvious choice for the Majlis Ittehad-ul-Muslimin, but the Congress Party too took these communal aspects into consideration and nominated Muslims in the constituencies with a Muslim majority.

The Jan Sangh did contest for the Muslim majority constituencies, but with Hindu candidates, hoping for a split of the Muslim votes among the Majlis and the Congress Party and for victory on the basis of the Hindu votes. In Hyderabad the Jan Sangh refrained from nominating Muslims as it did in some areas to counteract criticism directed at this party's communal bias. Also half of the Independent candidates are Muslims, two are former members of the Majlis. Three out of these five, however, stood in the Maharajganj constituency, where the Majlis was not on the scene. These Muslim Independents were not very successful at the polls: four of them received less than 500 votes. The high percentage of Muslims among the candidates suggests that there is certainly no lack of effort on the part of Muslims to represent their community in the State Assembly, but their performance at the polls also shows that the Muslim community does not stand solidly behind one party.

Table 3. *Religions of the candidates*

	Total	Congr.	C.P.I.	J.S.	Majlis	Swat.	S.S.P.	Indep.
Hindu	17	3	1	5	—	1	3	4
Muslim	15	4	—	—	5	1	—	5
Christian	1	—	—	—	—	—	—	1
Sikh	1	—	—	—	—	1	—	—
Total no. of candidates	34	7	1	5	5	3	3	10

The Sikh candidate was a retired lieutenant-colonel of the Indian Army, who had joined the Swatantra Party a few months before the elections and hoped—in vain—to win the votes of the ex-servicemen in his constituency. The Christian candidate was a thirty-eight-year-old masseur who had resigned from the Congress Party and contested as an Independent.

Four Hindu candidates (Table 4) were Brahmins, of which two belonged to the Jan Sangh. Only two candidates belong to the caste which so successfully preserved their traditional dominance in the rural power structure through the medium of modern politics: the Reddis. For obvious reasons Reddis are less numerous and less powerful in the city than in rural areas. Satyanarayan Reddy was the only C.P.I. candidate mentioned above, a Trade Union leader, who has emancipated himself from his family background. The other Reddy, Mrs Sarojini Pulla Reddy, was a Congress candidate, a municipal corporator and a former mayor of Hyderabad, who was elected from Malakpet, a partly urban and partly rural constituency. Two more Reddis had originally filed their nominations but retired in the course of the campaign, one in favour of Sarojini Pulla Reddy, one in favour of D. Goswami in the Sitarambagh constituency.

Three candidates belong to Vaishya castes, two Banyas and one Marwari. The two Banyas—an S.S.P. candidate and a Congress candidate—fought against each other in the Maharajganj constituency, the commercial centre of Hyderabad, which is considered to have a large Vaishya population. The Marwari contested on a Jan Sangh ticket in the heart of the town, the Charminar constituency. The majority of voters in this constituency are Muslims, but there is also a settlement of Hindu traders around the business centre of old Hyderabad. This candidate, although making efforts to win Muslim votes, clearly aimed at the support of his fellow caste-men and his co-religionists, successfully so, as he polled 10,402 votes, more than the Muslim Congress candidate.

Table 4. *Caste-wise break-up of the Hindu candidates*

		Total	Congr.	C.P.I.	J.S.	Majlis	Swat.	S.S.P.	Indep.
Brahmin		4	—	—	2	—	1	1	—
Kayasth		1	—	—	—	—	—	—	1
Vaishya		3	1	—	1	—	—	1	—
Gosai		1	—	—	—	—	—	1	—
Reddy		2	1	1	—	—	—	—	—
Naidu	Shudras	1	—	—	—	—	—	—	1
Munnur Kapu		1	—	—	1	—	—	—	—
Kammari		1	—	—	—	—	—	—	1
Gowd		2	1	—	—	—	—	—	1
No information		1	—	—	1	—	—	—	—
Total no. of candidates		17	3	1	5	—	1	3	4

Two candidates belong to castes which are not numerous in Andhra Pradesh. One is a Kayasth, whose family migrated from U.P. He contested for the Yakutpura constituency as an Independent, but in spite of the support he received from the C.P.I. (Right) he won only 997 votes. These votes may be interpreted as coming from secular-minded intellectuals in protest against the communal tinge of the campaign in this constituency. More successful was the other outsider, D. Goswami, a Gosai, who fought the elections for the S.S.P. in the Sitarambagh constituency. The main contest in this partly rural constituency was between a candidate of the Majlis and a Congress Muslim. The Majlis candidate won, but Sri Goswami received more votes than the Congress candidate. Also in this constituency the election campaign was dominated by communal issues and it can be safely assumed that this candidate paradoxically received the votes of the traditionalist Hindus (there was no Jan Sangh candidate in this constituency) and the secular-minded people from all communities as well, since he was known for his modernist views. Moreover he is a municipal corporator and claimed to have a personal following in his municipal constituency even among Muslims.

Given the peculiar caste structure of Andhra Pradesh,[1] the majority of the candidates belong to high castes. Strictly speaking, there are no Kshatriyas in A.P., but the *sat-shudra* peasant-proprietor castes of the Reddis, Kammas and Velamas claim Kshatriya status and rank high in secular terms. Two candidates belong to castes ranking slightly below the Reddis, a Munnur Kapu (a Jan Sangh candidate) and a Naidu (an Independent), but only two candidates belong to a low-ranking *shudra* caste, the Gowd (toddy tappers). One of them was elected from the Musheerabad constituency; the other, a *sarpanch* in the rural area of Malakpet, lost, but received a fair number of votes (6,991). Only one member of the scheduled castes filed a nomination, but retired later in favour of D. Goswami.

This break-up according to caste does not indicate an alignment between parties and certain castes—except perhaps in the case of the two Brahmins, contesting for the Jan Sangh. Since in four of the seven constituencies the crucial fight was between Muslims of different parties or between Hindus and Muslims, it is hardly relevant to correlate the electoral performance of these candidates with their caste backgrounds. Neither is there any sign of a war between different castes. I suggest that those Hindus who were either elected or polled a number of votes close to the elected candidate owed this to a combination of their party alignment and personal qualifications rather than to their caste membership. However, it is interesting to note that there are so few low caste candidates, considering that 12 per cent of the population of Hyderabad-Secunderabad belongs to the scheduled castes. This indicates that still—even in the city—few members of the low castes have an educational or financial background sufficient to carry out an election campaign (Secunderabad-Cantonment is a reserved constituency, thus one of the eleven M.L.A.s from Hyderabad-Secunderabad belongs to the scheduled castes).

---

[1] The caste-ranking is based on: H. Gray, 'Power and politics in Hyderabad', pp. 18–29; E. Kulke, 'Die allgemeinen Wahlen 1967 in Nalgonda, einem ländlichen Distrikt Andhra Pradeshs', manuscript to be published within the project mentioned on p. 137 n. 3), p. 5; cf. S. C. Dube, 'Ranking of castes in Telangana villages', *Eastern Anthropologist*, vol. 8, no. 3, 4, 1955.

3. LANGUAGES

A look at the language qualifications of these candidates reveals that almost all of them are proficient in several languages. Sixteen candidates listed Urdu as their mother-tongue, namely the fifteen Muslim candidates and the Kayasth from U.P. Thus the proportion of Urdu-speaking candidates corresponds roughly to the proportion of Urdu-speaking voters.

Although Telugu is spoken by 46·68 per cent[1] of the population of Hyderabad, only thirteen candidates considered this language to be their mother-tongue; four named Hindi and one candidate Punjabi. It is a reflexion of the polyglot character of Hyderabad that twenty-eight candidates speak more than one language;[2] five of them even know four languages. Only three candidates do not speak English at all; one of them (the Christian candidate of Musheerabad), however, speaks two Indian languages. Fifteen candidates speak their mother-tongue and English, two their mother-tongue and one Indian language, eleven speak more than two languages. Six of these know their mother-tongue, English and a second Indian language, five English and three Indian languages. While ten of sixteen candidates whose mother-tongue is not Urdu do in fact speak this language, only four of the candidates with Urdu as their mother-tongue also speak Telugu or any other Indian language. This is indicative of a persisting cultural pride on the part of the Urdu speakers and shows that Urdu is still largely a *lingua franca* in Hyderabad. Only six candidates speak no Urdu at all. One of these is the Sarpanch and Independent candidate in the rural part of the Malakpet constituency, the other five are all Jan Sangh candidates.[3] It is no wonder that the representatives of Hyderabadi Muslim culture feel threatened by this party.

4. EDUCATION (see Table 5)

It is often said that Indian candidates need first of all the capacity to raise large financial resources for their election campaigns. Our analysis suggests however that many more capabilities are necessary. In a multilingual area like Hyderabad it seems essential to be a polyglot. An analysis of the educational backgrounds of our candidates points in this direction too.

Only one candidate, the Sarpanch and Independent candidate for

---

[1] R. A. Khan, 'Social and economic features of Hyderabad', p. 4.
[2] Exact information on the second languages of five candidates was not available.
[3] It is possible that these Jan Sangh candidates do speak Urdu, but did not say so for ideological reasons.

the rural part of Malakpet, is illiterate (see Table 4), but almost one-third of the candidates have a university education. None, however, studied abroad.

Five candidates received a non-western education, a Jan Sangh, a Majlis and three Independent candidates. They are also among the oldest candidates: two are sixty and two between fifty and sixty years of age, only one is thirty-eight years old. Two out of the three candidates, who do not know English, belong to this group. Three are Muslims, two of them obtained a Diploma of Munshi Fazil (Oriental learning) and both are now journalists. The Majlis candidate for the Yakutpura constituency (who was elected) learned *unani* (traditional) medicine and practises as a *hakim*. The only Christian candidate and the youngest in this group was trained by his father, an *ayurvedic* doctor and by a *Guru*. He runs what he calls a 'Scientific Massage Centre' and likes to be addressed as 'Professor'.

Table 5. *Education of the candidates*

	Total	Congr.	C.P.I.	J.S.	Majlis	Swat.	S.S.P.	Indep.
Illiterate	1	—	—	—	—	—	—	1
Traditional Education	5	—	—	1	1	—	—	3
Elementary School	8	4	—	—	3	—	—	1
B.A.	9	1	—	4	—	—	1	3
M.A.	2	1	—	—	—	—	—	1
Interrupted University Education	2	1	1	—	—	—	—	—
Other Diplomas	3	—	—	—	—	—	2	1
Military Training	1	—	—	—	—	1	—	—
No Information	3	—	—	—	1	2	—	—
Total no. of candidates	34	7	1	5	5	3	3	10

Eight candidates went to the elementary school but only five matriculated. Also two of the thirteen university-educated interrupted their studies and did not obtain degrees. Three received Master's degrees, nine Bachelor's degrees, three two Bachelor's degrees. One candidate holds a diploma of engineering, two a diploma of a Hindi academy, one was trained as a military officer. Including these diploma holders, seventeen candidates—half of our sample—received a higher education and thus belong to a very small stratum in Indian society. It is remarkable that no graduate of a foreign university was tempted to contest the election in these constituencies. There is no holder of a degree higher than the M.A. As mentioned before, five candidates did not complete their school or university studies. However the repercussions of the Independence struggle and the post-war years were responsible for such interruptions in the education of these candidates.

A correlation of the educational qualifications and the party membership of candidates shows a fairly even distribution of educated and little-educated over all parties. It is remarkable that, while four out of the five Jan Sangh candidates hold B.A. degrees, no Majlis candidate is university-educated. In spite of the fact that the majority of the voters have little or no education at all, candidates with a university education tend to stress their degree and mention it on posters and hand-bills and in the slogans disfiguring every wall at election time.

5. OCCUPATIONS (see Table 6)

By far the largest professional group among our sample are businessmen (eight), closely followed by journalists. Although during the early period modern Indian politics were dominated by lawyers, only four candidates came from this profession. As mentioned earlier, two candidates practise traditional medicine—one *unani* and one *ayurvedic* medicine—two are farmers (in the constituency of Malakpet), one housewife, an army officer and an engineer.

A number of professions are conspicuous by their absence: school and university teachers, scientists, architects etc. Not only teachers but nowadays also a large number of scientists and engineers are civil servants, who need permission to take an active part in politics and contest elections. Therefore they are automatically excluded from the political elite. Graduates from foreign universities often belong to this group. Whereas it is not surprising that businessmen can apparently easily find time—and funds—to contest, the large number of journalists may be a reflexion of the unstable situation of this profession.

I have termed a group of five candidates professional politicians.[1] These are persons who have not exercised any other profession for ten years or longer and who are given other political appointments if they lose an election. The two youngest members of this group (Owaisi and Mrs Sarojini Pulla Reddy) have never had any other occupation. Significantly, four of these five are in the Congress Party, the only party in Andhra Pradesh so far which has offered sufficient scope for professional politicians. Four (not the same four) are members of the

---

[1] Béteille considers only professional politicians as belonging to the 'political elite'. See A. Béteille, 'Elites, status groups, and caste in modern India', in *India and Ceylon, Unity and Diversity* (edited by Ph. Mason), London 1967, p. 224.

outgoing Legislative Assembly, three for the Congress and one for the Majlis. Two candidates of this group lost the election (both Congress candidates), two were re-elected and one was elected for the first time.

Apart from the concentration of professional politicians in the Congress Party and the fact that three out of five Jan Sangh candidates are businessmen, hardly any relationship can be found between the parties and their candidates' occupations. But in some cases the candidate's profession corresponds to the prevalent occupation in the constituency. Thus two candidates in the Musheerabad constituency (an industrial area) are professional Trade Union leaders, the other three have been active in the Trade Union movement at one time or the other. Four of the seven candidates in the Maharajganj constituency are businessmen.

Table 6. *Occupations of the candidates*

	Total	Congr.	C.P.I.	J.S.	Majlis	Swat.	S.S.P.	Indep.
Businessman	8	1	—	3	1	—	2	1
Journalist	6	—	—	1	1	—	1	3
Lawyer	4	1	—	1	—	—	—	2
Professional politician	5	4	—	—	1	—	—	—
Trade-unionist	2	1	1	—	—	—	—	—
Army officer	1	—	—	—	—	1	—	—
Traditional medicine	2	—	—	—	1	—	—	1
Farmer	2	—	—	—	1	—	—	1
Housewife	1	—	—	—	—	1	—	—
Engineer	1	—	—	—	—	—	—	1
Unemployed	1	—	—	—	—	—	—	1
No Information	1	—	—	—	—	1	—	—
Total no. of candidates	34	7	1	5	5	3	3	10

6. SOCIAL MOBILITY

A discussion of social mobility is hampered by the difficulty in obtaining information on the occupations of the candidates' fathers. Only for two-thirds of our sample was it possible to collect the pertinent data. A comparison of the occupations of these twenty-one candidates with the occupations of their fathers shows that only in a few cases inter-generational mobility has taken place. Nine candidates work in the same profession as their fathers; six businessmen are sons of businessmen, the two farmers sons of farmers. A group of five have professions different from their fathers, but remain in the same social class. The army officer is the son of a translator at Osmania University, the father of one of the journalists was an officer in the Nizam's bodyguard, another journalist is the son of a *tahsildar*.

Only four of the twenty-one candidates have risen to occupational positions higher than their fathers: an M.L.A. and Trade Union leader is the son of an agricultural labourer, an engineer the son of a skilled worker. One of the lawyers and one of the 'professional politicians' are sons of (non-graduate) government employees.

Three candidates (out of the total of thirty-four) are descendants of the traditional elite, who have moved into the political elite, even into the ruling elite. Mir Ahmed Ali Khan, the Home Minister at the time of the elections, belongs to the Hyderabadi Muslim nobility, Mrs S. Pulla Reddy and the C.P.I. candidate for Musheerabad, Satyanarayan Reddy, hail from landowning families of one of the dominant agricultural castes. While the Muslim nobility has lost importance after the integration of Hyderabad into the Indian Union,[1] the rural landowning elite is still powerful. Two candidates belong to the business elite of Hyderabad: the S.S.P. and the Congress candidates for the Maharajganj constituency. Apart from these five candidates all others belong to the urban middle class by education and family background or by personal achievement.

Considering that only five candidates out of thirty-four are linked with established elites, I think it is justifiable to conclude that this sample of a political elite represents a new elite, risen from the middle class to the echelon in the political elite where they are nominated as candidates for the general elections (five candidates are sitting M.L.A.s and several have contested the general elections before). Politics do provide a channel for social mobility, but quick careers are rare.

7. THE POLITICAL BIOGRAPHIES OF THE CANDIDATES

A look at the length and nature of the candidates' association with politics shows that most of them have been active in politics for a long time, starting early in their lives.

Eleven candidates—almost one-third of our sample—were members of political movements or parties before the Police Action,[2] nineteen entered politics after 1948, but seven of these before the 1957 general elections. Six started their political activities in 1957 or between the second and third general elections, three in 1962. Only three candidates have joined the race since the last general elections. One of them, a

---

[1] Particularly after the Jagir abolition regulations of 1949. See H. Gray, 'Power and politics in Hyderabad', p. 19.

[2] For Hyderabad 1948, the year of the integration into the Indian Union, serves as a historical landmark.

48-year-old Independent candidate in Sitarambagh, was however a member of the Jamiat-ul-ulema-e-Hind (a non-party, pro-Congress congregation of learned Muslims).

The only two real newcomers are the Jan Sangh candidate for the Maharajganj constituency, M. Hanumanth Rao, and the Congress candidate for the Malakpet constituency, Mrs Sarojini Pulla Reddy. Both are thirty-five years of age and have been municipal councillors since 1964. Shri Hanumanth Rao lost, but Shrimati Pulla Reddy won, and is one of the few examples of a 'lightning' political career. She joined the Congress Party in 1963, contested and won the Municipal elections 1964, became mayor of Hyderabad from 1965 to 1966, received a Congress 'ticket' in 1967 and was elected to the Legislative Assembly. She owes this success to a combination of good looks and good rhetoric, an efficient organization of her campaign and support from prominent politicians on national and state level.

So far I have analysed the political biographies of the candidates in the perspective of the political history of Hyderabad. An analysis in the perspective of their personal lives is equally relevant. Seven candidates claim to have entered politics before the age of twenty (mostly as student leaders). Eleven said they started in their twenties, nine in their thirties. Only three became politicians after the age of forty. Remembering that only five candidates were sitting M.L.A.s and that no candidate is below thirty—the average age is just over forty—it is obvious that most candidates started their political lives a long time before they were nominated.

8. CONCLUSIONS

These thirty-four candidates represent a new elite which is not linked to the established elites. However they belong to a small stratum in Indian society, to the educated middle class, and half of them received a higher education. By education and occupation none of them can be considered as belonging to the lower classes. Yet 50 per cent of the population of Hyderabad is still illiterate. No candidate is from a scheduled caste, but a few belong to lower Shudra castes.

Politics provide a channel for social mobility, but the climb is slow. One-third of our sample was active in politics before 1948, for more than twenty years, and only twelve entered politics during the last decade. Considering that for an ambitious politician membership of the Legislative Assembly is only one stage in his career, we must conclude that there is little circulation among this elite.

M. N. ROY AND RADICAL HUMANISM: THE IDEOLOGY OF AN INDIAN INTELLECTUAL ELITE

D. G. DALTON

The aim of this chapter is to examine certain ideas of M. N. Roy as they evolved from his Marxist to radical humanist phases. The analysis will be concerned with the relationship of these ideas to those of three other Indian thinkers, Swami Vivekananda, Sri Aurobindo, and Mahatma Gandhi. It is hoped that this analysis will illustrate the significance of Roy's thought for a general study of ideology in modern India: that is, for a study of articulated attitudes, values, and presuppositions about man in society. Radical humanism, which is synonymous with the mature political and social thought of M. N. Roy, will be considered here as the ideology of an intellectual elite. For this purpose, the paper will focus on three concepts, freedom, power and leadership. These themes have been selected as central to Roy's thought and also because they provide convenient points of comparison with Vivekananda, Aurobindo and Gandhi.

M. N. Roy's thought, like the ideological tradition of modern India itself, is characterized by elements of continuity and innovation. In order to understand radical humanism as Roy's mature phase of thought, some understanding of the earlier nature and evolution of Roy's ideas is essential. The first part of this paper will accordingly be directed to this aim. At least four major phases of Roy's thought may be distinguished. The first of these begins at the turn of this century, with Roy as a young terrorist in Bengal under the personal leadership of Jatin Mukherjee and the intellectual influence of Vivekananda. It ends with Roy's conversion to Marxism in 1919. The second stage of his thought covers his active career as a devout Communist; this begins in Mexico and ends in India with his imprisonment in 1931. The third phase can be seen as a period of transition. It includes Roy's six critical years in prison, his brief flirtation with the Indian Congress, and his subsequent formation of the Radical Democratic Party (R.D.P.), in opposition to the Congress. The final phase of his thought provides the main source of the present study. It extends from Roy's transformation of the R.D.P. into the Radical Humanist Movement in 1948 until Roy's death in January 1954.

Roy remained throughout much of his life, and particularly during his Marxist phase, alienated from the Indian nationalist tradition.[1] This alienation was not concealed; it was outspoken and vehement. His Marxist writings, beginning in the early 1920s, are crammed with diatribes against India's 'much vaunted spiritualist tradition', her 'reactionary ideology' of Gandhism, and most of her political leaders.[2] On the basis of this open alienation, the orthodox interpretation of Roy's life and thought has seen him as a thoroughly de-nationalized emigre, significant chiefly for his contribution as a revolutionary Marxist. One Indian analyst regards Roy as 'the Indian Edward Bernstein' and he believes that the 'tragedy of M. N. Roy was that...he failed to strike roots in Indian society'.[3] This interpretation either ignores Roy's radical humanism altogether, or treats it as the discursive ramblings of a Marxist who has at last gone off the rails. The argument of this chapter will not be in accord with this interpretation. It will be suggested here that, while Roy was without roots in Indian nationalist politics, he nevertheless remained deeply grounded in Indian culture as a whole. Indeed, it was the very depth of these roots that led Roy, after his excursions into Marxism, back to a way of thinking which has much in common with Vivekananda, Aurobindo, and Gandhi. The thought and culture of the Indian nationalist tradition and the type of intellectual experience it nurtured, was a complex blend of structure and change, challenge, response and counter-response. From this cultural complex more than from anything else, Roy, as a youth in nationalist Bengal, recieved his early and decisive orientation.

I. ROY AND NATIONALISM IN BENGAL

Towards the end of his life Roy reflected on the early sources of his attitudes and those values that had guided his thought:

When as a boy of fourteen, I began my political life, which may end in nothing, I wanted to be free...In those days, we had not read Marx. We did not know about the existence of the proletariat. Still, many spent their lives in jail and went to the gallows. There was no proletariat to propel them.

[1] The term 'Indian nationalist tradition' will refer, throughout the chapter to the *ideological* tradition of nineteenth- and twentieth-century India; that is, to that common stock of myths and symbols, attitudes and ideas that have developed in India since Rammohun Roy and are found particularly in the thought of Vivekananda, Aurobindo, and Gandhi. For clarification of my own conception of the Indian ideolgical tradition since Rammohun Roy see D. G. Dalton, 'The Idea of Freedom in the Political Thought of Vivekananda, Aurobindo, Gandhi and Tagore', Ph.D. thesis (unpublished), University of London, 1965.

[2] M. N. Roy, *India's Message* (*Fragments of a Prisoner's Diary*, vol. II) (Calcutta: Renaissance Pub., 1950) second revised edition, p. 149.

[3] V. P. Varma, *Modern Indian Political Thought* (Agra: Lakshmi Narain Agarwal, 1961) p. 659–61.

They were not conscious of class struggle. They did not have the dream of Communism. But they had the human urge to revolt against the intolerable conditions of life...I began my political life with that spirit, and I still draw my inspiration rather from that spirit than from the three volumes of Capital or three-hundred volumes by the Marxists.[1]

Roy was born into an orthodox Brahmin family in a village near Calcutta in 1886. Bengal had already established itself as the centre of that flowering of thought and literature which later historians would call 'The Indian Renaissance'. For it was there, in this very decade, that Bankim Chandra Chatterjee was publishing his influential periodical, *Bengal Darsan*, and writing his renowned novels, notably *Anandamath* in 1882. Near Calcutta, too, a young University student, Narendra Nath Datta, soon to become Vivekananda, was frequenting a Kali temple on the Ganges to sit at the feet of an illiterate *bhakta*, Ramakrishna Paramahamsa. Educated Indians were speaking in enraptured tones of Keshub Chunder Sen's oratory, with reverence of Devendranath Tagore's saintly example, and Rammohun Roy's achievements were already passing into legend. Late nineteenth-century Bengal fostered a climate of opinion, an intense atmosphere of ideas and sentiments, that dominated India well into this century. The influence which it had upon those young revolutionary intellectuals growing up in its midst was immense. It was this early influence that set the pattern of M. N. Roy's political and social thought, in terms of explaining its underlying presuppositions, the way in which it developed, and to some extent its final form.

Roy begins his *Memoirs* abruptly with the year 1914, and biographical accounts are scarcely more informative about his first, and undoubtedly formative, twenty-eight years. This untold story, however, pieced together from various sources,[2] appears to be as follows. His father was a

[1] Roy, *New Orientation* (Calcutta: Renaissance, 1946) p. 183.
[2] Biographical sources include the following for Roy's early period:
   (a) Interviews with numerous figures in India both inside and out of the Radical Humanist Movement. The most helpful for this early period were with Aloke Nath Chakravarty (tape-recorded interview in Calcutta in May 1967) and K. K. Sinha (interview and response to questionnaire in Calcutta in May 1967). The former source was one of Roy's younger associates in the terrorist movement under Jatin Mukherjee. He stressed the influence on Roy of Jatin and Vivekananda and outlined Roy's religious affiliations at that time. The latter, Mr Sinha, was kind enough to make a lengthy written reply to my questionnaire, and to discuss points raised about Roy's early period in some detail.
   (b) Government of India Records: Statement (confession) of Fanindra Kumar Chakravarty in Simla Records 2. Government of India, Home Department Political-A. Proceedings January 1917, Nos. 299–301 & K. W. Mr Chakravarty reports that in 1911, after release from the 'Howrah Gang Case', 'Noren' (Roy) 'decided to become a sannyasi', and visited Banares. It appears that Roy did this more to escape the police than out of religious conviction.
   (c) Political Report: James Campbell Ker, I.C.S. (from 1907 to 1913 Personal Assistant

priest and a schoolteacher, who, as Roy himself remarked, 'spent his life in teaching Sanskrit to would-be clerks or prospective lawyers'.[1] Roy received his primary education in his village school, and then joined the National University founded by Aurobindo Ghose; he soon withdrew, however, to become committed, while still in his teens, to the Bengali extremist movement. From 1906 to 1914, Roy was implicated in a series of revolutionary offences, the major one being the Howrah Conspiracy Case of 1910, which led to an imprisonment of twenty months before acquittal for lack of evidence. During this time, moreover, he seems to have held strong religious beliefs, particularly in Vaishnavism, and while in prison he became engrossed in religious texts. On release, he rejoined the terrorist movement and rose quickly to become one of its bright young lights. Two influences were critical at this time. First, there was the intellectual impact of Vivekananda, whose speeches on *Karma Yoga*, *The Mission of the Vedanta* and *The Work Before Us* were avidly studied by Roy's circle. These provided a key source of his ideological inspiration. The other influence was a personal one. Soon after Roy joined the movement in 1906, Aurobindo Ghose became a power in it, but Aurobindo retired from politics to Pondicherry in 1909 and Roy never developed a personal relationship with him. Roy did become intimate with one of Aurobindo's successors, Jatin Mukherjee, who became the 'Commander and Chief of Staff' of the Bengali Revolutionaries. 'Jatinda' was a devout Hindu and a daring terrorist whose use of violence against the Raj led to his untimely execution in 1915. The personal influence which Jatin exercised on Roy lasted throughout his life. In his *Memoirs* Roy recalls that Jatin was 'the only man I ever obeyed almost blindly...I admired Jatinda because he personified the best of mankind.'[2] Following Jatin's orders, Roy left India on a revolutionary mission in early 1915; he was not to return until 1930.

In sum, one may discriminate at least three important elements in Roy's youthful experience in Bengal. First, there was his apparently happy childhood in a Brahmin family, his father a Sanskrit *pandit*. The

to the Director of Criminal Intelligence), *Political Trouble in India, 1907–1917* (Calcutta: Superintendent of Government Printing India, 1917) p. 400. See especially report on Norenda Nath Bhattacharji alias C. A. Martin.

(*d*) Periodicals and books: Various issues of *The Radical Humanist*, especially 7 Feb. 1954 and 25 Jan. 1956; biographical sketches in *Memoirs* (Intro. and Epilogue) by G. D. Parikh and V. B. Karnik; M. N. Roy, *Letters from Jail* (Calcutta: Renaissance, 1943); Niranjan Dhar, *The Political Thought of M. N. Roy* (Calcutta: Eureka Publishers, 1966) Introduction; Ramyansu S. Das, *M. N. Roy, The Humanist Philosopher* (Calcutta: Tower Publishers, 1956); A. K. Hindi, *M. N. Roy, The Man Who Looked Ahead* (Ahmedabad: Modern Publishing House, 1938); Gene D. Overstreet and Marshall Windmiller, *Communism in India* (Berkeley and Los Angeles: Univ. of California Press, 1959); Sibnarayan Ray(ed.) *M. N. Roy, Philosopher-Revolutionary* (Calcutta: Renaissance, 1959).

[1] Roy, *Memoirs* (London: Allen and Unwin, 1964) p. 567.   [2] *Ibid.* pp. 35–6.

Brahmanical outlook on life, which is so congenial to an elitist view of society, remained with Roy until the end, influencing in particular his theory of leadership. The second element appears in his marked receptiveness to the general ideological and religious climate of Bengal; that is, his acceptance of Vaishnavism, his attraction to Vivekananda, and his strong commitment to nationalism and terrorism. Finally, there was his active involvement in the revolutionary movement under the lasting personal influence of Jatin Mukherjee.

2. ROY AND MARXISM

When Michael Borodin baptized Roy into Marxism in 1919, Roy came from Indian nationalism to the new faith with the zeal commonly found amongst fresh converts. 'Marxism is a wonderful philosophy, is it not?' he exclaimed to a fellow Comrade in 1923. 'It has made of history such an exact science.'[1] Roy's first major work, *India in Transition* (1922), attempted to apply this 'exact science' in orthodox Marxist fashion to an analysis of British imperialism and Indian nationalism. For Roy it was evident that 'It is only the philosophy of Historic Materialism and the programme of Marxism, Socialism, that can show the way out.'[2] When an Indian Comrade expressed mild qualms over 'Bolshevism', Roy snapped back, 'Let me be brutally frank and tell you openly that the salvation of India lies through Bolshevism'.[3] Nowhere in Roy's early Marxist polemics does one find a hint of his later heresies. The Communist doctrines which he eventually repudiates are here vigorously employed in his analysis of Indian politics. In a tract of 1926, for example, Roy applies the Marxist theories of class struggle, dialectical materialism, economic determinism, and the proletarian revolution to establish the inevitability of a Communist conquest of India. The need of the masses is for revolutionary leadership and 'The Communist Party of India is called upon by history to play this role'.[4] This theoretical orthodoxy was matched in practice by a position of high status on the Comintern where Roy attained the height of his influence in 1926. Whether his subsequent decline and expulsion from the Comintern is attributed to Roy's own tactical blunders or Stalin's need for a scapegoat, it was certainly not as a result of any theoretical departure from Marxism. At least until 1931 when he entered his 'quiet country-town jail' in Cawnpore, Roy remained an orthodox Marxist.[5]

[1] Roy, *Political Letters* (Zurich: Vanguard Bookshop, 1924) p. 14.
[2] *Ibid.* p. 7.   [3] *Ibid.* p. 48.
[4] Roy, *The Aftermath of Non-Co-operation* (London: The Communist Party of Great Britain, 1926) pp. 13, 47.
[5] Roy, *Letters from Jail* (*Fragments of A Prisoner's Diary*, vol. III) (Calcutta: Renaissance, 1965) p. 1.

Roy was imprisoned for almost six consecutive years. Those who were closest to Roy have said that no experience had a more profound effect upon his thought than this. Pandit Nehru wrote of his own imprisonment that 'A person who was at all sensitive was in a continuous state of tension'.[1] Roy had plenty of sensitivity, but few of the special privileges accorded to prominent figures like Nehru. His *Letters From Jail* suggest the acute mental tension that he suffered as well as intolerable physical strain. An interesting sidelight on this experience and its impact on Roy's personality might perhaps be gleaned from Philip Spratt's 'Notes on jail psychology'.[2] Spratt, a British Communist in India, had a prison experience similar to Roy's. After his release, Spratt became one of Roy's close associates in the R.D.P. Spratt writes in these articles on jail psychology that a prolonged prison experience produces the effect of a 'psychological hothouse' where there is an overwhelming 'concentration of emotion upon the self'. This encourages latent elements of thought and feeling to rise and flourish through the stimulus of intense introspection. The element that flourishes best is man's 'urge towards religion'. Spratt regards jail as 'a forcing house for religion'; he relates that in his own case 'I had myself no religious belief, and had been very critical of religion, but I felt the force of its appeal.'

Roy did not experience in prison a mystical revelation like that claimed by his erstwhile Bengali leader, Aurobindo Ghose. Indeed the scorn which Roy pours on such 'revelations' in his essay 'Psychology of the Seer' (written in prison) would seem to make nonsense of any 'religious conversion' at this time. Yet, it remains true that a marked change in Roy's thought and personality did occur, and it may not be entirely wrong to see this change as a response to the sort of religious appeal which Spratt describes. One thing at least is certain: Roy's movement away from orthodox Marxism towards the foundations of radical humanism began in prison. The first clear sign of this shift appeared shortly after his release in the article 'Marxism is not a dogma'. First, this writing stresses the limitations of Marxism. New discoveries in science combined with those 'practical problems' and historical developments unforeseen by Marx establish the need to 'revise certain fundamental conceptions of classical Materialism'. 'The modern Marxist', Roy says, 'cannot follow literally the line predicted by Marx...we cannot say that developments here in India must necessarily follow the same line as Marx predicted for European developments.'[3] At this point, however,

[1] Jawaharlal Nehru, *Toward Freedom* (Autobiography) (Boston, Beacon Hill, 1961) p. 4.
[2] P. Spratt, 'Some notes on jail psychology', in *Modern Review*, June 1937, vol. LXI, no. 6, pp. 649–54, and July 1937, vol. LXII, no. 1, pp. 31–6.
[3] Roy, 'Marxism is not a dogma' in Roy and K. K. Sinha, *Royism Explained* (Calcutta: Saraswaty Press, 1938) pp. 22–3.

he insists that he remains nevertheless a Marxist and asserts the endur-
ing positive value of Marxism. He does this in a manner reminiscent of
Bengali reformers like Vivekananda who sought to reconstitute Hinduism by distinguishing between its 'spirit' and 'form'. Marxism, Roy
argues, is not a dogma, it is a 'philosophy of life'. As such, it is 'greater
than Communism', which is merely a particular 'phase of human
development'. Roy's aim now is to reinterpret Marxism as a liberal,
humanist philosophy. He discovers 'the essence of Marxism' in the idea
that Man is God, and therefore 'the master of history'. The old
emphasis upon economic determinism and historical inevitability have
disappeared; in their place is the view that 'the foundation of Marxism
is Rationalism' and the Marxist philosophy must be appreciated
together with its great heritage, the European Renaissance. The message
of Marxism for India is that the nation needs a 'Renaissance movement',
a 'philosophical revolution'.[1] This is the theme that is to develop
during the next decade, eventually providing one of the bases for
radical humanism. In 1947 Roy reflected back upon this critical
juncture in his thought and wrote: 'I still spoke as an orthodox Marxist
criticising deviations from or faulty understanding of the pure creed.
Nevertheless, the tendency to look beyond Communism was already
there in a germinal form.'[2] The nature and significance of this meta-
morphosis from Marxism to radical humanism will now be analysed
in the context of two major aspects of Roy's ideology, his conceptions of
freedom and of power.

3. ROY'S CONCEPTION OF FREEDOM

The use, in this discussion, of Roy's conceptions of freedom and power
is intended not only to illustrate the evolution of his thought, but also to
argue the close parallels which these two concepts ultimately developed
with the ideas of Vivekananda, Aurobindo, and Gandhi. The implication of this argument is not that these parallels emerged as a direct
result of the influence of these other thinkers. The point is rather that
the evolution of Roy's thought may be seen in terms of his continuing
response to the Indian nationalist tradition. And the broad implication
of this is that the ideological presuppositions of this tradition can be
analysed in the context of the similar way that Roy and the others
formulated their parallel views on freedom, power and leadership.

With Indian Marxists and Gandhi alike, Roy always asserted that
freedom meant more than political independence. India might gain her

---

[1] *Ibid.* pp. 23–5.
[2] Roy, *Scientific Politics* (Calcutta: Renaissance, 1947). Roy's Preface to the Second Edition,
p. vii.

independence from Britain, they all asserted, but freedom for the Indian people would not necessarily follow. However, there were two ways of interpreting this proposition. The Marxists contended that political independence did not equal freedom, since the latter involved economic rights and opportunities for the masses far beyond what mere political liberation from England implied. The Gandhians claimed to recognize the importance of economic reform, but they emphasized the 'moral' aspect of freedom. Gandhi thus preferred to use the term *swaraj*, which for him had two meanings: not only political independence but also (as he wrote as early as 1909) 'self-rule or self-control'.[1] This view of freedom in fact dominated the Indian nationalist tradition. Aurobindo often distinguished between 'internal' (moral) and 'external' (political and economic) freedom. Perhaps Vivekananda summed up the idea earliest and best whem he wrote at the close of the last century, 'One may gain political and social independence, but if one is a slave to his passions and desires, one cannot feel the pure joy of real freedom'.[2]

In 1937, Roy was much closer to the Marxist than the Gandhian view of freedom. In the very first issue of his weekly *Independent India*, Roy wrote, under the heading 'National Freedom', that 'Political independence is not the end, it is the means to an end which is radical transformation of the Indian society...The required change in the social structure of our country will be brought about primarily through the transfer of the ownership of land to the cultivator'; and, once this is attained, the transformation will be completed by 'a rapid growth of modern mechanized industry', the 'guarantee to the cultivator of... the entire product of his labour', the 'abolition of all privileges' and a wide and fair 'distribution of newly created wealth'.[3] This was the revolutionary programme, Roy believed, that would usher in 'real freedom'. At this point, then, Roy as a Marxist conceived of freedom and also social change in terms of sweeping economic reforms.

A fascinating aspect of Roy's thought may be seen in the way his conception of 'spiritual freedom' first appears, then co-exists for a decade with the 'materialist' view of freedom, and ultimately gains ascendancy to dominate the value-theory of the radical humanist period. As early as his *Fragments of a Prisoner's Diary*, we find Roy writing of the need for a new philosophy to 'indicate the way to real spiritual freedom'; a bit later he claimed that 'a true revolutionary is not ashamed of declaring that he is not fighting merely for wages... The revolution of our epoch will, for the first time, conquer spiritual

[1] M. K. Gandhi, *Hind Swaraj or Indian Home Rule* (Ahmedabad, Navajivan, 1938) p. 104.
[2] Swami Vivekananda, *The Complete Works*, 8 vols. (Calcutta: Advaita Ashrama, 1959) vol. V, p. 419.
[3] Roy, 'National Freedom', *Independent India*, 4 Apr. 1937.

freedom for humanity.'[1] And, as late as March 1945, Roy is holding forth the co-existent ideals of 'material and spiritual emancipation', although the emphasis at this time is clearly on political and economic rather than 'spiritual' or moral freedom. The decisive change in his thought was yet to occur.

In May 1946, the R.D.P. met in Dehra Dun for perhaps the most critical 'political study camp' of Roy's career. For Roy and his Party were meeting in the wake of two crucial events. The first was the complete defeat of the R.D.P. in the 1946 Spring elections. The Party had clearly been consigned to the political wilderness for at least the rest of Roy's life. The second event revolved around the direction of the world Communist movement, in India, Russia, and Eastern Europe. In his own country, Roy had long been under fierce attack from the Indian Communist Party; abroad, the ruthless ambitions of Stalin's dictatorship had become abundantly clear, and the result was Roy's profound disillusionment with Communism. The deep impact which the election experience and the direction of world Communism had upon Roy's thinking is amply illustrated throughout his lectures at the study camp. His indictment of the Indian election as 'fascist' is not surprising. What is noteworthy is that Communism is now grouped with fascism: they 'both sacrifice the individual on the altar of the collective ego'. 'Therefore, Communism has ceased to be an ideal which can inspire us and guide our steps in the march towards freedom.'[2] While Roy does distinguish between Communist practice and Marxist theory the association between them remains, and it is not long before Roy drops the distinction and develops the association.

The most striking development in Roy's thought seen in this volume of speeches (significantly entitled, *New Orientation*) does not appear with his attitude toward Communism, but rather in the unprecedented emphasis placed on the need for a 'moral philosophy', a 'philosophy of freedom', and a 'philosophical revolution' in India:

Human life must be guided by a philosophy. That philosophy may change from time to time. But there are certain values, certain principles, which transcend time and space...A philosophy, to be a guide for all forms of human action, must have some ethics, some morals, which must recognize certain things as permanent and abiding in humanity. And only a group of human beings—be it a political party or any other kind of organisation—primarily moved by those abiding (and I should say even permanent, as permanent as humanity itself) values, can claim to be the maker of the future...We must know what is freedom before we can be qualified as the architects of a free world. What the world needs is a philosophy of freedom.

[1] Roy, *India's Message*, p. 307, and *Scientific Politics*, p. 313.
[2] Roy, *New Orientation*, pp. 142-3.

The birth of the RDP was heralded by the declaration that India needs a philosophical revolution. Without a philosophical revolution, no social revolution is possible. We shall have to remember that.[1]

This passage suggests the nature of Roy's quest for 'permanent values' that characterized the radical humanist period. Marxism had now become of no help in this quest, and the extent of his departure from it is evident throughout the speeches. For example, he declares that the R.D.P. 'must be a party not of the economic man' but rather a 'party of moral men, moved by the ideal of human freedom'. Any connexion between the R.D.P. and a particular class is repudiated. The Party's allegiance can only be to the 'abiding values' of humanity, since 'ethical values are greater than economic interests'. 'Call this an idealistic deviation, if you please,' Roy tells his Party, 'I would plead guilty to the charge.'[2]

Throughout *New Orientation* Roy extols the ideal of spiritual freedom. It has now become the ultimate value of his system, a dimension of freedom which is both primary to the attainment of political or economic liberty, and yet beyond them, existing as a supreme state of philosophical wisdom. In his subsequent elaboration of the idea, Roy seems eventually to conceive of spiritual freedom in at least two senses. These correspond to the ways in which Vivekananda, Aurobindo and Gandhi understand the idea as well. First, Roy posits spiritual freedom as not only the ultimate value of radical humanism in its hierarchy of values, but also as the key motivating force of human action. 'The urge for spiritual freedom, though it has remained largely in the realm of the subconscious, has been the lever of entire human development, ever since the birth of the species.'[3] This conception of spiritual freedom as a kind of final cause may seem vague or mystical but the idea does have firm roots in the Indian nationalist tradition. Although Vivekananda, unlike Roy, chose to identify explicitly the idea of spiritual freedom with the ancient Hindu theory of *Mukti* or *Moksha*, he fully anticipated Roy in the view of freedom as both the cause and the ultimate value or goal of human development. 'Freedom,' Vivekananda wrote, 'is the one goal of all nature...everything is struggling towards that goal.' In this ideal is found the 'groundwork of all morality', and 'to advance oneself towards freedom, physical, mental and spiritual and help others do so, is the supreme prize of man.'[4] 'Political and social independence are well and good, but the real thing is spiritual independence—*Mukti*.'[5] The parallel with Roy is evident, but for Roy's rejection of the *Vedanta* and insistence that the value of spiritual free-

[1] *Ibid.* pp. 26–7.   [2] *Ibid.* pp. 200–1, 204–5.
[3] Roy, *Reason, Romanticism* and *Revolution* (Calcutta: Renaissance, 1955) vol. II, p. 297.
[4] Vivekananda, *The Complete Works*, vol. V, pp. 141–2.   [5] *Ibid.* p. 458.

dom somehow must be grounded in a 'materialist philosophy'. This analysis of Roy's ideology will not deal with his peculiar theory of materialism since it has no real logical relation to his ethical or political ideas. Rather it seems that Roy appropriated some aspects of materialist philosophy to justify in his own mind his appeals to rationalism and modern science. This attempt did not succeed. The consequence was an incongruous conglomeration of scientism, irrationalism and moralism that vitiates the claim of radical humanism to being a systematic philosophy.

The second sense in which Roy conceived of spiritual freedom was as a prerequisite for social and political freedom. Roy often argued in his last years that 'Spiritual liberation is the condition for social and political liberation. Radical humanism is the message of that liberation.'[1] This view of the primacy of spiritual freedom is suggested in the above passage from Vivekananda, and Gandhi wrote in similar terms, 'The outward freedom therefore that we shall attain will only be in exact proportion to the inward freedom to which we may have grown at a given moment.'[2] 'Spiritual liberation' in the sense that Roy uses it here depended upon the moral transformation of the individual in society, that is, the realization of those virtues which we shall see in a moment embodied in Roy's vision of the ideal leader. 'The burning problem of our time,' Roy concluded, 'is the problem of morality',[3] and for him in this final phase this problem had indeed become paramount. The former Marxist revolutionary has thus turned moralist, preaching the goal of spiritual freedom familiar to his tradition.

4. ROY'S CONCEPTION OF POWER

Roy's view of power, no less than that of freedom, underwent change in that critical decade of 1937–47. As a Congressman writing in 1937, Roy repeatedly called through the columns of *Independent India* for a more effective mobilization of the masses to prepare for the great goal, the 'capture of power' from the British. 'Ours is not a constitutional debate,' he insisted, 'it is a political struggle for the conquest of power.' The Congress must activate the people for the coming power struggle, and no holds should be barred in dealing with the imperialists. The theory of a peaceful transfer of power was thought insipid. Such senseless faith in the British could only 'obviate the necessity of the revolutionary mass action indispensable for the conquest of power.'

[1] Roy, 'Radical Humanism: theory and practice' in *The Radical Humanist*, 9 Mar. 1952, p. 111.
[2] Gandhi, *Young India* (Selections), 1927–8, III (Madras, 1935) 1 Nov. 1928, pp. 901–2.
[3] Roy, *Reason, Romanticism and Revolution*, vol. II, p. 272.

If the constitutional approach was misleading, then 'the humani-tarian idea of social service', with its associated moral trappings, was emasculating when applied to the revolution. Gandhism is emphatically rejected by Roy now as he had rejected it fifteen years earlier in *India in Transition*. The 'mass struggle for the capture of power...is incompatible with the moral dogmas, religious creeds, pseudo-philosophical doctrines that have been dominating our movement for political freedom'. Gandhi talks about 'human virtues and tests of sincerity' in negotiating with the British. Here and elsewhere he sets up impossible moral hurdles for the struggle. He should realize the hard revolutionary truth that 'anything instrumental for developing our fight for freedom should be considered proper'. The Congress effort has too often been undermined by the Ghandian insistence upon 'ethical' means. It has failed to appreciate that 'every crisis must be utilised for furthering and intensifying that decisive struggle for the capture of political power'.[1]

Once again, a decisive change of view appears in 1946 with Roy's *New Orientation*. Now Roy's attitude towards power follows from his moralistic approach to politics that has been discussed above. Communists, Roy remarks, have 'vulgarised' Marxism, so that it 'can no longer give us a strong enough inspiration. We shall have to set up higher ideas and find a nobler philosophy of life. Unprincipled power-politics inevitably results from the pragmatic view of history, the view that the end justifies the means.' Thus, while a decade earlier Roy had insisted that power was the only proper concern for politics, and argued against Gandhi that any means were legitimate in the struggle for power, now he denounces power-politics as 'unprincipled'. In words practically identical with those used by Gandhi, Roy writes: 'It is a fallacy to hold that the end justifies the means. The truth is that immoral means necessarily corrupt the end. This is an empirical truth.'[2] Whereas the great need in 1937 was for the mobilization of the masses in the struggle for power, Roy's desire now is for 'a decent politics, human politics [that] cannot be practised except as the expression of some higher moral urge, according to some philosophical principles'. Earlier Roy had scorned Gandhi's talk of the 'purification of politics'. Now Roy declares that he can remain in politics only if it is purified, for 'political practice without a philosophy is a vulgar scramble for power'.[3] The stage is set for Roy's withdrawal from politics. The obvious point might be made that he could do little else, given the hopeless political position of the R.D.P. Yet to reduce Roy's view of power to this would be misleading. Roy was not merely making a virtue of necessity. He was

---

[1] Roy, *Our Problems* (Editorials of *Independent India*, 1937) (Barendra Library, Calcutta, 1939) pp. 20, 38, 47–8, 66, 82, 244–5, 59.
[2] Roy, *New Orientation*, p. 248.   [3] *Ibid.* pp. 209–10, and 26.

creating an ideology; and the conception of power which he developed is representative of an important strand of Indian thinking about politics which one political scientist has aptly called, 'The Struggle Against Power'.[1] Roy articulated this strand of thought, with all its related assumptions about the nature of leadership, better than any of his contemporaries.

If this theme of the 'struggle against power' is analysed in the context of Roy's thought, it should be noted that Roy was not suspicious of power *per se*. What he feared and criticized was the *desire* for power. 'Power', he observed, 'will always have a place in human society', for 'it is precisely man's power which can make a better job of human society.' But, if the body politic is to be purged of evils like injustice, authoritarianism and corruption, then 'it must be free from the lust for power'. It is precisely the lust for power that leads to what Roy describes over and over again with disgust, the vulgar 'scramble for power'.[2]

The mad scramble for power usually culminates, according to Roy, in a concentration of power in the unworthy hands of a political party or dictatorship. This can only result in the suppression of individual freedom. Roy therefore asks for a leadership that will promote the widest possible diffusion of power in society. Since, however, the scramble and concentration of power emanate, in Roy's view, from the leader's lust for power, it follows that only a disinterested leadership, purged of normal political ambitions, can be trusted with the public welfare. Today, such men are not placed in positions of responsibility because an unenlightened public 'has been debased to the level of unthinking beasts, to serve the purpose of power politics'. The public thereby reproduces leaders corrupted by 'hatred, greed, lust for power'.[3] The remedy for this is to enlighten the people not through precept but example. If the right leadership sets a high moral example, it will compel the people's respect and will be given the opportunity to transform society. This attitude towards power was best summed up by Gandhi when he explained that the ideal leadership 'does not seize power. It does not even seek power—power accrues to it.'[4] Gandhi, as the Mahatma, discovered that power often 'accrued' to him in abundance. Roy, who never developed anything like Gandhi's ingenious style of leadership, failed in his early quest for power. Yet ultimately Roy came to share with Gandhi that conception of power which was deeply embedded in their common ideological tradition.

Closely allied to this dark view of power was, as one would suspect, a

[1] Myron Weiner, 'Struggle against power', in *World Politics*, VIII, Apr. 1956.
[2] Roy, *Politics, Power and Parties* (Calcutta: Renaissance, 1960) pp. 181, 72, 184, 122.
[3] *Ibid.*
[4] Gandhi in Mira Behn, *Gleanings* (Navajivan, Ahmedabad, 1949) p. 15.

grim estimate of the nature of politics itself. Once again, this position was not peculiar to Roy; it had been forecast decades earlier in Bengal. Vivekananda had denounced politics as 'trash', an unclean business unwisely imported from the west, and alien to the Indian tradition. 'The voice of Asia has been the voice of religion. The voice of Europe is the voice of politics.' 'Do not mix in politics' were his orders to his disciples. Yet Vivekananda gave his countrymen the apt advice, 'If you want to speak of politics in India, you must speak through the language of religion.'[1] Bengali extremists like Aurobindo had come to heed this advice by the time of Vivekananda's death in 1902. But for Aurobindo, politics soon proved to be not enough—as well as too much. Once he had followed Vivekananda's path to the seclusion and security of the *ashram*, he remained there until his death. From Pondicherry then came the word of 'the disease and falsehood of modern political life', the utter immorality of political leaders, and the demonic nature of the State.[2] Unlike Aurobindo, Gandhi remained absorbed throughout most of his life in the business of politics. However, Gandhi's fundamental assumption on the nature of politics was not unlike Aurobindo's: 'If I seem to take part in politics,' Gandhi said, 'it is only because politics encircle us today like the coil of a snake from which one cannot get out, no matter how much one tries. I wish therefore to wrestle with the snake.'[3] Until the end, Gandhi insisted that his 'work of social reform or self-purifica-tion...is a hundred times dearer to me than what is called purely political work.' Even these protestations, though, could not exempt Gandhi from the trenchant criticism of Rabindranath Tagore. The poet's suspicion of nationalist politics led him to admonish the Mahatma: 'Power in all its forms is irrational, it is like the horse that drags the carriage blind-folded.'[4] From the ensuing Gandhi–Tagore controversy emerged the poet's overwhelming repulsion from what M. N. Roy eventually denounced as the dominant trait of contemporary politics, the corrupting influence of power. 'All brands of politics', Roy wrote, 'as practised today are party-politics. If party politics is bad, politics is itself bad. It is easy to see how this system is bound to lead to demorali-sation.'[5] These impressions of power and politics, shared among Roy and the others, had far-reaching implications for their thinking on the problem of right leadership, the nature of the good society, and the method by which it might be achieved.

---

[1] Vivekananda, *Complete Works*, vol. VIII (1959) p. 77.
[2] Sri Aurobindo, 'The ideal of human unity' in *The Human Cycle, The Ideal of Human Unity, War and Self-Determination* (Pondicherry: Sri Aurobindo Ashram, 1962) pp. 388–91.
[3] Gandhi, *Young India*, 12 May 1920, cited in N. K. Bose, *Selections from Gandhi* (Ahmedabad: Navajivan, 1948) p. 45.
[4] Rabindranath Tagore in R. K. Prabhu and R. Kelekav (editors) *Truth Called Them Differently* (Ahmedabad: Navajivan, 1961) p. 14.   [5] Roy, *Politics, Power and Parties*, p. 70.

5. ROY ON LEADERSHIP, CHANGE AND THE GOOD SOCIETY

In the free state visualised by us as a practical possibility, detached individuals, modern versions of philosopher-kings—will be at the helm of public
affairs. Detached individuals, that is, spiritually free men, cannot be corrupted by power. A man susceptible to corruption is not spiritually free,
not detached, not a philosopher. Therefore, the doubt is not with regard to
the possibility of spiritually free men to be above corruption; it is about
the possibility of men ever becoming spiritually free. A Humanist philosophy
does not admit of that doubt...

We maintain that, given his essential rationality, it is possible for the
individual man to attain spiritual freedom, to be detached, and thus to be
above corruption. Such men would not hanker after power.[1]

This critical passage from a speech of May 1947 suggests the main
assumptions which Roy was to develop over the next six years, as well as
the relationships which he formed among his ideas of spiritual freedom,
political power, and right leadership.

Roy introduces here his conception of the ideal leader as the detached
individual, the 'philosopher-king'. For one who had been so recently a
Marxist and who still claimed to be a materialist, the attraction to the
vision of the philosopher-king, with all its Platonic associations, may
seem peculiar. Yet, Roy took not only the idea of the philosopher-king
but also its association with Plato very seriously indeed. Even as a
Marxist, Roy had argued that Plato's conception of the ideal state and
particularly his theory of the guardian elite, 'can guide not only political thinking, but even political practice of our time'.[2] Later, after
his departure from Marxism, Roy's affection for Plato, and especially for
the ideal of the philosopher-king, strengthened considerably. In defend-
ing Plato's *Republic* against the charge of 'fascism', Roy concludes:
'The philosopher in the Platonic sense is a person characterised by love
of truth and virtue, ability for detached objective judgment, disinclin-
ation to possess or accumulate any wealth and desire to teach others.'[3]
This, Roy says, is the type of leader that he wants to 'guide' his 'true
democracy'. Their guidance would assume the form not of political
power over others, but of 'creative and co-operative education of the
common people'. Such leaders could not have 'a contempt for the
unenlightened common man and seek consolation in some intellectual
privacy of their own'. Rather they would function through 'advisory
councils' 'to guide and not to control social conduct'.[4] Roy's vision of a
'true democracy' guided, served, and enlightened by a disinterested
moral elite could find parallels with a combination of western political

[1] *Ibid.* p. 81–2.
[2] Roy, *Nationalism, Democracy and Freedom* (Bombay: V. B. Karnik, 1943) p. 52.
[3] Roy, *The Radical Humanist*, 2 Dec. 1951, p. 556.   [4] *Ibid.*

thinkers. However, it can also be seen as a familiar theme of ideology in modern India, and it will be analysed here in that context.

The anarchist ideal of a society free from the 'scramble for power', from the oppressive interference of an unwanted government, indeed from the taint of politics itself: this is implicit throughout the writings of Vivekananda, Aurobindo, Gandhi, and Roy. The Marxist Utopia represents a form of anarchism and Roy's version might, at first glance, be identified with Marxism. This, however, would be to ignore one of the defining characteristics of Roy's ideal, a trait that establishes it clearly within the modern India context. For, while Roy's order is without government or politics, it is nonetheless a 'guided anarchy', a society directed toward righteousness by the moral example of a *karmayoga*-type elite. This leadership is invested with what Vivekananda called, 'the ideal Brahminness in which worldliness is altogether absent and true wisdom is abundantly present'. 'That', Vivekananda added, 'is the ideal of the Hindu race.'[1]

Vivekananda's portrayal of the *karmayogin* as a free man, spontaneously virtuous and uniquely capable of love and compassion, is not new to the Indian tradition; indeed, Ramakrishna saw the conception in this light. The development that emerges with Vivekananda lies in his emphasis upon the free individual as a national leader, a disinterested social reformer, working in a spirit of renunciation to secure values which were often foreign to the Indian tradition. 'We must prove', said Vivekananda, 'the truth of pure Advaitism in practical life. Shankara left this Advaita philosophy in the hills and forests, while I have come to bring it out of those places and scatter it broadcast before the work-a-day world and society.'[2] This was the role of the *karmayogin*: a part played by Vivekananda himself, in a social if not in a political sense. And the conceptual correspondences which he drew anticipated the emergence on the Indian political scene of a *karmayogin par excellence*, Mahatma Gandhi.

In writing of the 'traditional ideal of the *guru* or teacher, better called "spiritual advisor" '", Karl Potter observes in his study of classical Indian philosophy:

That those only are fit to guide who have gained mastery of their subject is a commonplace requirement; but the relationship of the student to his *guru*, an especially intimate one, requires the teacher not only to have mastered the variety of subject-matters included in the 'curriculum' but also, and more important, to have such insight and superior awareness—coupled with the ability to carry out the decisions that insight dictates—as to be always cognizant of his pupil's innermost needs as well as master of the exactly appropriate ways of satisfying them. It is no wonder, with this ideal

[1] Vivekananda, *Complete Works*, vol. III (1960) p. 197.   [2] Vivekananda, vol. VII, p. 162.

in mind, that the gifted teacher remains in contemporary India a figure highly fitted in the mind of the community to take on the added burdens of political leadership. Nor is it any wonder that, in the light of the correspondence we have noted between hero, saint, and teacher, the men who appeal to Indians as leaders have been respected and revered as being at one and the same time all three. Because of their superior understanding, such men are held to be worthy of everyone's trust and allegiance, even despite apparent external inconsistencies in their behaviour. The hero, the *yogi*, and the *guru* exemplify superior mastery of themselves and their environment; they, among men, most closely approximate the ideal of complete control or freedom.[1]

The *karmayogin* was indeed synonymous, in Vivekananda's view, with the classical conceptions of the hero and the *guru*; and it was this figure, embodying these three symbols rolled into one, surrounded with an aura of saintliness and spiritual power, that became a dominant image in modern Indian political thought. The *yogin* had realized his own nature and attained freedom, and was thus unquestionably fitted not only to serve mankind, but to lead it in all spheres of action.

The outstanding theoretical statement in recent Indian thought on the theme of a spiritual elite occurs in the concluding chapters of Aurobindo's *The Life Divine* with his vision of the 'gnostic beings', a monastic leadership that has much in common with Roy's philosopher-kings. In Aurobindo's eloquent description one discovers the archetypal Indian leader, acting selflessly, instinctively, for the good of humanity, endowed with spiritual freedom, above the temptation of power or of political ambition, conscious of the unity of mankind, and confident of his ability to 'turn and adapt [the world] to his own truth and purpose of existence; he will mould life itself into his own spiritual image'.[2] Roy too expresses his faith that carriers of spiritual freedom will transform humanity, 'leaving the politicians to their scramble for power, very soon they will multiply themselves to be five hundred and then thousands. The contagion will spread. . .'[3] Precisely the manner in which this momentum would grow was based upon a belief common to Aurobindo and Roy that the moral purity of a spiritual elite would prove irresistible. This belief is fundamental to the Indian tradition and particularly to the conceptions of power and leadership shared by those thinkers mentioned in this chapter. Gandhi expressed the belief lucidly when he remarked that the ideal government would consist of 'sages' and went on to explain: 'In modern times a "sage" is a person who has education, a spirit of service, and the qualifications

[1] Karl Potter, *Presuppositions of India's Philosophies* (N. J.: Prentice Hall, 1963) p. 5.
[2] Aurobindo, *The Life Divine* (Pondicherry: Sri Aurobindo Ashram, 1960) chapter on 'The gnostic being', p. 1163.
[3] Roy, 'Preconditions for Democracy', *The Radical Humanist*, 31 Aug. 1952, p. 410.

for rendering service in the largest measure. A man of this type will not seek power; but the people of their own desire will elect him and invest him with power, because they will realise that he is indispensable.'[1]

The same attitudes towards freedom and power that shaped the Utopian visions of Gandhi and Roy also directed their more practical programmes of social reconstruction. Their common suspicion of man's lust for power dictated a highly decentralized political structure, where infusion of social morality depended upon a wide diffusion of power. 'The end to be achieved', Gandhi wrote, 'is human happiness combined with full mental and moral growth...This end can be achieved under decentralization. Centralization as a system is inconsistent with a non-violent structure of society.'[2] Roy espoused neither Gandhi's doctrine of non-violence nor his aversion to industrialization but he set forth a theory of village democracy closely akin to Gandhi's. 'Ultimately', Roy argued, 'the problem of democratic political practice is that of decentralization.' 'Diffusion of power is the essence of democracy, because concentration of power leads to tyranny and dictatorship...' With Gandhi, Roy looks forward to 'the foundation of a decentralized State...laid in local republics which will combine all functions of the State as they affect the local life...Being thus reared upon a broad foundation of direct democracies the State will be really democratic.'[3] The village is the key unit in Roy's concept of direct democracy. Even in the early 1940s Roy is insisting as emphatically as Gandhi on the primacy of the village for development in India.[4]

We may look back to Vivekananda once again to introduce the final point of comparison between Roy and the other Indian thinkers discussed here; that is, their theory of the right method of social change.

There is a class [wrote Vivekananda] which still clings on to political and social changes as the only panacea for the evils in Europe, but among the great thinkers there, other ideals are growing. They have found out that no amount of political or social manipulation of human conditions can cure the evils of life. It is a change of the soul itself for the better that alone will cure the evils of life. No amount of force, or government, or legislative cruelty will change the conditions of a race, but it is spiritual culture and ethical culture alone that can change wrong racial tendencies for the better.[5]

This marks the beginning of a prolonged Indian indictment of the western parliamentary form of government with its alleged exclusive dependence on institutional or legislative reforms. It is a line of criti-

---

[1] C. S. Shukla, *Gandhi's View of Life* (Bombay: Bharatiya Vidya Bhavan, 1956) pp. 146–7.
[2] Gandhi, *Harijan*, 18 Jan. 1942.
[3] Roy, *Politics, Power and Parties*, pp. 75, 71, 77.
[4] Roy, *Scientific Politics*, pp. 240–1; and *Constitution of Free India* (Delhi: V. B. Karnik, 1945) chapter XIII, pp. 41–2.
[5] Vivekananda, *Complete Works*, vol. III, p. 182.

cism which extends from Vivekananda through Aurobindo and Gandhi, and on to Roy and Jayaprakash Narayan. The implication was generally that expressed by Vivekananda: political changes are inevitably superficial since they leave untouched the underlying cause of social ills as well as the potential source of their correction, the moral character of the individual. 'The most drastic changes', wrote Aurobindo, 'made by these [political] means change nothing; for the old ills exist in a new form: the aspect of the outward environment is altered, but man remains what he was...Only a spiritual change can make a real and effective difference.'[1] In most cases, this type of criticism was followed by a suggested remedy derived from the Indian tradition. The classic example is Gandhi's theory of *satyagraha*.

Roy's line of criticism on this issue is as forceful as that of any of the other thinkers. Referring to the 'crisis of modern civilisation' he says:

Others diagnose the disease as a crisis of political theories and institutions. They recommend that the parliamentary system would be improved by various ingenious devices. It is hardly necessary to go into an examination of the mechanical remedies suggested; they are bound to fail as long as greater importance is attached to institutions than to men. The central fallacy of these political theories is to place institutions above men, to ignore that institutions are created by men. Any attempt at social reconstruction to promote economic welfare and political liberty must begin with man.[2]

Roy does not proceed to identify his theory of the right method of social change with elements of the Indian tradition. However, the similarity on this point between Roy and the others discussed here is considerable. It rests upon a common view of what constitutes genuine social change as well as on the nature of the leadership that must initiate it.

'Society', Roy believes, 'is no more than an integration of individuals, and if you want a good society, you must have good individuals. Until now, we have put the cart before the horse, and said that we must have a good society in order to have good men.' The truth, however, is that 'Without moral men, there can be no moral society'.[3] Lasting and meaningful social change can occur only with a moral transformation of the individual in society. This approach to change, combined with Roy's views on power and politics, reinforced his belief that only a 'philosophical revolution', a fundamental re-orientation of attitudes on man and society, could have the desired results. Roy not only dismissed most political agencies as ineffective, he subjected the party system in particular to scathing criticism for its lustful pursuit of power and

[1] Aurobindo, *The Life Divine*, p. 1053.
[2] Roy, *New Humanism, A Manifesto* (Calcutta: Renaissance, 1961), p. 85.
[3] Roy, *Politics, Power and Parties*, p. 41.

corrosive influence upon public morality.[1] Therefore, only a year after Gandhi had advised the Congress organization to 'disband' and 'flower into a Lok Sevak Sangh', Roy officially transformed his R.D.P. into the Radical Humanist Movement. Writing in *The Radical Humanist* on 'The Mahatma's advice', Roy praised Gandhi's move as a sincere attempt to withdraw the Congress party 'from the scramble of power-politics and to concentrate on constructive work for the service and welfare of the people'.[2] In the years following Gandhi's death, Roy, although his attitude was ambivalent towards much of Gandhi's legacy, developed the theory of the social movement in a way which Gandhi would have approved.

In Roy's final phase he often recalled the early inspiration of that first leader of his Calcutta youth, Jatin Mukherjee. It is in a remarkable eulogy to Jatinda that Roy indicates the nature of the reconciliation of ideals which he has finally realized:

Good men are seldom given a place in the galaxy of the great. It will continue to be so until goodness is recognised as the measure of genuine greatness. Jatinda...did not belong to any age; his values were human and as such transcended space and time... Like all modern educated young men of his time, he tended to accept the reformed religion preached by Swami Vivekananda—a God who would stand the test of reason and a religion which served progressive social and human purpose. He believed himself to be a Karmayogi, trying to be at any rate, and recommended the ideal to all of us. Detached from the unnecessary mystic preoccupation, Karmayogi means a humanist. He who believes that self-realisation can be attained through human action, must logically also believe in man's creativeness—that man is the maker of his destiny. That is also the essence of Humanism. Jatinda was a Humanist—perhaps the first in modern India.[3]

The easy correspondence drawn here between *karmayoga* and humanism, which transforms a Hindu mystic into the first humanist of modern India, suggests where the roots of Roy's own humanism lay.

[1] *Ibid.* p. 70.
[2] Roy, 'The Mahatma's advice', in *Radical Humanist*, 29 May 1949, pp. 247–8. Roy's praise or condemnation of Gandhi is seldom unqualified; this article is no exception.
[3] Roy, 'Jatin Mukherji', *Independent India*, 27 Feb. 1949, p. 91.

THE ACADEMIC PROFESSION
IN INDIA[1]

EDWARD SHILS

I

Every society with a complex industrial technology, with transportation and communications networks based on complex technology, with a dense and comprehensive system of administration, has an elaborate higher educational system. Such higher educational systems either develop slowly over hundreds of years from a time before the emergence of modern technology and administration, or they have been created in connexion with the aspiration towards such a society from an already-formed model located in a foreign society or culture. In India a system of higher education was created from a European model.[2] It was intended to be a complement of its emerging modern sector which comprised rational or bureaucratic administration, modern forms of litigation and adjudication, technological construction, transportation and communication, the care of health, the improvement of agriculture and the diffusion of secular knowledge and information. It was expected that higher positions in the modern sector of Indian society would be filled by persons who became qualified for them to a large extent by the certified and systematic study of more of less codified bodies of knowledge.

Except for certain areas of legal and linguistic studies, the bodies of knowledge taught in the universities and in their affiliated colleges have all been of exogenous origin; they taught traditions which had grown up not in India but outside India. They have been criticized for the exogenous origin of what they have taught and even more for the conduct of their instruction and research in the English language. The academic profession is also a new one in India and it is criticized for not being the same as its traditional analogue, the *guru*.

In the land of the *guru*, the profession which has taken over his obligations is held in low esteem both by those who practise it and by

---

[1] In what follows I shall use the terms 'academics' or 'academic profession' to refer to university and college teachers. 'University teachers' will refer to those employed in universities, 'college teachers' to those employed in colleges.

[2] The most comprehensive scholarly account of the transplantation of the model is to be found in Eric Ashby and Mary Anderson, *Universities: British, Indian and African*, Weidenfeld and Nicolson, London, 1960, pp. 47–143.

others. In the numerous efforts to diagnose and prescribe for the ailing Indian universities, the *guru* as a spiritual guide and as a source of solicitude is often invoked as a standard in comparison with which the character of the contemporary Indian academic is regretted. The theme appears incessantly. I cite only a few from innumerable examples: 'In pre-British days, the relations between the teacher and the taught were very intimate as they lived together and no time limit was imposed on any particular course of study. Mass lectures were unknown and when they had any doubt or difficulty, they approached a senior student or the professor himself for its solution.'[1] 'In our ancient system of education, there was respect for the teacher as a result of personal contacts between the teacher and the student...Today, due to many factors, the position is different.'[2]

It is certainly true that there are very great differences between *gurus* and academics. The *gurus* of the past never did what a modern university teacher is required to do and those who are still functioning are not making any attempt to do this either. The modern academic profession seeks to transmit specialized bodies of knowledge established by systematic research, to add to knowledge by its own research, to prepare young persons to do such research and to qualify them to practise a wide variety of professions which require certified knowledge. *Gurus* supervised the memorizing of sacred texts and they sought to exemplify and inculcate wisdom. The teachings of the *gurus* were not subject to continuous renewal and revision by freshly acquired knowledge. One might indeed say that the expectation that academics should be *gurus* helps to make the Indian academic what he is. Articulate Indian public opinion which expresses a somewhat hypocritical admiration for *gurus* shows by the choice of its standard of assessment that it does not care enough for modern science and scholarship to enable the academic to be what an academic can be. It charges the academic with failure to take a parental interest in the student and with accepting a salary. It cares for incidentals and by-products—for a quiet student body, for degrees, for the enhancement of India's reputation internationally and for the production of 'qualified manpower'—but it does not care for modern scholarly and scientific knowledge. It respects saintliness—intermittently—and it defers to power, but it does not respect hard and persistent intellectual work and it shows little concern for the conditions under which an academic can be effective. The tasks of academics

[1] Surendrenath Sen, *Educational Reforms of Sir Asutosh Mookerjee* (Kirti Mandir Lecture Series No. XI), Dept. of Education, Baroda State, Government Press, Baroda, 1949, p. 4.
[2] M. S. Doraiswami (Vice-Chancellor of Osmania University) in *Indian University Administration: Proceedings of the Vice-Chancellors' Conference on University Administration convened by the Ministry of Education and Scientific Research from 30 July to 1 August 1957*, Ministry of Education, Government of India, Delhi, p. 85.

entail neither the exercise of power nor the practice of saintliness. An atmosphere of opinion which admires these is not likely to contribute to the well-being and fruitfulness of a profession which involves neither of these. This state of opinion which derogates the academic profession helps to confirm itself, and it produces no positive results.

All these criticisms, which have gained in strength in the present century, have been supported by sentiments affronted by the implicit judgement that the indigenous culture and languages and indigenous cultural institutions were inadequate to meet the needs set by new developments in Indian society and by an unarticulated doctrine of the integrity of national culture. According to the latter, whatever is not continuous with the past of a society lacks vitality; it cannot flourish if it does not emanate from an *essential* quality of the culture which is contained in language and which is expressed in traditional beliefs and institutions. Indian universities and colleges, and those who teach and have taught in them, have often been criticized for this departure from the paths indicated by the Indian past. There is great dissatisfaction in India with the structures of higher education formed in accordance with the exogenous model and there is great pressure to change the medium of academic instruction. Both of these are expressions of beliefs which are manifested for the most part in a negative form.

Of course, if the contemporary Indian higher educational system were more successful simply as a higher educational system, it would probably not be so injurious to Indian self-esteem and would not call forth to such an extent the nationalistic beliefs in the integrity of culture, etc. The failure of Indian universities and colleges to please their constituents is at least in part a result of their failure to conform with the standards which are inherent in modern higher educational systems. The argument that they do not conform with or continue from Indian traditional culture would still persist but it would probably be less frequent and less intense if they conformed more closely with the standards of effective teaching of advanced modern knowledge and if they themselves contributed more frequently to the advancement of knowledge.

II

The fact is that the Indian academic profession has a bad name among those Indians who make it up and those Indians who observe it. There is undoubtedly a good deal of truth in these negative evaluations. This essay offers some hypotheses to account for the relatively low intellectual effectiveness of the Indian academic profession.

I began by stating that there might well be some substantial validity in the assertions that Indian higher education has faltered because of its disjunctiveness with respect to traditional Indian philosophical, religious and 'scientific' culture. It is surely difficult for a model of a system of cultural institutions to be translated into reality in an alien culture—alien in language, in religion, in mores and in sensibilities to the culture from which it was taken. It is difficult enough to transplant a cultural institution from one society to another which shares the same culture, e.g. from Great Britain to Australia, New Zealand and English-speaking Canada. But, where the cultural postulates are different, it is even more difficult. The difference in cultures is only one factor among several and in this essay I shall concentrate my attention on the others.

One is the incapacity of the Indian university and college system to generate a compelling tradition of intellectual work of its own. In a certain sense, every university system is to some extent alien to the culture in which it operates—it is more differentiated, more critical, more innovative than its environing culture. It succeeds as an institution of higher education to the extent that it differentiates itself from the environing cultural traditions and generates its own traditions—institutional, professional and disciplinary—which sustain its efforts in teaching and research. It is to this failure that some of the present weakness of Indian higher education can be attributed. In what follows I shall attempt to explain why such traditions have not been able to grow up in Indian universities and colleges.

There is also another reason why Indian universities and colleges have not been successful. Universities are part of the central institutional system of their society; they are elite institutions. I do not refer to the class composition of the student body but to their functions as sources of personnel for various sectors of the elite, as sources of knowledge necessary for the making and implementation of policy in state, economy and society, as sources of high culture and as sources of critical and evaluative opinion. But a university is part of the centre of society in a sense additional to that of performing functions vital to the centre of society such as training, evaluating, informing. The tasks traditionally undertaken by universities have always postulated this participation in the centre of society. Such a relationship to the centre is not contained within written university constitutions but it is part of the unwritten culture of university systems. The image of the university which was imported into India carried with it the conception of the university as part of the centre of society.

This is where the Indian universities and colleges have encountered a fundamental obstacle. When Indian universities and colleges were founded in the nineteenth and twentieth centuries, India was a province of a bureaucratic empire. Indian society was not a society in the sense of being an autonomous, autocephalous collectivity. It had little or no civic life and much of what it had was in opposition to the alien political and bureaucratic elites. The religious life of Indian society prevailed apart from the academic system—the religious elite had no affinity or even relationship to the academic elite. Only towards the end of the period of British rule did the academic system begin to produce a substantial proportion of the bureaucratic elite (i.e. the Indian Civil Service). The political (counter-) elite of India stood in a hostile or at best attenuated relationship to the academic profession.

The Indian academic profession could not perform the various functions which are performed by the academic profession in autonomous and autocephalous societies, i.e. in societies which have their own fully developed centres. This was a severe burden on its morale. Still it might have felt itself to be in some measure part of the centre had it been able to perform in its own institutional sphere at a level sufficiently high to evoke its own self-esteem and the esteem of those abroad whom it in turn esteemed. Had it been an intellectual success, it might have been able to act as part of the centre of Indian society when India became independent. It could not however do so. In the following section, I shall try to explain the impediments which prevented the Indian academic profession from performing with distinction in its work of research and teaching and which have led it into becoming a *pariah* class rather than a self-confident and equal sector of the centre of Indian society. Then I shall attempt to explore some of the ways in which the segmented structure of the centre of the India of the Raj blocked the performance of other elite functions by the Indian academic.

III

Recruitment to the Indian academic profession lay from quite early on under the burden of the reservation of many of the best positions in the best colleges—the 'premier' government colleges—by foreigners. The Graded Educational Service and the Indian Educational Service were founded on the conviction that it would require well-educated Europeans to provide the stiffening within those colleges which government had destined to the role of setting an example to the rest of the more nondescript higher educational institutions. As late as 1922, the number of posts sanctioned for Indians in the Indian Educational Service only amounted to 162; while 171 were sanctioned for Europeans.[1]

The growing numbers[2] of non-government colleges were always

[1] Government of India, *Proceedings in the Department of Education and Health Education*, Oct. 1922, nos. 1–3.

[2] In 1857, there were 9 non-government colleges out of 27; in 1882, 34 out of 72; in 1901–2, 91 out of 115; in 1962–3, 1,333 out of 1,805; in 1963–4, 1,485 out of 1,983. Cf. Syed Nurullah and J. P. Naik, *A History of Education in India (British Period A)*, Bombay, Mac-

afflicted with poverty; they paid small salaries[1] and their ill-paid teachers commanded little respect. It was this way at the end of the last century and it has remained so up to the present.[2]

Under these circumstances, the profession has had little attractive power. India is a society in which many young men are still guided or directed to particular occupations by the decisions of their elders; I have not encountered one Indian academic who entered on his career under the pressure of the preferences of his elders. Parents encourage their offspring to enter government service, medicine, engineering and law but not university and college teaching. Those parents who are already highly educated are aware of the lowly estate of the Indian college and university teacher. (Very few, for example, who have entered the Indian academic profession are the offspring of members of the Indian Civil Service.) Those who are not educated are only dimly aware of its existence, but they do know about government service and insofar as their opinion is influential with their offspring, a barrier to the entry of the best into the academic profession is erected or maintained.

Even the academic profession does not encourage its best young men and women pupils to pursue academic careers. There are universities which are famous for encouraging and preparing their best pupils to enter the competitive examinations for the higher civil service—Madras and Allahabad are still the most outstanding in this regard. Occasionally a teacher encourages one of his best pupils to enter on a career of

millan and Co., 1951, pp. 279, 281, 286; *University Development in India: Basic Facts and Figures 1962/63*, University Grants Committee, New Delhi, 1963, p. 17; *University Development in India: Basic Facts and Figures 1963/64*, University Grants Committee, New Delhi, 1964, p. 20.

[1] In six non-government colleges in Calcutta in 1917, the average salary of teachers was Rs. 140 per month; in the *mofussil* in Bengal it was Rs. 131 per month; in second grade colleges, it was Rs. 99 per month. The highest salary of any individual teacher in a private *mofussil* college was Rs. 300 per month, while salaries of Rs. 50 to 70 were common. *Report of the Calcutta University Commisssion: 1917–1919*, Calcutta, 1919–20, vol. I, chapter XIII, pp. 374 ff.

[2] During the Second Five Year Plan (1956–61), the University Grants Commission sought to raise the level of remuneration of college teachers. Among the reasons given was that: 'It was felt that on account of the existing disparity between the salary scales in universities and those in affiliated colleges, it often became difficult to recruit and retain qualified staff.' (University Grants Commission, *Report for the Year 1961–62*, p. 25.) The new scales were to be: principal, Rs. 600–40–800 per month; head of departments, Rs. 400–25–700 per month; senior lecturers, Rs. 300–25–600 per month; lecturers, Rs. 200–15–320–25–500 per month; demonstrators/tutors, Rs. 150–10–200 per month. The Commission undertook to provide 50 per cent of the additional expenditure entailed in raising the scales in men's colleges and 75 per cent of the additional expenditure in women's colleges and would do so for a five year period provided that the State Government or the governing body of the institutions concerned undertook to provide the remainder and would bear the entire cost after five years. By the year 1963/64, 14,000 teachers in 461 colleges were covered by the scheme. At this time there were 2,111 colleges in India (University Grants Commission, *Report for the Year 1963–64*, pp. 17, 24); there were 57,112 teachers in affiliated colleges (*University Development in India 1963–64*, p. 44).

scientific research but, except possibly for Presidency College, Calcutta, I know of no higher educational institution in India where teachers encourage their best pupils to enter the academic profession. In fact many of the senior members of the academic profession take a very poor view of those who do enter the profession. Repeatedly in interviews, in writing and in oral testimony before government commissions, it is said that 'we only get the left-overs or dregs'.[1] This is no new development. Even before the post-independence expansion of the student body in higher education, such judgements were common.[2]

Before independence there were few rewarding professional careers for intellectually well-endowed young Indians—the higher levels of government service, medicine and the law were then the main attractions. Now, in addition to these, there are many more opportunities in science and technology and some in large business firms. The great expansion of opportunities for employment in scientific research in India since independence has taken place outside the universities;[3] the system of national laboratories under the sponsorship of the Council of Scientific and Industrial Research and the Department of Atomic Energy have provided the most remunerative posts and the best facilities for scientists. According to qualified judges, the non-academic laboratories have succeeded in attracting the most talented young and middle-aged scientists in the country. Thus, at a time when more Indians have been highly trained in science than ever before, and when university staffs have grown to about 70,000, the capacity of the universities to attract the best men has probably diminished.

IV

For those of high talent who do enter the university system, the situation which confronts them is not conducive to performance of a high order or to the morale which is necessary for it. Not only are academic institutions not highly regarded in India, but within the academic institutional system the pronounced internal stratification of academic life in India condemns a large part of the profession to inferior academic status. Ever since the University of Calcutta became a teaching as well

[1] '...faculty vacancies are being filled, generally, by craven left-outs from other vocations.' Professor B. R. Shenoy, letter to *The Times of India*, 2 Nov. 1967.
[2] The senior academics who presented evidence before the Radhakrishnan Commission in the second half of the 1940s frequently expressed such opinions.
[3] In 1901, according to the *Census of India*, there were 548 scientists.(In 1901, the 548 who included astronomers, meteorologists, botanists, naturalists, metallurgists, etc., must have been mainly in government survey organizations and a substantial proportion must have been British.) In the first half of the 1960s the number of scientists and technologists doing research has been estimated variously between 15,000 and 44,000. (In the 1960s practically all in the uncertain figure were Indians.)

as an examining and degree-granting institution, there has been a stratification which discriminates between the universities and their affiliated colleges.[1] More than 80 per cent of Indian academics teach in colleges.[2] The universities have better salary scales than the colleges; their conditions of service are better.[3] Their members teach less and they have more opportunity to teach more advanced and specialized subjects.[4] They have more security of tenure and there are more grades or ranks to which they can reasonably hope to advance. Except for the principalship, or the headship of a department in a large college, the college teacher has no ladder of advancement once he has reached the upper limit of his scale. Universities, even if not greatly esteemed, are at least nationally known; most colleges are unknown except in their immediate environments. There is some mobility of teachers between universities; there is very little between colleges. Syllabuses and examinations being university functions, decisions are usually made by college principals and by persons with university appointments, rather than by those who are confined to their colleges. The intellectual autonomy and initiative of the great mass of the teachers is thus so restricted as to be paralysing in its effects.

I have already indicated that in India the academic sector has a smaller proportion of the total research and development funds than it has in most countries with large university populations. Very little of these funds goes to teachers in colleges. Appointment in practically all Indian colleges is a predestination to exclusion from research ; it is also, given the prestige of research in the present-day academic profession— in India as well as elsewhere—predestination to the status of an academic *pariah*.

An additional and important element in the stratification system in the universities is the preponderance of the professor within each department. The great majority of the departments in Indian universi-

[1] Of the 66,634 university and college teachers in India in 1963/64, 57,112 taught in affiliated colleges. The majority of the colleges are private colleges and most of these are regarded internally and externally as inferior institutions. Cf. I. P. Desai, 'The Fortunate Few and The Miserable Many', *The Journal of University Education*, vol. I, no. 3, March 1963, pp. 211–20.

[2] In 1963/64 they taught 1,013,032 of 1,184,697 students or about 85 per cent of all the students in Indian institutions of higher education.

[3] In the universities and government colleges teachers enjoy legally guaranteed tenure; in private colleges, they are legally treated as employees in commercial establishments, dismissable at the will of the management committee. In fact, however, convention and usage give them indefinite tenure. Nonetheless many of them feel insecure and at the mercy of the managers, who almost always support the principal if there is a disagreement with the teaching staff. The rarity of disagreements is attributed by many teachers to their fear of their superiors.

[4] In 1963/4, they taught more than half of the M.Sc. students and 87 per cent of the Ph.D. students (*Report on Standards of University Education*, University Grants Commission, Delhi, 1965, p. 48).

ties have only one professor, who is also the permanent head of the department. (The department head has a similar hegemony in colleges.) He assigns tasks to his subordinates, he is the link which connects the department with the university (or college) and the world outside. Initiatives must pass through him—such as they are, they are usually blocked there. Applications for research grants, etc., must have his approval.[1] Heads of departments who vary this pattern and practise informal consultation and the delegation of authority are rare.

Above the professor stands the administrator. Professor B. R. Shenoy has recently written about this relationship in universities:

The relationship now obtaining between the teacher and the administrator is not one in which the administrator caters to the needs of academicians; it is very much a case of administrators issuing directives to the faculty in academic as well as other matters. They enjoy this topsy-turvy arrangement as much as the faculty resents receiving orders from less qualified people. Resentment leading to conflict between administrators and the faculty is common.

This has produced odd results. Faculty members have to put up with petty humiliations as if they were subordinates. Administrators may reprimand academicians with impunity. They have to accept discriminatory disposal of physical facilities as between themselves and adminstrators. Post-graduate departments may grow much more slowly than the administrative paraphernalia. Starting on the initial salary of the reader's grade, which his background permitted, the salary of a registrar in a certain university nearly doubled in five years and, including allowances, rose to three times as much in another six years; having just reached his salary ceiling, he is now placed on a higher grade, which, together with fringe

---

[1] A young Indian statistician, now teaching in the United States, had the following observation to make regarding his relationship to his professor in instruction and research. 'I was 21 years of age when I was appointed as a lecturer in ABC University. I worked very hard preparing for my classes and in working with students. The curriculum was out-dated and I spent many evenings working out a proposal for improving the content and teaching of statistics. When I presented the draft proposal to the head of the department for discussion, he showed no interest in introducing any change either in the curriculum or in the teaching methods...He made all the decisions pertaining to the department...The enthusiasm for wanting to do and to improve things began to corrode...I worked out a very good research proposal on a subject of interest to the Planning Commission. The research section of the Planning Commission returned the proposal saying that they do not entertain research proposals from anyone less than a reader. The head of the department was willing to lend his name if the proposal and the subsequent publication had his name first as the author. The departmental head had made it quite clear that he was neither interested in the research subject nor did he plan to contribute to the research work. The price of getting my research proposal accepted was to accept the departmental head as the senior author.' After two years the young man obtained an assistantship in an American university where in due course he obtained a Ph.D. and was appointed to its teaching staff where he still remains.

I owe this information to an unpublished paper 'Brain Drain: Uprootedness in Our Time' by Dr Kamla Chowdhry of the Indian Institute of Management in Ahmedabad. Numerous other cases have been reported by my interviewees over the decade 1955–65.

benefits, will make him the highest-paid official on the campus indeed, not excluding the vice-chancellor. By contrast, even distinguished academicians have had to await the arrival of the University Grants Commission for bettering their lot, and U.G.C. directives are often accepted with reluctance.

In the same university, the average expenditure on an administrator in the registrar's office rose by 98 per cent in less than ten years while that of a faculty member declined by 24 per cent. This is due to promotions much more than new recruitments in the upper administrative cadres. Faculty members were denied comfortable residences. Even when the U.G.C. provided the finance, substandard hutments alone were constructed; and, to add to the injury, even senior academicians were bracketed with clerks and stenographers of administrators in respect to allotment of the hutments.

Laboratories and buildings constructed from public funds may ill suit the needs of faculties. The ubiquitous presence of administrators is felt even when ordering slides, chemicals and other laboratory needs; considerations of 'economy' may prevail in taking decisions, not the possible margins of error in experiments. Administrators may be generally relied on to stretch a point against academicians.[1]

Thus, within the universities, between the universities and colleges and within colleges, as well as between government and most private colleges, there are profound differences in power and dignity. There is also a steep and discontinuous stratification of colleges. At the top are the 'premier' government colleges and a few missionary colleges, then a long drooping tail of mediocre and poor colleges mainly private but also including missionary colleges and the lesser government colleges. In a minority of colleges, there is a constant menace of dis-affiliation because of inability to conform with the minimal require-ments of the university with respect to libraries, teaching space and facilities, laboratories, even seating accomodation for enrolled students, etc. The standards are very undemanding and in fact even the most outrageously defective colleges are very seldom deprived of their affiliation to the university. Nonetheless those who are employed to teach in them know of their low standing and they believe that some of that low standing rubs off on them personally.

Although even the best Indian academic institutions are not fellow-ships of equals, the relationship between master and servant becomes more visible, more pronounced and more humiliating with descent in the hierarchy. Terms of employment are harsh; there is no protection in most private colleges from arbitrary dismissal, tasks are autocratically assigned and, as has been already indicated, scales of remuneration are very low as compared with the universities or with the best government and missionary colleges. There are, moreover, no compensations in relations with students or colleagues.

[1] 'University Administration: Forgotten Factors', *The Times of India*, 11 Oct. 1967.

It is appropriate at this point to say something about academic freedom and autonomy as they bear on the Indian academic. The Indian universities are legally autonomous corporations and their staffs enjoy the same guarantees of tenure as do university teachers in Great Britain or in most institutions of the United States. There are very few instances of the removal of academic staff members from their posts on political grounds. Teachers in colleges do not enjoy the same legal guarantees but on the whole they too enjoy a fairly high degree of freedom in the expression of their political attitudes. I myself have encountered, since independence, only one instance of a dismissal of a qualified teacher which constituted an infringement on academic freedom. This occurred in a Bombay College in the early 1950s; the victim was a well-trained historian who had raised a question as to whether Sankaracharya might not have been a crypto-Buddhist. The dismissal occurred because it was thought that the patrons of the college would take offence and discontinue their largesse to the college.

Nonetheless, Indian college and university teachers do feel themselves to be at the unpredictable and inclement mercy of their private managements and of the state governments. Some of their anxiety might be a function of the diffuse animosity which most academics in India have towards professional politicians, particularly those of the leading parties. But some of it is based on actual experience of interference by state governments in university affairs.[1]

State governments have power over the universities through influence over the selection of the vice-chancellor and therewith over the tone and style of the whole university. They also, through the system of state grants, have the vice-chancellor under their control. 'At every step...a university has either to 'go' with the Government or grind down to a halt. Since the second thing cannot happen sooner or later, every university goes with the Government.'[2] It is also known that some leading politicians regard senior administrative posts of the university, e.g. the vice-chancellorship and those in the registrary, as suitable objects of patronage. Thus, even though the actual substance of what is taught or investigated is left fairly inviolate by politicians, the administrative framework is much exposed to them and teachers are very aware of this, and often feel vulnerable.

The teaching of undergraduates has always been the main business

---

[1] Education in India is, according to the constitution, a 'state subject'. Only four universities in India are 'central universities', i.e. independent of state governments and dependent practically entirely on grants from the University Grants Commission. (This protects them from the intrusiveness of state governments but it does not spare them from most of the other ills of Indian higher educational institutions.)

[2] Amrik Singh, 'Universities and the Government' in A. B. Shah (ed.), *Higher Education in India*, Lalvani Publishing House, Bombay, 1967, p. 71.

of the Indian academic. This stems from a tradition of undergraduate instruction in the United Kingdom. Even though London University provided the model for its constitution, the powerful Germanic style of scientific and scholarly research developed there in the latter part of the nineteenth century, particularly in University College London, was not assimilated with the constitution. The Oxford model, devoted to the 'education of young men' took root in India. It was the intention of the founders and rulers of the Indian Educational Service that such a pattern should prevail, and thus the tradition of concern with under-graduates and of a disregard for research became established in India. Given the paucity of opportunities for research and the ready availa-bility of the pedagogical tradition, it would seem that the Indian academic should find his best gratification in teaching. Yet teaching in colleges and universities in India does not confer much satisfaction on those who practise it.[1]

Student–teacher ratios are high; they are higher in the colleges (nearly 18:1 in 1962–3) than in the universities, but even in the latter about twice as high as they are in the British universities. The students are ill-prepared for higher studies, their understanding of English, where English is still the medium of undergraduate instruction and even where it is only a 'library language', is insufficient. Where there has been a 'changeover' to the regional language, the amount of material presented is small and there is little literature available to the students— since they cannot usually read English well enough to cover much ground. In many colleges and universities, an improvised compromise between English and the regional languages is employed—the same thing being said in both languages. The students are restless and un-interested.

This attitude of the students and the half-heartedness of the teacher are both dominated by a belief in inevitable lack of career prospects for the graduate. From the 1880s onwards, there has been discussion about the poor employment prospects of graduates. As numbers increased— modestly by present standards—pessimism grew. A teacher who thinks that what he teaches has no value to the student to whom it is addressed— because the student cannot understand it or because he has no interest in it and because even if he understands and is interested in it he is

---

[1] Of the pre-1920s, to which some critics of the present state of the academic profession look back with admiration, as to a time of demigods, the Report of the Calcutta University Commission had this to say: 'They are deprived of the chance of kindling the interest of their students, and so winning their allegiance, because every inch of the ground they are to cover is marked out for them, and the students, bent simply on the examinations, are apt to resent any departure from examination coaching' (*Calcutta University Commission Report*, vol. II, p. 370). The teachers referred to are the British members of the Indian Educational Service, teaching at the best colleges and being paid more amply than any other college teachers in India!

doomed to a life in which what he has learned contributes nothing to it—such a teacher is not to be expected to have a high esteem for his calling. The belief in their own 'irrelevance' which one so often encounters among Indian academics, and the frequency with which they refer to the inevitable period of unemployment of their graduates, are closely connected.

Lack of enthusiasm among the students can scarcely be compensated by conditions in which a teacher lectures for 15–20 hours per week. (This is not the universal teaching requirement or practice but it is the load of the considerable majority of the teaching profession in Indian higher education.)[1] It should be emphasized that teaching at the undergraduate level is lecturing, often at dictation speed, to groups of students which are very small when they contain only twenty-five or thirty. Tutorial sessions have been recommended repeatedly but few institutions have made provision for them. Informal consultation by students and teachers is very rare by British or American standards—much criticized though these are today. The social tone which fosters and is fostered by so much lecturing and being lectured to, the distractions of the teacher, the shyness, bewilderment and aggressiveness of the students, work against informal intellectual guidance. And where can it take place? In many of the better colleges the teachers have only one common room, there are still many where only corridors are available for conversations between colleagues and between teachers and their pupils.[2]

There are admirable teachers in India—as there were before independence—who study their subjects thoroughly even though they publish very little, and who take a great personal interest in their pupils. They are however rare and they are not exhilarated by their rarity. Even those who believe that they are engaged in a noble calling and who try to live up to their obligations are depressed when they observe the long tail of their profession, the lifelessness of teaching and the dubious practices of Indian colleges and universities, and they are oppressed by the indignity to which their profession is condemned.

It cannot be said that most Indian academics are allowed to idle. The majority who teach in colleges not only are required to teach many hours but they often have to seek supplementary sources of income. Despite the efforts of the University Grants Commission to persuade state governments to share with them the costs of raising and standardizing the salary scale of college teachers, there has thus far

[1] The teaching burden is much lighter in universities than in colleges. Cf. University Grants Commission, *Report on Standards of University Instruction*, New Delhi, 1965, Appendix 18 'Workload of Teachers (Hours per Week)', pp. 215–19.

[2] As recently as 1964, the provision of cubicles for teachers was still regarded as an ideal to be attained.

been little success. Real incomes of college teachers have actually declined; from 1950–1 to 1965–6 the real incomes of college teachers (at constant prices) fell by 10 per cent.[1] Supplements must be found; private tuition—coaching of uncertain students—has for many years been a much discountenanced, much sought-after source of income for the more impecunious and less worldly teachers in universities and colleges[2] (especially the latter). The writing of 'notes' is another of the less agreeable by-products of the ineffectiveness of formal instruction. These comprise elucidations of passages of set texts, glossaries of difficult terms and model answers to past examination questions. 'Notes' are only a printed form of 'tuitions', made available more cheaply and to a wider student public. Both are directed towards examinations and attest both to the examination-orientation of the students and to the students' uncertainty about the efficacy of the instruction which they receive. The teachers' poverty probably contributes to another unseemly feature of Indian academic life, namely intrigue, particularly intrigue over appointments to examinerships, deanships, elections to boards and syndicates.

India is not unique in the fact that the readiness to perform these necessary and boring tasks of academic administration gives rise to conflict among competitors; India's uniqueness seems to be rather in the frequency and intensity with which such conflicts occur and the embittering ramification of their effects. Conflicts for ascendancy are taken so seriously by those for whom the stakes are greatest that they affect deeply the expectations and apprehensions of the more peripheral mass of teachers who believe that their future prosperity depends on being on the side of the winner. The winners might after all be able to influence appointments to higher grades, administrative posts and examinerships and they might be able to curb possible retaliation of the partisans of the losing side.

Sometimes these conflicts about the spoils of academic administration are complicated by the turmoil of national party politics. The penetration of state and national—more often state—politics into the university usually has little to do with issues of substantive public policy on the national and state levels. Politicians occasionally seek university office to obtain the power of patronage which enables them to reward and bind to themselves persons whose support they value; sometimes they seek membership on the governing bodies of universities because of the influence which they think such positions will

[1] The real incomes of university teachers rose by 5 per cent in this period, *Report of the Education Commission*, Government of India, New Delhi, 1966, Table 3.1, p. 47.

[2] The practice is strenuously disapproved by educational administrators and reformers but it seems inevitable as long as teachers' incomes are small and students are lacking in self-confidence.

permit them to exercise within the university and also because of the increment to their prestige which they think will result. The conflicts among politicians for these offices are not always simply the struggles of individuals for advantage; they are often exacerbated by caste loyalties and rivalries. Whatever the motives of the politicians in the governing bodies, they bring into action in the university conflicts which might otherwise be only latent.

The main significance of such intra-university conflicts is that, for periods of varying length and with differences in intensity of sentiment and in scale of involvement, they distract university and college teachers from their professional tasks of research and teaching, from the training and care of students and from the intellectual concerns which should be their primary obligations. It is not only energy and time which are lost but also self-respect. Self-respect is lost because many of those who become involved in these conflicts are not so corrupt that they do not know that they are sinning against the holy ghost of academic life. Many of them know—despite their aggressive self-righteousness while the battle is at its height and their obvious pleasure in combat—that their actions are unworthy of academic existence. Those who do not become immediately involved, either out of higher principle or timidity, are demoralized too. They cannot, even from a position of detachment, resist the belief that their institution and their profession are being degraded and that they themselves are also being degraded by the improprieties of their colleagues.

V

When the first Indian universities were founded in the middle of the nineteenth century, it was not thought in English-speaking countries that universities should be institutions for the conduct of research. Although marked changes began to occur in the next quarter-century in both Britain and the United States, the practice in India continued relatively unchanged. The recruits to the Indian Educational Service were intended by its promoters to raise the intellectual standard of Indian higher education through teaching and administration.[1] They came from an Oxford tradition which did not look upon research as an obligation of the academic man—the German orientalists among them were exceptions to this. Poverty, governmental niggardliness and snobbery permitted this tradition to continue, even at a time when the University of Calcutta was the scene of significant changes,[2] with

[1] My knowledge of the Indian Educational Service is drawn largely from the unpublished research of Miss Irene Gilbert of the University of Chicago.

[2] Calcutta University was the first to *teach* a scientific subject; its university department of chemistry was established in 1915. These developments were largely the result of the initiative of Sir Asutosh Mukerjee, when vice-chancellor of Calcutta University. In the

professorships created through endowments for the promotion of re-search, research scholarships, etc. The other Indian universities were slow to follow the path of Calcutta University but they too began to move in this same direction. Academic opinion about the necessity of research began to change. The Ph.D. has become more common and it is an indication of a somewhat more favourable attitude towards research. Indian students have gone abroad increasingly for post-graduate studies and not primarily for undergraduate work as they once did.

Since independence, the amount of financial resources made available for scientific research in India has increased a great deal. It is not however the universities which have been the beneficiaries of this increase. On the contrary, it is the non-academic, governmental research institutions which have got the lion's share. In the last decades before independence, opportunities for research, particularly in the medical sciences, were becoming more numerous but they were concen-trated largely in non-academic institutions. The Indian government of the period did not look on the universities as promising places in which to do important research.[1]

The early decision of the government of India—it was probably mainly Jawarhalal Nehru's decision—to promote scientific and techno-logical research through the national laboratories of the Council of Scientific and Industrial Research and the Department of Atomic Energy rather than through the universities continued this tradition. It was indicative of the low esteem in which the academic profession was held by the men who ruled India during the early years of its independence. Even the quite recent decision to establish the Indian Institute of Advanced Studies in Simla—far from the universities and cut off from them by the policy of long-term appointments—is a sign of this indifference to or denigration of the academic profession. What it

praise given to Sir Asutosh for this accomplishment, it is usually forgotten that one of the by-products of the development of postgraduate studies in the university was the frustration of the plans, initiated by Henry Roscher James, then principal of Presidency College, to develop the latter from a college restricted by the university into a self-governing, non-affiliating university (Calcutta University Commission, 1917–19, *Report*, vol. I, p. 416). It is a serious question whether India did not lose more by this refusal to allow this important innovation than it gained by the establishment of postgraduate studies in the university. Had James's aspirations been fulfilled, the soul-crushing 'academic lockstep' imposed by the affiliating university might have been alleviated.

[1] This attitude was not confined to the government of India. Indian opinion inclined in the same direction. The Indian Association for the Cultivation of Science, which occupies a significant place in the history of Indian science, was established by its Indian sponsors and patrons in Jadavpur entirely outside the academic system. Cf. also the observations in chapter XVI 'Science, Education and Research' in *Education and National Development: Report of the Education Commission (1964–1966)*, Ministry of Education, Government of India, New Delhi, 1966; also in *Minerva*, VI, 1 (1967), pp. 66–8, 74–5.

means however is that much of the talent which would be available for training research students and for inspiring college and university staffs is more or less isolated and without influence.[1] It leaves the mass of university and college teachers in the situation of 'second-class citizens' of the republic of science.

The thousands of college teachers who never] do any research have been affected by the enhanced prestige of research. They too have begun to accept the obligation to do research as part of the task of a teacher in higher education. In fact, however, they are virtually excluded from the increased opportunities which have in any case been very few in number.[2] As in the major university systems throughout the world at the present time, research is fashionable. Those who do not do it have the burden of proof laid upon them to justify their failure. Those who do no research are made to feel inferior.

Most Indian university teachers—like many university teachers else-where—do little or no research. They have not been trained to do research—the M.A. and the M.Sc. are examination and not research degrees.[3] Their colleges have not the equipment to do it. Yet they

[1] A certain amount of supervision of postgraduate students registered for advanced degrees in universities is done in some of the national laboratories. Cf. A. J. Kidwai, 'Collaboration between Universities and Government Laboratories', *Minerva*, IV, 3 (Spring, 1966), pp. 402–6.

[2] '...except in very few colleges, research facilities are totally non-existent' (*Report on Standards of University Education*, p. 41). Presidency College, Calcutta, is the only Indian college at which teachers had the opportunity to do, and actually did, important research. J. C. Bose, P. C. Ray, P. C. Mahalanobis *et al.* did much of their important research while at Presidency College. It was a unique exception. A young Indian scientist, recently interviewed in London, accurately portrayed the actual situation when he said: '...[if] you are trying to go back to teaching, which might mean a small pittance and having to teach first-year students upwards; this is a big strain on your work, and you might quite likely not get time to do research. The second class people would be more justified in staying here in a sense, except that there is an equally strong argument that they should go back if they want to teach; in fact, they are very well-qualified to teach. No one in Asia seems to be doing anything towards creating the sort of post in which a man can teach and actively do research and involve his students in research at the same time... if there was some sort of scheme by which a man doing research could teach also, I think there would definitely be an improvement' (Rathnakar Kini, 'Self-exiled Asians in the West', *The Hindu*, 24 Oct. 1967).

[3] In 1963–4, there were 2,251 research students in science in India (*University Development in India: Basic Facts and Figures 1963–1964*, p. 51). There were also 328 research students in engineering and technology, medicine, veterinary science and agriculture. If there were 28,000 teachers of scientific subjects and if their average term of service is thirty years there would have to be 300 new teachers at least each year, disregarding a highly probable expansion of teaching staff, associated with expansion of size of student bodies, and losses through death, migration and change of mode of employment. Assuming that a research degree takes three years to complete, it can be seen that the output of formally qualified scientists to meet the demand for academic scientific staff will be quantitatively inadequate. When we recall that conditions of service and work in the national and other government laboratories are much more attractive, and that the Tata Institute in Bombay has an especially great power of intellectual attraction, it seems inevitable that the teaching of science in Indian colleges and universities will have to be reinforced by those who have no training in research and whose

believe that it is expected of them and their failure to conform with expectations furthers their distress. Many of those who are interested in research and who have a considerable aptitude for it leave their universities or colleges for institutions like the Atomic Energy Commission, the Tata Institute of Fundamental Research, the national laboratories of the Council of Scientific and Industrial Research, the Indian Statistical Institute, or the Botanical, Geological and Archaeological Surveys of the government of India. The academic profession thus loses some of its 'highly qualified and talented teachers'.[1] Many others go abroad to make their careers.

Nonetheless, despite this diversion of research talent from the Indian universities, a good deal of research is done there. In 1962–3, research was done by perhaps as many as 2,000 out of a very rough total of 28,160 teachers of scientific and technological subjects.[2] The upshot of these figures is that only a very small proportion of Indian college

undergraduate training has for the most part been elementary, if not archaic. Such recruits to the academic staff, beginning below the present level of their subject by world and by Indian standards, naturally feel themselves outside the centres of intellectual activity.

[1] *Report on Standards of University Education*, p. 44.

[2] I have arrived at a figure of 825 authors of scientific papers by taking the annual average of authors of papers in twelve natural science fields in twenty-five universities over the years 1952–62, as presented in *Scientific Research in Indian Universities* by U. Sen, A. Rahman *et al.*, Survey and Planning of Scientific Research Unit, CSIR, New Delhi, 1965, Table 2, p. 15. The figure 825 assumes that each author did research once during the period in question and was active for only one year during the period covered. This is undoubtedly not the case and 825 is therefore an understatement; at the same time many of the authors were research students who appeared because they were co-authors. This results in an overstatement of the number of academics doing research. The estimate of 28,160 teachers of scientific and technological subjects is derived from *University Development in India: Basic Facts and Figures 1962–63*, University Grants Commission, New Delhi, pp. 39–40. The figure of 28,160 is arrived at by adding teachers of scientific subjects and teachers of scientific subjects in professional courses in university departments and university colleges (5,006) to teachers of science subjects in affiliated colleges (12,579) and teachers of scientific subjects in professional courses in affiliated colleges (10,575). The figure of 10,575 was derived by extrapolation of the proportion of teachers of scientific subjects in professional courses to the total of teachers of all subjects in professional courses in university departments and university colleges (73 per cent) to the total teachers of professional courses in affiliated colleges (14,486). (Dr Ward Morehouse presents a different calculation of 5,600 authors of research papers and 20,000 teachers of scientific subjects. Unpublished manuscript, pp. 127–9.) In 1964, a report of the Council of Scientific and Industrial Research estimated that in 1966/67 4,600 teachers in universities (and colleges) would be doing scientific research. The same report estimated that by 1970–1, 8,000 teachers would be engaged in research. (Zaheer, S. Husain, A. Rahman, and N. Sen, *Investment in Scientific and Technological Research during the Fourth Five Year Plan* [working paper], Council of Scientific and Industrial Research, Survey and Planning of Scientific Research Unit, New Delhi, 14 Sept. 1964, Table 3.1, column 2, not paginated.) These estimates were made in connexion with the Fourth Five Year Plan which was scrapped. Extrapolating backwards and bearing in mind the optimism of the CSIR estimates, I think that Dr Morehouse's figure is a considerable overstatement. The correct figure probably lies somewhere between Dr Morehouse's 5,600 and my 825. A very approximate total is, literally, nearer to the true figure than an approximate total? (Latin *proximus* = the nearest.)

and university teachers of scientific and technological subjects conduct research at a time when it is constantly stressed that teachers should do research, even if only for the sake of the quality of their teaching. Most of those who do research moreover do it under difficulties. The derogation from which the academic profession suffers in opinion is given more substantial form in the meagreness of financial support for academic research.

Expenditure on research by academic scientists is estimated to come to Rs. 6,000 per annum per scientist.[1] Those research workers employed by the Indian Council for Medical Research are supported to the extent of Rs. 16,000 per annum those supported by the Council of Scientific and Industrial Research are provided with Rs. 45,000 per annum; those in the Atomic Energy Department have Rs. 72,000.[2]

The hindrances to effective academic research in India are not only financial. We have already referred to the intra-departmental hierarchies which discourage initiative in research. Poverty as well as discriminatory attitude towards academic institutions limits financial support to research in academic institutions. But quite apart from these factors the inflexibility and slowness of a huge governmental administrative machine play their parts as well. Applications for foreign exchange to purchase equipment and material move slowly through the labyrinthine ways of the middle bureaucracy and this is especially sorely felt when India still has to import very much of its scientific equipment. Even where foreign exchange is not required, bureaucracy interposes itself with dampening influence on the desire to do research.[3]

Much of the research which is carried out is epiphenomenal to world science; most of it appears in Indian scientific journals which are

[1] According to another estimate, the expenditure per research worker in universities in 1963/64 was Rs. 10,470, *Research Expenditure and Manpower* (mimeographed document prepared for the Education Commission, undated, p. 1).

[2] In the United States it is calculated that a scientist requires $30,000 or between Rs. 180,000 and Rs. 240,000 per annum; at CERN $85,000 or Rs. 510,000 to Rs. 680,000 (Ward Morehouse, unpublished manuscript).

[3] A young crystallographer working at one of the universities in Gujerat a few years ago aroused through his work the interest of a colleague working on related problems in a South African university. The Indian scientist needed diamonds to carry his research further and since he could not obtain them from the resources available to him in India, his South African colleague generously sent him some diamonds *gratis* to enable him to get on with his research. The customs in Bombay, as soon as the diamonds arrived there, began to harass the Indian scientist, threatening to bring him into court because he had not obtained permission from the Reserve Bank of India to import the diamonds. The upshot was that the diamonds could not be cleared through customs until one of the governors of the university, well-connected in Delhi, made representations at the highest level of the relevant ministry and obtained a clearance for the parcel of diamonds. Unfortunately, many months had elapsed and the young scientist, having had enough of the harassment of the Bombay customs, had requested that the diamonds be returned to their sender. This had already been done by the time the clearance came through. As a result, the research could not be carried out.

not much noticed outside of India and even in India it is less regarded than foreign science.[1]

Nor is there the consolation available to those Indian academics who do research at their colleges and universities that what they do has the merit of serving the interest of national development. According to a long-prevailing principle, applied or technological research is not to be done in academic institutions. College and university teachers when they do research must do pure research and they must therefore compete with other scientists in a world arena. Very few do so successfully and most do not; their publications are hidden from the world's eye and the reward of their efforts is disregarded by a world-wide audience.

There is no compensation in a vigorously critical and understanding Indian audience. Specialized communities of scientists on an 'all-India' scale are few. Intercourse among Indian academics outside their own universities is rudimentary. It is hard for Indian scholars and scientists to travel abroad, but travel within India is not much easier. Many of them spend their entire academic life in one place or within a narrow radius. Inter-regional appointments—a Maharashtrian in Calcutta or a Bengali in Bombay—are rare. It is as if most Cambridge dons came from East Anglia or most members of the Harvard faculty had all their upbringing, education and academic experience in New England. Learned societies are not strong enough to form an intellectual community. Practically every academic subject has now reached such a degree of specialization that except for a few departments in a few subjects, an academic research worker engaged on particular subjects rarely has the advantage of frequent contact with another research worker engaged on a closely related subject. Stimulation is infrequent and so is the embodiment at close proximity of a high and exigent standard. Mr Nirad Chaudhuri observed not long ago that 'even brilliant research workers in history and science [in India] gave up all further work as soon as they had assured a satisfactory career for themselves. Among Indian professors there are very few who produce new works after their first research thesis.'[2] Mr Chaudhuri suggests that this decline in productive power is to some extent a function of the 'overstrain...due to the fact that the [modern] intellectual activities had only very recently been adopted and were in many cases imposed

---

[1] Cf. 'Classified Distribution of Research Papers in Indian and Foreigh Journals', *Scientific Research in Indian Universities*, Appendix I, Table 0·1, [p. 13] (not paginated). It may be noted that the scientific staff of the Tata Institute for Fundamental Research (Bombay), which is regarded as the most important centre of scientific research in India, published only 21 of their 107 published papers in one year (1965) in Indian journals. B. V. Rangarao, 'Scientific Research in India: An Analysis of Publication', *Journal of Scientific and Industrial Research*, vol. 26, no. 4 (1967), p. 174.

[2] Nirad C. Chaudhuri, *The Intellectual in India*, Vir Publishing House, New Delhi, 1967, pp. 32–3.

from the outside'.[1] There might well be considerable substance in Mr Chaudhuri's explanation but I would attribute no less importance in this fading of intellectual energy to the absence of the stimulus of a relatively densely-populated intellectual community in most of the fields of contemporary academic research. The relative immobility of Indian academics, their small numbers and the great distances which separate them, cut most of them off from personal contact with the most advanced work in their subjects, and in so doing it deprives them of the pressure of a high standard embodied in immediately present intellectual work.

Whether this often-noticed decline in intellectual energy is a consequence of the reassertion of a traditional religious anti-empirical attitude or whether it is a surrender to the obstacles to vital intellectual activity in the Indian academic environment is not by any means clear. What is clear is the high frequency of diminished interest in research and even in study of the literature of their subjects reported by many Indian academics. At present India is much concerned about the 'brain-drain'—although fifteen years ago, when it was as visible as it is now to an outside observer, it was denied on all sides. There is no doubt that the migration of Indian academics abroad is a reality, and since it involves many hundreds of Indians of high qualification and ability, it must represent an enfeeblement of the teaching and research capacities of the Indian academic profession.[2]

VI

A higher educational system is not exclusively a system of cultural institutions transmitting knowledge and advancing it. It is also closely linked with the economic, social and political systems of its society. It depends on the environing society for financial support whether it comes from private endowment, grants from the state or from students' fees. Its performance of its internal tasks are affected by the distribution of educational opportunity within the society and by the social origins of its students. It trains persons, specifically or generally, for the increasingly wide variety of occupations requiring systematic knowledge for their practice. It forms opinion, legitimatory and critical, with respect to the central institutional system of the society. In the minds of those who staff it and of those who exercise power in society—in the economy, in religion, in the polity—it occupies a place as part of the

[1] *Ibid.* p. 32.
[2] In 1966–7, there were about 1,000 Indians on the regular staffs of universities and colleges in the United States. About one-fourth of them were in the fifteen leading universities of the country. It is resonable to infer that these 250 or so were persons of considerable intellectual quality. CSIR, 'Indians Holding Faculty Positions in the U.S.A.,' *Technical Manpower, Bulletin of the Division for Scientific and Technical Manpower*, vol. X, no. 7 (July 1968), pp. 1–2.

centre. An effective university system must be an equal among equals in this central institutional system. If it is not, if it is pushed out to the periphery, it is hampered in its performance of both its purely cultural, i.e. its knowledge-transmitting and -discovering functions, and its civil functions.

The Indian university was formed on models taken from a civil society in which universities could perform both their cultural and their civil functions. It was established in a society in which it might have been able to perform its cultural functions, although the handicaps were very great. It was not however able to perform its civil functions, partly because the society in which it was established was not a civil society.

A heteronomous, heterocephalous society cannot be a civil society. Even the European members of the Indian Educational Service were kept at a distance from the Indian Civil Service as well as from the leaders of the British and Indian communities; the Indian members not less so. What was true of these peaks of the academic profession in the latter part of the nineteenth and the beginning of the twentieth centuries was all the more true of their foothills. (In addition the Indians did not mix outside the college with the European staff members.)

The social gap between the academics and rulers became more pronounced through the decades, as the number of private colleges increased. The latter were distrusted as loci of student agitation, they were also disliked as the manufactures of 'educated natives', a class much disliked by officials and the Anglo-Indian community generally. The dislike of the institutions was extended to dislike of those who manned them.

In the nineteenth century when moderate politics began to appear and even before then, in the reform movements, college teachers played a significant part. In Maharashtrian reform movements, Balshastri Jambhekar and Krishna Shastri Chiplunkar, who had both been college teachers, were leading figures. Later leaders included Mahadeo Govind Ranade, who was acting professor of English at Elphinstone College (1868–71), Naoroji Furunji, an assistant professor, and Dadabhai Naoroji, a professor, at the same institution. Ramkrishna Gopal Bhandarkar, who later became known as one of the greatest Indian indologists, was an active member of the *Prarthana Samaj*. By the beginning of the twentieth century, they had practically no successors, although the size of the academic profession increased markedly.

In the politicization of the educated class in Bengal which began in the last quarter of the nineteenth century,[1] the college teacher was

---

[1] Anil Seal, *The Emergence of Indian Nationalism: Competition and Collaboration in the later Nineteenth Century*, Cambridge University Press, 1968, pp. 194–244.

conspicuously absent. The Indian Association started in 1876 led by the *bhadralok* was governed by a committee of forty-eight; twenty-six of them were lawyers, eight journalists. There is no reference to any of them as teachers. Sixty-eight per cent of the membership of the Indian Association were lawyers.[1] Dr Gordon Johnson lists the members of the Councils formed after the 1892 Councils reform: of fourteen members in the 1893–5, 1895–7 and 1897–9 Councils, eleven were lawyers, two were *zamindars* and one, Surendranath Banerji,[2] was a journalist. Schoolmasters offered themselves for election to municipalities and district boards but not college teachers.[3]

Students (as well as schoolboys) took an active part in the Swadeshi movement but not college teachers. In the secret societies and brotherhoods in which Bengali terrorism was nurtured in the beginning of the twentieth century, secondary school and college students had a large part; so did secondary school teachers. College teachers seem to have abstained.

What was the reason for this gradual separation between academics and politics? In March 1890 the Governor-General in Council declared:

servants of Government have not the same liberty as private individuals and are bound to hold themselves aloof from many movements which are perfectly legitimate in themselves and which private persons are free to promote. Their participation in such movements is open to objection because their connection with them is likely to create and even to be appealed to for the purpose of creating, a false impression in the minds of ignorant persons that such movements have the countenance of Government, and because their influence with the community at large is liable to be impaired by their identifying themselves with the class by which the movement is promoted. For these reasons...(1) as a general rule, no officer of government should attend at a political meeting where the fact of his presence is likely to be misconstrued or to impair his usefulness as an official. (2) No officer of government may take part in the proceedings of a political meeting or in organizing or promoting a political meeting or agitation.[4]

In 1897, following the murders of the British officials, Rand and Ayerst, in Poona, the government of Bombay Presidency enunciated the following principle:

...the instruction of youth should be wholly dissociated from politics...as a consequence...teachers and professors should not take part in political agitation. The observance of this rule must be insisted on, not only in the

---

[1] *Ibid.* p. 215.

[2] He was also the founder and principal of Ripon College in Calcutta in 1882.

[3] Gordon Johnson, 'India Politics 1888–1908', unpublished manuscript.

[4] 'Engagement of Government Officials in Political Agitation', Office of the Director of Public Instruction, Allahabad, File no. X-19 of 1890–1.

case of educational institutions under the direct control of government, but in the case of all institutions which receive aid from public funds.[1]

In 1902 Charles Russell, an Oxford graduate who was recruited to the Indian Educational Service in 1899, organized a conference of teachers in arts colleges to be held on 29 September to discuss the recent Universities Commission Report. On 27 September a notice was circulated to the staff of Presidency College stating that in accordance with Home Department Rulings of 1890 and 1898 government servants could not attend meetings to discuss government policy. Russell, in a letter of 8 November 1902 addressed to Lord Curzon, protested against the prohibitory order, denying that the Report was government policy; he said that as a result of the prohibition, government educationists could not attend and the conference was a failure.

On 4 May 1907, Sir Herbert Risley, secretary to the Government of India, addressed the following communication to the Chief Secretaries of the government of Bengal, Eastern Bengal and Assam, and Burma:

I am directed to address you on the subject of the principles to be observed and the line of action to be followed with the object of protecting higher education in India from the dangers with which it is threatened by the tendency of both teachers and pupils to associate themselves with political movements and to take a prominent part in organizing and carrying out overt acts of political agitation...

A [college] professor is dealing with more advanced and more responsible material than a schoolmaster and it is everywhere recognized that he may claim a larger discretion in respect of the expression of opinion. But he also has his special obligations. If he abuses his position by diverting the minds of his students to political agitation, if he encourages them to attend political meetings or personally conducts them to such meetings, or if while avoiding open propagandism, he adopts a line of action which disturbs and disorganizes the life and work of the college at which he is employed and if the governing body of the college fails to check such abuse, then it is clearly the duty of the University to interfere in the interest of the educational efficiency of which it is the constituted guardian. If the University were to refuse to control its affiliated colleges in this respect, it would fail to carry out the educational trust with which the law has invested it and it would be the duty of the government to intervene.[2]

In 1909, J. A. Cunningham, a member of the Indian Educational Service, teaching at Presidency College, wrote a letter to the well-known liberal journalist, S. K. Ratcliffe, requesting him to cause a public protest to be made against the action of the government of Bengal in

---

[1] 'Protection of Higher Education from Dangers with which it is threatened by participation of teachers and pupils in Political Movements', Education Branch (A-June 1907), Nos. 76–9, p. 2.

[2] Government of India, *Proceedings in the Home Department*, Education Branch (A-June 1907), Nos. 332–4.

transporting a number of teachers charged with involvement in a terrorist episode. Cunningham said that the government's action 'will ultimately play into their hands'. For this Cunningham was severely censured, since such a proceeding was manifestly inconsistent with the responsibilities attaching to the position of a government servant.[1]

The firm hand of government over the Indian academic, however much it might have elevated the level of instruction in colleges where the Indian Educational Service operated, had a harmful effect on the academic profession's performance of its civil function. The coming of the Gandhian ascendancy in the Indian political movement was a further barrier. The academic profession was teaching a culture imported from abroad in the face of a political movement which denied the validity of that culture for India. It was serving the purposes of the alien regime through accepting employment in its institutions and through educating young persons who would aspire to employment in other governmental institutions. The academic institutions themselves were alien in inspiration and disjunctive *vis-à-vis* the Indian tradition. The medium of instruction was an alien one. Gandhism set itself against all these.

When the civil disobedience movement urged students to leave their colleges and many students responded, their Indian teachers ordinarily remained at their posts. In many cases they were sympathetic with the students and with the national movement but there were practically no instances of resignation by teachers from their academic posts. Academic persons played no part in the Congress Party, perhaps because they feared the heavy hand of the Risley circular, perhaps because they felt ill at ease in the resurgence of traditional Hinduism which was associated with the movement dominated by Gandhi.

To the isolation from civil life—there was really very little in Imperial India—and from the actuality of oppositional politics, Gandhism added the sense of isolation from India itself. Ever since the renascence of Hinduism which followed very soon after the short-lived occidentophilia of the first half of the nineteenth century, western culture, despite the universal fascination it held for the educated, had carried with it an overtone of betrayal. The acceptance of modern culture implied departure from the ancestral domain, not territorially but in the realm of the spirit. Gandhian populism, which sought unsuccessfully to avoid an exclusively Hindu idiom, turned to the peasantry and the poor as the true bearers of the Indian essence. Those who espoused and taught western culture were turning away from this Indian essence.

Who in India were the chief embodiments of western culture and thus most out of affinity with the Indian essence? Not the lawyers

[1] Government of India, *Proceedings of the Home Department*, Education Branch (A-May 1909), Nos. 12–16.

because, although they practised in an imported legal system, they were among the main actors in the national movement; not the business men because they usually were traditional in their domestic life and they financed the national movement; not the middle and lower ranks of the government service since they were generally not much immersed in western culture; not the small number of Indian members of the Indian Civil Service because they were powerful, and power—even hostile power—evoked awe; not even secondary school teachers because they were not so much implicated in western culture. It was the academic profession carrying on its work in the alien language and expounding the alien culture which was the most cut off from the Indian essence.

The highly educated Indian college or university teacher had no-where to turn. There was no civil life in India; oppositional politics were forbidden to him and they also refused him. He was barred from social intercourse with the educated British except for his own colleagues —aside from this there were few highly educated Britons in India except for members of the Indian Civil Service with whom any relationship was practically out of the question for academics. The peasantry too was out of the question; after all who, except civil servants, land-lords, money lenders, craftsmen, small merchants and other peasants associated with peasants anywhere? Nonetheless, the accusation of being 'out of touch with the masses' touched a tender spot, and politicians, even educated politicians, still exploit it.[1]

What I have been describing is the inherited 'subjective map' of the position of the academic in Indian public life as it appears by and large to the academic. In actual fact the situation is somewhat different. The gap is not as unbridgeable as the fundamental image has it. The two presidents of the Republic of India have both been former academics. In the present Indian cabinet, Dr V. K. R. V. Rao is now minister of education. In his earlier career he developed the Delhi School of Economics of the University of Delhi into the most interesting centre of economic analysis outside western Europe and the United States. Before that he was an academic economist of some merit. His predecessor was another academic, Dr Triguna Sen.[2] The deputy chairman

[1] Professor Sher Singh, until recently minister of state for education in the Government of India, said in justifying the government's campaign against the use of English as medium of instruction in higher education: 'Our masses have lost all contact with the intelligentsia who are living in an ivory tower' (*Indian Express*, 23 Sept. 1967). Academic intellectuals are criticized for excessive cosmopolitanism, for being 'content to write in English and to seek appreciation for our work outside India rather than in India' (President Zakir Husain, 23 Aug. 1967). 'The collaboration of Indian scholars with foreign scholars is justified only if Indian intellectuals were to convey their knowledge to the Indian people by writing in the Indian languages' (*Times of India*, 24 Aug. 1967). The theme is incessant.

[2] Dr Sen did not hesitate to use the conventional politician's criticisms of the Indian academic as 'being out of touch with the masses' during his ministry. Such criticism from a

of the Planning Commission is Dr D. R. Gadgil, one of the most eminent Indian economists and founder of the Gokhale Institute of Economics and Politics in Poona.[1] From time to time, since independence as well as before, academics, especially economists, are asked to serve on one panel or government commission or another. As consultants to government, Indian academics play a much more restricted role than they do in the United States or Great Britain. Professor P. C. Mahalanobis, who was statistical adviser to the Planning Commission and major consultant in matters of economic and science policy during the prime ministry of Jawaharlal Nehru, was an exception. Even in matters of science policy, Indian university scientists play a very modest role. The Ministry of Defence has had two leading academic scientists as its consultants but the Scientific Advisory Committee to the Cabinet with a membership of fifteen includes only one active academic scientist—the professor of botany of the University of Madras.

There is very little interchange between the higher civil service and the universities. Academics who leave the academic profession to enter government service ordinarily enter in the intermediate grades. Retired senior civil servants, if they do not retire completely, either go into business or if they are academically inclined become associated with non-university research institutions such as the Indian Institute of Public Administration.

Similarly, party politics involve very few academics in the work of the party. In recent years, except for Dr Humayan Kabir, who was once an esteemed teacher of philosophy in Calcutta (Presidency College), no significant Congress party figure has been a former university or college teacher. In the opposition parties, Hiren Mukerji (Communist Party of India), N. R. Malkani (Jana Sangh) and N. R. Ranga (Swatantra Party) have formerly been college teachers but on the whole, despite their quietly held anti-political and apolitical attitudes, Indian academics have held themselves apart from oppositional party activities nearly as much as from the activities of the long dominant Congress Party.

This atrophy of the civil organ of the academic profession manifests itself in matters with more immediate academic bearings. I have already referred to the feebleness of the learned and scientific professional societies in India in the purely scholarly and scientific sphere. They are more inert in making pronouncements or representations in matters which involve their expertise or their professional interests.

As individuals, they do not engage in the publicistic activity which is

former academic comes easily, not because it makes sense but because it is so widely shared, at least ambivalently, by so many academics. Cf. my 'The Implantation of Universities', *Universities Quarterly*, vol. 22, no. 2, March 1968, pp. 142–66, especially pp. 142–6.

[1] Itself, significantly enough, founded outside the University of Poona, although in the course of time relations became very intimate.

common among academics in Great Britain, Western Germany or the United States. It is seldom that one sees a turnover article in a leading Indian newspaper on some important current economic or political issue written by an academic. In the intense discussion or dispute about the medium of instruction which has been going on for some years, only teachers of law, engineering and medicine have expressed themselves in public individually and corporately on the question. The majority of college and university teachers—apart from a group at the University of Delhi—have been surprisingly silent, although many have definite opinions and all are bound to be affected by the outcome, whatever it is. Mr A. B. Shah, who was for many years professor of mathematics in Fergusson College (University of Poona) and who is an outstanding exception to the above proposition about the attrition of civility in the Indian academic profession, has written:

Nor have they proved capable of coming together over issues that demand their judgement unless it were in support of the Government. The proceedings of the various learned conferences make instructive reading in what they omit to discuss as in what they do not. For instance, the All-India Political Science Conference paid little or no attention to the question of the linguistic reorganisation of the states; nor did the All-India Economic Conference examine the question of nationalisation and democratic socialism until decisions were already taken independently of the academic world.[1]

VII

The Indian academic profession has suffered from having been born under three unlucky stars. It was unable, because of the poverty of the country, an unfortunately chosen constitutional model and an uncongenial cultural tradition, to develop vitality as an intellectual community with a variety of overlapping, more specialized intellectual sub-communities. Coming into existence in a society which was not a civil society, it could not develop a sense of affinity with the other sectors of the elites—alien and Indian—which ruled the Indian polity, economy and culture. And being more advanced in the scale on which it was carried on than the economic and social structure of the country, it could not function as an effective training stage for the central and lesser elites of the country. These latter two misfortunes accentuated the first. The attrition of civility and superfluity in the performance of its function in the Indian economy have inhibited intellectual ardour and hampered the growth of academic intellectual traditions.

[1] Cf. 'Public Opinion in Indian Democracy' in S. P. Aiyar and R. Srinivasan (eds.), *Studies in Indian Democracy*, Allied Publishers, Bombay, 1965, p. 530. Cf. also [A. D. Gorwala], 'The Public Voice', *Opinion* (Bombay), vol. IX, no. 35, pp. 7–10, for a severe criticism of the civil deficiencies of the Indian Economics Association.

All the above notwithstanding, India today, as the most effective democratic polity among all the new states and as an underdeveloped country with a growing modern sector, would not be what it is without the long and ill-rewarded labours of the Indian academic profession. Practically every eminent Indian scientist in the world today—and their number is not inconsiderable—started in the Indian higher educational system. Practically all Indian engineers have had much of their training in India. Nearly all the better Indian scholars in history, anthropology, sociology, linguistics, etc., have had at least their initial if not all their training in Indian colleges and universities. The same is true of the leading Indian journalists and the most progressive and imaginative of Indian politicians. Their outlook is inconceivable without that which they assimilated from their higher education in India. This is a remarkable accomplishment. One cannot imagine modern India without that accomplishment. It is an accomplishment which bears witness to the indomitability of the human spirit in India and to the existence of a nurturant tradition with which strong characters could make contact under the debris of historical misfortune. The paradox requires respectful and grateful acknowledgement and further study.

THE MERCHANTS OF SURAT,
c. 1700–50

ASHIN DAS GUPTA

From about the middle of the sixteenth century for about two hundred years the city of Surat in the *subah* of Gujarat was the major port of the Mughal Empire. Through this port much of northern and western India maintained cultural, political and commercial connexions with western Asia and the Indonesian world. At the turn of the eighteenth century, if not earlier, the city was the home of the largest commercial marine in India. The mercantile classes of this great trading metropolis naturally played an important role in the city and through it in the trading world of India. In this article I shall be concerned with some of the features to be associated with the role of the merchants of Surat in the first half of the eighteenth century. I have selected this period in order to look at the Indian world immediately before the establishment of the British Empire. But the sources for this study, as with any other study of Indian trade, are almost exclusively European. They comprise the archives of the Dutch and the English East India Company, supplemented by the papers of Sir Robert Cowan, governor of Bombay 1728–34, now preserved at the Public Record Office, Belfast. Needless to say these sources are neither satisfactory nor adequate, but they are contemporary, detailed and useful. I do not know of any Indian material directly bearing upon trade; however, the famous Persian history *Mirat-i-Ahmadi* completed in the 1750s by Ali Muhammad Khan, the last of the Imperial *dewans* at Ahmadabad, the capital of the *subah* of Gujarat, has some supplementary information on Surat, and so, to a lesser degree, has the biography of the Parsi merchant Rustamji Manakji written in 1711 at Surat.[1]

---

[1] The papers of the Dutch East India Company are preserved at the *Algemeen Rijksarchief*, The Hague, and the English papers at the India Office Library, London. As it will appear these papers contain, in addition to letters written from Surat to Bombay, Batavia, Amsterdam and London at the time, several diaries and journals kept in these years, different kinds of accounts and a number of letters and petitions written by the Indian merchants. The papers of Sir Robert Cowan are the earliest of such private collections and elucidate the magnitude and methods of trade of the European private merchants. Sir Robert had strong connexions with Surat and specially with the family of Seth Laldas Vitaldas Parak. I have studied this collection in microfilms at the India Office Library and I wish to acknowledge my most sincere gratitude to Dr Richard Bingle for drawing my attention to it. The Persian text of the *Mirat-i-Ahmadi*, edited by Syed Nawab Ali in two volumes, is available in the Gaekwad Oriental Series, nos. 33 and 34 [Baroda, 1927–8]. Ali Muham-

We have no reliable data on the population of Surat in our period and impressionistic estimates made at different times in the eighteenth century varied between 200,000 and 400,000.[1]

It is also quite impossible to tell what percentage of this population took part directly in trade, although indirectly everyone living in the town must have been connected to it. At this point it may be helpful to find out what other kinds of social groups were to be found at Surat. There was, obviously, an important group of administrative personnel, although Surat was never an important administrative centre. The centre for administration was the capital of the *subah* at Ahmadabad, a hundred and forty miles to the north of Surat. Ahmadabad was also an important manufacturing town in the eighteenth century and a variety of cottons and silks were made in it or in its neighbourhood, which was not the case with Surat.

At Surat, the civil administration was entrusted to a port-officer (*mutasaddi*) and the defence of the town was the responsibility of the commander of the local castle (*killadar*). The *mutasaddi*, early in the eighteenth century, was often an important *mansabdar* of the empire but gradually lesser people were appointed to this post. The *killadar* was never of this class, as is shown by the fact that he drew his income from only four *parganas* attached to Surat and the whole amounted to no more than Rs. 100,000.[2] Apart from these two there was a *darogha* for sea-

mad Khan also wrote an account of Gujarat as a supplement to this history. This work, called the *khatima*, is available in English translation by Syed Nawab Ali and C. N. Seddon, Gaekwad Oriental Series, no. 63 [Baroda, 1928].

An English translation of the *Mirat* by Professor M. Lokhandwala is also now available in the same series no. 146 (Baroda, 1965). [All references in this chapter are to Professor Lokhandwala's translation.] For the text of the biography of Rustamji Manakji, written by Jamshed Kaikobad, private tutor to Nowroji Rustumji, the third son of Rustam, in 1711, with extensive annotations and translations in English, see Sir J. J. Modi, *Asiatic Papers*, vol. 4 (Bombay, 1929), pp. 101–320.

[1] Alexander Hamilton, an English free trader using the port of Surat in the 1720s, estimated its population to be 200,000. See *A New Account of the East Indies*, W. Foster (ed.) (London 1930) vol. 1, p. 89. William Phipps, governor of Bombay, once described Seth Laldas Vitaldas as 'the principal of about four hundred thousand people' as opposed to Nowroji Rustumji, whose community, the Parsis, formed a small and, according to Phipps, despised section of the populace of Surat. See *B(ombay) P(ublic) P(roceedings)*, vol. 6, consultation 23 Feb. 1728. Walter Ewer, ex-member of the Court of Directors, on a visit to Surat in 1796 noted that 'the population was supposed to be about three hundred thousand', *Home Miscellaneous*, vol. 438, p. 37.

[2] The distinction between Ahmadabad and Surat is to be seen in the ranks of officers appointed to these two places. Thus Amanat Khan, who was the *dewan* at Ahmadabad, was appointed to be the *mutasaddi* at Surat in 1699, and Kartalab Khan, who was *mutasaddi* at Surat with the rank of 900 (*zat*) and 700 (*sawar*), do-*aspah, se-aspeh*, was promoted to be the governor of Ahmadabad with a rank of 5,000 (*zat*), 4,000 (*sawar*), do-*aspah, se-aspeh*: *Mirat-i-Ahmadi*, pp. 278–9 and 283. For a discussion of Mughal ranks, see M. Athar Ali, *The Mughal Nobility Under Aurangzeb* (Asia Publishing House, 1966), pp. 38–43. In 1720 Philip Sael, Dutch *directeur*, in a letter to Batavia expressed his apprehensions that now that lesser men were taking charge of the Gujarati towns it would affect the administration

customs as well as for land customs, a *kotwal* for policing the town and two *faujdars* of uncertain functions. Each one of them would have a personal retinue, none of which was large. There were a few other Imperial officials as well, like the reporters, public and confidential, who were to keep the court informed of events in the town, and the *desais* who were to supervise the collection of Imperial revenue. There was also a *kazi* to administer justice and three *muftis* as legal experts and registrars of legal documents. These men do not seem to have had any significant group of subordinate officials. At the beginning of the century men of this official class often came and went, but as the century wore on this movement gradually ceased and they became like any other local group.[1]

Apart from the officials of the city, Surat had an important group of religious men. Gujarat as a whole was an intensely religious part of the country and Surat had the added distinction of being the port of embarkation of pilgrims for the *haj*. Every year therefore a large concourse of Muslim pilgrims from the north and west of India converged on the town. I am unable to discuss the local religious hierarchy and the place of the individual Muslim divines in it, but both the Dutch and the English documents from time to time noted the important influence of men like Shaikh Fazal, Syed Sadulla and Syed Zainal Abidin in the affairs of the city. Syed Zainal Abidin in particular was the most outstanding man among them in the 1730s and, judging from the fact that the *dawat* of the Ismaili Bohras was at this time in Saurashtra and Malwa, it is possible that he was the *amil* of their *dai* at Surat. Some of these men were certainly interested in worldly affairs as well and took part in ordinary business transactions.[2] Together with the senior

---

adversely: *K(olonial) A(rchief)* 1839, p. 28. A memorandum drawn up in 1759 on the revenues of the Surat Castle is to be found in G. W. Forrest, *Selections from the State Papers of Bombay* (Home Series, vol. 2, Bombay 1887), pp. 108–16.

[1] Excellent discussions on the local official hierarchy are to be found in the memoirs of Hendrik Zwardecroon, 1702, in *H(ooge) R(egeering) te Batavia*, no. 834, pp. 16–30, and that of Jan Schreuder, 1750, *H.R.* no. 838, p. 61 ff. The transfers noted in the early years of the century in the notes kept at Surat gradually ceased. Thus Joan Diodati, a senior Dutch official, noted in his personal diary on 3 September 1699 that the *kotwal* of Surat was being replaced by an officer sent from Delhi: *K.A.* 1558, p. 369. Again in a letter to Batavia, the Dutch Council noted on 21 July 1708 that the higher officials at Surat had all been recently replaced by orders from the Court, including the *kazi*, the *harkara* (the Imperial reporter) and the *kotwal*: *K.A.* 1645, p. 235. No such comments are to be found later on.

[2] Early in 1713, the Dutch were in high hopes of getting the palace of Itibar Khan, lately *mutasaddi* at Surat, by virtue of an Imperial *firman*. These hopes however were frustrated mainly by the strenuous efforts of Shaikh Fazal supported by Syed Sadulla. They created a great tumult in town, threatened to leave in a body and finally persuaded the *killadar* to come out openly for them. Shaikh Fazal had lent Rs. 5,000 to the sons of Itibar, and thought that this money would be lost if the house went to the Dutch: *K.A.* 1710, pp. 341–4. Syed Zainal Abidin was repeatedly mentioned, usually as Zaid Zein, in the papers of the 1730s and, as will be seen below, was a leading signatory in Ahmad Chellaby's letter in 1732. In 1737 Syed Zainal was involved in a dispute with the English Company, who were trying to realize a large claim from their broker Seth Jagannathdas Laldas. Syed Zainal, who

officials and the leading divines, the principal merchants of Surat comprised what were called the 'principal inhabitants' of the town. In any public matter of great import, these 'principal inhabitants' were always consulted, and often invited to act in the interest of the city.

It would be instructive to look at two lists, one giving the names of some of the leading merchants in 1727, and the other a list of leading citizens, merchants, officials and religious leaders in 1734. It is also of interest to note the occasions of these lists. In 1727 the directeur of the Dutch Company at Surat, Abraham Weijns, was recalled to Batavia to answer charges against his administration and he was replaced by Herman Bruinink. But Weijns was very unwilling to go and, according to Bruinink, began to conspire with the *nawab* (i.e. the *mutasaddi*) against him. It was to prove this fact that Bruinink drew up a declaration which he had attested by the seals of 'the great merchants of the city, Muslim as well as Hindu', and their names were as follows: Mulla Muhammad son of Muhammad Ali, Haji Ahmad Chellaby, Ibrahim Chellaby, Hussain Chellaby, Shaikh Muhammad Kodsi, Hassan Badawi, Abdul Rahaman Sulaimanji, Omar Chellaby, Shaikh Ali Kaderi, Haji Hussain Abid, Muhammad Salebi Saketti, Haji Muhammad Baghdadi, Ilias Osman Baghdadi (?), Mustafa, Abdul Kader Kamal, Mustafa Sale, Muhammad Aref, Kika Dada, Vanarasidas Vallabhdas, Tapidas Revadas, and Vallabhdas Daldas.

The second list was enclosed in a letter to Robert Cowan, governor of Bombay, by Ahmad Chellaby dated at Surat, 24 September 1732. Ahmad Chellaby thanked Cowan for help received from the English during a recent rebellion led by the merchants against the *mutasaddi* of the town, and enclosed what he called 'a certificate under the seals of the Principal Inhabitants of this City, as well Syeds as officers and Merchants' testifying to the gratitude of the city for what the English had done. This list (drawn up in two columns) was as follows: Ahmad Chellaby, Abdul Kader, Abdul Gunny, Abdul Fattah, Abdul Rahman, Abdul Salem, Mahmud Sayyid, Ibrahim, Hasan, Ali Ibrahim, Abdul Rahman Sulaimanji, Rahim Mulla in one column, and, facing it in another, Syed Zainal Abidin, Syed Abdulla Ibn Xarift(?), Syed Abdul Kader Ibn Ahmad, Syed Ataula Ibn Ismael, Syed Sayyid Ibn Omar, Kazi Hydaitullah, Mufti Azimuddin, Mufti Lutfullah, the Third Mufti [without name], Haji Ahmad Soalia, and Mahmud Arifa.[1]

---

had also lent some money to Seth Jagannathdas, took possession of a house and a garden of the Seth as security, and the English had to appeal to the *mutasaddi* and have the Syed's peons removed from the premises: *S(urat) F(actory) R(ecords)*, vol. 21, entry 27 Mar. 1737. For the organization of the Ismaili Bohras, see S. C. Misra, *Muslim Communities in Gujarat* (Asia Publishing House, 1964), pp. 39–40.

[1] For Bruinink's list: *K.A.* 1970, pp. 197–8. The letter from Chellaby is in *B.P.P.*, vol. 6, 6 Oct. 1732, pp. 34–5. Needless to say, much ingenuity has to be exercised in reconstruct-

The first thing that strikes one is that, although these two lists were drawn up within five years of each other, of the twenty-one merchants in the first list only three figure in the second and even then one, Abdul Kader, must be regarded as doubtful. Too much importance should not however be attached to this as much depended on who was drawing up the list and who were available at the time. It is however interesting to note that Ahmad Chellaby who was the principal figure among the Chellaby clan at Surat did not think it necessary to include any of his clansmen in his list, although they were so prominent in the declaration of Bruinink. It is possible he thought his own attestation was sufficient for the purpose. Secondly, it is important to note the predominance of the Muslim merchants in the first list and the total exclusion of the Hindus from the second. Two explanations may be considered in this context. First, although the Hindus were numerically by far the largest group and no doubt controlled much of the wealth in town, individually the Muslim shipowners were the wealthiest and most influential. To this has to be added the fact that the administration was Muslim, which must have given some influence to the leading Muslim merchants, which the Hindus lacked. Secondly, the Hindu family which was undoubtedly the most influential in town also happened to be the family which worked in the interest of the English Company. Seth Laldas was the head of the family of Paraks and the broker to the English. Naturally enough Bruinink's list would not include him and if Chellaby's letter had been inspired by Cowan himself, as there is some reason to think that it was, it would not include the Paraks, because their support for the English would be taken for granted. There is one other important omission from both these lists, that of the leading Parsi family of the Rustumjis. But again, as this family provided some of the important brokers to the English during this half-century, their omission can be similarly explained. The fact that Armenian, Kashmiri, Jewish or Sindhi merchants were not included can be explained by the supposition that, although they carried on important trade in Surat, individually none of them merited inclusion. There is one other point to note before we leave these lists. These thirty or thirty-one men introduced to us as the leading merchants of Surat are for the most part men in shadows as far as our documentation is concerned. It is true we know a considerable amount about some of them, and a little about a few others, but many of these men are only names. Now the documents we have are always informative about anyone who took any important

ing the possible Indian names from their forms in European transmigration. The name Chellaby I have retained as this was the fairly consistent spelling in the English documents throughout. The *Mirat* has it as Chalabi and Chalapi, which are perhaps more accurate. A question mark indicates that I suspect my own ingenuity or that I admit defeat.

part in public affairs. Thus it seems fair to come to the conclusion suggested by common sense, that many of the rich merchants at Surat, though contributing in a general sense to the influence of their community, took no individual part in the affairs of the city but were content to fall in with the leading figures among them.

Let us now take a closer look at some of the men on these lists and see what kind of things are known about them and what conclusions these would suggest. The man who leads the list of Bruinink is undoubtedly the person deserving the most attention, although he was personally not very important at the time the list was drawn up. This man, Muhammad son of Muhammad Ali, must have been a very young lad at the time, as five years later when his father was murdered he was considered only a youth. It is significant that Muhammad Ali himself did not attest Bruinink's declaration, probably because he thought this sort of thing beneath his dignity. This he well might, as he was at the time virtually the governor of Surat, in all but name. The fortunes of this family of Ismaili Bohras had been founded by his grandfather, that is the great-grandfather of Muhammad who attested Bruinink's declaration, Mulla Abdul Gafur, in the second half of the seventeenth century. The members of this family were always called Mullas, sometimes Maulanas. This is curious, because they were neither particularly holy nor in any sense learned. It is possible as local legends seem to suggest that Abdul Gafur, before he built up his fortune through trade, was connected with a mosque, probably as a teacher. It is interesting to add at this point that another family fortune, that of the Rustumjis, was founded by a man who was of the priestly classes among the Parsis and very poor before he took to trade. The family of Seth Dayaram, broker to the Dutch East India Company in the 1720s, also had a similar introduction to prosperity. Ruidas, Dayaram's father, was a *munshi* at the Dutch warehouse at Surat and took to trade in a modest way, on which his sons built. There are a few other examples of this kind as well. Now from these it would seem that there was a certain openness about the world of the merchants at Surat. It was of course always a great help if one inherited a fortune, but without that one was not neccesarily in a hopeless position. It would also appear to be the case that men came to trade from other kinds of occupation, especially from genteel but indigent families.[1]

---

[1] For the local legends concerning Abdul Gafur, see *Gazetteer of the Bombay Presidency*, vol. 2 (*Surat*) (Bombay, 1887), p. 110 n. The immaturity and youth of Muhammad, the eldest son of Muhammad Ali, was commented on by directeur Pieter Phoonsen on 17 June 1733: *K.A.* 2213, p. 120. All the Mullas were always referred to as bohras. The fact that they were Ismailis is my conjecture from the private mosque the family had near their ancestral home. I believe the Sunni bohras usually went to public mosques. Further there is the fact that Ismaili Bohras at Surat are called Mulla bohras. As to the Rustumjis, in addition to the

The major concentration of the Mulla family was in shipping. Some data on the shipping controlled by the Mullas are available from the list of passes issued by the Dutch between the years 1707 and 1736, after which unfortunately this annual list disappears from the Dutch papers. It has to be noted that these lists were usually only 'extracts' from the total of passes issued in any year and they did not enumerate vessels which fell below a certain size. There is some reason to believe that the size of the vessels was usually understated. The largest ship on these lists did not go beyond 1,200 *khandis*, that is 400 tons, but other evidence indicates that ships of up to 600 tons were at the time owned by Indian merchants of Surat. We have no indication as to how the fee for these passes was collected, but there is the possibility that the fee went up according to size. If that was so, there would be a reason for understating the actual measurement. The passes gave the date of issue, the name of the ship, the name of its owner, the community to which he belonged, the name of the *nakhuda* who would command the ship during the intended voyage, the tonnage of the ship, the number of its guns and finally its destination. The cargo was never noted. Naturally the Dutch secretary who made out the passes was often not very sure about the Indian names, and the spellings varied considerably. Data about tonnage and the number of guns carried by a particular ship also varied over the years, but this variation was slight. Ships were lost fairly regularly either through natural causes at sea or by piracy. They were sometimes replaced by others with identical names, and this causes some confusion. But, bearing all this in mind, much reliable information can be gathered from these passes, especially when checked with data from other documents. In all, thirty-four vessels are shown against members of the Mulla family in these years. During the time of Abdul Gafur the total was eighteen, of which as many as fourteen were sent out together in the year 1707–8. This was the maximum figure for any year in this half-century, the usual number being about ten. It is therefore impossible to tell whether more than fourteen ships were ever owned by the family at any particular time. Abdul Gafur's son Abdulla Hai died shortly after his father and did not add to the fleet. But Muhammad Ali, the grandson, added thirteen, although these were for the most part smaller vessels. We do not know exactly how many he lost, but there is stray evidence of his losses. The son of Muhammad Ali, Mulla Muhammad, who later became Mulla Fakruddin, and his brother Mulla Aminuddin, are known to have added three more ships

biography of Rustum himself cited above, much information is available in P. S. Pissurlencar, *Portuguese Records on Rustom Manock* (Nova-Goa, 1936). The reader will have to ignore the variant spellings: it is the same man. The origins of the family of Dayaram of course can be traced in the Dutch records, especially in a letter to Batavia, 10 Feb. 1718, where Ruidas Commersie(?) was first mentioned: *K.A.* 1805, pp. 54–5.

to the family total, but again we do not know their losses and no exact information is available for the years after 1736. The largest ship of the Mullas was called the *Hussaini* of a declared tonnage of 400 tons, carrying twenty-five guns of unknown calibre.[1]

Of the leading merchants mentioned in the two lists of Bruinink and Ahmad Chellaby, at least six are repeatedly mentioned in the passes issued by the Dutch and it is possible that some more of them were ship-owners as well, although their names cannot be definitely identified. Haji Ahmad Chellaby, son of Haji Sale Chellaby, was himself an important shipping magnate, although the maximum number of his ships that I have come across in any one year is eight.[2] The remarkable thing about shipping at Surat is that very few of them were owned by the Hindus. The maximum number in any one year in the list of passes is nine out of fifty-seven in 1707–8. Five of these ships were very small, between 50 and 100 tons; one was 150, two of about 175 tons and one a large vessel of Tapidas Surji of Cambay of 1,000 *khandis* carrying seven guns, commanded by *nakhuda* Trimbakdas Trikamdas and sailing from Cambay to Munga-lore. Apart from Tapidas, there was another Cambay bania, Haridas Kal-yan, taking out a pass this year, the rest being all from Surat. We know very little about these men apart from the fact that they turned up from year to year in the list of passes and their number dwindled as the mercantile marine at Surat itself was gradually reduced. The Hindus who played a prominent role in the city, for example the five men mentioned in Bruinink's list, were all merchants, brokers and *sarafs*, but not shippers. It is safe to say that shipping at Surat was controlled by the Muslims as owners and sailors.

The number of ships owned by the Mullas should give us some idea, admittedly vague, of the wealth of the family. It is of course impossible to gain any precise information about this. At his death in 1718, Abdul Gafur is reputed to have left eight and a half million rupees in cash. This was presumably a conjecture formed at the bazaar at Surat but passed into local legend. In addition to his ships and a very consider-able amount in cash, Gafur also left a garden in the northern suburbs of the city, a family mansion in *Saudagar-pura*, the locality of the mer-chants within the city, at least one other house in its neighbourhood, a

---

[1] The shipping list for the season 1707–8 is in *K.A.* 1638, pp. 268–81. Mulla Abdulla Hai, son of Abdul Gafur, appears as a ship-owner only in the season 1719–20: *K.A.* 1839, pp. 202–3. Muhammad Ali begins to figure prominently from 1721–22: *K.A.* 1875, pp. 145–8. There is no list for the season in between. Muhammad Hussain's first appearance is in 1732–3: *K.A.* 2185, p. 1351. Of the evidence relating to the losses suffered by Muhammad Ali there is the interesting letter from him to Charles Boone, governor of Bombay in 1720, in which he urged upon Boone the necessity of a coalition against the Angria: G. W. Forrest, *Selections from the State Papers of Bombay* (vol. 2, Bombay, 1887), p. 18.

[2] The eight ships of Chellaby were noted, not in the pass list but in the list of arrivals, in the year 1729: *K.A.* 2060, pp. 190–1.

mosque probably also in the same neighbourhood, a wharf to the south of Surat and some landed property on an island near Gogo in the gulf of Cambay. Muhammad Ali, his grandson, expanded the wharf by acquiring a considerable amount of land in its neighbourhood, and developed the area into a suburban complex. He built a fort there, several houses, and even laid down a few streets. The whole thing he called Maghbulabad and there was a time in the late 1720s when it was thought that Maghbulabad would become a new Surat. Abdul Gafur himself is not known to have maintained any troops, although he must have had his slaves and retainers as all the wealthy Muslim merchants appear to have done. Muhammad Ali, however, in the early 1730s raised a small army of about 2,000 men, to defend himself against the *mutasaddi* Sohrab Khan. In addition to this we must remember the sailors who manned the fleet of the Mulla family and who would be available for several months of the year when the ships were at their home port. It is well to note at this point that the recruiting of troops by a merchant at Surat was a very unusual measure and the government frowned upon it. The army which Muhammad Ali gathered together became a cause of conflict between the port-officer and himself. At the same time there was a close rapport between these two, and Sohrab Khan leaned heavily upon Ali's purse to keep his position safe at the Imperial Court at Delhi.[1]

Such wealth and such influence were of course no common phenomenon. The position of the Mulla family was quite unique and we must not think of Surat as a city dominated by its leading merchants. Ahmad Chellaby, the second man on Bruinink's list, was also the second most important merchant in the city, but well behind Muhammad Ali in property and power. Unfortunately, we know even less about him than we do about the latter. Apart from being a large ship-owner,

---

[1] The garden of Abdul Gafur was often mentioned. For example in 1711 when Delawar Khan, newly installed governor of the city, was coming to Surat, he spent a few days in this garden before actually entering the town: *K.A.* 1721, p. 41. The family residence within the town was next to the English Factory. As Henry Lowther, Chief of the Factory, noted during the rebellion of 1732: 'As to my own part I shall endeavour all in my power to prevent a street fight any more and especially since we are so ill scituated [*sic*] on both sides of him [Ali]', Lowther to Cowan, 3 Aug. 1732, R(obert) C(owan) P(apers), India Office Microfilm 2034, under date. In 1721 the French Company leased a house from Muhammad Ali and later there was some correspondence about repairing this house. See Pondicherry to Surat, 10 July 1727, vol. C² 74, p. 170, and Pondicherry to Surat, 26 Jan. 1728, *ibid.* p. 292, at the *Archives Coloniales*, Paris. The family in fact owned the small island near Gogo where Muhammad Ali built a fort and tried to settle people. But there were so many snakes on the island that the plan had to be abandoned: *Mirat*, p. 457. The buildings and fortifications at Athwa were often referred to in the late twenties and early thirties of the century. Pieter Phoonsen once noted that it was becoming like 'a new Surat': in letter to Batavia dated 26 February 1730, *K.A.* 2060, p. 77. For the relations between Muhammad Ali and Sohrab Khan and the rebellion in 1732 see my article 'The Crisis at Surat, 1730–32' in *Bengal Past and Present*, LXXXVI, pp. 148–62.

Ahmad was the principal figure among the Turkish community settled at Surat, and it is possible he had links with Aleppo. There was a deadly enmity between the Chellabies and the Mullas and, while Muhammad Ali was at the peak of his power, Ahmad was once imprisoned by the governor of the town and on another occasion had to seek safety in flight. Ali also made a determined attempt to run him out of the Red Sea trade in which both of them were largely interested. Ahmad Chellaby in his turn did his best to ruin the Mullas and was instrumental in the final downfall of Muhammad Ali. Afterwards, for a brief period, he was the successor to the fallen giant in that he became the principal financial support of the *mutasaddi* and inherited Muhammad Ali's considerable influence in the affairs of the town. However this did not last long, and, after a humiliating setback in which he was worsted by the Paraks and the English, a mysterious murderer removed him from the scene in 1736.[1]

This brings us to some of the men who were not on either of the lists with which we started. The family of the Paraks comprised the leading group among the Banias of Surat. The family of the Rustumjis were the principal men among the Parsis. As between the Mullas and the Chellabies, there was a traditional and deadly feud between these two families. Because both the Bania and the Parsi family had close contacts with the English, we are somewhat better informed about the rise and progress of this enmity. In the year 1662, Bhimji Parak, along with his three brothers Kalyandas, Kissoo and Vitaldas, was appointed the broker of the East India Company by Sir George Oxenden. Kalyandas died 'soon after', although we do not know exactly when. We know he left a few children but again not their number or names. Bhimji, after a most successful career as the chief English broker, died in 1686. Kissoo and Vitaldas Parak looked after the office of the broker on behalf of themselves and Banwalidas and Shankardas Bhimji, the

---

[1] In the European documents this family is always called Turkish. In the *Mirat* they are Rumi, and, to the author of the biography of Rustamji, they are Turki by *jat*. I do not know whether they were ethnically Turks or a Syrian family who spoke Turkish. For the Syrian connexion, see Charles Fawcett (ed.), *English Factories in India* (New Series), vol. 3, p. 311 n. The hostility between the Mullas and the Chellabies would from time to time erupt into public disorder and were noted. Thus the *dag register* or the diary of daily events maintained at the Dutch Lodge described how, in January 1729, Muhammad Ali persuaded the custom-master to tax Chellaby's goods at a higher rate and in the difficulties which resulted had him arrested by the governor: *K.A.* 2029, pp. 272–3. On 2 July 1730 Sohrab Khan pressingly invited Chellaby to come and dine with him but Chellaby discovered it was a plot of Muhammad Ali, probably to have him poisoned, and declined: *Dag Register, K.A.* 2094, pp. 749–51. In October of that year he fled to Hormuz to avoid further persecution: *Dag Register*, 29 Oct. 1730, *ibid.* p. 825. The attempt to monopolize the Red Sea trade and its specially adverse effect on Chellaby was noted by the diarist on 28 September 1731: *K.A.* 2143, p. 889. The career of Chellaby after the death of Ali can be followed in *S.F.R.* vol. 18, pp. 79–170. For his death see *S.F.R.* vol. 20, p. 116.

children of their elder brother. In 1697 however the two Bhimjis became the sole brokers. For various reasons all the Indian merchants who were connected with the English came under severe pressure in the 1680s and the pressure continued for about twenty years thereafter. In 1703 Shankardas flung up the office of the broker and Banwalidas took over the sole concern. But soon after disputes arose between the English Company and the family of the Paraks and as a result of this Banwalidas was totally ruined. His two children were surviving 'on the charity of the caste' in the 1720s. The family revived with the emergence of an extremely able youth, Laldas son of Vitaldas, in about 1718. In that year Laldas carried through complicated negotiations on behalf of himself and other members of the extended family with Charles Boone, governor of Bombay, and at a great sacrifice salvaged something of the family fortune. It is interesting to note that, while conducting these negotiations in 1718 and again arguing the case of the Paraks later, Laldas maintained that the four brothers who had originally begun the family's business with the English Company were concerned in it as follows: Bhimji Parak as the eldest had eight shares, Kalyandas had five, Kissoo and Vitaldas had four each. Unfortunately we do not know why this division was made in twenty-one shares and what was the reason behind the specific allotments. It is also difficult to tell how long the original group of the four brothers and their children stayed together. We know that when Shankar gave up the office of broker in 1703, he also separated from his brother Banwali, so that he was untouched by the calamities which immediately afterwards over-whelmed the latter. Thus it would be safe to assume that other members of the family had separated from the two children of Bhimji Parak before 1703, probably in 1697 when they ousted their uncles from the broker's office. However, as the accounts of the Parak family with the English Company were concerned mainly with their transactions in the 1680s, Laldas Vitaldas repeatedly emphasized the division in the several shares and attempted to protect himself and the other members from a wholesale claim. He maintained that the concessions he made under threat in 1718 were severely criticized by the rest of the family. However, in the 1720s Laldas became the broker of the English Company and for about fifteen years the Paraks once again became a leading family at Surat.[1]

---

[1] A considerable amount of material on the Paraks and the Rustumjis is available in the papers of the English Company relating to Bombay and Surat, and also in the papers of Sir Robert Cowan. The most concise account of the Parak family was written by Seth Laldas himself and is to be found in *B.P.P.* vol 6., entered after consultation of 10 December 1725. Also in the same volume the defence of Laldas against the claims of the Company under date 7 Dec. 1725. The negotiations of 1718 and the emergence of Laldas is best studied in *S.F.R.* vol. 9, which is wholly devoted to the settlement with the Paraks reached in that year.

But already the great rivalry between the Paraks and the Rustumjis had begun. Rustumji Manakji rose to affluence in the last two decades of the seventeenth century and became the broker of the New English East India Company at the beginning of the eighteenth century. The two young Paraks, Banwalidas and Shankardas, were at the time the brokers of the Old Company and appear to have been out-generalled by Rustumji. In 1712 the United Company moved against Banawalidas for old debts and the sole brokerage was given to Rustum. The family of the Paraks went into eclipse only to emerge after the death of Rustumji in 1719. Seth Laldas Parak now managed to turn the tables against the three sons of Rustum, Framji, Bomanji and Nowroji Rustumji, who had succeeded their father in the office of broker. Laldas discovered evidence of systematic cheating of the English Company by the Rustumjis, and as a result the family were turned out of their office and large claims were made against them. Framji was imprisoned at Surat and Bomanji was arrested at Bombay while Nowroji managed to sail to England to plead the family's case before the Court of Directors. The master-stroke of Nowroji in England appears to have been the successful revival of an old claim against the Paraks. There is no evidence that Nowroji was directly responsible for this, but, while he was in London, the Court of Directors not only agreed to make large restitutions to the Rustumji family, but also bought from the family of Sir John Child, English Chief at Surat in the 1680s, an old claim they had against the Paraks, at Rs. 150,000. In 1725 when Nowroji returned to Surat he immediately spread the news of a disastrous claim soon to be made against Seth Laldas by the English Company. The instructions which the governor and council at Bombay received from London in the matter were very clear and it seemed that a persecution of the Paraks was about to begin just after the persecution of the Rustumjis had ceased. But Laldas fought a masterly rearguard action and Nowroji in the excitement of his triumph overplayed his hand. Laldas refused to acknowledge that the claim of the Child family was just and thus that the Company had any legal right to demand restitution from him for what it had paid the Childs. But, as he was the broker, he wished to please his employers, and 'solely for this reason' paid his four shares of twenty-one of the 150,000 paid in London. However, he was obliged to sign for the rest of the debt although he never acknowledged its validity. Nowroji on the other hand, when asked whether he would take over the office of the broker if Laldas failed to discharge the debt, made extravagant conditions including what amounted to a total control of the Company's affairs at Surat and the countenance of the Company's navy in his persecution of the Paraks. Friends of Laldas in the Bombay Council, among whom was the governor William Phipps himself, rejected these demands. Laldas was confirmed as the sole broker of the English Company.[1]

As long as Seth Laldas Vitaldas Parak lived Nowroji Rustumji was entirely unable to make any impression at Surat. In the late 1720s and the early 1730s, on the other hand, the Rustumji family built up a base at Bombay away from Surat. They acquired landed properties on the island and several members of the family began to live permanently there. The Paraks do not seem to have made any similar move and remained firmly based at Surat.[2] In these years the council at Bombay was dominated by the friends of the Paraks, among whom, after governor Phipps, governor Robert Cowan and Henry Lowther, chief at Surat, 1729–34, were outstanding. Lowther in particular was a close business associate and an admiring friend of Seth Laldas and helped to preserve the influence of the family after the sudden death of the latter in 1732. But the Rustumjis came back into the picture very strongly in the mid-thirties. Robert Cowan was recalled home in disgrace to answer charges against him before the Court of Directors. John Horne who succeeded Cowan was totally unsympathetic to the Paraks and was acting most probably in the Rustumji interest. Henry Lowther was soon in trouble and, rather than return to Bombay to face his enemies in the council, escaped from Surat in a private trading vessel to the Persian Gulf and thence made his way to London.[3] The persecution of

[1] In addition to references above in connexion with Rustumji Manakji and the family of the Paraks, see *B.P.P.* vol. 5, consultation 13 April 1722, 16 April 1722, 9 May 1722 and the report on the Rustumjis entered after the consultation of 2 November 1722. A typical private comment on this feud between the Bania and Parsi families was in Robert Cowan's letter to the ex-governor Charles Boone, 8 December 1724: 'If Nowros [Nowroji Rustumji] goes home [to England] Doubtless he expects you…will espouse him, if he resolves to go to Law and sue the Company, it will be many years before such a sute [*sic*] can be ended, and very flagrant proofs of the infidelity of that family will be sent from here [i. e. Surat], for no such inveterate Enemys [*sic*] are under the sun as these black fellows to one the other.' R. C. P., Microfilm 2013, under date. Also see Nowroji's memorandum setting out the conditions under which he was willing to accept the office of broker, entered after the consultation of 30 November 1728, *B.P.P.* vol. 6.

[2] The involvement of the Rustumjis at Bombay is clear from the documents relating to several law-suits in the thirties. See the petition of Nowroji Rustumji against Sagoon Sinay in 1730, Mayor's Court Proceedings, Range 416, vol. 103, pp. 2–3; Bomanji Rustumji *vs.* Chandaboy Boreah, vol. 109, p. 93; Bomanji *vs.* Ventu Morarset and others, vol. 110, pp. 62–4. Also the petition of Manakji Nowroji, son of Nowroji Rustumji, seeking permission to build a Parsi temple at Bombay in *1735*, *B.P.P.* vol. 8, p. 163. In 1731 Laldas asked permission to build a house at Bombay in the manner that the Rustumjis had already done, and although permission was granted the family do not seem to have followed it up, *B.P.P.* vol. 7, cons. 3 Dec. 1731.

[3] Henry Lowther wrote much in public and private to testify to the qualities of Seth Laldas. A typical example would be his letter to Cowan on 2 September 1731, when, discussing the difficulties in the trade in woollens, he wrote: 'Indeed it is very well, his [Laldas's] Genius is so well adapted to Trade besides having a spirit to undertake anything that has the least prospect of success.' R.C.P., Microfilm 2033, under date. For the developments subsequent to the death of Laldas, see *S.F.R.* vol. 21, 3 Jan. 1737 ff.

the Paraks now began in right earnest and the fortunes of the family were almost totally destroyed between 1736 when Seth Jagannathdas, eldest son of Laldas, was arrested at Bombay, and 1738, the year in which he escaped to the Marathas. In 1737 Nowroji Rustumji returned to Surat as the 'sole broker' of the English East India Company and had the satisfaction of personally conducting the sales of the property of the Paraks.[1] But tables were turned yet once more in the forties when the Rustumjis again retired to Bombay and Jagannath took up the functions of the broker, although much reduced in fortunes and influence.[2]

This particular rivalry between two of the leading families of Surat during the first half of the eighteenth century is thus known to us in some detail. The other rivalry, and obviously the more important one, between the Mullas and the Chellabies is known only in its barest outlines. We also have evidence that within the Rustumji family there were furious quarrels between its different branches, primarily between Manakji, son of Nowroji Rustumji, and Cowji, son of Framji Rustumji.[3] These rivalries therefore were marked features of the world of the Indian merchants at Surat. It would be a mistake, I think, to treat them as tensions among the different communities which comprised the mercantile society. They should rather be thought of as personal and accidental, but inexorable once they developed. What is clear from the accounts of these quarrels is that among each of the major communities at Surat there was at least one leading family the fortunes of which had been founded by the abilities of an outstanding individual. This family would gather round it other members of the community in relations of business, patronage or distant kinship ties. In a quarrel of the kind we have been considering the group would act in the interest of the head of the family.[4]

---

[1] For Jagannath's arrest, *B.P.P.* vol. 9, pp. 70–4. Nowroji's appointment in *ibid.* p. 113. A fierce denunciation of Nowroji, written in Gujarati, for the part he played in the persecution of the Paraks was dropped near the gate of the English Factory. I believe this document portrays more accurately the true feelings of a large number of Banias, attached to the Parak interest, than anything officially recorded by the English. See *S.F.R.* vol. 21, cons. 20 June 1737.

[2] For the developments in the 1740s, *S.F.R.* vol. 27, pp. 189–90, *S.F.R.* vol. 28, pp. 58–9 and *S.F.R.* vol. 32, pp. 79–81.

[3] This particular quarrel within the Rustumji family led to grave consequences in 1734 when the English Company's warships blocked Surat. Later John Braddyl of the Bombay Council enquiring into the incident thought that Henry Lowther, who had a grudge against Nowroji Rustumji, took advantage of this quarrel between the two cousins to embroil the Company in a way which would be to the disadvantage of Nowroji, *B.P.P.* vol. 8, pp. 180–1. For a few more details see below p. 218. It is interesting to note that, in the quarrel between the Paraks and the Rustumjis, the faction of Framji Rustumji was supporting the Paraks in 1737, *B.P.P.* vol. 9, p. 231.

[4] In each of the grave incidents connected with these leading families, several persons would be mentioned who stood by their principals. Thus Muhammad Aref and Muhammad Sayyid, relations of Muhammad Ali, shared all his troubles including a spell of imprison-

Now, if we turn from a consideration of the individual merchants and the families to which they belonged, and examine the varying occupations within the mercantile world which they followed, the picture is somewhat different. The multifarious activities all hung together, and were all directed to the end of gathering the production of northern and western India at the port of Surat and then exporting it to other Asian ports and to Europe, as also to the importing of a considerable amount of bullion from abroad and some amount of spices, silk and other items and distributing these through other networks into the interior of Gujarat and northern India. Naturally the Muslim ship-owners played an important role in this and we may think of them as the ultimate exporter or the first importers. If we concentrate on exports first, the thing to notice is that the final exporter always acted through another group of men called *dalal* or broker, at times *wakil*, which is best translated as representative, agent or attorney. It is important to realize that the 'broker' was not an institution invented for the convenience of the Europeans who did not know the country, but the ordinary indigenous institution through which all exporters would work. The amount of dependence upon the broker of course would vary according to the experience the exporter had of the local conditions and related factors. The Mulla family had two main brokers, both *banias*, called Rajaram and Jeddaram. We do not know the name of Ahmad Chellaby's broker, but in the late 1720s there was a quarrel between the two, and Muhammad Ali took advantage of it to have Chellaby imprisoned.[1]

There were two kinds of broker. The men we have been considering can be called general brokers and the other kind, usually called sub-brokers, would be more usefully called commodity-brokers. Exporters like Muhammad Ali, Ahmad Chellaby or the English Company handled a wide range of goods. The broker who took upon himself to

ment with him in 1732, *S.F.R.* vol. 17, pp. 36–7. There are also frequent references to the 'adherents' or more critically 'hangers-on' of each of the leading families. In January 1732 when Muhammad Ali was arranging a petition to Batavia against Pieter Phoonsen and his Council, Henry Lowther noted that this petition was to be signed 'by all his hangers-on and these are pretty numerous'. R.C.P., Microfilm 2034, Lowther to Cowan, 7 Jan. 1732.

[1] It is interesting to note that as the principal assistants to Muhammad Ali in all his financial dealings, Rajaram and Jeddaram were arrested along with Muhammad Aref and Muhammad Sayyid, *S.F.R.* vol. 17, pp. 36–7. The difficulties with Chellaby's broker were noted in *K.A.* 2029, p. 272. On 25 March 1732 Lowther wrote to Cowan, 'Chellaby I understand will not long escape this [persecution] owing to a complaint lately renewed by his Broker, whom he tortured very barbarously and afterwards took one lack of rupees from him'. R.C.P., Microfilm 2034, under date. In 1727 the Dutch offered the post of their warehouse *munshi* to a *Bania* called Girdhardas, who turned it down, as he said he was much better employed as broker to the leading Muslim merchant Abdul Rahman Sulaimanji, *K.A.* 1996, p. 62.

provide all of them did not himself deal in everything, perhaps in nothing at all. It was his business to get in touch with other men who dealt in various kinds of textiles and indigo and procure the different commodities through different brokers. The latter were the brokers for particular commodities. It was this ring of commodity-brokers who were in direct touch with the primary producer or in most cases their *patel* or headmen. We must also remember that for much of the period we are considering, little manufacture was done at Surat itself, and the general brokers at Surat procured their goods through their contacts at places like Broach or Ahmadabad. The man who can really be called a sub-broker is a general broker at a place, say Broach, acting as the *wakil* of another, also a general broker, at Surat. It is important to remember that between the primary producer and the ultimate exporter stood at least the *patel* and two different kinds of brokers.

It would seem that the Hindus and the Parsis were exclusively engaged in the profession of brokers. I have not come across a single instance of any other social group supplying a broker to the exporters or importers. The importers usually held public sale of their goods at Surat, which were attended by merchants dealing in particular commodities, brokers of the same kind and brokers or *wakils* of merchants interested in buying the goods but living away from Surat. A group of Kashmiri merchants, for example, permanently maintained at Surat their *wakils*, who bought a large amount of spices each year from the Dutch and sent these across to the northern cities where their principals lived. It is possible that, once the spices reached, say, Agra, Delhi or Lahore, another public sale would take place before they reached the retailers, who would finally dispose of them to the consumers, but we cannot be certain about this from documentation relating to Surat.[1]

Apart from the exporters and importers and the brokers, another important group of men formed part of the mercantile world. These were the merchants in money, usually called *sarafs* or *shroffs*. Their main business was the conversion of currency but they also lent money, bought and sold bills of exchange on distant places and undertook

---

[1] The two kinds of men engaged in brokerage were, of course, noted almost every year by the English and the Dutch. An interesting example was provided by Laldas when, in course of his investigations into the methods by which the Rustumjis used to provide the 'investment' for the English Company, he turned up two *Banias*, one at Nadiad, about thirty miles to the south of Surat, and the other, who had provided goods about 20 per cent cheaper than the rate the Rustumjis actually charged the Company, at Surat itself, *B.P.P.* vol. 5, the report on the Rustumjis entered after cons. 2 Nov. 1722. Girdhardas and Vanmalidas, two brothers, were brokers for a particular kind of silk cloth called *patol* at Ahmadabad. The Dutch tried to move them to Surat in 1734 and they said they would gladly have come but that they were unwilling to abandon their 'old master', Birsbukhandas, broker to the Dutch Lodge at Ahmadabad, *K.A.* 2247, pp. 145–6. For the Kashmiri merchants, *K.A.* 1946, pp. 82–3.

marine insurance and respondentia loans. Lending of money or selling bills was also done by ordinary merchants, but, because the *sarafs* as a group were the largest operators of this kind, they settled the rate of exchange, discount and interest. Again I have not come across any but Hindu names in this profession, but it is possible that at least the Parsis were engaged in it as well. However there can be no doubt at all about the absolute dominance of the Hindus in the money market and it is quite certain that no Muslim *saraf* was ever known.[1]

Now that we have seen how the different kinds of mercantile occupations were the specialities of the various social groups, we may ask the question whether these different social groups and men in these different but related occupations were organized in any common body, and, if not, what their reaction was to matters which affected them all. We have also to ask whether organizations existed at the lower level of particular occupations or a single social community. The answer to the first question is definitely in the negative. There is no evidence at all that the Bohras and the Turks, the Banias and the Parsis formed parts of a single organization, and it is quite clear from the rivalries among some of them that this did not exist. There was however a very real concern for the common good, and common action would often be undertaken in an emergency. Occasions for this became more frequent as law and order gradually gave way at Surat. The initiation of such common action was however left to one or other of the leading families in the town and there was no knowing whether and when such action would come and how much support it would get. In the period we are considering there were, however, common forms for such action. In the first place some of the leading merchants of the different communities would call upon the *mutasaddi* and ask him to redress whatever the grievance might be. Then, if unsuccessful, they would make representations to the Imperial Court through their *wakils*, and try to gather up more general support within the town by passing round a petition or a declaration setting forth the grievance. This would be accompanied by meetings of the merchants at the house of the leading figure who had taken the initiative in the matter. And, if the problem was not resolved, the merchants concerned would shut their shops and offices and sometimes leave the town and disperse into the surrounding villages, which happened in the case of the Hindus and Parsis to be their ancestral seats. The magnitude of such action varied according to the occasion. Thus in 1729 when Muhammad Ali had Ahmad Chellaby arrested by Sohrab Khan, the

---

[1] The best description of the money market at Surat was written by Jan Schreuder as part of his memoir, *H.R.* 838, pp. 54–5. The role of a *saraf* acting as an agent for respondentia loans was discussed in some detail in the case of Brindabandas Nanabhai, who negotiated a large sum for a ship freighted by Seth Jagannathdas going to Siam, *S.F.R.* vol. 26, pp. 88 ff.

mutasaddi, representations were repeatedly made at the *darbar* for Chellaby's release by Ibrahim Chellaby, Ibrahim Kodsi, Sidi Ambar, the
leading *sarafs* and, surprisingly, by Muhammad Hussain, son of Muhammad Ali. These representations were continued till Ahmad Chellaby
was set free with special marks of honour.[1] More serious trouble followed
shortly after when Ahmad Chellaby led a group of merchants, including some notable figures among the Hindus as well as the Muslims, to
the protection of the Castle, and issued a statement of grievances against
Sohrab Khan to be signed by prominent citizens in general. Sohrab on
his part rallied Muhammad Ali and several of the leading *sarafs* and
Armenian merchants to his side and a counter-petition setting forth the
wickedness of Chellaby, disturber of the public peace, was organized.
Some of the shops were shut but the governor forced them to reopen. He
also prohibited any soldier from enlisting with Chellaby. The *wakil*
of Chellaby at the Imperial Court however obtained instructions in his
favour which obliged Sohrab to retrace his steps. At this point a Muslim
holy man, Gazi Fazal Hassan, mediated between the parties and the dispute was made up amicably.[2] The most serious incident of this kind occurred in 1732 when for once Muhammad Ali made common cause with
Ahmad Chellaby and Seth Laldas Vitaldas, and the combined merchants
drove out the *mutasaddi* Sohrab Ali Khan as they had found his government too oppressive. They were however unable to change the nature of
government at Surat as the governor they selected for themselves
turned out to be just as oppressive. The complete unity which was
achieved in this instance was never recaptured.[3]

It would seem that at the level of relatively homogeneous communities and particular professions, in so far as they were the preserve of
particular communities, there was more organization and discipline.
But it should be noted that at this level European documentation is
extremely scanty and may well be misleading. However, we do have
evidence that the *sarafs* of Surat had a fairly disciplined organization of
their own. In the year 1733, Cowji Framji spread a rumour in the
town of Surat that Nowroji Rustumji, his uncle, had lost a hundred
thousand rupees he had invested in respondentia at Bombay and,
further, that the governor of Bombay had extorted forty thousand
rupees more from him. Once the rumour got about, a run started on
Manakji Nowroji, son of Nowroji Rustumji, at Surat, and he saved
himself from total ruin only through the powerful financial support of
several of the leading *sarafs* and merchants, among whom was included

---

[1] See the extracts from *Dag Register, K.A.* 2029, p. 271 ff.
[2] The two petitions circulated by Ahmad Chellaby and Sohrab Khan, in *K.A.* 2060, pp. 177–
20. The development of events is set out in the extracts from the daily diary cited above.
See A. Das Gupta, 'The Crisis at Surat, 1730–32', *Bengal Past and Present*, LXXXVI.

Ahmad Chellaby. Now, according to the information collected by Chellaby, a *saraf* called Shudas Parak had been the instrument of Cowji Framji in making this mischief. Chellaby therefore called two of the leading *sarafs*, Banarasidas Jewdas and Jagjivan Mehta, to his house and ordered them to expel Shudas Parak from their organization. Banarasidas and Jagjivan both agreed that 'no punishment can be too great for such a crime' but argued that 'as Shudass has a very honest and fair character, it would also be unjust to condemn him without either examining into the affair or hearing what he had to say for himself'. However, Chellaby bullied them into doing what he desired, and 'the poor timorous banians for fear signed a paper whereby they declared Shudass Parrack expelled the community of shroffs without mentioning his crime'.[1] I believe that the strict organization suggested by this piece of evidence was the result of the dominating position of the *banias* in the profession of *saraf*. There is also evidence that the *banias* of Surat taxed themselves by common consent in order to support the hospitals for animals which they maintained in the town.[2] The social composition of a profession was therefore the crucial factor in determining the character of its organization. Because of the paucity of evidence, however, all conclusions on this point must be regarded as strictly tentative.

Thus it appears that the mercantile communities at Surat, when united on any particular issue, was an important counter-weight to the political hierarchy in the town. The family of the Mullas by themselves could for a time claim this distinction. But we should remember that the officials at Surat were lesser men compared with those in charge of the capitals of the various Mughal *subahs*, not to mention the Imperial cities in the north. Unity among the merchants was comparatively a rare phenomenon and the Mullas were a very exceptional family. The influence of the merchants was essentially defensive, in the sense that they were in a position to redress particular grievances although this might set them at odds with the local port officer. In the period we are discussing a defensive reaction was the only natural one as mercantile property was more and more threatened by political pressure. It would however be wrong, I believe, to put the influence of the merchants in any stronger terms than these. Thus I doubt whether we are justified in saying that the merchants were able to inffluence 'the commercial policy of the Mughals'. I do not think the Mughals ever had anything which can be called a commercial policy. The Imperial Government

---

[1] *S.F.R.* vol. 18, pp. 45–6.
[2] In an anonymous description of the *pinjrapole* (hospital for animals) in the outskirts of Surat written in 1841, the author noted the rates of contribution levied by the *mahajan* upon the *banias* for the maintenance of the establishment, 'Notes on Gujarat', European Manuscripts A 28, vol. 729, pp. 157–8. All the eighteenth-century travellers in Gujarat of course noted these hospitals and the fact that they were maintained by the *banias*, but only in general terms.

was naturally concerned with the revenue from sea-customs, and if the merchants could show that a particular administrative measure would be likely to affect it adversely, this would be seriously considered. The merchants of Surat, although they appear to have had some organization at certain levels, never evolved a comprehensive impersonal body to take care of all their common interests. Although common actions were often undertaken they were always open to certain risks and frequently foundered in fruitless compromise. Intense competition and bitter personal rivalry were the marked features of the mercantile world.

It remains for us to consider the relations of the merchants of Surat with the rural society from which they drew their exports, and their connexions with the Europeans who were, at least some of the time, setting an example of combined action. Information about the first problem is scanty and, again, may well be misleading. It is however clear that the pull of the export market was felt mainly along the major roads connecting Surat with Baroda, Broach, Ahmadabad and Cambay. The principal 'villages' like Ankleswar, Pitlad and Dholka which were often mentioned as centres of supply were on these roads. Each centre of this kind would have a weaving population of its own and also villages in the neighbourhood up to a maximum radius, which I should guess at about twenty miles, would send in their cloths to it. This was also true of the major towns like Broach and Surat. Now, most of the merchants of Surat were probably village-based in the sense they had ancestral villages with which they retained some connexion, but none of them owned land outside the town of Surat. The kind of property we hear of is always a house or a garden in the town of Surat. They were thus in no position to influence the village-world round them. Further, the wealthiest among them, the ship-owners and general brokers, dealt with the weavers through the intermediary of commodity-brokers or brokers in localities away from Surat. The headman of the weavers came between any broker and the men who actually produced the goods. Thus men who had the money operated at a certain distance from the system of production which turned out the stuff they wanted. Neither through local influence nor through direct contact could they hope to break through to the primary producer. It has to be added that we have no evidence to suggest that they ever attempted this and failed. Weavers were in fact sometimes displaced and wandered from one centre to another, but these were the results of natural calamities or political disasters and there is nothing to show that the merchants of Surat ever took advantage of these to expand production under their own supervision.[1]

[1] One of the reasons for thinking that the maximum distance of a village from its market in town was perhaps no more than twenty miles is a statement in a memorandum on the

The wealthiest of the merchants at Surat—the group of Muslim shippers—had no direct connexions at all with the European companies. Their names are never mentioned in the sales of the European imports and of course never in connexion with the procurement of European exports. They were in fact the rivals of the Europeans in the market at Mocha and the Persian Gulf, especially in the matter of procuring freight from Surat to these places. Below this level, the families of the Paraks and the Rustumjis are good examples of men growing rich and influential through a European 'connexion'. It must be realized, however, that the brokerage they earned from the Company must have been a very small fragment of their total profit through this connexion. The major advantage of such a post was obviously the credit which it brought with it and the trading connexions it opened up. The management of most English private trade at Surat appears to have been a perquisite of the office of the broker. However the fortunes acquired by these men were modest in this period. When Seth Laldas died he left about five hundred thousand rupees in all kinds of property. And, as is clear in the case of the Rustumjis, a demand in the neighbourhood of three hundred thousand was enough to send them crashing. None of the families which were connected with the Dutch could arrive at affluence, and the other Europeans were of no importance at Surat in this period.[1]

Towards the middle of the eighteenth century, sustained plunder of mercantile property by local officials drove several of the middling merchants of Surat into taking the 'protection' of the English and the Dutch Company. Of the top-ranking men only Mulla Fakruddin, the great

revenues of the Castle at Surat, drawn up in 1759. The memorandum noted that some of the villages of the *pargana* of Ankleswar paid their revenues to the *killadar* at Surat and the distance of this *pargana* from Surat was twenty miles. Then it went on to observe: 'This district being at such a distance from Surat, and the people not necessitated to bring their grain or other produce hither to market is the occasion that its revenue is most troublesome to recover, for the other districts and villages that pay the Castle Jagheer are all situated near, and bring their produce hither to the best market which makes them keep on good terms.' *Selections from Bombay State Papers* (Home Series, vol. 2), p. 109. The fact that most of the Parsis lived in villages and only some had by 1750 come to the towns, was emphasized by Schreuder in his memoir on the trade of Gujarat, *H.R.* 837, section 105. There is no direct statement of this kind about the Banias, but there are occasional references to *sarafs* living in villages, e.g. *K.A.* 2143, p. 788. The Muslim merchants on the other hand appear to have been exclusively urban. The fact that the weavers worked usually under headmen can be gathered from occasional references, but there is one clear statement of the distribution of the English 'investment' in 1741 among the weavers at Surat from which it appears that much of the money advanced was to seventeen 'chief weavers' who had each about a hundred corges (twenty pieces) to supply. At the end of the list it was added that in addition to these 101 'particular weavers' were also employed, *S.F.R.* vol. 27, pp. 28–32.
[1] The statement about his inheritance was made by Seth Jagannath in 1736 and there was corroboration of it from two other merchants, *B.P.P.* vol. 8, p. 174. For the fortunes of the families of Kissendas and Ruidas, see *K.A.* 1946, pp. 378–81, and the appendix to the memoir of Jan Schreuder, where he lists the value of property owned by the leading merchants of Surat in 1750.

grandson of Mulla Abdul Gafur, retired to Bombay for a short time before finally returning to Surat. The Chellabies never deserted Surat and remained hostile to the development of English influence within the city, which they saw as a threat to their freight trade to the Red Sea. The Rustumjis made Bombay their home fairly early in the century and soon became the leading merchants there. It has sometimes been suggested that the Parsis as a community possessed certain entrepreneurial qualities which other Indian groups lacked, and this led to their prosperity in the nineteenth century. I am not here concerned to examine this proposition in detail but from the evidence relating to the first half of the eighteenth century, it would seem there was no difference between the Parsis and the Banias or Bohras at Surat as far as business was concerned. It is on the other hand possible to suggest that the Parsis were a small community at Surat and could never hope to match the influence of the Banias, among whom the Paraks, the deadly enemies of the Rustumjis, were the most prominent men. This might have been a factor behind their early removal to Bombay. But the new structure of business at Bombay is best explained from an exact examination of the historical developments, with all the accidents in them as they came, rather than from immutable qualities of particular peoples. The evidence I have seen seems to suggest that those with influence and power at Surat were very unwilling to move even when faced with disaster, while others with less at stake moved with less reluctance.

EUROPEAN AND INDIAN
ENTREPRENEURSHIP IN INDIA,
1900–30[1]

AMIYA KUMAR BAGCHI

I

In the mythology of 'explanations' of economic stagnation in India during the British rule, caste restrictions or the other-worldly features of Indian value systems figure prominently. Authorities coming from backgrounds as diverse as those of Vera Anstey,[2] Kingsley Davis,[3] and Max Weber[4] are to be found ranged behind this complex of views and attitutes regarding the interpretation of modern Indian economic history. In all these explanations the inhibitions of indigenous entrepreneurial groups figure prominently. There is, however, little discussion in the existing literature of the reason for the emergence and the survival or disappearance of indigenous and foreign entrepreneurial groups in India. Recently, two books have indeed focused on the question of the emergence and growth of the Indian capitalist classes, but both suffer from the telescoping of about five centuries of Indian economic history into one single volume.[5]

My aim is to gather some of the relevant facts about the functioning of European and Indian capitalist groups in India roughly from the years of the 'high noon' of the British empire to the beginning of

[1] I am indebted to Pramit Chaudhuri, Ashin Das Gupta, Ashok Desai, Moses Finley and Edmund Leach for valuable comments on this paper. None of them is responsible for any remaining errors.

[2] Vera Anstey: *The Economic Development of India* (London, 1957).

[3] Kingsley Davis: *The Population of India and Pakistan* (Princeton, N. J., 1951), pp. 213–20. Davis does attach some importance to the depressing effects of alien rule.

[4] Max Weber: *The Religion of India* (Glencoe, Illinois, 1958). Weber's thesis has been critically examined by Professor M. D. Morris in his article, 'Values as an Obstacle to Economic Growth in South Asia: An Historical Survey', *The Journal of Economic History*, Vol. XXVII, no. 4, Dec. 1967, pp. 588–607. Unfortunately, Professor Morris fails to investigate the impact of British rule on the differential advantages enjoyed by Indians and Europeans in India.

[5] B. B. Misra: *The Indian Middle Classes* (London, 1961) and V. I. Pavlov: *The Indian Capitalist Class* (New Delhi, 1964). Misra's book suffers particularly from taking little account of the recent work on the economic history of Bengal done by Professors N. K. Sinha and Amalesh Tripathi; it also suffers from attributing to British rule many changes which had already occurred before the British conquest of India. Pavlov's book is far more balanced but its interest tends to peter out at the end of the nineteenth century.

definitely protectionist policies.[1] An explicit distinction is made between the capitalist groups operating in western, eastern, southern and northern India. This helps to lay bare some features of the domination of the Indian economy by European capital which are obscured in aggregative analysis, since the trade and industries of Bengal and Madras far outweighed the trade and industries of Bombay, up to 1914, and the European domination of the industries in the first two Provinces is translated into the European domination of Indian industries as a whole. A regionally orientated analysis at once brings out that in Bombay Indian and European capitalists were less unequal than in other parts of India. The pre-eminent position of the Parsis among the Indian capitalist groups is also seen to be more closely connected with the development of Bombay and western India. Whether the Parsis were more Protestant than other Indian communities may be an interesting question in the history of economic thought; but, if the Parsis were favoured by very tangible elements in the political and economic development of western India, and if their rise as a business community was also accompanied by similar activity of other Indian capitalist groups for whom claims of Protestantism are not made, then the discovery of specifically Protestant elements in the social and religious values of the Parsis loses much of its significance.[2] We shall concentrate mainly on the situations in Bombay and in Calcutta because (a) these two cities were the major centres of industrial growth and (b) while Bengal was the first extensive province to be conquered by the British, Maharashtra was among the last to be formally annexed by them, so that the differing degrees of political domination can be expected to have worked their effects out to the greatest extent in the two provinces.

British paramountcy in India in 1900 was very much in evidence. The unchallenged political supremacy of the British favoured, among other things, the exercise of economic power by Europeans resident in India who derived special advantages from linguistic and racial identification with the rulers of India. It is curious that, while the benefits or evils wrought by imperialism in India have been discussed often enough, and while the roots of imperialism have also attracted the attention of liberals, Marxists, nationalists and allegedly objective historians, the mechanics of the operation of imperialism in India have escaped any

---

[1] Although the policy of 'discriminating protection' was adopted by the Government of India in 1923, the only major industries which were substantially protected before 1930 were iron and steel and paper. The depression forced the Government of India to raise customs duties all round, because of the fall in government revenues from normal sources.

[2] For an analysis claiming specifically Protestant virtues for the Parsis see Robert E. Kennedy: 'The Protestant Ethic and the Parsis', *The American Journal of Sociology*, Vol. 68 (1962–3), pp. 11–20, reprinted in N. J. Smelser (ed.): *Readings in Economic Sociology* (Englewood Cliffs, N. J., 1965), pp. 16–26.

detailed analysis. Perhaps the liberal defenders and critics of British rule alike have turned away in horror from the suggestion that the rule of the British Parliament over India could be and was translated into gains for individual European businessmen in India. Even more horrifying is the suggestion that it was a racial and cultural affinity claimed by all European businessmen with the British rulers rather than specifically British birth that gave the former an edge over Indians in all public affairs including the affairs connected with making money.[1] But the businessmen themselves were quite clear that they were identified by the colour of their skin and the so-called European heritage rather than by their British nationality: this was the basis on which chambers of commerce and trade associations were organized and represented before official bodies.[2] Contemporary observers also commented on the feeling of racial differentiation obtaining among Indians and Europeans.[3]

One other factor which seems to have prevented the recognition of the special advantages enjoyed by European businessmen just because of their birth is the supposedly hostile attitude of the Government of India towards private business during the late nineteenth century. Lord Curzon is supposed to have been the first Viceroy to try to aid commerce and industry by government action.[4] Even if this is true, it would merely mean that all businessmen would be treated with some suspicion by the top bureaucrats; but it would not make it any less probable that given the background of suspicion the European would still get a better deal than the Indian in the same walk of life. Furthermore, there are enough instances of the Government of India trying to widen the channels of trade and commerce for the benefit of private business for one to be sceptical about the strength of the hostility to private business. The development of the railways and ports are the best examples of Government response to the demands of private

[1] The sense of community of the British *politicians* and administrators and their sense of distance from the Indians is more widely recognized. It is even recognized by some that, in fact, the 'guardians' (to use Philip Woodruff's epithet characterizing the British administrators of India) were possessive of their power and their privileges. See an anonymous review ('Anglo-Indian Attitudes') of Martin Gilbert: 'Servant of India, A Study of Imperial Rule from 1905 to 1910' as told through the correspondence and diaries of Sir James Dunlop Smith (London, 1967) in the *Times Literary Supplement*, 18 May 1967, p. 418.

[2] As just one example among many that could be cited see the evidence of R. Steel representing the Bengal Chamber of Commerce in *Minutes of Evidence taken before the Royal Commission on Opium between 18th November and 29th December 1893, with Appendixes* (U. K. Parl. Papers, 1894, LXI), p. 161. The phrases 'white man's burden' and 'black town' recall the racial basis of moral and physical demarcation from the 'natives'.

[3] See, for example, C. E. Buckland: 'The City of Calcutta', *Journal of the Society of Arts*, No. 2,776, LIV, 2 Feb. 1906, pp. 275–94, at p. 292.

[4] Lovat Fraser: *India under Curzon and After* (London, 1911), Chapter IX.

businessmen in the late nineteenth century.[1] One can claim also that, since, up to 1930 or so, the basic policy of the Government of India was one of free trade, which encouraged the activities of exporting raw materials and food-grains and the importing of manufactured products, no specific government help for industries was necessary. The Europeans automatically enjoyed enormous privileges over Indians simply through their control of the major part of the external trade of India. In the specific instances in which government patronage to industry was important, the Europeans far outdistanced the Indians in the enjoyment of such patronage; the industries which were, with a few exceptions, entirely in European hands.[2] When a pioneer enterprise was handed over to private business, it was handed over to private European business.[3] When the growth of a new industry was encouraged, it was encouraged under European auspices.[4]

One important industry where government patronage was crucial and where Indians were rarely to be found was the engineering industry. Large government contracts for construction and engineering were rarely, if ever, given to Indian firms. Since engineering firms in a poor economy with little industry had to depend mainly on contracts placed by public authorities, there were practically no large Indian firms. Sir Rajendra Nath Mookerjee made a name for himself in the construction of water works for the Calcutta corporation. But he found that, as T. C. Mookerjee and Company, his firm could not obtain the

[1] For a detailed description of how the development of the railways and ports in Bombay responded to the demands of the European businessmen organized in the Bombay Chamber of Commerce, see R. J. F. Sulivan: *One Hundred Years of Bombay* (Bombay, 1937), Chapters X–XIII, XXI–XXIV. For an analysis of the true import of the *laissez faire* policy of the Government of India in the nineteenth century, see S. Bhattacharya: 'Laissez Faire in India', *The Indian Economic and Social History Review*, Vol. II, No. 1, Jan. 1965.

[2] The paper industry was heavily dependent on the Government purchase of stores; of the paper mills existing in 1914, only one Indian-controlled mill, the Upper India Couper Paper Mills of Lucknow, accounting for a small fraction of the total domestic output sold a substantial portion of its output to the Government. The case of the woollen industry was similar.

[3] The government of Madras, under the imaginative direction of Alfred Chatterton, started the first aluminium ware industry in India; after the commercial possibilities of this enterprise had been proved, it was handed over to Eardley Norton, a European barrister of Madras, and half of the net profit of Rs. 60,000 made by the Department of Industries, Madras, from the manufacture of aluminium ware was made over as a free gift to the Indian Aluminium Company, which Mr Norton had started: *Report of the Indian Industrial Commission, 1916–18* (U.K. Parl. Papers, 1919, XVII), Appendix J.

[4] The Army Boot and Equipment Factory of Cawnpore was started in 1880 or 1881 by W. E. Cooper. 'The firm in 1883 secured their first boot contract from Government. and obtained a large advance of money on the understanding that they were to build pits and carry out the manufacture of leather after the methods employed in the Government factory. It now holds the contract for the supply of boots to the whole British army in India...The factory also does a large trade with other Government departments in addition to a most flourishing private business...' H. R. Nevill: *Cawnpore: A Gazetteer, being Vol. XIX of the District Gazetteers of the United Provinces of Agra and Oudh* (Allahabad, 1909), pp. 78–9.

contracts for the construction of water-works in the United Provinces though theirs were the lowest tenders. He then had to join forces with Acquin Martin and adopt the name of Martin and Company in order to obtain the contracts.[1]

The Government of India by its policy decisions kept alive the belief that 'British is best', a belief that was not often tested by the free market. The share of Britain in the imports of iron and steel into India on private account was declining before the First World War, mainly because European steel was cheaper.[2] The Government of India, however, continued to buy only British-made iron and steel products for all its purposes; the railways also—whether managed by the State or by companies based in London, or based in India but controlled by British or British-Indian firms—would buy, with rare and insignificant exceptions, railway materials made of iron and steel only from the U.K. One could argue that although this policy might discriminate against imports of manufactures of iron and steel products in India,[3] this was not specifically directed against the Indians. But the policy had the effect of stunting the growth of railway industries in India, even though railway workshops were set up by all the important railway lines. British manufacturers of locomotives had a monopoly of the Indian market, and several attempts at manufacturing locomotives by the railways themselves in India proved futile—although, when the necessity arose, the railway workshops successfully manufactured locomotives—because of lack of official support. In Great Britain, railway industries were considered the best training ground for the training of mechanical engineers.[4] The suppressing of railway industries, combined with the discrimination practised against Indians in the training of apprentices in the railway workshops, virtually closed this avenue of technical education for them. Government ordnance factories also rarely trained Indians for supervisory posts.[5]

---

[1] K. C. Mahindra: *Sir Rajendra Nath Mookerjee* (Calcutta, 1962, reprint of the first edition, 1933), pp. 103–13.

[2] S. B. Saul: *Studies in British Overseas Trade* (Liverpool University Press, 1960), pp. 198–203.

[3] The Government of India or the Railway Board had refused to guarantee purchases of steel products from the Bengal Iron and Steel Company, which was owned and managed by British capitalists.

[4] See the evidence of the Peninsular Locomotive Company in the Indian Tariff Board, *Minutes of Evidence on the Steel Industry*, Vol. II (Calcutta, 1924), p. 280; for corroboration see S. B. Saul: 'The Engineering Industry', in D. H. Aldcroft (editor): *The Development of British Industry and Foreign Competition, 1875–1914* (London, 1968), pp. 186–237. On the importance of mechanical engineering, see Sir Alfred Chatterton's evidence in *Minutes of the Evidence Recorded by the Indian Fiscal Commission*, Vol. III (Calcutta, 1923), p. 1016. For evidence of 'economic imperialism' in the supply of locomotives to India, see F. Lehmann: 'Great Britain and the Supply of Railway Locomotives of India: A Case Study of "Economic Imperialism"', *The Indian Economic and Social History Review*, Vol. II, No. 4, Oct. 1965.

[5] Brigadier General H. A. Young, director of ordnance factories in India from 1917 to 1921, stated: 'There has been little attempt to train the Indians for posts of responsibility in the

Much of this kind of discrimination arose from oversight and the prejudice of various departmental heads or other responsible officers rather than from high government policy. But there were other aspects of government policy which were quite deliberate. There was the decision to limit the technical education of Indians because the Government found it difficult to provide for the few that the engineering colleges turned out,[1] since it was not prepared to alter the policy of recruitment of the officers of the Public Works Departments and other technical departments in England, and it was even less prepared to interfere with the recruiting policies of private firms. Not only did the Government of India recruit the officers for its technical departments, it also maintained a Royal Engineering College at Coopers Hill, England, at its own expense, for the training of engineers who might or might not join the service of the Government of India. Indians were excluded from admission except at the discretion of the President of the College in case of spare accommodation being available, when up to two natives of India might be admitted.[2]

This framework of policy was sustained by the administrative machinery of the Government of India and the railways in which very few Indians had any share in decision-making power. Although the junior posts in the hierarchy of officers were coming more and more to be occupied by Indians, their chances of promotion to the superior posts were rather slender, and the latter remained the almost exclusive province of Europeans.[3] The advantages which European businessmen derived from this set of circumstances are quite obvious, although they are more difficult to document because their channels were informal. Whereas Indian businessmen would complain about delays in the transport of goods on the railways and differential treatment by railway staff, Eurpoean businessmen would be able to remove any difficulty through informal meetings with senior executives of the railways.[4]

Ordnance Factories'. 'The Indian Ordnance Factories and Indian Industries', *Journal of the Royal Society of Arts*, 1 Feb. 1924, p. 181.

[1] See, for a short but good survey of the educational policy of the Government of India, J. R. Cunningham: 'Education' in L. S. S. O'Malley (ed.): *Modern India and the West* (London, 1941).

[2] *Reports and Correspondence Relating to the Expediency of Maintaining the Royal Indian Engineering College, and Other Matters* (U.K. Parl. Papers, 1904, LXIV), Appendix I, Prospectus of the Royal Indian Engineering College, Coopers Hill.

[3] See *Report of the Royal Commission on the Public Services in India* (U.K. Parl. Papers, 1916, VII), pp. 24–6; *Report of the Committee appointed by the Secretary of State for India to enquire into the administration and working of Indian Railways*, p. 58 (U.K. Parl. Papers, 1921, X).

[4] The Reports of the Committee of the Indian Jute Mills Association from 1902 to 1914 contain examples of such amicable settlements almost every year.

The Reports of the Mackay Committee (1908) and the Acworth Committee (1921) on the railways, and the minutes of evidence taken before the Indian Industrial Commission 1916–18 contain numerous references to the complaints of Indian businessmen about differential treatment in railway facilities.

II

The European businessmen in their turn had established organizations and institutions for building up their advantages and protecting them against intruders all over India. They were organized in Chambers of Commerce to which very few Indians were admitted. The Bengal, Madras and Upper India Chambers of Commerce had practically no Indian members before the First World War. Only the Bombay Chamber of Commerce had Indians—all Parsis.[1] These chambers of commerce looked after the interests of a host of trade associations. In eastern India, the jute trade was almost entirely in European hands, and traders were organized into associations whose general interests were looked after by the Bengal Chamber of Commerce. For other commodities and other regions, except for western India, the same situation obtained. Some of the associations had explicit clauses barring Indians from membership. But most of them did not need such clauses, for any aspiring Indian could be excluded from membership by the existing members. The chambers of commerce and trade associations provided excellent means for adjusting the interests of different groups to one another, and for eliminating unnecessary competition. The European traders and businessmen were great believers in reasonable compromise and mutual accommodation among themselves, however much they might believe in the virtues of competition for others. The compromises were often facilitated by recognition of one association as the leader for a group of trades; for instance, the Indian Jute Mills Association normally acted as the spokesman for both the jute trade and the jute industry.

Thus, in most fields, the European businessmen were well organized to maintain something approaching collective monopoly. This collective monopoly in most industrial fields in most regions of India could also fight off new entrants, for the lock gates to the various channels of trade were under European control. Ocean shipping was in predominantly European hands; so was most of coastal and inland shipping; it was only in Bombay that there still were ships owned by Indians or other Asians.[2]

Most of the external trade was in European hands, including the most lucrative trades in opium, tea, jute, and later in coal. The trade in cotton and cotton yarn and in opium produced in western India was, however,

---

[1] R. J. F. Sulivan: *One Hundred Years of Bombay* (Bombay, 1937), Chapter II.

[2] The Bombay Steamship Company Limited, registered in 1906, had a board of directors in 1914 consisting of two Europeans, one Jew (Sir David Sassoon), one Parsi and four other Asians; it had acquired the navigation business known as Shepherds Steamers from the owner and vendor Hajee Ismail Hassum. *Investor's India Year-Book 1914* (Calcutta, 1914), pp. 400–2.

in Indian hands. There were few challenges to the European monopoly in shipping; these were easily beaten off by companies which had much vaster financial resources than their challengers and enjoyed patronage from public authorities and from the most powerful private firms.[1] The European shipping companies plying along the coast and across the oceans enjoyed mail subventions from the governments of India and the U.K. During the First World War, the British Government subsidized British shipping companies in other ways; but the attempts to get the Government of India to protect Indian shipping against unfair competition failed.[2]

The near-monopoly of Europeans in foreign trade was supplemented and buttressed by their control of its organized money market. The Banks of Bengal and of Madras never had an Indian director on their boards between 1876, when they were constituted as Presidency Banks, and their amalgamation into the Imperial Bank of India in 1921, except for a year or two at the very end. But the Bank of Bombay had Indian directors on its board and the latter often had a majority. The Presidency Banks had the right to use deposits from the Government and other public bodies free of interest; these deposits constituted, in 1900, about a fifth of their total deposits.[3] Of the Presidency Banks, the Bank of Bengal was easily the biggest. The other major joint-stock banks such as the Mercantile Bank, the Alliance Bank of Simla, and the Allahabad Bank were controlled by Europeans, although the last named bank had originally been organized by Indians. Not only were the directors of these banks Europeans, the senior officials were almost without exception Europeans, since the bias in favour of European business was very heavily built into the financial structure. It was only from 1906 onwards that large Indian joint-stock banks came into existence; of these only the Punjab National Bank and the Bank of India achieved any prominence before the First World War and survived.[4]

---

[1] See the story of the ruin of the steamship company of an elder brother of Rabindranath Tagore by the European Flotilla Company in Rabindranath Tagore: *My Reminiscences* (London, 1917), pp. 252–5; see also George Blake: *B.I. Centenary* (London, 1956), p. 170. Jamsetji Tata's attempt to break the monopoly of European liners in the carrying trade between India and China failed owing to drastic rate-cutting extending even to 'the unusual offer of carrying cotton to Japan free of charge' by the P. & O. and its associates; see F. R. Harris: *Jamsetji Nusserwanji Tata* (Bombay, 1958), Chapter V. Similar tactics were employed by the inland steamship companies.

[2] S. N. Haji: *State Aid to Indian Shipping* (Indian Shipping Series, Pamphlet No. 1, Bombay, 1922) and the memorandum of the Indian National Steamship Owners' Association, Bombay, in *Report of the Fiscal Commission, 1949–50, Volume Three* (Written evidence) (Delhi, 1952), pp. 185–276.   [3] *Investor's India Year Book 1911* (Calcutta, 1911), pp. 43–8.

[4] The Central Bank of India, organized mainly by the Parsi businessmen of Bombay, ultimately became the largest Indian-controlled private joint-stock bank, but it had not achieved such prominence before the First World War. Another large Bombay bank controlled by Indians was the Indian Specie Bank, but it crashed in 1913 primarily owing to involvement in speculation in silver.

All the so-called exchange banks, which also received deposits and lent money in India, were in European hands.[1] The total weight of the European-controlled banking institutions can be gauged roughly from the following figures (in £000):

	Capital reserve and rest	Deposits in India	Cash balances in India
Presidency Banks:			
1900	3,731	10,458	3,363
1910	4,607	24,387	7,567
Exchange Banks:			
1900	—	7,000	1,600
1910	—	16,200	2,900
'Indian' Joint-Stock Banks:			
1900	850	5,380	790
1910	2,510	17,110	1,870

SOURCE: J. M. Keynes: *Indian Currency and Finance* (London, 1913), Chapter VII.

In 1900 there were practically no Indian-controlled joint-stock banks of any importance; taking the Bank of Bombay as representing an institution jointly controlled by Europeans and Indians, we find that the total deposits of that bank in that year came to £3,471,049 out of total deposits amounting to £22,830,000 in that year. Even in 1910, the total deposits of Bank of Bombay, Bank of India, Central Bank of India (the figure of deposits for 1912 was used), People's Bank, Indian Specie Bank, Bombay Merchants' Bank, Bengal National Bank, Benares Bank, Oudh Commercial Bank, Punjab Banking Co., Punjab National Bank and Punjab Co-operative Bank[2] amounted to about Rs. 26,62,32,000 or about £17,748,000 out of total deposits of £57,697,000 for all the banks together. This figure used as an index of Indian control over the organized banking sector will almost certainly exaggerate it since two of the most important banks included in our calculation, the Indian Specie Bank and the People's Bank, crashed in 1913.

It is not easy to find out the extent to which European industry borrowed its working capital from the banks, but, from old share registers and evidence given before the Indian Tariff Board, it appears that most European managing agency houses had arrangements for cash credit or overdrafts for the companies under their control with

[1] The National Bank of India originated in 1863 as the Calcutta City Banking Corporation, with three European and four Indian directors. But its head office was transferred in 1866 to London, and the Indian directors lost their seats on the board. See G. W. Tyson, *100 years of Banking in Asia and Africa* (London, 1963), Chapters II and III.
[2] The figures were taken from *Investor's India Year-Books 1911–1914*.

the Presidency Banks, or with other European-controlled banks when the Presidency Banks did not have conveniently situated branches. Joint-stock banks lent money only for working capital; but, so long as a business was supposed to be credit-worthy, banks did not bother to check the uses to which the credit was put. Hence businessmen could and did use some short-term loans for long-term purposes. In any case, the financing of working capital by banks released all the capital of the businessmen for purposes of long-term investment in buildings, machinery etc.

According to the evidence of Sir W. B. Hunter before the Indian Industrial Commission, Indian industry also received a substantial value of its working capital in Madras from the Bank of Madras, even before the First World War.[1] No comparable figures were available for other banks before the war. According to the evidence given by Norman Murray, one of the managing governors of the Imperial Bank of India before the Royal Commission on Indian Currency and Finance of 1926, the advances by the Imperial Bank to purely industrial concerns were distributed between regions and communities as follows:

Advances to purely industrial concerns (figures in Rs. lakhs)

	Indian	European	Total
Bengal	3·74	5·74	9·48
Bombay	8·50	0·65	9·15
Madras	0·90	1·31	2·21

SOURCE: *Royal Commission on Indian Currency and Finance*, Vol. IV, *Minutes of Evidence taken in India before the Royal Commission on Indian Currency and Finance* (London, 1926), p. 479.

These figures related obviously to advances over a short period of time and may or may not be average figures but it is fair to judge that the situation must have been more biased in favour of European concerns before the war, when the Banks of Bengal and Madras had been under purely European management, and when Indian industrial control was even weaker.[2] It can be argued that we are exaggerating the

---

[1] According to Hunter, during the busy season, between Rs. 175 and Rs. 200 lakhs were lent to industrial concerns (including cotton mills, rice mills, cotton gins and presses, oil mills and sugar factories). He also claimed that of this amount about Rs. 110 lakhs were lent to Indian concerns and about Rs. 80 lakhs to European concerns. See *Minutes of Evidence taken before the Indian Industrial Commission 1916–18, Vol. III* (U.K. Parl. Papers, 1919, XIX), pp. 275–6.

[2] From a written statement submitted by Norman Murray it also appears that Europeans as a community accounted for a much larger fraction of total advances than of total deposits. This discrepancy is most extreme in Bengal. See *Royal Commission on Indian Currency and Finance, Vol. II, Appendices to the Report of the Royal Commission on Indian Currency and*

importance of European control over joint-stock banking, for indigenous bankers probably controlled a much vaster quantity of capital than did joint-stock banks. But the point is that the rates of interest in the modern sector of the money market were lower than those in the traditional sector and that the joint-stock banks had access to public deposits and the money market outside India. The importance of such cheap and easy credit for industry is obvious.

One can question whether the greater European control over industry and trade may not have been due to the fact that most of the capital was invested in India from Europe. As far as the period from 1900 to 1914 is concerned, this was not so. Keynes, after a careful consideration of figures of net remittances by Europeans in India and the new capital invested in India from Europe (or, rather, the United Kingdom), came to the conclusion that the net inflow of foreign private capital into India was roughly zero over the period up to 1910.[1]

Most of the capital invested in the enterprises controlled by Europeans came from their earnings in trade, industry, banking, and employment in the army or various government departments in India. Although all this must figure as investment of 'foreign capital' in India, it represented no real transfer of resources from the industrialized countries of Europe to India. Since the railway rates were geared to the transport of goods to and from the ports, they favoured foreign trade as did the general free trade policy of the Government. This not only served to keep India as a very valuable member in the imperial payments system, but also to increase the earnings of Europeans who had a monopoly of the financing of foreign trade and who had a near-monopoly of foreign trade itself except in Bombay. The recruitment policies of the Government, the enormous differences between the income of an average Indian—between £2 and £3 per year in 1900 according to the optimistic calculations of Lord Curzon and F. J. Atkinson—and the income of a salaried European earning between £300 at the lowest and £7,000 at the highest (excluding the Viceroy) further increased the pool of incomes in European hands out of which capital could be supplied.[2] Assuming a lognormal distribution of incomes among Europeans, and taking the geometric mean as the appropriate average, the average income of a salaried European would come to

Finance (London, 1926), Appendix no. 48. This is of course consistent with what one would expect in a situation where there is a larger fraction of businessmen among Europeans than among ordinary Indian depositors.

[1] J. M. Keynes's review of Sir Theodore Morison: *The Economic Transition in India* (London, 1911) in *Economic Journal* 1911, p. 430.

[2] Income tax rates were very low, but military officers were given special exemptions even from these low rates. Secretaries and agents of the Presidency Banks earned between £750 and £7,000 (without taking account of fringe benefits such as free housing).

about £1,450. There was naturally hardly any complaint by European businessmen giving evidence before the Indian Industrial Commission about the scarcity of capital for worthwhile enterprises.

III

We now turn to the regional aspects of European control over industry in India. India was a very poor country in 1900, and, even though by 1900 about 25,000 miles of railways had been built, the interior parts were still largely unconnected with one another except through the ports. The currency system of India, with different notes for different 'currency circles', also led to the fragmentation of the economic space. Hence if in an industry some protection against foreign competition existed in the shape of transport costs from abroad or in the interior and in the form of some public patronage, it was easy to set up a regional monopoly in the products, since the local market was small. Of the three major ports of India, Calcutta commanded the largest trade, and one result of the greater European involvement in the commerce of India in eastern India was the greater relative difference between exports and imports in that part than in other parts of India. One other result was that they had a very much bigger base for the accumulation of capital than the Indian businessmen in Bombay. The fact that the seat of Government was in Calcutta also meant a much larger share of Government patronage for Calcutta than for Bombay—at any rate, until the irrigation works of Sind demanded a much larger amount of construction in that part of India.

We have already referred to the facility with which European businessmen arrived at compromises minimizing competition and the threat of challenges from outside. This had quite tangible results in major industrial fields, such as the short-time agreements which the Indian Jute Mills Association organized, whenever the need arose, from 1885 onwards, until the arrangements broke down under the dual stress of the depression of the 1930s and the entry of new, primarily Indian-controlled firms. The jute mill companies regularly negotiated collective agreements with the steamship companies of eastern India for the carriage of jute and jute goods. The steamship companies themselves entered into a series of agreements with one another for the division of the market and the fixing of rates and fares. The two major European-controlled paper mills of eastern India entered into agreements about prices before the First World War, and such co-operation continued throughout the interwar period.

The straddling of different fields by the same managing agency house, and the concentration of capital in the hands of a few European managing agency houses facilitated the maintenance of individual or collective monopolies, and British businessmen fully appreciated the advantages of such monopolies for themselves. Thus when Parry and Company, in conjunction with the Commercial Bank of India, floated the East India Distilleries and Sugar Factories, Limited, the prospectus claimed: 'the Company will...secure the practical control of the Spirit and Sugar Trade throughout the Madras Presidency'.[1] The substance of this claim lay in the monopoly of supplying sugar to the troops stationed in the Madras Presidency and Burma, and of supplying spirits to Mysore, and the control of all big sugar- and spirits-producing factories in the Madras Presidency except one that was managed by Binny and Company. This last obstacle to the exercise of effective monopoly was removed when Binny and Company had to hand over the management of the Deccan Sugar and Abkhari Company Limited to Parry and Company in 1902, because of large losses sustained mainly in sugar trade.[2] Similar local European monopolies existed in the case of breweries in north and north-western India, and in the field of supply of army boots, blankets and other equipment; these monopolies were often based on an initial government patronage.[3]

More important perhaps than the domination of individual industries by individual companies or managing agency houses was the domination of all the major industries by a small group of European managing agency houses in eastern, southern and northern India. An analysis of the rupee companies listed in *Investor's India Year Book 1911* revealed that the seven managing agency houses Andrew, Yule and Company, Bird and Company, Begg, Dunlop and Company, Shaw, Wallace and Company, Williamson, Magor and Company, Duncan Brothers, and Octavius, Steel and Company controlled 55 per cent of the jute companies, 61 per cent of the tea companies, and 46 per cent of the coal companies. In the case of jute, Andrew Yule and Company and Bird and Company alone controlled fourteen out of twenty-nine rupee companies, and their control increased during the decade 1910–20; the inclusion of sterling companies would tend to decrease the degree of concentration measured by control over capital and looms.

---

[1] *Issues 1897 advertised in the Times* (London), 14, July–Dec. 1897, p. 269.
[2] Hilton Brown, *Parry's of Madras: A Story of British Enterprise in India* (Madras, 1954), pp. 162–5.
[3] The Murree Brewery Limited and, E. Dyer and Company Limited, both connected with the Dyer family, controlled the trade and manufacture of spirits in north and north-west India: Somerset Playne (compiler) and Arnold Wright (editor): *The Bombay Presidency, The United Provinces, the Punjab etc.* (London, 1920), pp. 157–64, 566–8, 633–8. Government patronage was enjoyed by the Army Boot and Equipment Factory and by the Cawnpore Woollen Mills and Army Cloth Manufacturing Company Limited. See H. R. Nevill, *Cawnpore: A Gazetteer, being Vol. XIX of the District Gazetteers of the United Provinces of Agra and Oudh* (Allahabad, 1909), pp. 78–9; and S. K. Sen, *Studies in Economic Policy and Development of India, 1848–1926* (Calcutta, 1926), p. 38.

An analysis of data from *Investor's India Year-Book* 1911 and *Capital* (Calcutta), 5 January 1911 and 4 January 1912, showed that, out of the total number of 32,711 looms in the jute mills of Bengal in 1910–11, Bird and Company controlled 4,707, Thomas Duff and Company controlled 3,724, Andrew Yule controlled 3,302, Jardine Skinner controlled 2,177, Ernsthausen controlled 2,150 and George Henderson controlled 2,040 looms.

Most of the coal companies were rupee companies, and the biggest of them such as Bengal Coal Company and Burrakur Coal Company were controlled by Andrew Yule and Bird respectively. The inclusion of sterling tea companies would seem to make a material difference to our measurement of the degree of concentration. According to an estimate made by G. D. Hope, Chief Scientific Officer, India Tea Association, out of a total nominal capital of £30·2 million of joint-stock companies registered in India only £4·3 million were accounted for by rupee companies.[1] However, a scrutiny of the list of sterling tea companies registered by 1914, and operating in India, published by the Mincing Lane Tea and Rubber Shares Brokers' Association Limited and the Indian Tea Share Exchange Limited, reveals that out of 124 companies so listed, forty-two were controlled by George Williamson and Company, Octavius Steel and Company, Walter Duncan and Company and R. G. Shaw and Company, which were the London correspondents of four firms appearing in our list of the top seven managing agency firms in Calcutta.[2]

The seven listed firms were probably not the biggest ones; in terms of influence and involvement, possibly Jardine Skinner and Company, Martin and Company, and F. W. Heilgers and Company would be bigger than some of the seven firms cited earlier. Nor does the control of the jute, coal and tea industries alone give a proper measure of concentration. The same group of British managing agency houses also controlled other fields. Andrew Yule were important in the field of steam navigation, Bird and Martin in the field of engineering, and Gillanders, Arbuthnot, and Martin in the field of railways. F. W. Heilgers and Balmer Lawrie controlled the two important paper mills of India before 1914. The degree of concentration cannot be measured by a mere listing of the companies or their capital under the control of the managing agency houses: there was an enormous degree of interlocking of boards of directors under the control of different managing agency houses: there was an enormous degree of interlocking of boards of

[1] G. D. Hope: 'The Tea Industry of Bengal and Assam' in Somerset Playne (compiler) and Arnold Wright (editor): *Bengal and Assam, Behar and Orissa* (London, 1917), p. 387.

[2] *Tea Producing Companies 1914* (London, 1914) and *Tea Producing Companies 1923–24* (London, 1924). The latter publication was utilized in those cases in which a company had been registered by 1914 but for some reason had been omitted from the earlier publication.

directors under the control of different managing agency houses.[1] Apart from the formal and informal associations and clubs of which the companies under the control of British managing agency houses and their managers were members, this interlocking of directorates also facilitated the smooth working of various types of price agreements or market-sharing arrangements.

It is not suggested that this degree of concentration of control was unusual in the field of Indian industry; although no rigorous estimate of changes in the degree of concentration of economic power has been worked out, all indications point to the conclusion that the 1920s witnessed a further increase in the concentration of control in the hands of the top British managing agency houses.[2] But the supremacy of the group of British managing agency houses began to be challenged seriously with the entry of new Indian entrepreneurial groups into the industrial field.

The control of the managing agency houses over the resources of eastern and northern India also extended to the supply of labour. By a series of laws the Government of India had facilitated and regulated the recruitment of labour for the tea gardens of Assam, and the scope of legal recruitment had been extended practically to the whole of India except the Bombay Presidency. Up to 1908 an indenture system had been adopted for the plantations of Assam, and the employers had enjoyed the right of private arrest of labourers for alleged breach of contract.[3] The local agents who were registered under Section 59 of the Assam Labour and Emigration Act, I consisted in 1900 entirely of the large managing agency houses of Calcutta such as Begg, Dunlop and Company, Balmer, Lawrie and Company, Macneill and Company, Williamson, Magor and Company, Octavius, Steel and Company, Finlay, Muir and Company, Shaw, Wallace and Company, and some other European firms or persons.[4]

The existence of an elaborate agency for the recruitment of labour for

---

[1] The Bank of Bengal itself was controlled by the leading managing agency houses. According to an article in *Capital* (Calcutta), 2 Sept. 1909, 'the directorate of the Bank of Bengal has always been a very close borough, confined to certain favoured firms, some sixteen in number. Of these sixteen again, nine had folded their business, so that the directors were drawn from only seven firms of which two firms Jardine, Skinner and Gillanders, Arbuthnot had had directors in the Board of the Bank of Bengal during the previous half-century at least.' The relevant extract from the article is given in Royal Commission on Indian Finance and Currency: *Appendices to the Final Report of the Commissioners (Third Volume of Appendices)* (London, 1914), p. 649.

[2] A merger of the interests of Bird and Company with those of Heilgers and Company was probably the single most important factor in this; the take-over of Burn and Company, the biggest engineering complex in India outside the works of the Tata Iron and Steel Company, by Martin and Company, was another important event.

[3] See R. K. Das: *Plantation Labour in India* (Calcutta, 1931), Chapter III; S. K. Bose: *Capital and Labour in the Indian Tea Industry* (Bombay, 1954), pp. 67–113.

[4] Government of India, Department of Revenue and Agriculture, Emigration, October 1900, A Proceeding nos. 15 and 16, p. 796.

the tea plantations meant that it could also be utilized for recruiting labour for jute mills and coal mines. The tea plantations were by far the biggest employers of labour among the enterprises controlled by Europeans; labour probably got lower wages there and was less free than in almost any other industry. Hence it was necessary for the managing agency houses to use elaborate methods for recruiting labour from the poorer parts of India since local labour in Bengal and Assam generally earned higher wages than were paid by the plantations. The recruitment of labour for jute mills never proved a problem once a flow of labour to the east from other parts of India could be ensured. Unlike the situation in Bombay before the First World War, there was very little complaint about the supply of labour to jute or cotton mills in Bengal.[1] The legal machinery of the Government and the monopolistic position of British managing agency houses were effectively utilized by the latter to ensure a supply of cheap labour from all over India, even though local labour was relatively expensive.

One can say that, when a company was registered in India, the capital had been predominantly raised from Europeans (and a small group of Indians) who were living in India or who had lived in India in the recent past and had close connexions with India. However, it is not true that, when a company was registered in London, the capital came predominantly from residents of Britain. This is obvious when one looks at the history of most of the tea companies under the control of British managing houses. The tea estates were organized into companies after they had already been worked, at least partially, for some years and an estimate of the profits that are likely to be made by the companies had been arrived at.[2] Many of the sterling companies managed by the managing agency houses were closely held, and their shares were not quoted on the stock exchange.

The European residents in India made their money, as we have pointed out earlier, in trade, government, railway, banking service or in the army. The salaries of government and military officers were high,[3] the rates of income tax were extremely low, and, as we have seen, even then military officers obtained special exemption from income tax rates. Most of the big managing agency houses made their money in trade or as labour contractors. Andrew Yule started in trade and entered the fields of coal and steamships before they took up the jute

---

[1] See in particular *Report of the Labour Enquiry Commission* (Bengal) (Calcutta, Bengal Secretariat Press, 1896), pp. 49–50.

[2] See, for example, the prospectuses of Cachar and Dooars Tea Company Limited and East India and Ceylon Tea Company Limited in *Issues 1895 advertised in the Times* (London), no. 10, July–Dec. 1895, the entries for 18 October and 16 October respectively.

[3] A senior collector in 1915, for instance, earned about 500 times an ordinary Indian and 30 times an ordinary Englishman. See also p. 233 above.

industry. Bird and Company made their money first as labour con-tractors for the East Indian Railways.[1] Binny and Company, the managers of Buckingham and Carnatic Mills, were probably the largest produce merchants in Madras around 1914 and acted as the landing agents for Madras Port Trust. The major managing agency houses continued to have large export and import departments after they had entered industry in a big way.[2] Among items of trade, imports of Manchester piecegoods remained extremely important among the operations of British managing agency houses; Calcutta was the largest single piecegoods market of the East, and the control of import trade by European businessmen resulted in a virtual monopoly of the wholesale trade in cotton piecegoods in ports other than Bombay. The imports of machinery and hardware also constituted an important item. Among the exports, raw jute, jute goods, opium, leather, oilseeds, indigo, tea, coffee, and spices were important, although both opium and indigo exports grew less important with time.[3]

Two other points are to be noticed about the British managing agency houses in eastern India. First, most of the firms which came to straddle different industries and counted as big firms had been started primarily by traders, contractors and financiers. Very few of the pioneering planters, apart from those who were involved with the early stages of the Assam Company and had managed to buy up large amounts of land suitable for tea cultivation, went on to become industrialists. The indigo planters remained primarily large farmers with strong features of the usual Indian landlords—receiving rent and doing very little to help change the methods of cultivation of the tenants. Apart from Martin and Company, no engineering firm by itself grew up to absorb or launch firms in other fields.

[1] Godfrey Harrison: *Bird and Company of Calcutta, A History produced to mark the firm's centenary 1864–1964* (Calcutta, 1964), Chapters II, III and IV. The labour department of the firm dealing with two railway companies, two steamer companies, and the Port Commissioners of Calcutta continued to be one of the most important departments of the firm. See *ibid.* pp. 50–3.

[2] Somerset Playne (compiler) and Arnold Wright (editor): *Southern India* (London, 1915), pp. 135–9.

[3] Although both W. R. Macdonell representing the Bombay Chamber of Commerce and R. Steel representing the Bengal Chamber of Commerce before the Royal Commission on opium claimed that they personally had nothing to do with opium, the official posi-tion of both the Chambers was in favour of continuation of the opium policy of the Govern-ment of India including unrestricted exports of opium to China: *Minutes of Evidence taken before the Royal Commission on Opium between 18th Nov. and 29th Dec. 1883 with Appendices,* Vol. II (U.K. Parl. Papers, 1894, LXI), pp. 160–2 and 439–52, and *Minutes of Evidence taken before the Royal Commission on Opium from 29th Jan. to 22nd Feb. 1894 with Appendices,* Vol. IV (U.K. Parl. Papers, 1894, LXII), pp. 314–16. By far the largest proportion of opium exports (two-thirds or more of total exports) were shipped from Calcutta after public auctions of opium produced in farms licensed and supervised by the Government, so it is natural to suppose that European traders had the major share of the profits.

The second point to be noticed is that the managing agency houses with strong industrial interests continued to have strong interests in trade. In fact, sometimes it was the industrial interest which led to an interest in trade in the raw material.[1] The engineering firms generally also dealt in imported engineering stores and hardware.[2] One of the results of this combination of interests was that the attitudes of the different managing agency houses to questions of tariff protection or state aid were often ambivalent. This ambivalence led to definite opposition to protectionist policies in the case of those firms whose primary interests lay in the field of exports and imports and which had little to do with producing industrial products for the domestic market.[3]

We can trace the operation of Indian entrepreneurship in eastern India against this background of domination of all fields of wholesale trade and modern industry by European business. The usual explanations for the late emergence of Indian industrial entrepreneurship generally follow one of three lines: (a) the Bengali middle classes were averse to trade and industry and preferred the liberal professions; (b) the Indian businessmen in general were interested in trade and would not enter industry because it did not promise a quick return;[4] (c) the big merchants of eastern India had been eliminated by the Permanent Settlement and eastern India had been converted into 'a landlords' paradise' so that investment in land was much more attractive than other types of investment.[5]

---

[1] Somerset Playne (compiler) and Arnold Wright (editor): *Bengal and Assam, Behar and Orissa* (London, 1917), 'Birkmyre Brothers', p. 85. The Birkmyre brothers had owned a small jute mill at Greenock and had dismantled the works and started in 1874 a highly mechanized jute company, viz. the Hastings Jute Mills, near Calcutta. 'Recently Birkmyre Brothers have given their attention to the baling of their own marks of jute for export to Dundee and in Continent, and they have already been successful in introducing these to the favourable notice of spinners.'

[2] Martin and Company, for example, were described in Somerset Playne and Arnold Wright, 1917, p. 157, as in all probability the leading importers of engineering tools and plant. Martin and Company were at that time the managing agents also for Bengal Iron and Steel Company.

[3] See the written evidence of Turner, Morrison and Company and the oral evidence of W. S. J. Wilson of the same Company in *Minutes of the Evidence Recorded by the Indian Fiscal Commission*, Vol. II (Calcutta, 1923), pp. 381–8.

[4] For an authoritative statement of the first two propositions see *Report of the Indian Industrial Commission, 1916–18* (U.K. Parl. Papers, 1919, XVIII), pp. 64–5; for an earlier statement of a similar import by one of India's foremost historians, see Jadunath Sarkar: *The Economics of British India* (Calcutta, 1911), particularly the preface ('To my countrymen'), and Chapters II and VII. For a modern, if not very sophisticated, statement of the second proposition, in a widely used textbook, see R. Chatterjee, *Indian Economics* (Calcutta, 1959), p. 134.

[5] For a contemporary exposition of this view, applied to the whole of India, see Barrington Moore, Jr.: *Social Origins of Dictatorship and Democracy* (London, 1967), pp. 345–70. For a description of the process of conversion of the Indian merchants into landlords, see N. K. Sinha: *The Economic History of Bengal*, Vol. I (Calcutta, 1961), and Vol. II (Calcutta, 1962), particularly Chapters VII–IX.

On the first explanation, even if one grants the aversion of the Bengalis to business independently of the relative attractiveness of the kinds of business open to them and the professions open to them,[1] the question still remains why the Marwaris, who were traditionally a trading and banking community, did not enter the industrial field on any large scale before the First World War. The traditional answer that Indian businessmen were addicted to enterprises which would yield quick returns is inadequate, for most of the European business houses were also engaged in trade on a large scale. The simpler explanation is that entry into modern industry was barred by European control over foreign trade, wholesale trade, and finance. It required a loosening of this grip—facilitated both by the First World War and the greater importance of internal trade in relation to external trade which came about in the 1920s and 1930s—before Indian businessmen could effectively challenge the Europeans in the industrial field.

It is important to notice that before the First World War many Indians from the professional classes had entered industry either on their own or in association with other businessmen. Nilratan Sarkar and P. C. Roy in Bengal,[2] Lala Harkishan Lal in the Punjab,[3] and Balchandra Krishna Bhatwadekar and Kirloskar in Bombay and pioneers of the glass and match industries in north India[4] had entered the field of industry; but industry which was not backed by a large trading and financing organization was not destined to succeed. Of these pioneers

[1] The date of the absolute decline of Bengalis in trade and industry has recently been brought forward from the time of the Permanent Settlement to the middle of the nineteenth century—more precisely to the year 1846 when Dwarakanath Tagore died; see B. Kling: 'The Origin of the Managing Agency System in India', *The Journal of Asian Studies*, Vol. XXVI, No. 1, Nov. 1966, pp. 37–48, and N. K. Sinha: 'Indian Business Enterprise: Its Failure in Calcutta (1800–1848)', *Bengal Past and Present*, Diamond Jubilee Number, July–Dec. 1967, pp. 112–23.

[2] Dr Nilratan Sarkar started the National Tannery and Dr P. C. Roy started the Bengal Pharmaceutical and Chemical Works; see *Minutes of Evidence taken before the Indian Industrial Commission, 1916–18*, Vol. II, Bengal and Central Provinces (U.K. Parl. Papers, 1919, XVIII), pp. 34–52, 78–88, 335–347.

[3] See Somerset Playne (compiler) and Arnold Wright (editor), 1920, 'Bharat Insurance Company Limited'. Lala Harkishan Lal, an Arora by caste and a lawyer by training, was the founder of Bharat Insurance, and the promoter of a host of companies including cotton mills, and the Lahore Electric Supply Company Limited.

[4] The following firms were represented before the Indian Industrial Commission, 1916–18: Bande Mataram Match Factory, Calcutta, Match Factory, Kota, Bilaspur District, C.P., Jubbulpore Glass Factory, Jubbulpore, the North Indian Matches Ltd, Bareilly, Western India Glass Works Limited, B.B. and C.I. Railway, Paisa Fund Glass Works, Telegawn, and Upper India Glass Works, Ambala. Of these, North Indian Matches Ltd, Bareilly, was controlled by the British managing agency house, Cooper, Allen and Company. Commenting on the Indian glass industry Alfred Chatterton wrote: 'The industry seems to have had a peculiar fascination for Indians, who undeterred by the failures of comparatively large concerns run by Europeans, started sixteen glass factories on a smaller scale between the years 1906 and 1913.' Indian Munitions Board, *Industrial Handbook, 1919* (Calcutta, 1919), p. 262.

only the house of Kirloskar survived as one of the seventy-five business groups of modern India.[1]

Before the First World War, not only the jute industry but the wholesale trade in jute also had been controlled by European and American businessmen. This control was maintained not only because the whole export trade in raw jute was in European hands and the internal consumers of jute, namely the jute mills, were European-controlled, but also because the trade associations explicitly or more often implicitly forbade the entry of Indian traders as members. The First World War saw the departure of many assistants and managers in European concerns for military service and Indians had the opportunity to move into the jute trade in force. Indian brokers also managed to buy up a sizeable proportion of the shares of British companies that were actually traded on the stock exchange. This was more true of Calcutta than of Madras or Cawnpore, where organized stock exchanges did not come into existence for a very long time. Whereas in 1914 Haji Sawood Beg Mohammad was the only Indian firm to rank among the first fifteen firms engaged in the export of jute fabrics[2] by the end of the First World War, Sarupchand Hukamchand and Company, and Birla Brothers had emerged as leading exporters of raw jute and jute fabrics. These firms were among the first Indian business houses to enter the jute industry after the First World War. During the 1920s, the further shift of exports of Indian raw jute away from the U.K. led to the almost complete loss of entrepot trade by the U.K. and gave an opportunity to the Indians to enter the field of exports directly. Further, political levers were utilized to allow Indians to participate in the jute trade in London also.[3] The amalgamation of the Presidency Banks to form the Imperial Bank of India and the strengthening of Indian-controlled Banks such as the Central Bank of India, the Bank of India and the Punjab National Bank also aided the Indians in their competition with the British businessmen in India.

A further opportunity for capturing the control of industrial capital by Indians came with the great depression of the 1930s. The drastic contraction of the export and import trade hit European business badly; the adoption of protectionist policies helped the growth of industries primarily for the domestic market. There was a considerable amount of repatriation of British capital from India during this period.

---

[1] R. K. Hazari: *The Corporate Private Sector, Concentration, Ownership and Control* (London, 1966), pp. 261–3, and *Report of the Monopolies Inquiry Commission 1965* (Delhi, 1965), pp. 73–4; G. B. Baldwin: *Industrial Growth in South India: Case Studies in Economic Development* (The Free Press, Glencoe, Illinois, 1959), pp. 284–303.

[2] Indian Jute Mills Association: *Report of the Committee for the Year ended 31st December, 1914* (Calcutta, 1915), Statement XIX.

[3] Frank Moraes, *Sir Purshotamdas Thakurdas* (Bombay, 1957), p. 44.

Indian businessmen with large trading enterprises entered the cement, sugar and paper industries; the almost complete displacement of imports of cotton piecegoods by Indian mill production was effected during the 1920s and 1930s.

It remains slightly puzzling that European businessmen should fail to take advantage of the protectionist policies adopted by the Government of India. One explanation would be that Europeans had really failed to keep their marketing techniques abreast of the times so that where their differential advantage was smaller, as in internal trade, they had to give place perforce to the Indians—or the Japanese—whose marketing methods were superior. This would seem to be a good explanation of the failure of the Europeans to make much of the opportunities offered by the cotton mill industry: Greaves, Cotton and Company had become one of the biggest managing agency houses controlling the cotton mill industry in the beginning of the century but they had become specialized in exporting low-quality yarn to China; when the exports to China were severely affected by Japanese competition, Greaves, Cotton suffered enormous losses. They had ultimately to give up their cotton mills although they retained very profitable agencies in cotton textile and other kinds of machinery. Many other Indian firms had faced a similar situation and survived and prospered by producing cotton piecegoods for the domestic market.

However, even in the cotton mill industry there were British firms producing for the Indian market before the First World War: there was the group of cotton mills at Cawnpore, there were the Buckingham and Carnatic Mills under the management of Binny and Company in Madras City, and there were the spinning mills under the control of A. and F. Harvey in the Madras Presidency. The Buckingham and Carnatic Mills became one of the most prosperous companies in India, producing fine-quality cloth and employing automatic looms long before Indian firms had adopted them. In the paper industry, the Titaghur Paper Mills and Bengal Paper Mill remained the leaders in the industry, controlling well over 60 per cent of total paper output in India right up to 1936 or 1937, and claiming tariff protection and benefiting from it like other Indian firms.

Hence orientation to the export market will not adequately explain the relative stagnation of British enterprise in India after 1914. One has here to look for specifically political factors including the gradual but steady transfer of the levers of power to Indian hands—at first, mainly the hands of collaborators with the British but increasingly into the hands of those who were definitely hostile to British rule. Probably the decreasing importance of foreign trade and finance to the British economy played its part. Perhaps some kind of group solidarity

transcending individual profit calculations prevented British businessmen from taking as much advantage of the protectionist policies in
India as they might have otherwise done because of the (mistaken)
belief that tariff protection was mainly directed against imports from
Britain.[1] Furthermore, in the 1920s and 1930s some European businessmen preferred the Far East as a field of investment since, although
conditions were unsettled there, wages were low, labour legislation was
practically non-existent and there was no government which wanted to
propitiate nationalists with concessions which European businessmen
considered damaging to their own interests. This factor was however
obviously connected with the political developments of the period.[2]

IV

If we turn our attention to Indian entrepreneurship in western
India, the contrast with eastern and northern India could not have
been greater. British interests were there in strength, buying raw cotton,
cleaning it in ginning presses, and baling it for export; spinning yarn
out of cotton; in the case of Finlay and Swan mills, and the mills
under the control of Indo-British managing agency houses, weaving
cloth for the Indian market. Killick, Nixon and Company were the
leading managing agency house of Bombay, developing and managing
light railways all over India. The exchange banks of Bombay were
exclusively in European hands, until the Eastern Bank was organized
under the leadership of E. D. Sassoon and Company. The senior
officers of the administration and the railways of Bombay and Sind were
Europeans as in other parts of Bombay. The Bombay Port Trust was
also European-controlled.

But the Indians had a toehold in the export business. They had been
ship-owners and also ship-builders until the activities of the Bombay
dockyard had been discontinued by governmental decision.[3] The cotton

---

[1] Professor Amartya Kumar Sen suggested that the social ethos of the rulers might explain
the failure of British businessmen to invest in certain fields, particularly the cotton textile
industry. See A. K. Sen: 'The Commodity Pattern of British Enterprise in Early Indian
Industrialization, 1854–1914', *Deuxième Conférence International D'Histoire Economique, Aix-en-
Provence, 1962* (Paris, 1965), pp. 781–808. While this was only partly true before the First
World War, in view of the involvement of Greaves, Cotton and Company, Binny and Company and A. and F. Harvey and others in the cotton mill industry, this was far more true
in the 1920s and 1930s when the social ethos was reinforced by the straitened circumstances
of the British economy and in particular of the investor in Britain and by the threat of
dissolution of positions of privilege in India.

[2] The trading and industrial interests of the Sassoon family were transferred to the Far East
from India because of political developments and because of a greater degree of competition
from Indian firms. See Cecil Roth: *The Sassoon Dynasty* (London, 1941), pp. 226–8.

[3] See the *Gazetteer of Bombay City and Island*, Vol. I (Bombay, 1909), pp. 390–1; see also V. I.
Pavlov: *The Indian Capitalist Class* (New Delhi, 1964), pp. 146–54. D. F. Karaka: *History of
the Parsis*, Vol. 2 (London, 1884), listed a number of Parsi ship-owners.

trade was mainly in Indian hands; the Indians also had a hand in the opium trade, particularly since the opium originated in native states where the Indians had a little more say in the conduct of political and commercial affairs than in British territory.

This difference in the position of the Indians is reflected not only in the greater percentage of industrial capital controlled by the Indians but also in the greater degree of collaboration between Indian and European businessmen. As we mentioned above the Bombay Chamber of Commerce was primarily a European organization but it also had several Indian members. The Bank of Bombay had an Indian majority on the board of directors, although the president was generally an Englishman. There was often an Indian majority in the boards of directors of companies under the control of managing agency houses such as Bradbury and Company, and Killick, Nixon and Company.[1]

This relative importance of Indian businessmen and their collaboration on a basis of something like equality in western India is often obscured by the extolling of the virtues of Parsis and the description of the evils caused by the caste system, or other-worldly values of Hinduism or Jainism. The Parsis certainly played a part in industry which was disproportionate to their numbers.

But this cannot be explained adequately only in terms of the attitudes of the Parsis to business, training, or technical education.[2] Some other tangible factors will help explain their early pre-eminence, and the later erosion of their position; one was the shift of the centre of commerce from Surat to Bombay, and the early shift of the Parsis from the region around Surat to Bombay;[3] there was also the 'special relationship' between the British and the Parsis evidenced by the fervent loyalty towards the Queen and her ancestors displayed by the educated Parsis, the recognition of Parsi merit by the British in the form of titles, and the association of the Parsis as junior or even equal partners in many British enterprises.[4] The values of the Parsis were probably more

[1] See, for example, the companies listed under 'Railways' and 'Cotton' in *Investor's India Year-Book, 1914* (Calcutta, 1914).

[2] The emergence of the Parsis cannot be explained in terms of a minority which had to seek outlets in trade because other professions were barred to them. Before they came into contact with the Europeans the Parsis had been a peaceable, largely rural community, engaged in all the professions that were open to other Indians. See D. F. Karaka: *History of the Parsis*, Vol. II, pp. 1–10. The Parsis, however, did not develop a caste-system and this may have made them more flexible when new opportunities were opened up.

[3] For an account of the later period of the decline of Surat as a port (from 1800 to 1875), see Gazetteer of the Bombay Presidency, *Gujarat: Surat and Broach*, Vol. II (Bombay, 1877), pp. 166–77.

[4] I am indebted to an unpublished paper by Dr Ashok Desai and to subsequent discussions in writing with him, for the conviction that there was a 'special relationship' between the British and the Parsis.

Jamsetjee Jeejeebhoy and Sons were the Bombay correspondents of Jardine Matheson and

important in their selection by the British for this kind of partnership than for pre-eminence in purely commercial and industrial activities.[1]

The growth of Bombay and of its foreign trade conferred a differential advantage on the traders associated with Bombay. Since the Parsis had been a ship-building and ship-owning community from the early days of Bombay, they could participate in the profits made in foreign trade—and, in particular, in the trade in cotton and opium. The resistance of the Marathas to British occupation meant that western India was not subject to British exploitation during the days when the East India Company and its servants treated India as the prize of victory in the most literal sense. It also meant that the native merchants were not eliminated from the fields of high finance as they were in eastern India; it is even probable that the merchant classes gained by lending money to the various powers during their struggle.

The differential advantage gained from the longer political independence of western India and the continuation of large parts of territory under the rule of native states applied to the merchants of all communities of western India, but it applied especially to Bombay. The merchants of Ahmedabad and the Baroda State as well as Bombay benefited from the opium trade;[2] the pioneers of the cotton mill industry in western India were a Parsi merchant and a Gujarati Brahman who had been a civil servant under the British. The American Civil War and the consequent cotton boom of Bombay made that city even more pre-eminent; the opening of the Suez Canal soon made it as important a port in India as Calcutta. The initial advantages of the Parsis because of early association with Bombay and the British and because of their part in the export trade became unassailable and the challenge of newcomers could not dislodge them from their position, although it could and did diminish the degree of their pre-eminence, over time.[3]

Company, who were one of the largest British firms trading with China. See Michael Greenberg: *British Trade and the Opening of China* (Cambridge, 1951), pp. 146–51, 164; Matheson described the Parsi firm as 'the best-managed business this side of the Cape', *ibid.* p. 164 n.

[1] Our belief in the 'special relationship' of the Parsis with the British is strengthened by the fact that whereas other Indian traders and bankers from Bolvia or Hindu *banya* communities were found in territories such as East Africa in the first half of the nineteenth century that were not controlled by the British, the Parsis were not to be found there. See in this connexion R. Coupland: *East Africa and its Invaders from the Earliest Times to the Death of Seyyid Said in 1856* (Oxford, 1965), pp. 182–3, 300–3, 324–5; K. B. Vaidya: *The Sailing Vessel Traffic on the West Coast of India and Its Future* (Bombay, 1945), pp. 18–26; L. W. Hollingsworth, *The Asians of East Africa* (London, 1960), Chapters III, V and XI, and G. S. Graham: *Great Britain in the Indian Ocean: A Study of Maritime Enterprise 1810–1850* (Oxford, 1967), pp. 209–11.

[2] *Gazetteer of the Bombay Presidency*, Vol. IV, Ahmedabad (Bombay, 1879), p. 64.

[3] According to the figures given by Andrew Brimmer, quoted in C. A. Myers: *Labour Problems in the Industrialization of India* (Cambridge, Mass., 1958), p. 22, the percentage of gross assets of public registered companies in the Bombay province controlled by Parsis

The difference in the control of industries by Indians and others in different parts of India is clearly brought out in figures of the relative distribution of directorships of companies and ownership of factories. (Table 1.)

The table is obviously incomplete: one does not know how the 'more important industrial concerns' were chosen, and there are glaring omissions. For example, cotton spinning and weaving mills are excluded from the C.P. and Berat, the United Provinces (not reproduced here) and Madras, although all of these provinces contained large cotton mills—primarily under Indian control in the first province and primarily under European control in the last two provinces. Still it does show some important features which are unlikely to be vitiated by the incompleteness of coverage. The proportions of companies controlled by Indian directors are very different in Assam, Bengal, Bihar and Orissa taken together and in Bombay, and the C.P. and Berar taken together; plantations are dominated by Europeans; so are engineering and machinery workshops, and railway workshops. One reason for the European control of engineering and machinery workshops was that government and railway patronage was important for most of them; when the patronage of private industry—for reasons of prejudice or common 'racial' background—was added to government and railway patronage, it was very difficult for any new Indian enterprise to compete with the European enterprises in this field.

In interpreting this table it is important to remember that, in most fields, the companies controlled the biggest enterprises, although there were exceptions, particularly in the case of engineering workshops, plantations and the industries demanding smaller units in general. No detailed figures of the distribution of directorships among various Indian communities are available. But the following analysis of the figures of ownership of privately owned factories—that is factories which were not owned by joint-stock companies or by public authorities, and of the management of all factories in the Bombay Presidency in 1911 will give some idea of the wide distribution of ownership and management

increased between 1912 and 1935; this finding seems to go against the other indices of growth and may primarily be due to the sampling techniques used by Brimmer.

It is difficult to know to what extent the Parsis exercised discrimination against other Indian communities and thus actively obstructed their entry into business either as owners or as managers. But it is known, for instance, that in the Central India Spinning, Weaving, and Manufacturing Company Limited, controlled by the house of Tata, and probably the most successful cotton mill of India ever, although a system of apprenticeship had been instituted from the very beginning and 202 men, including 23 university graduates, had been trained, almost all the apprentices up to 1916 had been Parsis. Sir Bezonji Dadabhoy Mehta, the Manager of the Mills, gave as the reason: 'We found it difficult to take other communities because they would not stand our discipline and our rules', *Minutes of Evidence taken before the Indian Industrial Commission 1916–18*, Vol. II (U.K. Parl. Papers, 1919, XVIII), pp. 518–21. The quotation is from p. 521.

Table 1. *Ownership and management of the most important industrial concerns*

Province and nature of factory etc.	Number owned by companies of which the directors are			Number privately owned		Number managed by	
	Europeans and Anglo-Indians	Indians	Of both races	Europeans and Anglo-Indians	Indians	Europeans and Anglo-Indians	Indians
Assam							
Tea plantations	494	12	—	55	48	536	73
Bengal							
Tea plantations	158	18	—	46	18	193	47
Collieries	53	6	21	7	43	66	63
Jute presses	50	16	—	7	36	64	45
Jute mills	49	—	—	1	—	50	—
Machinery and engineering workshops	22	—	—	4	7	30	7
Brick and tile factories	7	3	4	10	136	8	153
Oil mills	4	4	—	—	118	4	115
Printing presses	11	4	1	17	65	32	71
Bihar and Orissa							
Indigo plantations	12	—	—	93	14	117	2
Collieries	80	11	5	6	99	87	112
Mica mines	10	—	1	4	37	14	38
Lac factories	1	—	—	1	46	2	46
Bombay							
Cotton etc. ginning, cleaning and pressing factories	13	92	13	—	194	10	304
Cotton etc. spinning, weaving and other mills	12	92	25	—	18	43	106
Flour and rice mills	1	14	3	—	39	6	51
Machinery and engineering workshops	5	—	2	4	2	10	3
Printing presses	8	8	—	5	36	16	45
Railway workshops	13	—	—	—	—	12	1
C.P. and Berar							
Manganese mines	15	3	—	1	21	20	20
Cotton ginning, cleaning and pressing mills	5	56	1	—	91	7	146

Table 1 (*cont.*)

Province and nature of factory etc.	Number owned by companies of which the directors are			Number privately owned		Number managed by	
	Europeans and Anglo-Indians	Indians	Of both races	Europeans and Anglo-Indians	Indians	Europeans and Anglo-Indians	Indians
Madras							
Coffee planta-tions	30	6	1	56	11	86	18
Tile factories	7	9	—	2	23	10	30
Rice mills	2	23	—	—	57	3	78
Railway work-shops	23	—	—	—	—	23	—
Printing presses	11	16	1	1	19	15	36
Tanneries	3	26	—	1	36	3	64

SOURCE: *Census of India, 1911*, Vol. I, INDIA, Part I. Report by E. A. Gait (Calcutta, 1913), Subsidiary Table XII (p. 446).

Note: 'Europeans and Anglo-Indians' included Armenians also.

among the different Indian communities.[1] Of the total number of 798 factories covered, 453 were privately owned. Of these 20 were owned by Europeans or Anglo-Indians, 125 by Vanis, 85 by Zoroastrians, 40 by Bohoras, 31 by Brahmans, 21 by Kunbis, 21 by Khojas, 14 by Kumbhars, 13 by Memons, 13 by Shaikhs, 9 by Khatris, and 5 by Jews. None of the 194 privately owned ginning, cleaning and pressing factories belonged to Europeans: 84 of them were owned by Vanis, 34 by Zoroastrians, 20 by Bohoras, 12 by Brahmans, and 12 by Kunbis. Only 19 out of 148 spinning, weaving and other mills (textile groups) were privately owned. Of these 5 were owned by Vanis, 3 by Zoroastrians and 2 by Bohoras.[2]

Among the managers of spinning, weaving and other mills, the Parsis (45) outnumbered both the Europeans and Anglo-Indians (43) and the Vanis (28); but 149 of the managers of ginning, cleaning and pressing factories were Vanis as against 46 Zoroastrians, 44 Brahmans, 16 Kunbis, 10 Europeans and Anglo-Indians, and 10 Lingayats. Of the total number of managers of the 798 factories analysed, 135 were Europeans and Anglo-Indians, 233 Vanis, 150 Zoroastrians, 86 Brah-

[1] The figures are taken from *Census of India, 1911, Vol. VII, Bombay, Part II*, Imperial Tables by P. J. Mead and G. L. Macgregor (Bombay, 1912), pp. 518–21 (Table XV, Part E, Parts III and IV).

[2] It is an interesting illustration of the obsession of official India with caste that the writers of the report on Bombay concluded in defiance of the evidence that 'with the exception of the Parsis—the caste which is concerned with a certain handicraft is most intimately connected with the same craft when it has become a large commercial concern'. *Census of India*, Vol. VII, *Bombay Part I*, report by P. J. Mead and G. L. Macgregor (Bombay, 1912), pp. 324–5.

mans, 32 Kunbis, 22 Bohoras, 18 Kumbhars, 17 Shaikhs, 16 Khojas and 12 Memons.

From these figures, and from the information obtained from other sources, such as the *Investor's India Year Book 1914*, it appears that the Parsis controlled a larger fraction of the bigger enterprises, particularly in the cotton mill industry, than did the other Indian communities— particularly the Vanis. The lead of the Parsis over the Vanis in the management of cotton mills was only partially due to the larger degree of control over them exercised by the former; it was also due to the lead the Parsis had in general education and, in particular, in technical education over the other communities.

Even before the First World War, the lead of the Parsis in the cotton mill industry was probably diminishing, for the mill industry of Ahmedabad, where the Vanis—either Jains or Vaishnavs—predominated, grew much faster than the mill industry of Bombay.[1] But this was compensated by the extraordinary feats of entrepreneurship displayed by the house of Tata in the development of the iron and steel industry and in the promotion and management of the hydro-electric works to supply cheap electric power to Bombay.[2]

In Bombay, as in other parts of India, the Indians owning smaller amounts of capital or suffering from a late start invested in industries which needed smaller volumes of capital: rice mills, oil mills, cotton or jute pressing and baling factories, cotton ginning and pressing factories, small collieries attracted their capital. But Indians were also attracted to enterprises which the Europeans left alone as too risky, perhaps because the internal competition here was not too obvious. C. A. Innes, the then Director of Industries, Madras, wrote in his evidence for the Indian Industrial Commission: 'The "Competent businessmen" in the [Madras] Presidency are mostly Europeans, and the majority of them seem to find trade and commerce sufficiently profitable to render it unneccessary for them to embark upon the more uncertain field of new industries. Indians are more enterprising and are continually starting new industries in a small way. But most of these ventures seem to fail sooner or later and as far as I can judge from the information on record in my office, bad management is often the cause of failure.'[3] Lack of experience and bad management could not survive competition unless it was backed by a large amount of capital; and for

---

[1] In 1900–1 Ahmedabad had 5,861 looms and 485,706 spindles, and Bombay had 22,563 looms and 2,608,527 spindles; in 1913–14, Ahmedabad had 18,359 looms and 963,093 spindles, and Bombay had 47,790 looms and 3,044,148 spindles.

[2] For a description of the early stages of the two schemes, see F. R. Harris: *Jamsetji Nusserwanji Tata: A Chronicle of his Life* (Bombay, 1958), Chapters VIII–XI.

[3] *Minutes of Evidence taken before the Indian Industrial Commission, 1916–18*, Vol. III (U.K. Parl. Papers, 1919, XIX), p. 149.

large amounts of capital to be available for new enterprises from Indian sources in the areas dominated by Europeans, new conditions such as the eruption of big Indian trading and the existence of some degree of tariff protection had to emerge. Hence no real break-through could be made by Indian capital in Bengal, Madras or the United Provinces until the end of the 1920s and the beginning of the depression.

We finally come to the question whether after all in Bengal and in parts of Madras it was the system of Permanent Settlement which was responsible for the relative lack of Indian enterprise in the field of industry before the First World War. This question cannot be fully answered without a much more detailed study of the incomes of the *zamindars* in the respective provinces and the relative profitability of investment in land and in trade or industry than has yet been attempted. There are complaints voiced by many traders and industrialists that because investment in land is so safe and profitable it is difficult to raise capital for industry.[1] There is little doubt that the capital market was extremely imperfect and the small industrialist in particular faced difficulties in raising capital for his enterprise. But it would be mis-leading to suggest that landlords were immune to the lure of profit or that they stuck to their semi-feudal privileges so steadfastly as to ignore the changes going on around them. India was after all a colony ruled over by the first industrialized country of the world, and the example of freebooting Europeans might not elevate but might certainly convert even the most snobbish of the pseudo-aristocrats among India's native princes and landlords.

In eastern and southern India there were landlords starting indus-trial enterprises and successful traders buying up land even in the beginning of this century. Maharaja Manindra Chandra Nundy of Cossimbazar started the Calcutta Pottery Works in collaboration with Baikunthanath Sen, another landlord;[2] the Raja of Baraon started a sugar factory which failed;[3] a little later the Raja of Baneli started the Kirtyanand Iron and Steel Works Limited, which manufactured iron and steel castings.[4] The Maharajas of Durbhanga and Burdwan in-vested in modern industry on a large scale. In south India, S.R.M.A.R. Chettiar and S.R.M.M.A. Annamalai Chettiar, enormously suc-cessful bankers in South East Asia, were buying up *zamindaris* and

---

[1] See the evidence of Rai Sitanath Roy Bahadur of Bengal, and of Rao Bahadur K. Suryanara-yanamurti Nayudu of Madras, in *Minutes of Evidence taken before the Indian Industrial Commission 1916–18*, Vol. II (U.K. Parl. Papers, 1919, XVIII), p. 279, and Vol. III (U.K. Parl. Papers, 1919, XIX), p. 88, respectively.

[2] Henry Hemantakumar Ghosh: *The Advancement of Industry* (Calcutta, 1910), p. 90.

[3] Somerset Playne (compiler) and Arnold Wright (editor): *The Bombay Presidency, United Provinces, Punjab etc.* (London, 1920), p. 423.

[4] Indian Tariff Board: *Evidence on Steel*, Vol. II (Calcutta, 1924), p. 257.

founding the Indian Bank of Madras.[1] There were other bankers and
traders who had built up their fortunes on the basis of successful collaboration with the British—often rendering the latter important
services at the time of the Mutiny—and who combined trade, ownership of land and of industrial enterprises without appearing to be
revolutionary innovators.[2] In Delhi, old banking families were founding
textile mills such as the Delhi Cloth and General Mills and Krishn
Mills.[3] In the Punjab proper, the landed money-lending castes were often
improving landlords and industrial entrepreneurs—though they generally operated only small-scale enterprises.[4] In central India, Jain
banyas were setting up cotton mills, often with money made from trade
in opium.[5] In central and western India, particularly, native princes
were eager to help Indian capitalists set up new industries in their
territories. There might be differences in the degrees of co-operation
between the British rulers on the one hand, and the Scindia, the
Holkar and the Gaekwar on the other, but there were no important
differences in their attitudes to the development of industry—primarily
on the basis of private enterprise. Thus the factor of political separateness of the native states of western India—however circumscribed that
separateness might be by the policies imposed by the British government
—was probably more beneficial for the development of private Indian
capital than the uniformity of European control under direct British
rule in eastern India.

As far as the land tenure systems of Bengal, Bombay, and Madras
were concerned, in spite of important initial differences, there was a
large degree of 'convergence' over time.[6] The greater degree of activity
of industrial capital in western India may have been to some extent due
to the relative unattractiveness of becoming a landlord. It is also

[1] S. Playne (compiler) and A. Wright (editor): *Southern India* (London, 1915), p. 479;
Investor's India Year-Book 1911 (Calcutta, 1911), p. 55; and *Debrett's Peerage, Baronetage and
Companionage for 1941* (London, 1941), p. 973. Annamalai Chettiar was knighted and
became the hereditary Raja of Chettinad in 1929.

[2] See, for example, the history and connexions of the firm of Sitalprasad Kharagprasad,
Agrawal Vaishyas from the Punjab, in S. Playne (compiler) and A. Wright (editor): *Bengal
and Assam, Behar and Orissa* (London, 1917), pp. 686–91. The family had bought in 1908 the
Bahrat Abhyuday Cotton Mills and expanded the concern, spinning yarn for local consumption.

[3] Punjab District Gazetteers, Vol. V A, *Delhi District, with Maps*, 1912 (Lahore, 1913), p. 77;
S. Playne (compiler) and A. Wright (editor): *The Bombay Presidency, United Provinces,
Punjab, etc.* (London, 1920), pp. 659–60.

[4] See M. L. Darling, *The Punjab Peasant in Prosperity and Debt* (London, 1928), pp. 187, 210–
13.

[5] S. Playne and A. Wright, 1920, p. 886 ('The Binod Mills'), pp. 896–8 ('Rai Bahadur
Onkarji Kastoorchand Kasliwal'), pp. 898–901 ('Rai Bahadur Seth Saroopchand Hukamchand'), pp. 887–8 ('The Hukamchand Mills').

[6] See H. H. Mann, 'The Agriculture of India', *Annals of the American Academy of Political and
Social Science*, Vol. 145, 1929, pp. 72–81.

possible that the marginally higher degree of participation of Indian capital in industrial enterprises in south India than in eastern India was due to the fact that only a part of the Madras Presidency was under the system of *zamindari* settlement. Without more detailed work it is not possible to conclude that there *was* a greater degree of participation by Indian capital in southern India before the First World War. If there was a lower degree of participation by Europeans in industrial enterprises it may have been as much due to the smaller scale of the enterprises and their lower profitability as to the greater willingness of Indian capital to enter into industry. There were no amazingly rich coal mines, no golden fibres, no indigo, and no rich tea gardens comparable to those of Assam to lure Europeans to south India to the same degree. The Buckingham and Carnatic Mills which later proved extremely profitable had not been very profitable in the initial years. There was no failure of a European enterprise comparable to Arbuthnot and Company in 1907 in eastern India for the period from 1900 to 1914. The bigger 'export base' of northern and eastern India and the location of the capital in Calcutta thus have may attracted a greater degree of European domination.

We do not mean to minimize the importance of the land tenure system in determining the pace of industrial and agricultural development of India. But the land tenure system was part of the fabric of British rule; it sustained a certain distribution of income in the country, it provided a method of realization of the surplus by wealthy Indians, wealthy Europeans and by the State apparatus under the control of the British. It was connected with the methods of financing of consumption of the poorer peasants and workers; it was one of the major factors governing the level of consumption of ordinary Indians and therefore the degree of profitability of investment in industries catering for such consumption. In view of all this, it would be misleading to suggest that the land tenure system *only* or even *mainly* affected industrial development through the restriction of investment in industry by wealthy Indians even though such investment was profitable. The evidence relating to the period before the First World War points in fact to the opposite conclusion, namely, that the surplus available for investment in industry could not be profitably utilized there in full, given the macroscopic (and microscopic) requirements of the British imperial system. From this point of view, the conspicuous consumption of many landlords and most princelings was only 'functional' wastage helping to preserve the stability of the imperial structure.

One of the marks of the Parsi collaboration with the British was the shower of knighthoods and baronetcies conferred upon them at the end of the nineteenth and the beginning of the twentieth century. But the

benefits to the rulers from the collaboration of a small community—
however wealthy and however articulate—plainly decreased with time;
on the other side, as other communities made their fortunes in industry
and trade, they also wanted to share in the honours that were going,
not least because they could be utilized to seize new opportunities for
making profit.[1] After having created two Parsi baronets (Jejeebhoy and
Jehangir), two Jewish baronets (Sassoon and David), one Muslim
baronet (Currimbhoy Ebrahim), the British Government chose in 1913
as the first Hindu baronet Chinubhai Madhowlal, the grandson (by
adoption) of the founder of the cotton mill industry of Ahmedabad.[2]

After the First World War, the political benefits of collaboration
decreased significantly; with drastic reductions in government capital
expenditure in the thirties and with the emergence of tariff protection,
the direct economic benefits derived by the Indian capitalists from
collaboration with the British also decreased, but they did not disappear.
The house of Tata still found it useful to employ former civil servants
(such as J. C. K. Peterson and S. K. Sawday) or former railway officials
(such as R. H. Mather) in high positions. The Indians in eastern India
began to take their positions on boards of companies controlled by
British managing agency houses, by virtue of their greater financial
stakes: the Goenkas and Jatias were joined by the Bangurs and the
Birlas; because of the managing agency system, the managerial control
of Indians lagged behind their financial control.

These major changes in the control of industry by Indians as against
Europeans stand out much more clearly than the changes in the control
by different groups of Indians themselves. In the rise of groups of
Indians, it is the connexion with trade and with big money that counted
far more than daring or the much-advertised Protestant virtues. One
does not find the Brahmos or the Prarthana Samaj people among the
ranks of the new business magnates. The enterprising intellectuals,
professional men or landlords who had shown courage and patriotism
in starting new industrial enterprises, particularly during the period of
political ferment after the partition of Bengal, rarely came out on top,
when the unstable 1920s had been succeeded by the disastrous 1930s.
Cotton mills, jute mills, oil mills, rice mills, cotton gins and presses, jute
presses and sugar factories used agricultural raw materials and skill in
buying the material and selling the finished product, and the ability to

---

[1] Acquin Martin and Rajendra Nath Mookerjee had been equal partners in Martin and
Company from the beginning. But, when Acquin Martin was knighted, Mookerjee volun-
tarily offered him a half-anna more in the partnership, thus recognizing him as the senior
partner. 'It was an offering from one sincere and cordial friend to another—a participation
in the high dignity conferred on Acquin Martin and a shrewd realization of the value of the
honour for purposes of business.' K. C. Mahindra: *Sir Rajendra Nath Mookerjee* (Calcutta,
1962), p. 128.   [2] *Debrett's Peerage, Baronetage, Companionage etc.*, 1915 and 1924.

finance the holding of stocks counted far more than acquaintance with the technical processes of manufacture; naturally traders and bankers beat the professional men at this game. Again and again, in industry, good management proved to be far more important than an enterprising spirit: one can almost conclude that 'patient attention to detail is the better part of entrepreneurship'.[1]

Lack of technical education had been used as a justification for the exclusion of Indians from responsible posts in industry and government before the First World War, and some belated attempts had been made to send scholars from India under both government and private auspices. But it was recognized even before 1914 that technically qualified men could not be expected to become captains of industry without financial backing.[2]

Technical experience could not be acquired without working in industry; however, unless there were industrialists willing to give the technically qualified person an even chance, he was unlikely to progress far in his profession. The cotton industry was almost certainly a more demanding industry technically than the jute industry; yet the European managers and masters of various departments in the cotton mills of Bombay came to be displaced over time, first by Parsis and then by members of other Indian communities,[3] whereas there were practically no Indians in supervisory positions in the jute mills of Bengal.[4]

The caste system as a pattern of stratification into endogamous groups survived intact over the period we are studying: but, already by 1901 in Bengal and even more in Calcutta, many castes—particularly the upper ones—had been largely divorced from their traditional occupation.[5] This 'liberalizing' tendency did not, however, throw up new entrepreneurial groups of any major significance from among the Bengalis. Even more ironically, many of the new trading and banking groups which emerged into industrial entrepreneurship—the Chettiars,

---

[1] Fortunately there is one well-documented record of the value of good management, namely F. R. Harris: *Jamsetji Nusserwanji Tata* (Bombay, 1958), Chapter II.

[2] *Report of a Committee appointed by the Secretary of State for India to inquire into the System of State Technical Scholarships established by the Government of India in 1904* (U.K. Parl. Papers, 1913, XLVII), p. 26: 'To expect a young man who has just quitted a technological school to set up a new industry on a large scale is probably absurd. Such a man has usually no capital of his own and he is very unlikely to find anyone to lend it to him.'

[3] See S. M. Rutnagur: *Bombay Industries: the Cotton Mills* (Bombay, 1927), pp. 288–309.

[4] The Alliance Jute Mills around 1916, for instance, employed a supervisory staff consisting entirely of Scotsmen. See S. Playne (compiler) and A. Wright (editor), 1917, p. 80. By 1932 or 1933, when D. H. Buchanan wrote, the situation in this respect had not changed at all for most of the jute mills: D. H. Buchanan: *The Development of Capitalist Enterprise in India* (New York, 1934), pp. 210–11, 254.

[5] See *Census of India 1901, Vol. VI, Bengal, Part I; Report* (Calcutta, 1902), Chapter XII; and *Vol. VII, Calcutta, Town and Suburbs, Part IV, Report (Statistical)* (Calcutta, 1902), Chapters XI and XII.

the Jains, and the Hindu *banyas*—were much addicted to the building of temples, *dharamsalas*, and the endowing of institutions of astrological and Sanskritic learning. One is permitted to doubt after reading the history of the period under consideration whether there was any positive connexion between westernization and success in making money in a big way.

One final aspect of entrepreneurship—namely the ability to innovate —may be noticed before we finish. While the introduction of any new industry into a poor country must be accompanied by some degree of skilled adaption, European industrialists in India were not particularly noted for innovations. Jamsetji Tata is reported to have helped in the development of ring spindles and their adaption under Indian conditions; the manager of his Nagpur mills, Sir Bezonji Dadabhoy Mehta, later claimed that he and his staff suggested many changes in the machinery used and they were generally accepted by the manufacturers of machinery.[1] This spirit of innovation seems to have atrophied later, as witnessed by the difficulties of the Bombay cotton mill industry in the interwar years. On the other side of India, the jute mill industry had become technically stagnant: no major changes in production methods had taken place after the 1880s. An official sub-committee appointed by the Indian Jute Mills Association reported in 1933 that 'there is no industry in the world which knows so little about its business as the jute industry'.[2] The Indian Jute Mills Association in 1934 invited Dr S. G. Barker, Director of Research, Wool Industries Research Association, to report on the manufacturing aspects of the jute industry; Dr Barker found the mills on the Hooghly particularly wanting in respect of innovations in methods and in products produced.[3] Thus foreign control of industry in India brought neither technical knowledge to the Indians without some political pressure[4] nor did it bring any extraordinary ability to adjust to changing conditions. It can be argued that by increasing the reverse flow of dividends from India to the west and by obstructing the emergence of Indians into positions of leadership in industry it may even have increased the degree of economic backwardness of India and aggravated her problems of adjustment to a world of aggressive capitalism.

[1] S. D. Mehta: *The Cotton Mills of India, 1854 to 1954* (Bombay, 1954), pp. 43–5; the evidence of Sir B. D. Mehta in *Minutes of Evidence taken before the Indian Industrial Commission, 1916–18*, Vol. II (U.K. Parl. Papers, 1919, XVIII), p. 521.

[2] *Report of the Bengal Jute Enquiry Committee*, Vol. I (Calcutta, 1934), p. 64.

[3] S. G. Barker: *Report on the Scientific and Technical Development of the Jute Manufacturing Industry in Bengal* (Calcutta, 1935), particularly pp. 38–40.

[4] When firms under European control benefited from tariff protection, there was pressure on them to take in more Indians in managerial and supervisory positions. But this pressure only had marginal effects as is evidenced, for instance, by the policies pursued by the Titaghur Paper Mills and the Bengal Paper Mill during the interwar period.

INDEX